KNOWLEDGE MANAGEMENT
SYSTEMS AND PROCESSES

KNOWLEDGE MANAGEMENT
SYSTEMS AND PROCESSES

IRMA BECERRA-FERNANDEZ
AND RAJIV SABHERWAL

FOREWORD BY CYRUS F. GIBSON

M.E.Sharpe
Armonk, New York
London, England

Library of Congress Cataloging-in-Publication Data

Becerra-Fernandez, Irma, 1960–
  Knowledge management : systems and processes / by Irma Becerra-Fernandez
and Rajiv Sabherwal.
      p. cm.
  Includes bibliographical references and index.
  ISBN 978-0-7656-2351-5 (cloth : alk. paper)
  1. Knowledge management. 2. Information technology. I. Sabherwal, Rajiv. II. Title.

HD30.2.B438 2010
658.4′038—dc22   2009018627

Printed in the United States of America

The paper used in this publication meets the minimum requirements of
American National Standard for Information Sciences
Permanence of Paper for Printed Library Materials,
ANSI Z 39.48-1984.

CW (c)   10   9   8   7   6   5   4   3

Contents

PART II. KNOWLEDGE MANAGEMENT TECHNOLOGIES AND SYSTEMS

PART III. MANAGEMENT AND THE FUTURE OF KNOWLEDGE MANAGEMENT

Foreword

The phrase "Knowledge Management" (KM) has faced severe competition over the last decade, and particularly since the publication of the first edition of this book in 2004. We hear "Business Intelligence" and "Collective Intelligence" that are close to KM in definition and implications. But now "Web 2.0," "Enterprise 2.0," and "Collaboration" are adding new ingredients to the KM pot, namely end-user social computing. With the hype cycles competing and vendors, consultants, and academics often pushing their particular phrases, it is important to have a foundation of terms and ideas that are durable and will enable us to adopt into KM what is good about new approaches while rejecting what is rehashed under a new name.

Knowledge Management: Systems and Processes has the depth and frameworks to provide this foundation of terms and ideas. For one important thing, it recognizes that organizational culture, behavior, and work processes must be made integral with the technical for an effective system to result. For another, it provides a clear set of definitions and frameworks, which, once shared among suppliers and users of information, will make the building, use, and adaptation of KM systems more efficient and effective.

It will be most interesting to see what happens over the next few years as organizations confront, adopt, resist, and adapt the new Web 2.0 technologies. The use and business value of wikis, blogs, Twitter, and the like is catching on for many individual advocates. It is truly a bottoms-up, generational thing. It is being questioned, examined, and experimented with by many organizations.

It seems clear that social computing and Web 2.0 is a big thing, perhaps comparable to the PC and the introduction of Web 1.0. I suppose one could argue that the emerging Web 2.0 tools and their adoption and adaptation going forward could really change the meaning and nature of KM. What may not be clear is how much organizations will have to change for these technologies and work practices to be beneficial. We can be sure that disciplined thinking and experimentation, guided by the terminology and ideas of KM, will be necessary to ride and exploit the benefits of this wave. A lot of work is reflected in this.

Knowledge Management: Systems and Processes is a comprehensive coverage of KM, including the explication and connection of the human and the technical side of the discipline so necessary for success now and in the future. The book is rich in information and detail, and is very clearly written with many good examples and illustrations. Congratulations to the authors!

Cyrus F. (Chuck) Gibson
Massachusetts Institute of Technology
Sloan School of Management
Center for Information Systems Research

Preface

Knowledge Management: Systems and Processes is for students and managers who seek detailed insights into contemporary knowledge management (KM). It explains the concepts, theories, and technologies that provide the foundation for KM; the systems and structures that constitute KM solutions; and the processes for developing, deploying, and evaluating these KM solutions. We hope this book will help readers acquire the relevant suite of managerial, technical, and theoretical skills for managing knowledge in the modern business environment.

The purpose of this book is to provide a thorough and informative perspective on the emergent practices in knowledge management. Information technology has been, and will continue to be, an important catalyst of this innovative field. Web-based technologies including Web 2.0, artificial intelligence, expert systems, analytics, and collaborative technologies continue to support and transform the field of KM. However, these technologies would not be effective without the day-to-day social aspects of organizations such as "water-cooler conversations," brainstorming retreats, and communities of practice. To further complicate matters, the current business environment renders new skills obsolete in years or even months.

Knowledge management is defined in this book as *doing what is needed to get the most out of knowledge resources.* KM is an increasingly important discipline that promotes the discovery, capture, sharing, and application of the firm's knowledge. Indeed, we are witnessing a new era with advanced industrial economies being revolutionized with the advent of the knowledge age and highly skilled knowledge-based workers replacing industrial workers as the dominant labor group. Although the benefits of KM may be obvious, it may not necessarily be so obvious to know how to effectively manage this valuable resource. In this book, the discussion of KM reflects the intimacy the authors have with this topic from a theoretical as well as a practical standpoint and through their substantial and diverse experiences.

The book is divided into three parts:

Part I, Principles of Knowledge Management—This part provides a more detailed discussion of the concepts of knowledge and knowledge management and describes the key constituents of KM solutions including infrastructure, processes, systems, tools, and technologies. The four types of KM processes are described and illustrated: knowledge application, knowledge capture, knowledge sharing, and knowledge discovery systems. The section also examines and provides examples of the ways in which KM impacts contemporary organizations.

Part II, Knowledge Management Technologies and Systems—This section is devoted to a discussion of the underlying technologies that enable KM systems associated with the four types of KM processes. The four different types of KM systems are described: knowledge discovery systems, knowledge capture systems, knowledge sharing systems, and knowledge application systems. The mechanisms and technologies to support these KM systems are discussed, and case studies related to their implementation are presented.

Part III, Management and the Future of Knowledge Management—Some of the issues related to management practices and the future of knowledge management are presented here. The section describes how KM can benefit from emergent practices and technologies, including social networks, communities of practice, wikis, and blogs. It also examines the factors that affect KM and identifies the specific effects of these factors. Moreover, the overall leadership and evaluation of KM are described here. This section and the book conclude by examining aspects that are likely to be important in the future of KM, including crowd sourcing or collective intelligence and concerns related to privacy and confidentiality.

This book may be adapted in several different ways, depending on the course and the students. It can be used as a one-semester course on KM for graduate MIS students by covering selected topics from Parts I, II, and III. An instructor teaching a course for engineering or computer science students may opt to concentrate on KM technologies and systems by covering Chapters 1, 6, 7, 8, 9, and 10. Alternatively, if the course is being taught to MBA students, a number of case studies could be assigned to complement the discussions presented in the book, and the discussion of Chapters 6, 7, 8, and 9 could be emphasized less.

To complement the text and enhance the learning and pedagogical experience, we provide the following support materials through the instructor's Web site:

1. Solutions to the end-of-chapter problems.
2. PowerPoint slides for each chapter that describe the key concepts explained in the text.
3. Sample syllabus and sample student projects.
4. List of relevant accompanying case studies.
5. References to KM software providers.

In addition, instructors adopting the book are encouraged to share with the authors any relevant material that could be included on the Web site to reinforce and enhance the students' experience.

ACKNOWLEDGMENTS

We have so many people to acknowledge! First, we want to recognize our families who were so supportive during the time we spent with our heads buried in our laptops.

We further thank those organizations that provided us with the fertile ground to develop many of our ideas about KM: NASA-Kennedy Space Center, Goddard Space Flight Center, Ames Research Center, NAVY Center for Advanced Research in Artificial Intelligence, and the Institute for Human and Machine Cognition, among others. We especially thank the individuals at these organizations who made it possible for us to formalize some of the concepts and techniques presented in this book. We also thank all the authors that individually contributed to the many vignettes and case studies presented throughout.

We also thank our administrators, who were very understanding when our other academic commitments couldn't be completed in time. These include Joyce Elam and Christos Koulamas at Florida International University and Keith Womer, Tom Eysell, and Ashok Subramanian at the University of Missouri-St. Louis. Our sincere thanks are also directed to Avelino Gonzalez of the University of Central Florida, who coauthored the previous edition of this book and selflessly contributed to some of the material contained in this book.

We also gratefully acknowledge the contributions of the students who previously worked at the FIU Knowledge Management Lab and who collaborated in the development of some of the KM systems described here. Finally, we are deeply indebted to many individuals at M.E. Sharpe, Inc. who enabled us to publish this book, especially the two individuals with whom we have directly worked: our editor, Harry Briggs, and associate editor, Elizabeth Granda.

KNOWLEDGE MANAGEMENT
SYSTEMS AND PROCESSES

1 Introducing Knowledge Management

The scientific endeavor that culminated on July 20, 1969, with the first American walking on the moon is considered one of the most significant accomplishments in the history of humankind. What is especially noteworthy about this undertaking is that when President John F. Kennedy issued the promise in 1961 that the United States would land a man on the Moon and return him safely to Earth before the end of that decade, most of the scientific and technological knowledge required to take this "one small step for man, one giant leap for mankind" did not exist. The necessary science and technology knowledge had to be discovered and developed in order to accomplish this extraordinary task. However, many of those technological advances now have permanent presence in the landscape of our lives, from cordless tools to cellular phones. These first missions to space carried less computer power on board than what some of us typically lug around airports on our portable computers. The computers on board Apollo 11, considered "state-of-the-art" in the 1960s, had 4 KB of RAM, no disk drive, and a total of 74 KB of auxiliary memory! From the knowledge management (KM) perspective, how did they manage the extraordinary quantities of knowledge that had to be developed in order to accomplish the task? The required knowledge about space travel, rocketry, aerodynamics, control systems, communications, biology, and many other disciplines had to be developed and validated prior to being used in the space mission. From the knowledge creation perspective, this was an extraordinarily successful endeavor. On the other hand, a closer look reveals that attempts to elicit and capture the knowledge resulting from these efforts may have been largely unsuccessful, and some studies even suggest that NASA may have actually lost that knowledge. In fact, in the words of Sylvia Fries, who was NASA's chief historian between 1983 and 1990 and who interviewed 51 NASA engineers who had worked on the Apollo program:

> The 20th anniversary of the landing of an American on the surface of the Moon occasioned many bittersweet reflections. Sweet was the celebration of the historic event itself. . . . Bitter, for those same enthusiasts, was the knowledge that during the twenty intervening years much of the national consensus that launched this country on its first lunar adventure had evaporated . . . a generation of men and women who had defined their lives to a large extent in terms of this nation's epochal departure from Earth's surface was taking its leave of the program they had built (Fries 1992).

In this book, we hope to impart what we know about the important field of knowledge management—what it is and how to implement it successfully with the tools provided by the technological advances of our times. The book presents a balanced discussion between theory and application of knowledge management to organizations. The reader will find an overview of knowledge management theory and implementation, with a special emphasis on the technologies that underpin knowledge management and how to successfully integrate those technologies. The book includes implementation details about both knowledge management mechanisms and technologies.

In this chapter, we first discuss what knowledge management is and what the forces are that drive it. We also discuss organizational issues related to knowledge management. Specifically, we introduce knowledge management systems and their roles in the organization. Finally, we discuss how the rest of the book is organized.

WHAT IS KNOWLEDGE MANAGEMENT?

Knowledge management (KM) may simply be defined as *doing what is needed to get the most out of knowledge resources.* Although KM can be applied to individuals, it has recently attracted the attention of organizations. KM is viewed as an increasingly important discipline that promotes the creation, sharing, and leveraging of the corporation's knowledge. Peter Drucker (1994), whom many consider the father of KM, best defines the need for it:

> Knowledge has become the key resource, for a nation's military strength as well as for its economic strength . . . is fundamentally different from the traditional key resources of the economist—land, labor, and even capital . . . we need systematic work on the quality of knowledge and the productivity of knowledge . . . the performance capacity, if not the survival, of any organization in the knowledge society will come increasingly to depend on those two factors (pp. 66–69).

Thus, it can be argued that the most vital resource of today's enterprise is the collective knowledge residing in the minds of an organization's employees, customers, and vendors. Learning how to manage organizational knowledge has many benefits, some of which are readily apparent, others not. These benefits may include leveraging core business competencies, accelerating innovation and time-to-market, improving cycle times and decision-making, strengthening organizational commitment, and building sustainable competitive advantage (Davenport and Prusak, 1998). In short, they make the organization better suited to compete successfully in a much more demanding environment. Organizations are increasingly valued for their intellectual capital. An example of this fact is the widening gap between corporate balance sheets and investors' estimation of corporate worth. It is said that knowledge-intensive companies around the world are valued at three to eight times their financial capital. Consider for example Microsoft Corporation, the highest-valued company in the world, with a market capitalization that was estimated at around $282 billion as of April 2007. Clearly, this figure represents more than Microsoft's net worth in buildings, computers, and other physical assets. Microsoft's valuation also represents an estimation of its **intellectual assets**. This includes structural capital in the form of copyrights, customer databases, and business-process software. Added to that is human capital in the form of the knowledge that resides in the minds of all of Microsoft's software developers, researchers, academic collaborators, and business managers.

In general, KM focuses on organizing and making available important knowledge, wherever and whenever it is needed. The traditional emphasis in KM has been on knowledge that is recognized and already articulated in some form. This includes knowledge about processes, procedures, intellectual property, documented best practices, forecasts, lessons learned, and solutions to recurring problems. Increasingly, KM has also focused on managing important knowledge that may reside solely in the minds of organizations' experts.

Consider, for example, the knowledge of the Shuttle Processing Director at NASA-Kennedy Space Center (KSC). By 1999, the Shuttle Processing Director at NASA had been supervising shuttle launches for twenty years and had supervised each of the shuttle launches until its lift-off (Becerra-Fernandez and Sabherwal 2005). During the countdown, he was responsible for making the final call if an anomaly justified calling off the mission. As Shuttle Processing Director, he depended on his experience in order to weigh the severity of the problem and decide on the spot if indeed it required stopping the mission. A decision to stop the launch could cost the organization millions of dollars, but on the other hand it could save lives—a priceless alternative. With retirement looming, how can an organization like NASA KSC elicit and catalog this person's knowledge so that new generations may benefit?

KM is also related to the concept of **intellectual capital**, which is considered by many as the most valuable enterprise resource. An organization's intellectual capital refers to the sum of all its knowledge resources, which exist in aspects within or outside the organization (Nahapiet and Ghoshal 1998). There are three types of intellectual capital: human capital, or the knowledge, skills, and capabilities possessed by individual employees; organizational capital, or the institutionalized knowledge and codified experience residing in databases, manuals, culture, systems, structures, and processes; and social capital, or the knowledge embedded in relationships and interactions among individuals (Subramaniam and Youndt 2005).

FORCES DRIVING KNOWLEDGE MANAGEMENT

Today, organizations rely on their decisionmakers to make "mission critical" decisions based on inputs from multiple domains. The ideal decisionmaker possesses a profound understanding of specific domains that influence the decision-making process, coupled with the experience that allows her to act quickly and decisively on the information. This profile of the ideal decisionmaker usually corresponds to someone who has lengthy experience and insights gained from years of observation. Although this profile does not mark a significant departure from the past, the following four underlying trends are increasing the stakes in the decision-making scenario:

1. INCREASING DOMAIN COMPLEXITY

The complexity of the underlying knowledge domains is increasing. As a direct consequence, the complexity of the knowledge required to complete a specific business process task has increased as well. Intricacy of internal and external processes, increased competition, and the rapid advancement of technology all contribute to increasing domain complexity. For example, new product development no longer requires only brainstorming sessions by the freethinking product designers of the organization, but instead it requires the partnership of interorganizational teams representing various functional subunits—from finance to marketing to engineering. Thus, we see an increased emphasis from professional recruiters around the world seeking new job applicants who not only possess excellent educational and professional qualifications, but who also have outstanding communication and team-collaboration skills. These skills will enable them to share their knowledge for the benefit of the organization.

2. ACCELERATING MARKET VOLATILITY

The pace of change, or volatility, within each market domain has increased rapidly in the past decade. For example, market and environmental influences can result in overnight changes in an organization. Corporate announcements of a missed financial quarterly target could send a company's capitalization, and perhaps that of a whole industry, in a downward spiral. Stock prices on Wall Street have become increasingly volatile in the past few years resulting in the phenomenon of day trading, where many nonfinancial professionals make a living from taking advantage of the steep market fluctuations.

3. INTENSIFIED SPEED OF RESPONSIVENESS

The time required to take action based upon subtle changes within and across domains is decreasing. The rapid advance in technology continually changes the decision-making landscape, making it imperative that decisions be made and implemented quickly, lest the window of opportunity closes. For example, in the past, the sales process incorporated ample processing time, thus allowing the stakeholders a "comfort zone" in the decision-making process. Typically in response to a customer-request, the sales representative would return to the office, discuss the opportunity with his manager, draft a proposal, and mail the proposal to the client, who would then accept or reject the offer. The time required by the process would essentially provide the stakeholders sufficient time to ponder the most adequate solution at each of the decision points. Contrast yesterday's sale process with today's, like for example the process required by many online bidding marketplaces thriving on the Web. Consider the dilemma faced by a hotel manager that participates in an Internet auctioning market of hotel rooms: "Should I book a $200 room for the bid offer of $80 and fill the room or risk not accepting the bid hoping to get a walk-in customer that will pay the $200?" Confronted with a decision to fill a room at a lower rate than what the hotel typically advertises poses an important decision that the hotel manager must make within minutes of a bid offer.

4. EMPLOYEE TURNOVER

Organizations continue to face employee turnover due to voluntary (i.e., decided by the employee, for example, due to opportunities for career advancement) as well as involuntary (i.e., for reasons beyond the employee's control, such as health-related problems and termination of employment by the employer). Employee turnover is especially important in tough economic conditions such as those being faced in the 2008 to 2009 period, when several large companies laid off large numbers of employees. Such employee turnover inevitably leads to the organization losing some of the knowledge possessed by the departing individuals. Moreover, in some cases these individuals might have knowledge that would be valuable to competitors. According to Kenny (2007), "As staff leave, retraining is necessary. This strains company resources and hinders growth. Replacing a full-time, private-sector worker costs, at a bare minimum, 25 percent of his or her total annual compensation, estimates the Employment Policy Foundation. Productivity nosedives, ultimately cutting into profitability."

So, what does this mean? Faced with increased complexity, market volatility, accelerated responsiveness, and employee turnover, today's manager feels less adequate to make the difficult decisions faced each day. In the decision-making scenario described above, it is evident that knowledge can greatly assist the decisionmaker. In the past, this knowledge resided mostly in the decisionmaker. The complications seen above indicate that in modern organizations, the knowledge necessary to make good decisions cannot possibly all reside with the decisionmaker, hence the need to provide her with the requisite knowledge for making correct, timely decisions.

Perhaps nothing has made more evident the need for KM than the corporate **downsizing** trend at public and private organizations that marked the re-engineering era of the 1990s, a well-known feature of the economic landscape of the late twentieth century. The dominant driver of downsizing in most organizations is well understood: Rapidly reduce costs in order to survive against competitors. Clearly, a negative side effect of downsizing is the dissipation of the knowledge resources, resulting in devitalized organizations. Some of the symptoms of such organizations are: decreased morale, reduced commitment, inferior quality, lack of teamwork, lower productivity, and lost of innovative ability (Eisenberg 1997). The fact is, many individuals who were laid off as a result of downsizing had performed significant tasks and had acquired considerable and valuable skills over the years. Many companies are typically not prepared for downsizing, and few take any steps to prevent the escape of knowledge that usually follows. To minimize the impact of downsizing, organizations should first identify what skills and information resources will be needed to meet **mission-critical objectives**. Therefore, effective **methodologies**, including tools and techniques to capture vital knowledge, are essential for an organization to maintain its competitive edge.

KM is important for organizations that continually face downsizing or a high turnover percentage due to the nature of the industry. It is also important for all organizations since today's decisionmaker faces the pressure to make better and faster decisions in an environment characterized by a high domain complexity and market volatility, even though she may in fact lack the experience typically expected from a decisionmaker, and even though the outcome of those decisions could have a considerable impact on the organization. In short, KM is important for everybody. Box 1.1 illustrates this fact.

KNOWLEDGE MANAGEMENT SYSTEMS

Rapid changes in the field of KM have to a great extent resulted from the dramatic progress we have witnessed in the field of information technology (IT). Information technology facilitates sharing as well as accelerated growth of knowledge. IT allows the movement of information at increasing speeds and efficiencies. For example, computers capture data from measurements of natural phenomena, and then quickly manipulate the data to better understand the phenomena it represents. Increased computer power at lower prices enables the measurement of increasingly complex processes, which we possibly could only imagine before. According to Bradley (1997):

> Today, knowledge is accumulating at an ever-increasing rate. It is estimated that knowledge is currently doubling every 18 months and, of course, the pace is increasing. . . . Technology facilitates the speed at which knowledge and ideas proliferate (p. 54).

Thus, IT has provided the major impetus for enabling the implementation of KM applications. Moreover, as learning has accrued over time in the area of social and structural mechanisms, such as mentoring and retreats that enable effective knowledge sharing, it has made it possible to develop KM applications that best leverage these improved mechanisms by deploying sophisticated technologies.

In this book, we therefore place significant focus on the applications that result from the use of the latest technologies used to support KM mechanisms. Knowledge management mechanisms are organizational or structural means used to promote KM. The use of leading-edge information technologies (e.g., Web-based conferencing) to support KM mechanisms in ways not earlier possible (e.g., interactive conversations along with instantaneous exchange of voluminous documents among individuals located at remote locations) enables dramatic improvement in KM. We call the applications resulting from such synergy between the latest technologies and social/structural mechanisms **knowledge management systems**, as described in Chapters 6 through 9 of this book. Knowledge management systems utilize a variety of KM mechanisms and technologies to support the knowledge management processes. Based on observations on the KM systems implementations under way at many organizations, a framework emerges for classification of KM systems as:

1. Knowledge Application Systems (discussed in Chapter 6)
2. Knowledge Capture Systems (discussed in Chapter 7)
3. Knowledge Sharing Systems (discussed in Chapter 8)
4. Knowledge Discovery Systems (discussed in Chapter 9)

Artificial intelligence and machine-learning technologies play an important role in the processes of knowledge discovery, capture, sharing, and application, enabling the

Box 1.1

Is Knowledge Management for Everybody?

John Smith owns an independent auto repair shop in Stillwater, Oklahoma, which he established in 1985. Prior to opening his own shop, he had been repairing foreign cars as a mechanic for the local Toyota dealership. In these days of increasing complexity in automobiles, he had to learn about such new technologies as fuel injection, computer-controlled ignition, and multi-valve and turbocharged engines. This has not been easy, but he managed to do it, and at the same time created a successful business, one with an outstanding reputation. As his business grew, he had to hire mechanics to help him with the workload. At first, training them was easy since cars were simple. That has radically changed in the last ten years. He now finds himself spending more time training and correcting the work of his mechanics instead of working on cars himself, which is what he truly enjoys. To further complicate matters, his mechanics are so well-trained that the local Toyota dealership is hiring them away from him for significant salary increases. Being a small business he cannot afford to compete with them, so he finds himself doing more and more training and correcting all the time. The turnover has now begun to affect the quality of the work he turns over to his customers, increasing complaints and damaging his hard-earned reputation. Basically, he has a knowledge problem. He has the knowledge and needs to capture it in a way that it is easy to disseminate to his mechanics. He must find a way to manage this knowledge in order to survive. How successful he is will dictate his future survival in this business.

development of KM systems. We provide a short introduction to these technologies in each of these chapters. Because KM systems provide access to explicit company knowledge, it is easy to learn from previous experiences. **Experience management** is another recent term also related to knowledge management. Basically, experience develops over time to coalesce into more general experience, which then combines into general knowledge. Experiences captured over time can be managed by the use of technology. We will discuss how intelligent technologies are used to manage experiences as well as create new knowledge.

ISSUES IN KNOWLEDGE MANAGEMENT

In practice, given the uncertainty in today's business environments and the reality of continuing layoffs, what could make employees feel compelled to participate in knowledge management initiatives? Although many attempts have been made to launch KM initiatives, including the design and implementation of KM systems, not all KM implementations have been successful. In fact many KM systems implementations, for example of lessons learned systems (discussed in Chapter 8), have fallen short of their promise. Many KM systems implemented at organizations have failed to enable knowledge workers to share their knowledge for the benefit of the organization. The case in point is that effective KM is not about making a choice between "software vs. wetware, classroom vs. hands-on, formal vs, informal, technical vs. social" (Stewart 2002). Effective KM uses all the options available to motivated employees in order to put knowledge to work. Effective KM depends on recognizing that all of these options basically need each other.

One of the primary differences between traditional information systems and KM systems is the active role that users of KM systems play on building the content of such systems. Users of traditional information systems are typically not required to actively contribute to building the content of such systems, an effort typically delegated to the MIS department or to information systems consultants. Therefore, traditional IS research has concentrated much of its efforts in understanding what are the factors leading users to accepting, and thereby using, IT[1]. As we'll see later in Chapter 8, users of lessons learned systems will not only utilize the system to find a lesson applicable to a problem at hand but will typically also contribute lessons to the system database. As a result, the successful implementation of KM systems requires that its users not only effectively "use" such systems as in traditional information systems but that in fact that they also "contribute" to the knowledge base of such systems. Therefore, seeking to understand the factors that lead to the successful implementation of KM systems is an important area of research that is still in its infancy.

Whereas technology has provided the impetus for managing knowledge, we now know that effective KM initiatives are not only limited to a technological solution. An old adage states that effective KM is 80 percent related to organizational culture and human factors and 20 percent related to technology. This means that there is an important human component in KM. This finding addresses the fact that knowledge is first created in the people's minds. KM practices must first identify ways to encourage and stimulate the ability of employees to develop new knowledge. Second, KM methodologies and technologies must enable effective ways to elicit, represent, organize, reuse, and renew this knowledge. Third, KM should not distance itself from the knowledge owners but instead celebrate and recognize their position as experts in the organization. This, in effect, is the essence of knowledge management. More about the controversies surrounding KM will be presented in Chapters 3, 5, and 13.

TEXT OVERVIEW

PART I. PRINCIPLES OF KNOWLEDGE MANAGEMENT

This section of the book includes the overview of knowledge management that we have presented in this chapter, including the role that IT plays in KM and the relevance of KM to modern organizations. Chapter 2 discusses the concept of knowledge in greater detail and distinguishes it from data and information, summarizes the perspectives commonly used to view knowledge, describes the ways of classifying knowledge, and identifies some key characteristics of knowledge. Chapter 3 explains in greater detail the concept of knowledge management. It also describes knowledge management foundations, which are the broad organizational aspects that support KM in the long-term and includes KM infrastructure, KM mechanisms, and KM technologies. KM foundations support KM solutions. Chapter 4 describes and illustrates KM solutions, which include two components: KM processes and KM systems. Chapter 5 describes the variety of ways in which KM can affect individuals and various aspects of organizations.

PART II: KNOWLEDGE MANAGEMENT TECHNOLOGIES AND SYSTEMS

This section of the book is devoted to a discussion of the underlying technologies that enable the creation of knowledge management systems. Chapter 6 introduces the reader to artificial intelligence (AI), its historical perspective, its relationship with knowledge, and why it is an important aspect of knowledge management. This chapter then discusses **knowledge application systems**, which refer to systems that utilize knowledge and summarize the most relevant intelligent technologies that underpin them, specifically rule-based expert systems and case-based reasoning. Case studies of knowledge application systems are discussed. In Chapter 7 we introduce the reader to **knowledge capture systems**, which refer to systems that elicit and preserve the knowledge of experts so that it can be shared with others. Issues related to how to design the knowledge capture system, including the use of intelligent technologies, are discussed. In particular the role of RFID technologies in knowledge capture is presented. Specific examples of knowledge capture systems are discussed. The chapter also includes a discussion on mechanisms for knowledge capture and the use of storytelling in organizations, and it concludes with a short discussion on research trends on knowledge capture systems. In Chapter 8 we describe **knowledge sharing systems**, which refer to systems that organize and distribute knowledge and comprise the majority of the KM systems currently in place. This chapter also discusses the Internet, the World Wide Web, and how they are used to facilitate communications. Search techniques used in Web-based searches are also discussed. Design considerations and special types of knowledge sharing systems are covered: lessons learned systems and expertise locator systems. Case studies of knowledge sharing systems are discussed based on the experience gained from their development. Finally, in Chapter 9 we introduce **knowledge discovery systems**, systems and technologies that create knowledge. The chapter presents a description of knowledge discovery in databases and data mining (DM), including both mechanisms and technologies to support the discovery of knowledge. The material covers design considerations and the CRISP-DM process. Two very relevant topics, DM and its relationship to discovering knowledge on the Web and to customer resource management (CRM), are also presented including the importance of "knowing" about your customer. Barriers to the use of knowledge discovery are discussed. Case studies of knowledge discovery systems are also presented. The chapter includes a discussion on mechanisms for knowledge discovery and the use of socialization to catalyze innovation in organizations.

PART III: MANAGEMENT AND THE FUTURE OF KNOWLEDGE MANAGEMENT

This section of the book presents some of the issues related to management practices and the future of knowledge management. Chapter 10 presents emergent KM practices including a discussion of social networks and communities of practice, how they facilitate knowledge sharing, and how they benefit from communication technologies. This chapter also incorporates a discussion of such emergent technologies as wikis, blogs, and open source development and examines how they enable KM. Chapter 11 describes some of the factors influencing KM, including a discussion of the impact of the type of knowledge, the business strategy, and the industry environment on KM. It also describes a methodology to prioritize implementation of KM solutions based on knowledge, organizational, and industry characteristics. Chapter 12 presents a mechanism for the evaluation and management of KM solutions in an organization. It describes the reasons why such an assessment is needed as well as alternative approaches to conducting the evaluation. Finally, it discusses some overall approaches for managing KM. Finally, Chapter 13 presents some issues on organizational leadership and the future of KM. As KM becomes widely accepted in corporate organizations, it will increasingly become critical for corporate managers to supply adequate leadership for it as well as important safeguards for insuring the security and adequate use of this knowledge. Also in this chapter, we present a discussion on the future of KM. In the future, knowledge management systems are expected to help decisionmakers make more humane decisions and enable them to deal with "wicked," one-of-a-kind problems. We anticipate a future where people and advanced technology will continue to work together, enabling knowledge integration across diverse domains and with considerably higher payoffs.

SUMMARY

In this chapter, you have learned about the following knowledge management issues as they relate to the learning objectives:

1. A description of KM ranging from the system perspective to the organizational perspective.
2. A discussion of the relevance of KM in today's dynamic environments that are augmented with increasing technological complexity.
3. Benefits and considerations about KM are presented, including an overview of the nature of the KM projects currently in progress at public and private organizations around the world.
4. Finally, IT plays an important role in KM. The enabling role of IT is discussed, but the old adage of "KM is 80 percent organizational, and 20 percent about IT" still holds today.

KEY TERMS

Experience management	Knowledge management systems
Intellectual asset	Mission-critical objectives
Intellectual capital	Structural capital
Knowledge management (KM)	

REVIEW

1. Describe knowledge management.
2. Discuss the forces driving knowledge management.

3. What are knowledge management systems? Enumerate the four types of KM systems.
4. Describe some of the issues facing knowledge management.

APPLICATION EXERCISES

1. Identify an example of a knowledge management initiative that has been undertaken in your organization. Has the initiative been successful? What are some of the issues, both technical and nontechnical, that were faced during its implementation?
2. Design a knowledge management initiative to support your business needs.
3. Describe the nontechnical issues that you will face during its implementation.
4. Consider the four forces driving KM described in this chapter. Think of another example that illustrates each of these forces.

NOTE

1. Much of the IS research has concentrated on the development of the technology acceptance model (TAM; Davis 1989), which identifies two factors associated with user acceptance of information technology to be *Perceived Usefulness* and *Perceived Ease of Use.*

REFERENCES

Becerra-Fernandez I. and Sabherwal R. 2005. Knowledge management at NASA-Kennedy Space Center. *International Journal of Knowledge and Learning,* 1(1/2), 159–170.

Bradley, K. 1997. Intellectual capital and the new wealth of nations. *Business Strategy Review,* 8(1) 53–62.

Davenport, T.H. and Prusak, L. 1998. *Working knowledge: How organizations manage what they know.* Boston: Harvard Business School Press.

Davis, F. 1989. Perceived usefulness, perceived ease of use, and user acceptance of information technology. *MIS Quarterly,* 13(3), 319–340.

Drucker, P. 1994. The age of social transformation. *The Atlantic Monthly,* 274(5), 53–70.

Eisenberg, H. 1997. Healing the wounds from reengineering and downsizing. *Quality Progress,* May.

Fries, S. 1992. NASA Engineers and the Age of Apollo. Washington, DC. (NASA SP-4104).

Kenny, B. 2007. The coming crisis in employee turnover. *Forbes,* April 25.

Nahapiet, J. and Ghoshal, S. 1998. Social capital, intellectual capital, and the organizational advantage. *Academy of Management Review,* 23, 242–266.

Stewart, T. 2002. The case against knowledge management. *Business 2.0,* February.

Subramaniam, M. and Youndt, M.A. 2005. The influence of intellectual capital on the types of innovative capabilities. *Academy of Management Journal,* 48(3), 450–463.

PART I

PRINCIPLES OF
KNOWLEDGE MANAGEMENT

2 The Nature of Knowledge

In the previous chapter, we provided an introduction to the basic concepts of knowledge management. This chapter takes the next step by explaining in detail what we mean by **knowledge**. It also distinguishes knowledge from **data** and from **information** and illustrates these three concepts using some examples. This chapter also summarizes some of the perspectives commonly used to view knowledge, including both subjective and objective viewpoints. Moreover, it describes some of the ways to classify knowledge and identifies some attributes that may be used to characterize different types of knowledge. It also relates knowledge to the concept of **intellectual capital** and its various dimensions. Finally, the chapter also explains the various reservoirs, or locations, in which knowledge might reside.

WHAT IS KNOWLEDGE?

"Knowledge" is quite distinct from "data" and "information," although the three terms are sometimes used interchangeably. However, they are quite distinct in nature. In this section, we define and illustrate these concepts and differentiate among them. This discussion also leads to our definition of knowledge.

Data comprise facts, observations, or perceptions (which may or may not be correct). By itself, data represent raw numbers or assertions and may therefore be devoid of context, meaning, or intent. Let us consider three examples of what is considered to be data. We will then build upon these examples to examine the meaning of information and knowledge.

Example 1: That a sales order at a restaurant included two large burgers and two medium-sized vanilla milkshakes is an example of data.

Example 2: The observation that upon tossing a coin it landed heads also illustrates data.

Example 3: The wind component (*u* and *v*) coordinates for a particular hurricane's trajectory, at specific instances of time is likewise considered data.

Although data are devoid of context, meaning, or intent it can be easily captured, stored, and communicated using electronic or other media.

Information is a subset of data, only including those data that possess context, relevance, and purpose. Information typically involves the manipulation of raw data to obtain a more meaningful indication of trends or patterns in the data. Let us continue with the three aforementioned examples:

Example 1: For the manager of the restaurant, the numbers indicating the daily sales (in dollars, quantity, or percentage of daily sales) of burgers, vanilla milkshakes, and other products are information. The manager can use such information to make decisions regarding pricing and raw material purchases.

Example 2: Let us assume that the context of the coin toss is a betting situation where John is offering to pay anyone $10 if the coin lands heads but take $8 if the coin lands tails. Susan is considering whether to take up John's bet, and she benefits from knowing that the last 100 times the coin was tossed, it landed heads 40 times and tails on 60 occasions. The result of each individual toss (head or tail) are data, but is not directly useful. It is therefore data but not information. By contrast, that 40 heads and 60 tails resulted from the last 100 tosses are also data, but they can be directly used to compute probabilities of heads and tails and hence to make the decision. Therefore, they are also information for Susan.

Example 3: Based on the *u* and *v* components, hurricane software models may be used to create a forecast of the hurricane trajectory. The hurricane forecast is information.

As can be seen from these examples, whether certain facts are information or only data depends on the individual who is using those facts. The facts about the daily sales of burgers represent information for the store manager but only data for a customer. If the restaurant is one out of a chain of 250 restaurants, these facts about daily sales are also data for the CEO of the chain. Similarly, the facts about the coin toss are simply data for an individual who is not interested in betting.

Knowledge has been distinguished from data and information in two different ways. A more simplistic view considers knowledge as being at the highest level in a hierarchy with information at the middle level and data at the lowest level. According to this view, knowledge refers to information that enables action and decisions or information with direction. Hence, knowledge is intrinsically similar to information and data, although it is the richest and deepest of the three, and is consequently also the most valuable. Based on this view, data refer to bare facts void of context, for example a telephone number. Information is data in context, for example a phone book. Knowledge is information that facilitates action, for example, individuals who are the domain experts within an organization. An example of knowledge includes recognizing that a phone number belongs to a good client who needs to be called once per week to get his orders.

Although this simplistic view of knowledge may not be completely inaccurate, we feel it doesn't fully explain the characteristics of knowledge. Instead, we use a more complete perspective, according to which knowledge is intrinsically different from information. Instead of considering knowledge as a richer or more detailed set of facts, we define knowledge in an area as *justified beliefs about relationships among concepts relevant to that particular area.* This definition has support in the literature (Nonaka 1994). Let us now consider how this definition works for the above examples.

Example 1: The daily sales of burgers can be used, along with other information (e.g., information on the quantity of bread in the inventory), to compute the amount of bread to buy. The relationship between the quantity of bread that should be ordered, the quantity of bread currently in the inventory, and the daily sales of burgers (and other products that use bread) is an example of knowledge. Understanding of this relationship (which could conceivably be stated as a mathematical formula) helps to use the information (on quantity of bread in the inventory and daily sales of burgers, etc.) to compute the quantity of bread to be purchased. However, the quantity of bread to be ordered should itself be considered information and not knowledge. It is simply more valuable information.

Example 2: The information about 40 heads and 60 tails (out of 100 tosses) can be used to compute the probability of heads (0.40) and tails (0.60). The probabilities can then be used, along with information about the returns associated with heads ($10 from Susan's perspective) and tails (−$8, again from Susan's perspective) to compute the expected value to Susan from participating in the bet. Both probabilities and expected values are information, although more valuable information than the facts that 40 tosses produced heads and 60 produced tails. Moreover, expected value is more useful information than the probabilities; the former can directly be used to make the decision, whereas the latter requires computation of expected value.

The relationship between the **probability** of heads, the number of times the coin lands heads, and the total number of tosses (i.e., that probability of heads, or $p_H = n_H/(n_H + n_T)$, assuming that the coin can only land heads or tails) is an example of knowledge. It helps compute the probability from the data on outcomes of tosses. The similar formula for probability of tails is knowledge as well. In addition, the relationship between expected value (EV) and the probabilities (p_H, p_T) and returns (R_H, R_T) for heads and tails (i.e., $EV = p_H*R_H + p_T*R_T$) is also knowledge. Using these components of knowledge, probability of heads and tails can be computed as 0.40 and 0.60, respectively. Then, the expected value for Susan can be computed as 0.40*(+$10) + 0.60*(−$8) =−$0.80.

Example 3: The knowledge of a hurricane researcher is used to analyze the *u* and *v* wind components as well as the hurricane forecast produced by the different software models, to determine the probability that the hurricane will follow a specific trajectory.

Figure 2.1　**Data, Information, and Knowledge**

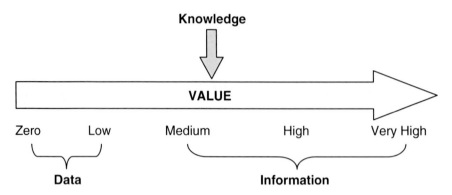

Thus, knowledge helps produce information from data or more valuable information from less valuable information. In that sense, this information facilitates action such as the decision of whether to bet or not. Based on the new generated information of the expected value of the outcome as well as the relationship with other concepts, such as Susan's anticipation that the coin may be fair or not, knowledge enables Susan to decide whether she can expect to win at the game. This aspect of the relationship between data and information is depicted in Figure 2.1, which shows the relationship between data (which has zero or low value in making the decision), and information (which has greater value than data, although different types of information might have differing values).

The above relationships between data, information, and knowledge are illustrated using Example 2 in Figure 2.2. As may be seen from the figure, knowledge of how to count helps convert data on coin tosses (each toss producing a head or tail, with the set of 100 tosses producing 100 such observations, shown as H and T, respectively) into information (number of heads and number of tosses). This information is more useful than the raw data, but it does not directly help the decisionmaker (Susan) to decide on whether to participate in the bet. Using knowledge of how to compute probabilities, this information can be converted into more useful information—that is, the probabilities of heads and tails. Moreover, combining the information about probabilities with information about returns associated with heads and tails, it is possible to produce even more information—that is, the expected value associated with participation in the bet. In making this transition, knowledge of the formula for computing expected value from probabilities and returns is utilized. Figure 2.2 illustrates how knowledge helps produce information from data (e.g., probabilities based on outcomes of tosses of 60 heads and 40 tails) or more valuable information (expected value) from less valuable information (e.g., probabilities and payoffs associated with heads and tails).

The above distinctions among data, information, and knowledge is consistent with Nonaka and Takeuchi's (1995) definition of knowledge as "*a justified true belief.*" It is also consistent with Wiig's (1999) view of knowledge as being fundamentally different from data and information:

Figure 2.2 **An Illustration of Data, Information, and Knowledge**

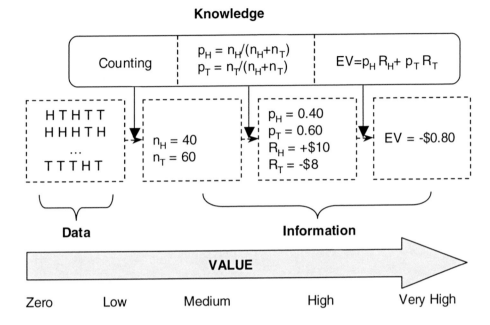

Knowledge consists of truths and beliefs, perspectives and concepts, judgments and expectations, methodologies, and know-how. It is possessed by humans, agents, or other active entities and is used to receive information and to recognize and identify; analyze, interpret, and evaluate; synthesize and decide; plan, implement, monitor, and adapt—that is, to act more or less intelligently. In other words, knowledge is used to determine what a specific situation means and how to handle it.

Figure 2.3 depicts how knowledge, data, and information relate to information systems, decisions, and events. As discussed, knowledge helps convert data into information. The knowledge could be stored in a manual or computer-based information system, which receives data as input and produces information as output. Moreover, the use of information to make the decision requires knowledge as well (e.g., in the context of the second example above, the knowledge that expected value above zero generally suggests that the decision is a good one). The decisions, as well as certain unrelated factors, lead to events, which cause generation of further data. The events, the use of information, and the information system might cause modifications in the knowledge itself. For example, in the context of example 1 on ordering raw materials based on sales, information about changes in suppliers (e.g., a merger of two suppliers) might cause changes in the perceived relationship (i.e., knowledge) between the quantity on hand, the daily sales, and the quantity to be ordered. Similarly, in example 2 on betting on the outcome of a coin toss, the individual's risk aversion, individual wealth, and so forth, might cause changes in beliefs related to whether expected value above zero justifies the decision to participate in the bet.

Figure 2.3   **Relating Data, Information, and Knowledge to Events**

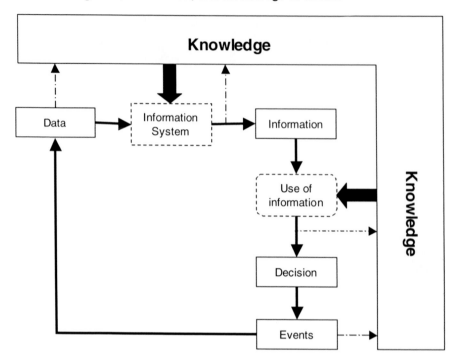

ALTERNATIVE VIEWS OF KNOWLEDGE

Knowledge can be viewed from a subjective or objective stance. The subjective view represents knowledge using two possible perspectives: as a state of mind or as a practice. On the other hand, the objective view represents knowledge in three possible perspectives: as an object, as access to information, or as a capability. The perspectives on knowledge are shown in Figure 2.4.

SUBJECTIVE VIEW OF KNOWLEDGE

According to the subjective view, reality is socially constructed through interactions with individuals (Schultze 1999). Knowledge is viewed as an ongoing accomplishment that continuously affects and is influenced by social practices (Boland and Tenkasi 1995). Consequently, knowledge cannot be placed at a single location, as it has no existence independent of social practices and human experiences. According to the subjective view, knowledge could be considered from two perspectives, either as a state of mind or as practice.

Knowledge as State of Mind

This perspective considers knowledge as being a state of an individual's mind. Organizational knowledge is viewed here as the beliefs of the individuals within the organization.

Figure 2.4 **Various Perspectives on Knowledge**

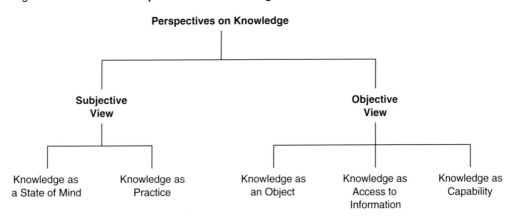

Moreover, to the extent the various individuals have differing experiences and backgrounds, their beliefs and hence knowledge, could differ from each other. Consequently, the focus here is on enabling individuals to enhance their personal areas of knowledge so that they can apply them to best pursue organizational goals (Alavi and Leidner 2001).

Knowledge as Practice

According to this perspective, knowledge is also considered as subjective but it is viewed as being held by a group and not as being decomposable into elements possessed by individuals. Thus, from this perspective, knowledge is "neither possessed by any one agent, nor contained in any one repository" (Schultze 1999, p. 10). Moreover, knowledge resides not in anyone's head but in practice. Knowledge is comprised of beliefs, consistent with our definition earlier, but the beliefs themselves are collective rather than individual, and therefore, are better reflected in organizational activities rather than in the minds of the organization's individuals. Viewed from this perspective, knowledge is "inherently indeterminate and continually emerging" (Tsoukas 1996, p. 22).

OBJECTIVE VIEW OF KNOWLEDGE

The objective view is the diametrical opposite of the subjective stance. According to the objective view, reality is independent of human perceptions and can be structured in terms of *a priori* categories and concepts (Schultze 1999). Consequently, knowledge can be located in the form of an object or a capability that can be discovered or improved by human agents. The objective view considers knowledge from three possible perspectives.

Knowledge as Objects

This perspective considers knowledge as something that can be stored, transferred, and manipulated. Consistent with the definition of knowledge as a set of justified beliefs, these knowledge objects (i.e., beliefs) can exist in a variety of locations. Moreover, they can be of several different types, as discussed in the next section.

Knowledge as Access to Information

This perspective considers knowledge as the condition of access to information (Alavi and Leidner 2001). Thus, knowledge is viewed here as something that enables access and utilization of information. This perspective extends the above view of knowledge as objects, emphasizing the accessibility of the knowledge objects.

Knowledge as Capability

This perspective is consistent with the last two perspectives of knowledge as objects or as access to information. However, this perspective differs in that the focus here is on the way in which knowledge can be applied to influence action. This perspective places emphasis on knowledge as a strategic capability that can potentially be applied to seek a competitive advantage.

Thus, the five perspectives discussed above differ in their focus in viewing knowledge, but they are all consistent in viewing knowledge as a set of beliefs about relationships. The first perspective, knowledge as a state of mind, focuses on beliefs within human minds; while the second perspective, knowledge as a practice, focuses on beliefs implicit to actions or practice. In either case, the beliefs, and the knowledge they comprise, are considered subjective. In contrast, the last three perspectives (knowledge as objects, knowledge as access to information, and knowledge as a capability) view knowledge as objective, focusing on beliefs as objects to be stored and managed, as the condition of access to information, and as a capability that affects action. We recognize all five perspectives as important, and consider them as simply providing different ways of examining knowledge. However, in the remainder of the book, we adopt a position that is more objective than subjective. This is due to the desire to make this textbook useful for students and managers responsible for managing knowledge in their organizations; an objective view facilitates making practical recommendations about how organizations should manage knowledge, whereas a subjective view helps with understanding knowledge management but may be less valuable in recommending actions for knowledge management.

We next examine the different forms of knowledge, which are clearly consistent with the objective perspective of knowledge. However, an argument could also be made that at least some types of knowledge discussed below (e.g., tacit) are not inconsistent with a subjective view either.

DIFFERENT TYPES OF KNOWLEDGE

Knowledge has been classified and characterized in several different ways. For example, knowledge has been categorized as individual, social, causal, conditional, relational, and pragmatic (Alavi and Leidner 2001) and also as embodied, encoded, and procedural (Venzin et al. 1998). In this section, we examine some of the more important classifications of knowledge. It is important to understand the nature of these various types of knowledge because different types of knowledge should be managed differently, as discussed in detail in some of the later chapters.

PROCEDURAL OR DECLARATIVE KNOWLEDGE

The first distinction we examine is that between **declarative knowledge** (facts) and **procedural knowledge** (how to ride a bicycle) (Kogut and Zander 1992; Singley and Anderson 1989). Declarative knowledge (or substantive knowledge, as it is also called) focuses on beliefs about relationships among variables. For example, all other things being equal, a greater price charged for a product would cause some reduction in its number of sales. Declarative knowledge can be stated in the form of propositions, expected correlations, or formulas relating concepts represented as variables. For example, stating that the sum of the square of the sine of an angle and the square of the cosine of the same angle would equal one is an example of declarative knowledge. Similarly, identifying the specific product features a specific customer likes is also an example of declarative knowledge.

Procedural knowledge, in contrast, focuses on beliefs relating sequences of steps or actions to desired (or undesired) outcomes. An example of such procedural knowledge is the set of justified beliefs about the procedure that should be followed in a government organization in deciding on whom to award the contract for a particular area (e.g., information system development).

Declarative knowledge may be characterized as "know what," whereas procedural knowledge may be viewed as "know-how." To further understand the difference between these two types of knowledge, let us consider the example of a hypothetical automobile manufacturing firm. An instance of declarative knowledge in this context is the set of justified beliefs about the effect that the quality of each component would have on the final product. This could include the effect of quality on such features as reliability, fuel consumption, deterioration over time, and quality of the ride of a particular model. Such declarative knowledge, combined with information about the set of components needed for each model and the prices of various alternatives for each component, would help determine the specific components that should be used in each model. An example of procedural knowledge in the same context would be the set of beliefs about the process used to assemble a particular model of the car. This could include such things as the steps in the engine assembly process, which tasks can be performed in parallel, the amount of time that each step should take, the amount of waiting time between successive steps, and so on.

TACIT OR EXPLICIT KNOWLEDGE

Another important classification of knowledge views it as tacit or explicit (Nonaka 1994; Polanyi 1966). **Explicit knowledge** typically refers to knowledge that has been expressed into words and numbers. Such knowledge can be shared formally and systematically in the form of data, specifications, manuals, drawings, audio- and videotapes, computer programs, patents, and the like. For example, the basic principles for stock market analysis contained in a book or manual are considered explicit knowledge. This knowledge can be used by investors to make decisions about buying or selling stocks. It should also be noted that although explicit knowledge might resemble data or information in form, the distinction mentioned earlier in this chapter is preserved; although explicated, the principles of stock market analysis are justified beliefs about relationships rather than simple facts or observations. Also the rules about how to process a travel reimbursement, which becomes embedded in an enterprise resource planning system, is considered explicit knowledge.

In contrast, **tacit knowledge** includes insights, intuitions, and hunches. It is difficult to express and formalize, and therefore difficult to share. Tacit knowledge is more likely to be personal and based on individual experiences and activities. For example, through years of observing a particular industry, a stock market analyst might gain knowledge that helps him make recommendations to investors in the stock market regarding the likely short-term and long-term market trends for the stocks of firms within that industry. Such knowledge would be considered tacit, unless the analyst can verbalize it in the form of a document that others can use and learn from. Tacit knowledge may also include **expertise** that is so specific that it may be too expensive to make explicit; therefore, the organization chooses to let it reside with the expert.

As discussed above, explicit and tacit forms of knowledge are quite distinct. However, it is possible to convert explicit knowledge into tacit, as occurs, for example, when an individual reads a book and learns from it, thereby converting the explicit knowledge contained in the book into tacit knowledge in the individual's mind. Similarly, tacit knowledge can sometimes be converted into explicit knowledge, as happens when an individual with considerable tacit knowledge about a topic writes a book or manual formalizing that knowledge. These possibilities are discussed in greater detail in the next chapter on knowledge management solutions.

GENERAL OR SPECIFIC KNOWLEDGE

The third classification of knowledge focuses on whether the knowledge is possessed widely or narrowly (Sabherwal and Becerra-Fernandez 2005). **General knowledge** is possessed by a large number of individuals and can be transferred easily across individuals. For example, knowledge about the rules of baseball can be considered general, especially among the spectators at a baseball park. One example of general knowledge in this context is recognizing that when a baseball player takes the fourth "ball," he gets a walk; when he takes the third "strike," he is out. It is general because everyone with a basic understanding of baseball would possess this knowledge.

Unlike general knowledge, **specific knowledge**, or "idiosyncratic knowledge," is possessed by a very limited number of individuals, and is expensive to transfer (Hayek 1945; Jensen and Meckling 1996; Sabherwal and Becerra-Fernandez 2005). Consider the distinction between a professional coach and a typical fan watching a baseball game. The coach has the knowledge needed to filter, from the chaos of the game, the information required to evaluate and help players through advice such as when to try to hit the ball, when to steal a base, and so on. For example, if Albert Pujols is at bat, a slow man is on first, his team has two outs and is behind by one run against a left handed pitcher, Pujols should be allowed to swing away. Few fans may have this knowledge, and so it is considered specific.

Specific knowledge can be of three types: technology-specific knowledge, context-specific knowledge, and context-and-technology-specific knowledge. **Technology-specific knowledge** is deep knowledge about a specific area. It includes knowledge about the tools and techniques that may be used to address problems in that area. This kind of knowledge is often acquired as a part of some formal training and is then augmented through experience in the field. Examples include the scientific knowledge possessed by a physicist and the knowledge about computer hardware possessed by a computer engineer. Within the engineering directorate at NASA-Kennedy Space Center, the knowledge of project management techniques (such as PERT charts and critical path analysis) is technology specific, as it pertains to project management in general without being specific to NASA or Kennedy Space Center.

On the other hand, **context-specific knowledge** refers to the knowledge of particular circumstances of time and place in which work is to be performed (Hayek 1945; O'Reilly and Pondy 1979; Sabherwal and Becerra-Fernandez 2005). Contextually specific knowledge pertains to the organization and the organizational subunit within which tasks are performed. For example, the detailed knowledge a design engineer possesses about the idiosyncrasies of the particular design group in which she is working is contextually specific. Another example is a baseball catcher's knowledge of the team's pitching staff. Contextually specific knowledge cannot be acquired through formal training but instead must be obtained from within the specific context (such as membership in the same design group or baseball team). Within the engineering directorate at NASA-Kennedy Space Center, the knowledge of the mechanisms used to patent and license NASA-developed technology for public use is context-specific, because it depends primarily on the Kennedy Space Center's context with minimal effect of the particular technical discipline.

A third kind of specific knowledge, which may be called **context-and-technology-specific knowledge**, is specific in terms of both the context and the technical aspects. Context-and-technology-specific knowledge simultaneously involves both rich scientific knowledge and an understanding of the particular context (Machlup 1980; Sabherwal and Becerra-Fernandez 2005). For example, knowledge of how to decide on the stocks to acquire within an industry is context-and-technology-specific; it blends an understanding of that industry's dynamics as well as the tools used to analyze stock performance. Similarly, in the engineering directorate at NASA-Kennedy Space Center, the knowledge of how to plan and develop ground and flight support systems is context-and-technology-specific because it depends on both the design context of flight systems at Kennedy Space Center and principles of engineering.

COMBINING THE CLASSIFICATIONS OF KNOWLEDGE

The above classifications of knowledge are independent. In other words, procedural knowledge could be either tacit or explicit and either general or specific. Similarly, declarative knowledge could be either tacit or explicit and either general or specific. Combining the above three classifications and considering technically specific and contextually specific knowledge as distinct, 12 ($2 \times 2 \times 3$) types of knowledge can be identified as indicated and illustrated in Table 2.1.

KNOWLEDGE AND EXPERTISE

We define **expertise** to be knowledge of higher quality. It addresses the degree of knowledge. That is, one who possesses expertise is able to perform a task much better that those who do not. This is specific knowledge at its best. The word "expert" can be used to describe people possessing many different levels of skills or knowledge. A person can be an expert at a particular task irrespective of how sophisticated that area of expertise is. For example, there are expert bus drivers just as there are expert brain surgeons. Each of them excels in the performance of tasks in their respective field.

Thus, the concept of expertise must be further classified for different types of domains. The skill levels of experts from different domains should not be compared to each other. All experts require roughly the same cognitive skills. The difference lies in the depth of their expertise when compared to others from their own domains. For example, a highly skilled bus driver has greater abilities than a novice driver, just as an expert brain surgeon has greater skills than a surgical intern. Prior empirical research on expertise indicates the importance of knowledge management: "It takes time to become an expert. Even the most gifted performers need a minimum of ten years of intense training before they win international competitions" (Ericsson et al. 2007, p. 18).

Expertise can be classified into three distinct categories. Expert systems have had varying degrees of success when representing expertise from each of these categories. These categories, discussed in the following subsections, are (1) associational (black box), (2) motor skills, and (3) theoretical (deep) expertise.

Associational Expertise

In most fields, it is usually desirable that experts have a detailed understanding of the underlying theory within that field. But is this absolutely necessary? What about the television repair technician considered an expert repairman but who does not understand all of the complex internal workings of a transistor or a picture tube? He can associate the observations of the performance of the device to specific causes purely based on his experience. This individual may have expert-level **associational understandings** of these devices and may be able to fix almost any problem encountered. However, if he encounters a new, previously unseen problem, he may not know how to proceed because he does not understand the inner workings of the device.

Motor Skills Expertise

Motor skill expertise is predominantly physical rather than cognitive; therefore, knowledge-based systems cannot easily emulate this type of expertise. Humans improve these skills by repeated and coached practice. While some people have greater

Table 2.1

Illustrations of the Different Types of Knowledge

	General	Contextually Specific	Technically Specific
Declarative			
Explicit	A book describing factors to consider when deciding whether to buy a company's stock. This may include price to earnings ratio, dividends	A company document identifying the circumstances under which a consultant team's manager should consider replacing a team member who is having problems with the project.	A manual describing the factors to consider in configuring a computer so as to achieve performance specifications
Tacit	Knowledge of the major factors to consider when deciding whether to buy a company's stock.	A human relations manager's knowledge of factors to consider in motivating an employee in a particular company.	A technician's knowledge of symptoms to look for in trying to repair a faulty television set.
Procedural			
Explicit	A book describing steps to take in deciding whether to buy a company's stock.	A company document identifying the sequence of actions a consultant team's manager should take when requesting senior management to replace a team member having problems with the project.	A manual describing how to change the operating system setting on a computer so as to achieve desired performance changes.
Tacit	Basic knowledge of the steps to take in deciding whether to buy a company's stock.	A human relations manager's knowledge of steps to take in motivating an employee in a particular company.	A technician's knowledge of the sequence of steps to perform in repairing a television set.

abilities for these types of skills than others, real learning and expertise result from persistent guided practice. For example, consider the tasks of riding a bicycle, hitting a baseball, and downhill snow skiing. When you observe experts performing these activities, you notice that their reactions seem spontaneous and automatic. These reactions result from the experts' continual and persistent and coached practice. For example, when a skilled baseball player bats, he instinctively reacts to a curveball, adjusting his swing to connect with the ball. This appropriate reaction results from encountering thousands of curveballs over many years and the coaches' recommendations on how to hit the ball in a particular situation. A novice batter might recognize a curveball being thrown, but due to a lack of practice reacts slower and consequently may strike out.

These processes do not involve conscious thinking per se. The batter merely reacts instinctively and almost instantaneously to the inputs. In fact, many coaches maintain that thinking in such situations degrades performance. Of course, some cognitive activity is necessary—the batter must follow the track of the ball, recognize its motion (curve, changeup, etc.), and make a decision on what to do (swing, let it go, etc.). The issue, however, is that the result of the decision-making is manifested in very quick physical actions and not in carefully pondered statements.

Box 2.1

Deep Theoretical Knowledge Enables Competitive Advantage

During the 1980s, two firms were involved in competition for a long-term (multiple decades) and large (multibillion dollar) government contract for tactical missiles. Neither company had a significant performance advantage over the other.

A scientist at one of the firms, who was not a member of the project team, broke the stalemate. He had deep expertise in developing missiles due to over 20 years of experience in this area. He was well regarded as a technical expert, and when he called a meeting of the major participants in the project they all came. For several hours, he enchanted them with a comprehensive description of design changes that he had identified within a single week of committed effort. Making no use of any kind of notes, he guided them through the reconfiguration of the entire missile. To implement the extensive changes he suggested in hardware, wiring, and software, 400 individuals would need to work full-time for a year and a half. However, the expert's audience was convinced that the redesign would produce tremendous competitive advantage. His proposal led to a frenzy of activity and enabled his firm to win the contract. More than 20 years later, in 2004, the redesign that this individual with deep expertise had created was still producing benefits.

Source: Compiled from Leonard and Swap 2004.

Theoretical (Deep) Expertise

Finding a solution to a technical problem often requires going beyond a superficial understanding of the domain. We must apply creative ingenuity—ingenuity that is based on our theoretical knowledge of the domain. This type of knowledge allows experts to solve problems that have not been seen before and, therefore, cannot be solved via associational expertise.

Such deeper, more theoretical knowledge is acquired through formal training and hands-on problem-solving. Typically, engineers and scientists who have many years of formal training possess this type of knowledge. Box 2.1 illustrates **deep theoretical knowledge**.

SOME CONCLUDING REMARKS ON THE TYPES OF KNOWLEDGE

In addition to the above types of knowledge, some other classifications also deserve mention. One of these classifications views knowledge as either simple or complex. Whereas **simple knowledge** focuses on one basic area, **complex knowledge** draws upon multiple distinct areas of expertise. Another classification focuses on the role of knowledge within organizations. It divides knowledge into: **support knowledge**, which relates to organizational infrastructure and facilitates day-to-day operations; **tactical knowledge**, which pertains to the short-term positioning of the organization relative to its markets, competitors, and suppliers; and **strategic knowledge**, which pertains to the long-term positioning of the organization in terms of its corporate vision and strategies for achieving that vision.

Based in part on the above types of knowledge, a number of characteristics of knowledge can be identified. One such characteristic is explicitness of knowledge, which reflects the extent to which knowledge exists in an explicit form so that it can be stored and transferred to others. As a characteristic of knowledge, explicitness indicates that rather than simply classifying knowledge as either explicit or tacit, it may be more appropriate to view explicitness as a continuous scale. Explicit and tacit kinds of knowledge are at the two ends of the continuum, with explicit knowledge being high in explicitness and tacit knowledge being low in this regard. Any specific knowledge would then be somewhere along this continuum of explicitness.

Zander and Kogut (1995) argue that instead of considering explicit and tacit knowledge, we should consider two characteristics of knowledge—codifiability and teachability. **Codifiability** reflects the extent to which knowledge can be articulated or codified, even if the resulting codified knowledge might be difficult to impart to another individual. In contrast, **teachability** reflects the extent to which the knowledge can be taught to other individuals, through training, apprenticeship, and so on. Of course, some knowledge could be high in both teachability and codifiability, while some knowledge could be low in both teachability and codifiability. The former would clearly be considered explicit, whereas the latter would clearly be considered tacit. But, teachability and codifiability need not be correlated. In other words, some knowledge could be high in teachability but low in codifiability—for instance, knowledge of how to play basketball. Alternatively, some knowledge could be high in codifiability but low in teachability—for instance, knowledge of how to fix problems in a personal computer.

Specific knowledge is directly related to the concept of knowledge specificity (Choudhury and Sampler 1997). A high level of knowledge specificity implies that the knowledge can be acquired and/or effectively used only by individuals possessing certain prior knowledge (Jensen and Meckling 1996). Knowledge specificity implies that the knowledge is possessed by a very limited number of individuals and is expensive to transfer (Choudhury and Sampler 1997). Taking a step further, technically specific and contextually specific knowledge lead us to break down knowledge specificity into **contextual knowledge specificity** and **technical knowledge specificity**. Of course, contextually specific knowledge and technically specific knowledge are high in contextual knowledge specificity and technical knowledge specificity, respectively.

In addition, the distinction between simple and complex knowledge may be represented using complexity as a knowledge attribute. Similarly, the organizational role of knowledge reflects the distinction among support, tactical, and strategic knowledge.

An organization does not have only one of the above types of knowledge. Instead, in any given organization, multiple different types of knowledge exist together. In Box 2.2, we provide an example of how different types of knowledge exist together within an organization.

LOCATIONS OF KNOWLEDGE

Knowledge resides in several different locations or reservoirs, which are summarized in Figure 2.5. They include people, including individuals and groups; artifacts, including practices, technologies, and repositories; and organizational entities, including

Box 2.2

Different Types of Knowledge at Hill and Knowlton

Founded in 1927, Hill and Knowlton is a leading international communications consultancy headquartered in New York, with 74 offices in 41 countries and an extensive associate network. It is part of WPP Group Plc, which is one of the world's largest communications services groups and provides services to local, multinational, and global clients. Among other things, the company is hired by organizations to manage their product launches, media relations, and communication during crises.

In the late 1990s, turnover rates in certain practices in public relations, such as those related to technology, increased from 15 percent to over 30 percent. The loss of talented individuals led to a leakage of important knowledge as well as information about specific projects. In 1988, in response to concerns by several key clients of the company, the Worldwide Advisory Group (a summit of the company's 200 managers) considered ways of addressing this issue of knowledge leakage. This group identified three broad types of knowledge that were important to the company. One of these was the company's internal knowledge about its own products and services. The second was external knowledge, such as economic forecasts and other related research by outside experts. The third type of knowledge related to clients including budgets, templates, and account activity.

Subsequently, Ted Graham was appointed as Hill and Knowlton's worldwide director of knowledge management. He concluded that while the company was performing well in terms of capturing the structured knowledge such as case studies, proposals, and staff bios, it was not doing so well in capturing unstructured knowledge such as knowledge embedded in speeches, e-mail messages, and other information that had not been classified in any fashion. To deal with this problematic situation, the advisory group decided to replace the current global Intranet with "hK.net," a "Web-based virtual workspace" serving the company's offices across the world. Based on Intraspect Software Inc.'s Salsa application and a password-protected Web site, hK.net was designed to enable both the employees and clients to access internal and external repositories of information and knowledge such as news about the company and the industry, client-related budget information and e-mail archives, staff biographies, presentations, spreadsheets, case studies, pictures, video clips, conference notes, research reports, and so on. Clients as well as Hill and Knowlton executives appreciated hK.net because it reduced the time spent in educating new members of project teams as well as training new employees.

Source: Compiled from Meister and Mark 2004, http://www.hillandknowlton.com/.

---

organizational units, organizations, and interorganizational networks. These locations of knowledge are discussed in the rest of this section.

KNOWLEDGE IN PEOPLE

A considerable component of knowledge is stored in people. It could be stored either at the individual level or within a group or a collection of people (Felin and Hesterly 2007).

Some knowledge is stored in *individuals* within organizations. For instance, in professional service firms, such as consulting or law firms, considerable knowledge resides within the minds of individual members of the firm (Argote and Ingram 2000; Felin and Hesterly 2007). The knowledge stored in individuals is the reason several companies continually seek ways to retain knowledge that might be lost because of individuals retiring or otherwise leaving the organization.

Figure 2.5 **The Reservoirs of Knowledge**

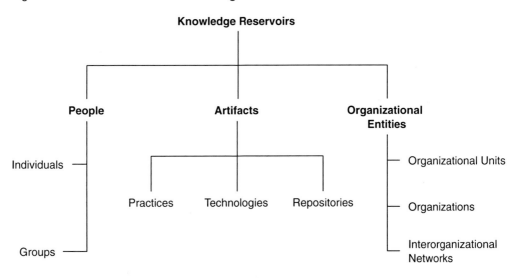

In addition, considerable knowledge resides within *groups* because of the relationships among the members of the group (Felin and Hesterly 2007). When three individuals have worked together for a long time, they instinctively know each other's strengths and weaknesses, understand the other's approach, and recognize aspects that need to be communicated and those that could be taken for granted (Skyrme 2000). Consequently, groups form beliefs about what works well and what does not, and this knowledge is over and above the knowledge residing in each individual member. In other words, the collective knowledge is synergistic—greater than the sum of their individual knowledge. Communities of practice that first develop as individuals interact frequently with each other (physically or virtually) to discuss topics of mutual interest, and they illustrate such embedding of knowledge within groups.

KNOWLEDGE IN ARTIFACTS

Over time, a significant amount of knowledge is stored in organizational artifacts as well. Some knowledge is stored in *practices,* organizational routines, or sequential patterns of interaction. In this case, knowledge is embedded in procedures, rules, and norms that are developed through experience over time and guide future behavior (Levitt and March 1988). For example, fast-food franchises often store knowledge about how to produce high-quality products in routines (Argote and Ingram 2000).

Considerable knowledge is also often stored in *technologies* and systems. As discussed earlier in this chapter, in addition to storing data, information technologies and computer-based information systems can store knowledge about relationships. For example, a computerized materials requirement planning system contains considerable knowledge about relationships among demand patterns, lead times for orders, and reorder quantities.

Knowledge repositories represent a third way of storing knowledge in artifacts. Knowledge repositories could either be paper based such as books, papers, and other documents, or electronic. An example of a paper-based repository is a consultant's set of notes to herself about the kind of things the client might focus more on, when examining the proposals submitted by the consultant firm's and its competitors. On the other hand, a Web site containing answers to frequently asked questions (FAQs) about a product represents an electronic knowledge repository.

Knowledge in Organizational Entities

Knowledge is also stored within organizational entities. These entities can be considered at three levels: organizational units (parts of the organization), an entire organization, and in interorganizational relationships (such as the relationship between an organization and its customers).

Within an *organizational unit,* such as a department or an office, knowledge is stored partly in the relationships among the members of the units. In other words, the organizational unit represents a formal grouping of individuals, who come together not because of common interests but rather, because of organizational structuring. Over time, as individuals occupying certain roles in an organizational unit depart and are replaced by others, the incumbents inherit some, but not all, of the knowledge developed by their predecessors. This knowledge may have been acquired through the systems, practices, and relationships within that unit. Moreover, contextually specific knowledge is more likely to be related to the specific organizational unit.

An *organization,* such as a business unit or a corporation, also stores certain knowledge, especially contextually specific knowledge. The norms, values, practices, and culture within the organization, and across its organizational units, contain knowledge that is not stored within the mind of any one individual. The way in which the organization responds to environmental events is dependent, therefore, not only upon the knowledge stored in individuals and organizational units but also in the overall organizational knowledge that has developed through positive and negative experiences over time.

Finally, knowledge is also stored in *interorganizational relationships.* As organizations establish and consolidate relationships with customers and suppliers, they draw upon knowledge embedded in those relationships. Customers who use the focal organization's products, and suppliers who provide the basic components from which the products are made, often have considerable knowledge about the strengths and weaknesses of those products. Consequently, organizations often learn from their customers' experience with products about how these can be improved. They can also learn about new products that might be appealing to customers.

Knowledge Locations and Forms of Intellectual Capital

An organization's intellectual capital refers to the sum of all its knowledge resources, which may be within or outside the organization (Stewart 1997; Subramaniam and

Youndt 2005; Youndt et al. 2004). **Intellectual capital** has been viewed as being of different types in terms of where the knowledge resides. Intellectual capital has recently been classified into three types (Subramaniam and Youndt 2005; Youndt et al. 2004): *human capital,* or the knowledge, skills and capabilities possessed by individual employees; *organizational capital,* or the institutionalized knowledge and codified experience residing in databases, manuals, culture, systems, structures, and processes; and *social capital,* or the knowledge embedded in relationships and interactions among individuals. These three types of intellectual capital relate directly to the locations discussed above: Human capital relates to knowledge in people, structural capital relates to knowledge in artifacts, and organizational capital relates to knowledge in organizational entities.

SUMMARY

In this chapter, we have explained the nature of knowledge in considerable detail. Knowledge is distinguished from data and information; highlighting that knowledge should best be considered as fundamentally different from data and information rather than considering data, information, and knowledge as being part of a hierarchy. We defined knowledge in an area as *justified beliefs about relationships among concepts relevant to that particular area.* Furthermore, we examined subjective and objective perspectives for viewing knowledge, including perspectives that consider knowledge as a state of mind, as practice, as an object, as access to information, and as a capability. We then distinguished between procedural and declarative knowledge, between tacit and explicit knowledge, and between general and specific knowledge. Some other ways of classifying knowledge were also described. Based on the various classifications of knowledge, we introduced knowledge characteristics such as tacitness, specificity, and so on. This chapter also described the possible locations of knowledge including people, artifacts, and organizational entities, and related these locations to different types of intellectual capital. The next chapter builds on this one by explaining knowledge management and describing the various aspects of KM infrastructure.

KEY TERMS

Associational expertise	Information
Data	Intellectual capital
Declarative knowledge	Knowledge
Deep expertise	Motor skills expertise
Expertise	Procedural knowledge
Explicit knowledge	Specific knowledge
General knowledge	Tacit knowledge

REVIEW

1. How do the terms data and knowledge differ? Describe each term with the help of a similar example, elucidating the difference between the two.
2. Information contains data but not all data are information. Justify this statement.
3. Explain why the same set of data can be considered as useful information by some and useless by others. Further, could this useful information be termed as knowledge? Why?
4. Describe the ways in which knowledge differs from data and information. Justify your answer with a relevant diagram.
5. Explain the importance of knowledge in creation and utilization of information.
6. How does the subjective view of knowledge differ from the objective view? Explain how knowledge can be viewed as a state of mind, as a practice, as objects, as access to information and as capability.
7. What is the difference between knowledge characterized as know what and know-how? In the above situations, how would you classify the knowledge a computer programmer has?
8. Does a player in a card game use tacit or explicit knowledge? Why? Define and explain the difference between the two.
9. What is general knowledge? How does it differ from specific knowledge? Describe the types of specific knowledge with suitable examples.
10. What is expertise? Distinguish among the three types of expertise.
11. Contrast the differences between knowledge in people and knowledge in artifacts. Describe the various repositories of knowledge within organizational entities.
12. What is intellectual capital? What are the three types of intellectual capital, and how do they relate to different knowledge locations?

APPLICATION EXERCISES

1. Consider five decisions you have made today. (They could be simple things like taking a turn while driving or even choosing a soda at a convenience store.) In each case determine the data, information, and/or knowledge that were involved in the decision. Now consider how those decisions would have been influenced by the lack of pre-existing data, information, or knowledge.
2. You have recently invented a new product. Collect demographic data from a sample population and determine how you would use this data and convert it into information for marketing the product. Give an example about knowledge that may be useful in converting the data into information.
3. Interview a manager in a manufacturing organization and one in a services-based organization. Determine the contrasting views of knowledge between the two due to the nature of their businesses.
4. Determine the various locations of knowledge within your organization (or that of a friend/family member). Classify them appropriately. Now speculate on the negative effects of not having one or more of those knowledge reposi-

tories and accordingly determine which repository is the most critical to the organization. Which is the least?

5. Determine the various types of knowledge you used to read this chapter. You should be able to state at least one of each type.

6. Interview organizations in your area to determine the explicit and tacit knowledge within the organization. Rank the explicit knowledge on the basis of its codifiability and teachability. Further, suggest ways in which the tacit knowledge could be made explicit.

7. You are considering buying a new 2009 Ford Taurus. Gather tacit knowledge and explicit knowledge on buying cars from various resources: for example, Ford Web site (http://www.ford.com). List your findings and explain what source of knowledge is important for your choice.

8. Suppose you desperately need technical advice on an Apple Inc. product. You have several options. Four of them are: (a) Call Apple's technical support; (b) use Apple's online customer support; (c) use Apple's online discussion groups; and (d) visit the genius bar at the nearest Apple store. Define your preferred option and briefly explain your choice with the concepts of accessibility to knowledge reservoir.

9. Wal-Mart Stores, Inc. (http://www.walmart.com) is said to be one of the leading employers of older workers and consider seniors vital to its unique corporate culture. Store managers are encouraged to recruit from senior citizen groups, local AARP chapters, and churches. Analyze Wal-Mart's above strategy in terms of knowledge management.

10. Use any organization with which you are familiar to answer this question. This organization could be one where you currently work or one where you have previously worked. For this organization, describe one example of knowledge that would be classified as structural capital, one example of knowledge that would be classified as organizational capital, and one example of knowledge that would be classified as social capital.

REFERENCES

Alavi, M. and Leidner, D. 2001. Knowledge management and knowledge management systems: Conceptual foundations and research issues. *MIS Quarterly,* 25(1), 107.

Argote, L. and Ingram, P. 2000. Knowledge transfer: Basis for competitive advantage in firms. *Organizational Behavior and Human Decision Processes,* 82(1) (May), 150–169.

Boland, R.J. and Tenkasi, R.V. 1995. Perspective making and perspective taking in communities of knowing. *Organization Science,* 6(4), 350–72.

Choudhury, V., and Sampler, J. 1997. Information specificity and environmental scanning: An economic perspective. *MIS Quarterly,* 21(1), 25–53.

Ericsson, K.A., Prietula, M.J., and Cokely, E.T. 2007. The making of an expert. *Harvard Business Review,* July–August, 114–121.

Felin, T. and Hesterly, W.S. 2007. The knowledge-based view, nested heterogeneity, and new value creation: Philosophical considerations on the locus of knowledge. *Academy of Management Review,* 32(1), 195–218.

Hayek, F.A. 1945. The use of knowledge in society. *American Economic Review, XXXV*(4) (September), 519–530.

Jensen, M.C., and Meckling, W.H. 1996. Specific and general knowledge, and organizational structure. In *Knowledge Management & Organizational Design,* ed. P.S. Myers, 17–38. Newton, MA: Butterworth-Heinemann.

Kogut, B. and Zander, U. 1992. Knowledge of the firm, combinative capabilities and the replication of technology. *Organization Science,* 3(3), 383–397.

Leonard, D. and Swap, W. 2004. Deep smarts. *Harvard Business Review,* 82(9) (September), 88–97.

Levitt, B. and March, J.G. 1988. Organizational learning. *Annual Review of Sociology,* 14, 319–340.

Machlup, F. 1980. *Knowledge: Its creation, distribution and economic significance,* Volume 1. Princeton, NJ: Princeton University Press.

Meister, D. and Mark, K. 2004. *Hill & Knowlton: Knowledge management.* Case #9B04E003. London, ONT: Ivey Publishing.

Nonaka, I. 1994. A dynamic theory of organizational knowledge creation. *Organization Science,* 5(1), 14–37.

Nonaka, I., and Takeuchi, H. 1995. *The knowledge creating company.* New York: Oxford University Press.

O'Reilly, C.A. and Pondy, L. 1979. Organizational communication. In *Organizational behavior,* ed. S. Kerr, 119–150. Columbus, OH: John Wiley & Sons.

Polanyi, M. 1966. *The tacit dimension.* London: Routledge and Keoan.

Sabherwal, R. and Becerra-Fernandez, I. 2005. Integrating specific knowledge: Insights from Kennedy Space Center. *IEEE Transactions on Engineering Management* 52(3).

Schultze, U. 1999. Investigating the contradictions in knowledge management. In *Information systems: Current issues and future changes,* ed. T.J. Larsen, L. Levine, and J.I. De Gross, 155–174. Laxenberg: International Federation for Information Processing.

Singley, M. and Anderson, J. 1989. *The transfer of cognitive skill.* Cambridge, MA: Harvard University Press.

Skyrme, D.J. 2000. Developing a knowledge strategy: From management to leadership. In *Knowledge management: Classic and contemporary works,* ed. D. Morey, M. Maybury, and B. Thuraisingham, 61–84. Cambridge, MA: The MIT Press.

Stewart, T.A. 1997. *Intellectual capital.* New York: Doubleday-Currency.

Subramaniam, M. and Youndt, M.A. 2005. The influence of intellectual capital on the types of innovative capabilities. *Academy of Management Journal,* 48(3), 450–463.

Tsoukas, H. 1996. The firm as a distributed knowledge system: A constructionist approach. *Strategic Management Journal,* 17 (Winter), 11–25.

Venzin, M., von Krogh, G., and Roos, J. 1998. Future research into knowledge management. In *Knowing in firms: Understanding, managing and measuring knowledge,* ed. G. von Krogh, J. Roos, and D. Kleine. Thousand Oaks, CA: Sage Publications.

Wiig, K. 1999. Introducing knowledge management into the enterprise. In *Knowledge management handbook,* ed. Jay Liebowitz, 3–1 to 41. Boca Raton, FL: CRC Press.

Youndt, M. A., Subramaniam, M., and Snell, S. A. 2004. Intellectual capital profiles: An examination of investments and returns. *Journal of Management Studies,* 41(2), 335–361.

Zander, U., Kogut, B. 1995. Knowledge and the speed of the transfer and imitation of organizational capabilities: An empirical test. *Organization Science,* 6, 76–92.

3 Knowledge Management Foundations: Infrastructure, Mechanisms, and Technologies

In Chapter 2, we examined the nature of knowledge as well as its various forms and locations. This chapter explains in greater detail the concept of knowledge management. It also describes knowledge management solutions, which refer to the variety of ways in which **knowledge management** can be facilitated. **KM solutions** include two components: KM processes and KM systems. KM solutions depend on three foundations: KM mechanisms, KM technologies, and KM infrastructure. This chapter describes these three **KM foundations**. It is followed by a discussion of KM solutions—that is, KM processes and KM solutions—in Chapter 4.

In this chapter we first discuss knowledge management, and then we describe the five components of KM solutions. We subsequently describe and illustrate KM mechanisms, KM technologies, and KM infrastructure followed by a brief discussion of the management of these KM foundations and some concluding remarks.

KNOWLEDGE MANAGEMENT

Managing any resource may be defined as doing what is necessary to get the most out of that resource. Therefore, at a very simple level, knowledge management may be defined as *doing what is needed to get the most out of knowledge resources.* Let us now consider this simple definition in some detail by providing a few elaborations.

First, it is important to stress that this definition can be applied at the individual as well as organizational levels. Depending on the level, knowledge resources might be those resources that are relevant to the decisions, goals, and strategies of an individual or an organization. The "organization" may be a corporation, a firm, a field office of a firm, a department within a corporation or firm, and so forth. Moreover, the term knowledge resources refers not only to the knowledge currently possessed by the individual or the organization but also to the knowledge that can potentially be obtained (at some cost, if necessary) from other individuals or organizations.

Second, get the most reflects the impacts of knowledge management on the goal achievement of the individual or the organization. Considering the impact knowledge can have on individuals and organizations (as summarized in Chapter 1 and to be discussed in greater detail in Chapter 4), the objective of knowledge management is to enhance the extent to which knowledge facilitates the achievement of individual or organizational goals. Furthermore, a cost/benefit assumption is implicit here. In other words, the objective is to enhance the impact of knowledge in a cost-effective fashion, such that the benefits of knowledge management exceed the costs of doing so.

Finally, the things needed refers to a variety of possible activities involved in knowledge management. These activities are broadly intended to: (a) discover new knowledge, (b) capture existing knowledge, (c) share knowledge with others, or (d) apply knowledge.

Based on these elaborations, a more detailed definition of knowledge management can now be offered.

> Knowledge management can be defined as performing the activities involved in discovering, capturing, sharing, and applying knowledge so as to enhance, in a cost-effective fashion, the impact of knowledge on the unit's goal achievement.

Another important emergent technology related to knowledge management—**business intelligence (BI)**—is sometimes used interchangeably with KM. Although KM and BI are somewhat interrelated, they are quite distinct. BI focuses on providing decisionmakers with valuable information and knowledge by utilizing a variety of sources of data and structured and unstructured information (Sabherwal 2007, 2008), via the discovery of the relationships that may exist between these sources of data and information.

Unlike KM, which starts with information and knowledge as inputs, BI begins with data and information as inputs. KM directly results in the discovery of new knowledge, the conversion of knowledge from one form to another (i.e., from tacit to explicit or vice versa), the sharing of knowledge, or the application of knowledge while making a decision. In contrast, BI directly results in information (which is presented in a friendly fashion, such as through dashboards) and newly created knowledge or insights obtained by revealing previously unknown connections or patterns within data and information. Thus, KM is by and large not directly concerned with data (with the exception of knowledge discovery from data and information using techniques such as data mining, which represents an area of overlap between KM and BI). In contrast, data are critical to BI, which often depends on activities like data warehousing and data mining. However, the results of BI can be, and often are, useful inputs to KM.

KM incorporates **knowledge capture**, **sharing**, and **application** in addition to **discovery**. On the other hand, BI focuses on data access, analysis, and presentation. The connection between BI and knowledge is limited to **knowledge creation** (by discovering patterns based on existing explicit data and information). Even in this respect, BI focuses directly on discovery of explicit knowledge whereas KM concerns discovery of both tacit and explicit knowledge. In other words, only explicit knowledge can directly result from BI, whereas KM is concerned with activities that produce both explicit and tacit knowledge.

Finally, KM involves using both social aspects as well as information technology, and is sometimes viewed as being more social than technical. On the other hand, BI is primarily technical in nature, and does not incorporate social mechanisms related to knowledge discovery, such as meetings and **brainstorming retreats**.

The above distinctions between knowledge management and business intelligence are summarized in Table 3.1.

Table 3.1

A Comparison of Knowledge Management and Business Intelligence

	Knowledge Management	Business Intelligence
Intellectual Components	Primary: Knowledge (Explicit and Tacit)	Primary: Data
	Secondary: Information, Data	Secondary: Information, Explicit Knowledge
Processes	Knowledge Capture, Sharing, Application, and Discovery	Data Access, Analysis, and Presentation
Key components	Social Mechanisms and Information Technology	Mainly Information Technologies

KNOWLEDGE MANAGEMENT SOLUTIONS AND FOUNDATIONS

Knowledge management depends on two broad aspects: KM solutions, which are specific in nature; and KM foundations, which are broader and more long-term. **KM solutions** refer to the ways in which specific aspects of KM (discovery, capture, sharing, and application of knowledge) can be accomplished. KM solutions include KM processes and KM systems. **KM foundations** are the broad organizational aspects that support KM in the short- and long-term. They include KM infrastructure, KM mechanisms, and KM technologies. Thus, KM solutions depend on KM foundations, as shown in Figure 3.1. Next, we briefly explain the three components of KM foundations and the two components of KM solutions.

KM infrastructure reflects the long-term foundation for knowledge management. In an organizational context, KM infrastructure includes five major components (e.g., organization culture and the organization's information technology infrastructure).

KM mechanisms are organizational or structural means used to promote knowledge management. They may (or may not) involve the use of information technology, but they do involve some kind of organizational arrangement or social or structural means of facilitating KM. They depend on KM infrastructure and facilitate KM systems.

KM technologies are information technologies that can be used to facilitate knowledge management. Thus, KM technologies are intrinsically no different from information technologies, but they focus on knowledge management rather than information processing. KM technologies also support KM systems and benefit from the KM infrastructure, especially the information technology infrastructure.

KM processes are the broad processes that help in discovering, capturing, sharing, and applying knowledge. These four KM processes are supported by KM systems and seven important types of KM subprocesses (e.g., exchange). KM processes are described and illustrated in Chapter 4.

KM systems are the integration of technologies and mechanisms that are developed to support the above four KM processes. KM systems are described further in Chapter 4, and each of the four kinds of KM systems is then discussed in considerable detail in Part II of the book.

Thus, KM infrastructure, which is at the organizational level, supports KM mecha-

Figure 3.1 **An Overview of Knowledge Management Solutions and Foundation**

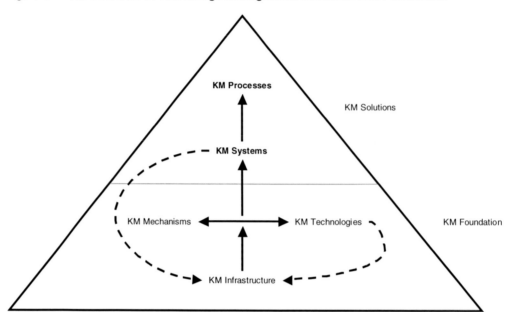

nisms and technologies. KM mechanisms and technologies are used in KM systems, with each KM system utilizing a combination of multiple mechanisms and multiple technologies. Moreover, the same KM mechanism or technology could support multiple KM systems. KM systems enable KM processes, with a KM system focusing on one specific KM process. Therefore, KM processes and KM systems are specific solutions for KM needs whereas KM infrastructure, mechanisms, and technologies are broader: KM mechanisms and technologies support multiple KM solutions, and the KM infrastructure supports (through KM mechanisms and technologies) all KM solutions. However, over time, KM infrastructure itself benefits from KM mechanisms and technologies as well as KM processes, as shown by the curved arrows in Figure 3.1.

The remainder of this chapter describes the three components of the KM foundation—that is, KM infrastructure, mechanisms, and technologies—in further detail. The two aspects of KM solutions—KM processes and systems—are described in Chapter 4.

KNOWLEDGE MANAGEMENT INFRASTRUCTURE

KM mechanisms and technologies rely on the KM infrastructure, which reflects the long-term foundation for knowledge management. In an organizational context, **KM infrastructure** includes five major components: organization culture, organization structure, information technology infrastructure, common knowledge, and physical environment. These components are discussed in greater detail the next five sections.

ORGANIZATION CULTURE

Organization culture reflects the norms and beliefs that guide the behavior of the organization's members. It is an important enabler of knowledge management in organizations. Indeed, a survey of KM practices in U.S. companies (Dyer and McDonough 2001) indicated that the four most important challenges in knowledge management are nontechnical in nature and include, in order of importance: (1) The organization's employees have no time for knowledge management; (2) the current organization culture does not encourage knowledge sharing; (3) inadequate understanding of knowledge management and its benefits to the company; and (4) inability to measure the financial benefits from knowledge management.

Though the second of the above challenges specifically mentions organization culture, the first and third challenges are also directly dependent on organization culture—a supporting organization culture helps motivate employees to understand the benefits from knowledge management and also to find time for knowledge management. Indeed, getting people to participate in knowledge sharing is considered the hardest part of KM. For example, individuals are usually reluctant to contribute knowledge to knowledge repositories, as illustrated by the following comment by one knowledge worker "If I share my knowledge, others may take advantage of that. Will they do the same for me?" (Standing and Benson 2000, p. 343). It is often believed that of the organizations trying to implement KM, less than 10 percent have succeeded in making it part of their culture (Koudsi 2000).

Attributes of an enabling organizational culture include understanding the value of KM practices, management support for KM at all levels, incentives that reward knowledge sharing, and encouragement of interaction for the creation and sharing of knowledge (Armbrecht et al. 2001). In contrast, cultures that stress individual performance and hoarding of information within units encourage limited employee interaction, and lack of an involved top management creates inhibited knowledge sharing and retention. Moreover, people are often afraid of asking others if they know the answer to a certain question, and especially if posting a question for the entire company to see, fear it might reveal their ignorance (Koudsi 2000).

A case study of a baby food manufacturer revealed that built-in competition within the corporate structure inhibited knowledge sharing practices that could have significantly increased revenues. The performance of front-line salespeople was evaluated comparing it to that of other salespeople. Because of this, a group of front-line salespeople found a market niche in selling baby food to aging adults who could no longer eat hard food, but they kept knowledge of their customer base to themselves and let only their successful sales figures reveal their find. Because the company's culture bred competition among employees and offered incentives based on a curve, the firm missed out not only on increased revenues across the organization but also through additional sales in that niche market and also on potential product development to better address the needs of this niche market (DeTienne and Jackson 2001).

In another case study, the CEO of a Web consulting company instituted several measures to enhance the use of the company's KM system (Koudsi 2000). He started publicly recognizing people who stood out as strong knowledge contributors. He

Box 3.1

Incentives for Knowledge Sharing at Hill and Knowlton

Hill and Knowlton, which was founded in 1927, is a leading international communications consultancy headquartered in New York with 74 offices in 41 countries and an extensive associate network. It is part of one of the world's largest communications services groups (WPP), and provides services to local, multinational, and global clients. The company is hired by organizations to manage their product launches, media relations, and communication during crises.

Hill and Knowlton offered "Beenz," which was a system of micropayments, each worth $0.001, to encourage employees to contribute case studies and bios. Employees could redeem Beenz online for CDs, books, and other items. For example, an employee could win a weekend for two in a Caribbean villa for 110,000 Beenz. After the company offering Beenz shut down on August 17, 2001, some offices started rewarding employees through gift certificates and pizza parties.

Hill and Knowlton also offered bonuses to individuals managing departments that were active in knowledge sharing. This was based on two criteria: whether the department made knowledge contributions and whether the department extracted and used knowledge from another department. Bonuses varied from one year to the next.

Hill and Knowlton also established a "best-seller" list to publicize the contributions that were most frequently accessed. Users were encouraged to discuss their rank on the best-seller list during conversations about advancement opportunities.

Source: Compiled from: Meister and Mark 2004; http://www.hillandknowlton.com/.

also made usage of the KM system a part of everyone's job description. He even started paying employees to use this system. Each task on the KM system was assigned points. If a consultant placed his résumé in the system, he would receive one point. If a consultant created a project record, she would receive five points. The company's knowledge manager acted as judge, deciding if entries deserved points. The totals were tallied every three months, and the resulting score accounted for 10 percent of a consultant's quarterly bonus. Before these metrics were introduced in January 1999, only a third of the company's employees were rated as good or better in the usage of the KM system, but two months later, that usage had almost doubled (Koudsi 2000).

Providing appropriate incentives is one way of building a culture that supports knowledge sharing. Some companies (e.g., Shell Oil Company and Giant Eagle, Inc.) provide informal recognition for individuals sharing knowledge by mentioning their accomplishments in a newsletter, an e-mail, or during a meeting. Halliburton Company uses a "most valuable player" program, acknowledging each month the person who provides the best idea. The prestigious consulting firm Bain & Company provides its employees only with two annual awards, and one of them is for the employee that best carried on the goals of knowledge management and innovation. Companies often incorporate knowledge sharing within employees' formal job reviews; some companies make employees' promotions and bonuses subject to their sharing knowledge, while some other companies use it as one factor in the overall evaluation process (Paul 2003). Box 3.1 illustrates the use of incentives for knowledge sharing at Hill & Knowlton, Inc., a company we examined earlier in Box 1.2.

Organization Structure

Knowledge management also depends to a considerable extent on the **organization structure**. Several aspects of organization structure are relevant. First, the **hierarchical structure** of the organization affects the people with whom each individual frequently interacts, and to or from whom he is consequently likely to transfer knowledge. Traditional reporting relationships influence the flow of data and information as well as the nature of groups who make decisions together, and consequently affect the sharing and creation of knowledge. By decentralizing or flattening their organization structures, companies often seek to eliminate organizational layers, thereby placing more responsibility with each individual and increasing the size of groups reporting to each individual. Consequently, knowledge sharing is likely to occur with a larger group of individuals in more decentralized organizations. In addition, matrix structures and an emphasis on "leadership" rather than on "management" also facilitates greater knowledge sharing primarily by cutting across traditional departmental boundaries.

Second, organization structures can facilitate knowledge management through **communities of practice**. A community of practice is an organic and self-organized group of individuals who are dispersed geographically or organizationally but communicate regularly to discuss issues of mutual interest (Lave and Wenger 1991). For example, a tech-club at DaimlerChrysler included a group of engineers who didn't work in the same unit but met regularly, on their own initiative, to discuss problems related to their area of expertise. Similarly, at Xerox Corporation, a strategic community of IT professionals, involving frequent informal interactions among them, promotes knowledge sharing (Storck and Hill 2000). Box 3.2 further illustrates communities of practice, using the example of Montgomery Watson Harza.

Communities of practice provide access to a larger group of individuals than possible within traditional departmental boundaries. Consequently, there are more numerous potential helpers, and this increases the probability that at least one of them will provide useful knowledge. Communities of practice also provide access to external knowledge sources. An organization's external stakeholders—for example, customers, suppliers, and partners—provide a far greater knowledge reservoir than the organization itself (Choo 1998). For instance, relationships with university researchers can help new biotechnology firms to maintain their innovativeness.

Although communities of practice are usually not part of a company's formal organization structure, company executives can facilitate them in several ways. For example, they can legitimize them through support for participation in them. Moreover, they can enhance the perceived value of participation in communities of practice by seeking advice from them. They can also help communities of practice by providing them with resources, such as money or connections to external experts and access to information technology that supports their virtual meetings and knowledge sharing activities. Communities of practice benefit considerably from other emergent information technologies, including blogs and social networking technologies.

Third, organization structures can facilitate knowledge management through *specialized structures and roles* that specifically support knowledge management. Three possibilities deserve special mention. First, some organizations appoint an

Box 3.2

Communities of Practice at Montgomery Watson Harza

Montgomery Watson Harza[1] (MWH) is a global engineering firm with over 3,600 specialists spread across about 200 offices in 38 countries. From 1995 to 1999, its KM efforts had focused primarily on information technologies and had encountered problems.

In 1999, it adopted a new KM approach characterized as "People First, Technology as Support." This approach led to a new name being given to the KM strategy: "KnowledgeNet." KnowledgeNet relied on formal and informal communities of practice, which would be supported by establishing a global Intranet, called KNet. Each formal community—called a Knowledge Center and partially funded by management—also established its theme as well as specific business objectives. Each informal community, called a Knowledge Base, was locally driven and easier to set up. Whereas Knowledge Centers were created from the top down to facilitate strategic initiatives, Knowledge Bases were organic and started by practitioners themselves. Knowledge Bases could also be networked together to represent a larger theme. Moreover, if a Knowledge Base became strategic to the entire company, it could be converted into a Knowledge Center.

The implementation of this new strategy began in 2000. By early 2004, MWH had three Knowledge Centers (a fourth center was being established) and 120 Knowledge Bases. MWH had about 6,000 employees at that time, and about 1,600 of them belonged to one of these formal or informal communities. The new KM strategy based on communities of practice received positive responses from top management, other employees, and clients. Top management perceived KnowledgeNet as having provided the company with a competitive advantage in terms of obtaining client accounts.

Source: Compiled from Parise, Rolag, and Gulas 2004.
[1]See http://www.mwhglobal.com/.

individual to the position of Chief Knowledge Officer and make this individual responsible for the organization's KM efforts. Second, some organizations establish a separate department for knowledge management, which is often headed by the Chief Knowledge Officer. Finally, two traditional KM units—the R&D department and the corporate library—also facilitate knowledge management, although they differ in focus. Whereas the R&D department supports management of knowledge about the latest, or future, developments, the corporate library supports business units by facilitating knowledge sharing activities and serving as a repository of historical information about the organization, its industry, and competitive environment. The leadership of the KM function is further examined in Chapter 12.

INFORMATION TECHNOLOGY INFRASTRUCTURE

Knowledge management is also facilitated by the organization's **information technology** (IT) **infrastructure**. Although certain information technologies and systems are directly developed to pursue knowledge management, the organization's overall information technology infrastructure, developed to support the organization's information systems needs, also facilitates knowledge management. The information technology infrastructure includes data processing, storage, and communication technologies and systems. It comprises the entire spectrum of the organization's information systems, including transaction processing systems and management information systems. It consists of **databases (DB)** and **data warehouses**, as well as enterprise resource planning systems. One possible way of systematically viewing the IT infrastructure is to consider the capabilities it provides in four important aspects: *reach, depth, richness,* and *aggregation* (Daft and Lengel 1986; Evans and Wurster 1999).

Reach pertains to access and connection and the efficiency of such access. Within the context of a network, reach reflects the number and geographical locations of the nodes that can be efficiently accessed. Keen (1991) also uses the term reach to refer to the locations an IT platform is capable of linking, with the ideal being able to connect to "anyone, anywhere." Much of the power of the **Internet** is attributed to its reach and the fact that most people can access it quite inexpensively. Reach is enhanced not just by advances in hardware but also by progress in software. For instance, standardization of cross-firm communication standards, and languages such as XML, make it easier for firms to communicate with a wider array of trading partners, including those with whom they do not have long-term relationships.

Depth, in contrast, focuses on the detail and amount of information that can be effectively communicated over a medium. This dimension closely corresponds to the aspects of bandwidth and customization included by Evans and Wurster (1999) in their definition of richness. Communicating deep and detailed information requires high bandwidth. At the same time, it is the availability of deep and detailed information about customers that enables customization. Recent technological progress—for instance, in channel bandwidth—has enabled considerable improvement in depth.

Communication channels can be arranged along a continuum representing their "relative richness" (Carlson and Zmud 1999). The *richness* of a medium is based on its ability to: (a) provide multiple cues (e.g., body language, facial expression, tone of voice) simultaneously; (b) provide quick feedback; (c) personalize messages; and (d) use natural language to convey subtleties (Daft and Lengel 1986). Information technology has traditionally been viewed as a lean communication medium. However, given the progress in information technology, we are witnessing a significant increase in its ability to support rich communication.

Finally, rapid advances in IT have significantly enhanced the ability to store and quickly process information. This enables the *aggregation* of large volumes of information drawn from multiple sources. For instance, data mining and data warehousing together enable the synthesis of diverse information from multiple sources, potentially to produce new insights. **Enterprise resource planning systems** (ERPs) also present a natural platform for aggregating knowledge across different parts of an organization. A senior IS executive at PricewaterhouseCoopers LLP, for example, remarks: "We're moving quite quickly on to an Intranet platform, and that's giving us a greater chance to integrate everything instead of saying to people, 'use this database and that database and another database.' Now it all looks—and is—much more coordinated" (Thomson 2000, p. 24).

To summarize, the above four IT capabilities enable knowledge management by enhancing common knowledge or by facilitating the four KM processes. For example, an **expertise locator system** (also called knowledge yellow pages or a people-finder system) is a special type of knowledge repository that pinpoints individuals having specific knowledge within the organization. These systems rely on the reach and depth capabilities of IT by enabling individuals to contact remotely located experts and seek detailed solutions to complicated problems. Another IS solution attempts to capture as much of the knowledge in an individual's head as possible and archive it in a searchable database. This is primarily the aim of projects in artificial intelligence, which capture the expert's knowledge in systems based on various technologies, including rule-based system and case-based reasoning, among others (Wong and Radcliffe 2000). But the most sophisticated systems for eliciting and cataloging experts' knowledge in models that can easily be understood and applied by others in the organization (see for example Ford et al. (1996) require strong knowledge engineering processes to develop. Such sophisticated KM systems have typically not been advocated as frequently for use in mainstream business environments, primarily because of the high cost involved in the knowledge engineering effort.

COMMON KNOWLEDGE

Common knowledge (Grant 1996) represents another important component of the infrastructure that enables knowledge management. It refers to the organization's cumulative experiences in comprehending a category of knowledge and activities and the organizing principles that support communication and coordination (Zander and Kogut 1995). Common knowledge provides unity to the organization. It includes: a common language and vocabulary, recognition of individual knowledge domains, common cognitive schema, shared norms, and elements of specialized knowledge that are common across individuals sharing knowledge (Grant 1996; Nahapiet and Ghoshal 1998). The following comment by a senior executive at NASA-Kennedy Space Center illustrates problems that might arise due to a lack of common knowledge (Sabherwal and Becerra-Fernandez 2005, p. 302):

> I used to consider myself a systems engineer. When I was in the shuttle program a systems engineer was somebody who was an expert on a particular shuttle system. In the outside world a systems engineer has a completely different definition. I was a technical expert on the shuttle toilet. I called myself a systems engineer, my position description said I was a systems engineer, but I could go over to the Payloads' IT department and ask them what their competency was, what their key effort was, and they would say "systems engineering." And I would say, "what system?" Because from my frame of reference, I was doing systems engineering, from theirs, they were doing something called systems engineering.

Common knowledge helps enhance the value of an individual expert's knowledge by integrating it with the knowledge of others. However, because the common knowledge is based on the above definition common only to an organization, this increase in value is also specific to that particular organization and does not transfer to its competitors. Thus, common knowledge supports knowledge transfer within the organization but impedes the transfer (or leakage) of knowledge outside the organization (Argote and Ingram 2000).

PHYSICAL ENVIRONMENT

The **physical environment** within the organization is often taken for granted, but it is another important foundation upon which knowledge management rests. Key aspects of the physical environment include the design of buildings and the separation between them; the location, size, and type of offices; the type, number, and nature of meeting rooms; and so on. Physical environment can foster knowledge management by providing opportunities for employees to meet and share ideas. Even though knowledge sharing there is often not by design, coffee rooms, cafeterias, water coolers, and hallways do provide venues where employees learn from and share insights with each other. A 1998 study found that most employees thought they gained most of their knowledge related to work from informal conversations around watercoolers or over meals rather than from formal training or manuals (Wensley 1998).

A number of organizations are creating spaces specifically designed to facilitate this informal knowledge sharing. For example, the London Business School created an attractive space between two major departments, which were earlier isolated, to enhance knowledge sharing between them. Reuters News Service installed kitchens on each floor to foster discussions. Moreover, a medium-sized firm in the United States focused on careful management of office locations to facilitate knowledge sharing (Stewart 2000). This company developed open-plan offices with subtle arrangements to encourage what one senior executive calls *knowledge accidents*. Locations are arranged in this company so as to maximize the chances of face-to-face interactions among people who might be able to help each other. For example, an employee might walk down the hall so that she might meet someone who knows the answer to her question, and she will meet such an individual not due to chance but because a snack area is positioned where four project teams' work areas intersect.

Table 3.2 summarizes the five dimensions of KM infrastructure, indicating the key attributes related to each dimension.

KNOWLEDGE MANAGEMENT MECHANISMS

Knowledge management mechanisms are organizational or structural means used to promote knowledge management. They enable KM systems, and they are themselves supported by the KM infrastructure. KM mechanisms may (or may not) utilize technology, but they do involve some kind of organizational arrangement or social or structural means of facilitating KM.

Examples of KM mechanisms include learning by doing, on-the-job training, learning by observation, and face-to-face meetings. More long-term KM mechanisms include the hiring of a Chief Knowledge Officer, cooperative projects across departments, traditional hierarchical relationships, organizational policies, standards, initiation process for new employees, and employee rotation across departments. To illustrate KM mechanisms, we briefly examine in Box 3.3 the approach one company, Viant Corporation, takes to manage knowledge.

Box 3.4 provides some additional examples of the use of KM mechanisms to facilitate knowledge management.

KNOWLEDGE MANAGEMENT TECHNOLOGIES

As mentioned earlier, KM technologies are information technologies that can be used to facilitate knowledge management. Thus KM technologies are intrinsically no different from information technologies, but they focus on knowledge management rather than information processing. KM technologies also support KM systems and benefit from the KM infrastructure, especially the information technology infrastructure.

Table 3.2

A Summary of Knowledge Management Infrastructure

Dimensions of KM Infrastructure	Related Attributes
Organization Culture	Understanding of the value of KM practices
	Management support for KM at all levels
	Incentives that reward knowledge sharing
	Encouragement of interaction for the creation and sharing of knowledge
Organization Structure	Hierarchical structure of the organization (decentralization, matrix structures, emphasis on "leadership" rather than "management")
	Communities of practice
	Specialized structures and roles (Chief Knowledge Officer, KM department, traditional KM units)
Information Technology Infrastructure	Reach
	Depth
	Richness
	Aggregation
Common Knowledge	Common language and vocabulary
	Recognition of individual knowledge domains
	Common cognitive schema
	Shared norms
	Elements of specialized knowledge that are common across individuals
Physical Infrastructure	Design of buildings (offices, meeting rooms, hallways)
	Spaces specifically designed to facilitate informal knowledge sharing (coffee rooms, cafeterias, water coolers)

KM technologies constitute a key component of KM systems. Technologies that support KM include **artificial intelligence** (AI) technologies including those used for knowledge acquisition and case-based reasoning systems, electronic discussion groups, computer-based simulations, databases, decision support systems, enterprise resource planning systems, expert systems, management information systems, expertise locator systems, videoconferencing, and information repositories including best practices databases and lessons learned systems. KM technologies also include the emergent **Web 2.0 technologies**, such as wikis and blogs, which are discussed in detail in Chapter 10.

Examples of the use of KM technologies include World Bank's use of a combination of video interviews and hyperlinks to documents and reports to systematically record the knowledge of employees that are close to retirement (Lesser and Prusak 2001). Similarly, at BP plc, desktop videoconferencing has improved communication and enabled many problems at offshore oil fields to be solved without extensive traveling (Skyrme 2000).

Box 3.5 provides one example of the use of technologies to facilitate knowledge management.

Box 3.3

Knowledge Management Mechanisms at Viant

Viant[1] is a Boston-based consulting company specializing in helping clients build e-commerce businesses. It considers knowledge management as a key objective of the processes through which new employees are initiated into the organization and existing employees are rotated across functions and locations as mechanisms for knowledge management. Viant makes excellent use of the orientation process to provide newcomers with knowledge of key clients, some company-specific skills, and the beginnings of an informal network. New employees begin their Viant career with three weeks in Boston. On arrival employees receive their laptop, loaded with off-the-shelf and proprietary software. Later that week they learn team skills and take a course in the company's consulting strategy and tools. For the next two weeks they switch back and forth between classroom work and teams, participating in a mock consulting assignment. They bond, meet all the officers, listen to corporate folklore, and party with the CEO. Employee rotation also plays an important role in knowledge management at Viant. In fact, conventional reporting relationships do not work here. Because people rotate in and out of assignments, consultants have no fixed relationship to a boss; instead, senior managers act as "advocates" for a number of "advocados." Performance reviews emphasize the growth in the employee's own skill level, and stock options recognize the knowledge they share.

Source: Stewart 2000.
[1]See http://www.viant.com.

Box 3.4

Knowledge Management Mechanisms from Three Organizations

At Phonak, Inc., a worldwide leader in digital hearing instruments, a series of events occur throughout the year (every six weeks or so) enabling employees to get to know each other through informal interactions including barbecues, company days out, and bicycle tours.

BP Amoco Chemical Company has benefitted from retrospect meetings at the conclusion of projects. Each retrospect meeting is facilitated by someone outside that project team and focuses on the following questions: What was the goal of the project? What did we accomplish? What were the major successes? Why? How can we repeat the successes? What were the significant disappointments? Why? How can we avoid them in the future?

Katzenbach Partners uses light-hearted contests and events to facilitate knowledge management. One example is "Stump Niko," in which the managing director, who had the reputation that he knew everything that was going on, would be asked a question about knowledge management and the knowledge management system would then be asked the same question. The objective was to demonstrate the potential of the knowledge management system.

Source: Compiled from: Burgelman and Blumenstein 2007; Hoegl and Schulze 2005.

MANAGEMENT OF KNOWLEDGE MANAGEMENT FOUNDATIONS (INFRASTRUCTURE, MECHANISMS, AND TECHNOLOGIES)

Knowledge management infrastructure, mechanisms, and technologies are the underlying foundations for any organization's KM solutions. KM infrastructure is of fundamental importance with long-term implications and needs to be managed carefully, with close involvement from top executives. In any case, all components of KM infrastructure (i.e., organization structure, organization culture, IT infrastructure,

---

Box 3.5

KM Technologies at Cisco

Cisco Systems Inc., utilizes Directory 3.0, which is its internal Facebook, in which the employee listings are designed to identify the employee's expertise area and promote collaboration. To further promote knowledge sharing, it utilizes a variety of technologies including: Ciscopedia, which is an internal document site; C-Vision, which is Cisco's version of YouTube; and the Idea Zone, which is a wiki for employees to post and discuss business ideas. Cisco has also been developing a companywide social computing platform to enable knowledge creation and sharing through strengthening of existing networks and facilitation of new connections (Fitzgerald 2008). According to Cisco's VP, Communication and Collaboration IT[1]: "Blogs and wikis are popping up all over the Cisco website at an exciting pace. But we're finding that actual adoption of wikis is outpacing that of blogs at an exponentially higher rate. This is most likely because wikis are part of the natural workflow—they are where work gets done. People are more driven to wikis because it is a primary form of communication and collaboration within a group."

Cisco's CIO remarked in 2008 (Fitzgerald 2008): "CIOs need to consider issues of privacy, data security, and the ability to scale across a global organization. It's no good, if 15 different business units develop 15 different online communities "that can't talk to each other."

[1]See Interview with Sheila Jordan, VP, Communication and Collaboration IT, "Cisco—Making the Most of Technology Now!" *Strategic Path,* 16 April 2008. http://www.strategicpath.com.au/page/Sponsor_Articles/CISCO/Cisco_-_Making_the_most_of_Technology_Now_Ciscos_Sheila_Jordan_reveals_how_Cisco_is_Embracing_Web_20/.

---

common knowledge, and physical environment) affect not only KM but also all other aspects of the organizational operations. Therefore, KM infrastructure does receive attention from top management, although it is important that KM be explicitly considered in making decisions regarding these infrastructural aspects. In this regard, a strong relationship between the leaders of the KM function (discussed in Chapter 12) and the top executives of the organization plays an important role.

KM mechanisms and technologies work together and affect each other. KM mechanisms depend on technology, although some mechanisms do so to a greater extent than others. Moreover, improvement in KM technologies could, over time, lead to changes (either improvements in, or in some cases, reduced emphasis on) in KM mechanisms. In managing KM mechanisms and technologies, it is important to recognize such interrelationships between mechanisms and technologies. Moreover, it is important to achieve an appropriate balance between the use of technology and social or structural mechanisms. Technological progress could lead to people focusing too much on technology while ignoring structural and social aspects. On the other hand, an organization with weak IT infrastructure may rely on social and structural mechanisms while ignoring potentially valuable KM technologies.

Consequently, some organizations focus more on KM technologies, some focus more on KM mechanisms, and some make a somewhat balanced use of KM technologies and mechanisms. For example, senior executives at Groupe Danone (Groupe Danone 2009), which is a leading consumer-goods company with headquarters in Paris and is known as Dannon in the United States (it is discussed in greater detail later in Chapter 11, Box 11.1), believe that using IT to share knowledge would not work as well for the company, and therefore rely primarily on social and structural mechanisms (Edmondson et al. 2008).

Several other organizations switch from a focus on mechanisms to a focus on technology, or vice versa. For example, Katzenbach Partners, LLC, relied almost entirely on social and structural mechanisms to manage knowledge until 2005, but then, in the light of its organizational growth, started focusing much more on KM technologies, first using an Intranet and then using Web 2.0 technologies (which we discuss in greater detail in Chapter 10). This is in contrast to Montgomery Watson Harza (MWH Global, Inc.), which as discussed in Box 3.2 earlier in this chapter (p. 46), focused primarily on information technologies from 1995 to 1999, and then switched to a KM strategy based on "People First, Technology as Support" (Parise et al. 2004).

SUMMARY

Building on the discussion of knowledge in Chapter 2, we have described the key aspects of knowledge management in this chapter. We have provided a working definition of knowledge management and discussed KM solutions as involving five components: KM processes, KM systems, KM mechanisms, KM technologies, and KM infrastructure. We have also discussed and illustrated three foundational components—KM mechanisms, KM technologies, and KM infrastructure—and briefly talked about how they could be managed. The next chapter examines the other key aspects of KM solutions including KM systems, KM mechanisms and technologies, and KM infrastructure.

KEY TERMS

Business intelligence	Knowledge management infrastructure
Common knowledge	Knowledge management mechanisms
Community of practice	Knowledge management solutions
Information technology infrastructure	Knowledge management technologies
Knowledge application	Knowledge sharing
Knowledge capture	Organization culture
Knowledge discovery	Organization structure
Knowledge management	Physical environment
Knowledge management foundations	

REVIEW

1. What is knowledge management? What are its objectives?
2. What is business intelligence? How does knowledge management differ from business intelligence?
3. Describe the ways to facilitate knowledge management and give suitable examples.

4. Distinguish between KM foundation and KM solutions. What are the components of KM foundation and KM solutions?
5. What is common knowledge? What does it include, and how does it support knowledge management?
6. State the role of organizational culture in the development of a good knowledge management infrastructure.
7. State the role of organizational structure in the development of a good knowledge management infrastructure.
8. In what way does information technology infrastructure contribute to knowledge management within an organization?

APPLICATION EXERCISES

1. Interview a manager of an organization where knowledge management practices have recently been implemented. Use the interview to study the nature of the KM infrastructure and the ways in which its components are helping or inhibiting those KM practices.
2. Consider an organization where you currently work, or are familiar with (either through your own prior experience or through interactions with someone who works there). What kind of mechanisms does this organization use to manage knowledge? What are their effects?
3. Determine ways in which a local hospital would benefit from communities of practice. Conduct interviews if necessary.
4. Consider a high school with which you are familiar. How can knowledge management at this high school benefit from information technologies? What kinds of technologies does it currently use, and how could they be improved?
5. Interview at least three managers from local organizations that have recently implemented knowledge management. Contrast the differences in organization culture, structure, IT Infrastructure, common knowledge, and physical environment within the organizations.

REFERENCES

Argote, L. and Ingram, P. 2000. Knowledge transfer: Basis for competitive advantage in firms. *Organizational Behavior and Human Decision Processes,* 82(1) (May), 150–169.

Armbrecht, F.M.R., Chapas, R.B., Chappelow, C.C., Farris, G.F., Friga, P.N., Hartz, C.A., McIlvaine, M.E., Postle S.R., and Whitwell, G.E. 2001. Knowledge management in research and development. *Research Technology Management,* 44(4), 28–48.

Burgelman, R.A. and Blumenstein, B. 2007. *Knowledge management at Katzenbach Partners LLC.* Stanford Graduate School of Business, Case SM162.

Carlson, J.R. and Zmud, R.W. 1999. Channel expansion theory and the experiential nature of media richness perceptions. *Academy of Management Journal,* 42(2), 153–170.

Choo, C.W. 1998. *The knowing organization: How organizations use information to construct meaning, create knowledge, and make decisions.* New York: Oxford University Press.

Daft, R.L. and Lengel, R.H. 1986. Organization information requirements, media richness, and structural design. *Management Science,* 32(5), 554–571.

DeTienne, K.B. and Jackson, L.A. 2001. Knowledge management: Understanding theory and developing strategy. *Competitiveness Review,* 11(1), 1–11.

Dyer, G. and McDonough, B. 2001. The state of KM. *Knowledge Management,* May, 31–36.

Edmondson, A., Moingeon, B., Dessain, V., and Jensen, D. 2008. *Global knowledge management at Danone.* Harvard Business School Publishing, Case 9–608–107, April 16.

Evans, P. and Wurster, T.S. 1999. Getting real about virtual commerce. *Harvard Business Review,* 77(6) (November-December), 85–94.

Fitzgerald, M. 2008. Why social computing aids knowledge management. *CIO.com,* June 13.

Ford, K.M., Coffey, J.W., Cañas, A.J., Andrews, E.J., and Turner, C.W. 1996. Diagnosis and explanation by a nuclear cardiology expert system. *International Journal of Expert Systems,* 9, 499–506.

Grant, R.M. 1996. Toward a knowledge-based theory of the firm. *Strategic Management Journal,* 17, 109–122.

Groupe Danone. 2009. http://www.danone.com/?lang=en.

Hoegl, M. and Schulze, A., 2005. How to support knowledge creation in new product development: An investigation of knowledge management methods. *European Management Journal,* 23(3), 263–273.

Keen, P. 1991. *Shaping the future: Business design through information technology.* Boston: Harvard Business School Press.

Koudsi, S. 2000. Actually, it is like brain surgery. *Fortune,* March 20.

Lave, J. and Wenger, E. 1991. *Situated learning: Legitimate peripheral participation.* Cambridge, England & New York: Cambridge University Press.

Lesser, E. and Prusak, L. 2001. Preserving knowledge in an uncertain world. *Sloan Management Review,* Fall, 101–102.

Meister, D. and Mark, K. 2004. *Hill & Knowlton: Knowledge management.* Case #9B04E003. London, ONT: Ivey Publishing.

Nahapiet, J. and Ghoshal, S. 1998. Social capital, intellectual capital, and the organizational advantage. *Academy of Management Review,* 23(2), 242–266.

Parise, S., Rolag, K., and Gulas, V. 2004. *Montgomery Watson Harza and knowledge management.* Harvard Business School Publishing, Case BAB102, November 15.

Paul, L.G. 2003. Why three heads are better than one (How to create a know-it-all company). *CIO Magazine,* December.

Sabherwal, R. 2007. Succeeding with business intelligence: Some insights and recommendations. *Cutter Benchmark Review,* 7(9), 5–15.

———. 2008. KM and BI: From mutual isolation to complementarity and synergy. *Cutter Consortium Executive Report,* 8(8), 1–18.

Sabherwal, R. and Becerra-Fernandez, I. 2005. Integrating specific knowledge: Insights from the Kennedy Space Center. *IEEE Transactions on Engineering Management,* 52(3), 301–315.

Skyrme, D.J. 2000. Developing a knowledge strategy: From management to leadership. In *Knowledge management: Classic and contemporary works,* ed. D. Morey, M. Maybury, and B. Thuraisingham, 61–84. Cambridge, MA: The MIT Press.

Standing, C. and Benson, S. 2000. Knowledge management in a competitive environment. In *Decision support through knowledge management,* ed. S.A. Carlsson, P. Brezillon, P. Humphreys, B.G. Lundberg, A.M. McCosh, and V. Rajkovic, 336–348. Stockholm, Sweden: Department of Computing Systems Sciences, University of Stockholm and Royal Institute of Technology.

Stewart, T.A. 2000. The house that knowledge built. *Fortune,* October 2.

Storck, J., and Hill, P. 2000. Knowledge diffusion through "strategic communities." *Sloan Management Review,* 41(2), 63–74.

Thomson, S. 2000. Focus: Keeping pace with knowledge. *Information World Review,* Issue 155 (February) 23–24.

Wensley, A. 1998. The value of story telling. *Knowledge and Process Management,* 5(1), 1–2.

Wong W. and Radcliffe D. 2000. The tacit nature of design knowledge. *Technology Analysis and Strategic Management,* 12(4), 493–512.

Zander, U., Kogut, B. 1995. Knowledge and the speed of the transfer and imitation of organizational capabilities: An empirical test. *Organization Science,* 6, 76–92.

4 Knowledge Management Solutions: Processes and Systems

In Chapter 3, we provided an introductory discussion of **knowledge management solutions**, which refer to the variety of ways in which knowledge management can be facilitated. We indicated that KM solutions include KM processes and KM systems and that KM solutions depend on **KM foundations** which include KM mechanisms, technologies, and infrastructure. We discussed KM foundations in detail in Chapter 3. This chapter provides a detailed discussion of KM solutions, including KM processes and systems.

The next section describes and illustrates the various processes used to manage knowledge including processes for applying knowledge, processes for capturing knowledge, processes for sharing knowledge, and processes for creating knowledge. In discussing these KM processes, we also examine the seven subprocesses that facilitate them. The discussion of KM processes is followed by a discussion of KM systems, followed by a discussion of the processes for managing KM processes and systems, and then some concluding remarks.

KNOWLEDGE MANAGEMENT PROCESSES

We earlier defined knowledge management as *performing the activities involved in discovering, capturing, sharing, and applying knowledge so as to enhance, in a cost-effective fashion, the impact of knowledge on the unit's goal achievement.* Thus, knowledge management relies on four main kinds of KM processes. As shown in Figure 4.1, these include the processes through which knowledge is discovered or captured. It also includes the processes through which this knowledge is shared and applied. These four KM processes are supported by a set of seven KM subprocesses, as shown in Figure 4.1, with one subprocess—socialization—supporting two KM processes (discovery and sharing). Of the seven KM subprocesses, four are based on Nonaka (1994). Focusing on the ways in which knowledge is converted through the interaction between tacit and explicit knowledge, Nonaka identified four ways of managing knowledge: socialization, externalization, internalization, and combination. The other three KM subprocesses—exchange, direction, and routines—are largely based on Grant (1996) and Nahapiet and Ghoshal (1998).

Figure 4.1 **Knowledge Management Processes**

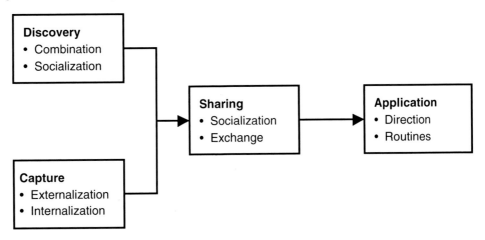

KNOWLEDGE DISCOVERY

Knowledge discovery may be defined as *the development of new tacit or explicit knowledge from data and information or from the synthesis of prior knowledge.* The discovery of new explicit knowledge relies most directly on combination, whereas the discovery of new tacit knowledge relies most directly on socialization. In either case, new knowledge is discovered by synthesizing knowledge from two or more distinct areas with explicit knowledge from two areas being synthesized through combination, and tacit knowledge from two areas being synthesized through socialization. Combination and socialization are discussed now.

Combination

New explicit knowledge is discovered through **combination**, wherein the multiple bodies of explicit knowledge (and/or data and/or information) are synthesized to create new, more complex sets of explicit knowledge (Nonaka 1994). Through communication, integration, and systemization of multiple streams of explicit knowledge, new explicit knowledge is created—either incrementally or radically (Nahapiet and Ghoshal 1998). Existing explicit knowledge, data, and information are reconfigured, recategorized and recontextualized to produce new explicit knowledge. For example, when creating a new proposal to a client, explicit data, information, and knowledge embedded in prior proposals may be combined into the new proposal. Also, data mining techniques may be used to uncover new relationships amongst explicit data that may be lead to create predictive or categorization models that create new knowledge.

Socialization

In the case of tacit knowledge, the integration of multiple streams for the creation of new knowledge occurs through the mechanism of socialization (Nonaka 1994).

Box 4.1

Knowledge Discovery at Xerox

Julian Orr, who was earlier an anthropologist at Xerox's Palo Alto Research Center (PARC), studied the actions of customer service representatives who fix Xerox machines. One day, he observed a representative working with an especially troublesome machine, which had been recently installed but had never worked properly. Each time the machine failed, it generated a different error message. Following the prescribed process for each particular message, such as adjusting or replacing parts, failed to correct the overall problem. Moreover, the messages did not make sense when considered together.

Frustrated with his inability to fix the troublesome machine, the representative called a specialist, but the specialist also failed to understand why the machine was behaving in this fashion. Subsequently the representative and the specialist spent the afternoon cycling the machine repeatedly, waiting for its crashes and recording its state when it crashed. While doing this, they discussed other incidents of apparently similar problems. "The afternoon resembled a series of alternating improvisational jazz solos, as each man took the lead, ran with it for a little while, then handed it off to the other, this all against the bass-line continuo of the rumbling machine" (Brown and Duguid 2000, p. 78).

During this process, the representative and the specialist gradually brought their different ideas closer together toward a shared understanding of the machine. Finally, late in the day, everything clicked. The erratic behavior of the machine, the experiences of the representative and the specialist, and the stories they both shared eventually formed a single, coherent account. They were able to make sense of the machine and figure out how to fix it. Thus, by bringing very different perspectives and experiences and then sharing them during their conversation—with the problems encountered with the machine providing a common context—they were able to create new knowledge and thereby solve the problem. Very soon, this new solution was passed around for other technicians to use if they faced the same problem.

Source: Compiled from Brown and Duguid 2000.

Socialization is the synthesis of tacit knowledge across individuals, usually through joint activities rather than written or verbal instructions. For example, by transferring ideas and images, apprenticeships help newcomers to see how others think. Davenport and Prusak (1998) described how conversations at the watercooler helped knowledge sharing among groups at IBM.

In Box 4.1, we illustrate the knowledge discovery process using the example of Xerox.

KNOWLEDGE CAPTURE

As we discussed in Chapter 2, knowledge can exist within people (individuals or groups), artifacts (practices, technologies, or repositories) and organizational entities (organizational units, organizations, interorganizational networks). Moreover, knowledge could be either explicit or tacit. It might sometimes reside within an individual's mind without that individual being able to recognize it and share it with others. Similarly, knowledge might reside in an explicit form in a manual but few people might be aware of it. It is important to obtain the tacit knowledge from individuals' minds as well as the explicit knowledge from the manual, such that the knowledge can then be shared with others. This is the focus of **knowledge capture**, which may be defined as

---

Box 4.2

Knowledge Capture at Viant

Viant, the Boston-based company that we discussed in Box 3.3, uses a variety of means to capture knowledge. It employs a number of simple but unavoidable forms. Before every project, consultants are required to complete a *quicksheet* describing the knowledge they will need, what aspects of knowledge can be leveraged from prior projects, and what they will need to create along with the lessons they hope to learn that they can share with others later. A longer report, a sunset review, is produced at a team meeting to document what worked and what did not work well. Forgetting these reports is hard due to several reasons: "First, almost every document ends up on Viant's internal Web site, hot-linked every which way. Second, sunset reviews are done with a facilitator who wasn't on the team, which helps keep them honest. Third, every six weeks Newell's knowledge management group prepares, posts, and pushes a summary of what's been learned."

Source: Stewart 2000.

---

the process of retrieving either explicit or tacit knowledge that resides within people, artifacts, or organizational entities. Also, the knowledge being captured might reside outside the organizational boundaries including consultants, competitors, customers, suppliers, and prior employers of the organization's new employees.

The knowledge capture process benefits most directly from two KM subprocesses—externalization and internalization. Based on work by Nonaka (1994), externalization and internalization help capture the tacit knowledge and explicit knowledge, respectively.

Externalization involves converting tacit knowledge into explicit forms such as words, concepts, visuals, or figurative language (e.g., metaphors, analogies, and narratives; Nonaka and Takeuchi 1995). It helps translate individuals' tacit knowledge into explicit forms that can be more easily understood by the rest of their group. This is a difficult process because tacit knowledge is often difficult to articulate. Nonaka (1994) suggested that externalization may be accomplished through the use of metaphor—that is, understanding and experiencing one kind of thing in terms of another. An example of externalization is a consultant team writing a document that describes the lessons the team has learned about the client organization, client executives, and approaches that work in such an assignment. This captures the tacit knowledge acquired by the team members.

Internalization is the conversion of explicit knowledge into tacit knowledge. It represents the traditional notion of **learning**. The explicit knowledge may be embodied in action and practice so that the individual acquiring the knowledge can re-experience what others have gone through. Alternatively, individuals could acquire tacit knowledge in virtual situations, either vicariously by reading manuals or others' stories or experientially through simulations or experiments (Nonaka and Takeuchi 1995). An example of internalization is a new software consultant reading a book on innovative software development and learning from it. This learning helps the consultant, and her organization, capture the knowledge contained in the book.

Box 4.2 provides an illustration of knowledge capture.

KNOWLEDGE SHARING

Knowledge sharing is the process through which explicit or tacit knowledge is communicated to other individuals. Three important clarifications are in order. First, knowledge sharing means effective transfer, so that the recipient of knowledge can understand it well enough to act on it (Jensen and Meckling 1996). Second, what is shared is knowledge rather than recommendations based on the knowledge; the former involves the recipient acquiring the shared knowledge as well as being able to take action based on it, whereas the latter (which is direction, discussed in the next section) simply involves utilization of knowledge without the recipient internalizing the shared knowledge. Third, knowledge sharing may take place across individuals as well as across groups, departments, or organizations (Alavi and Leidner 2001).

If knowledge exists at a location that is different from where it is needed, either knowledge sharing or knowledge utilization without sharing (discussed in the next section) is necessary. Sharing knowledge is clearly an important process in enhancing organizational innovativeness and performance. This is reflected in the fact it was one of the three business processes for which General Electric Company CEO Jack Welch took personal responsibility (the others were allocation of resources and development of people) (Stewart 2000).

Depending on whether explicit or tacit knowledge is being shared, exchange or socialization processes are used. Socialization, which we have discussed above, facilitates the sharing of tacit knowledge in cases in which new tacit knowledge is being created as well as when new tacit knowledge is not being created. There is no intrinsic difference between the socialization process when used for knowledge discovery or knowledge sharing, although the way in which the process may be used could be different. For example, when used to share knowledge, a face-to-face meeting (a mechanism that facilitates socialization) could involve a question-and-answer session between the sender and recipient of knowledge, whereas when used to create knowledge a face-to-face meeting could take more the form of a debate or joint problem-solving, as seen in Box 4.1.

Exchange, in contrast to socialization, focuses on the sharing of explicit knowledge. It is used to communicate or transfer explicit knowledge among individuals, groups, and organizations (Grant 1996). In its basic nature, the process of exchange of explicit knowledge does not differ from the process through which information is communicated. An example of exchange is a product design manual being transferred by one employee to another, who can then use the explicit knowledge contained in the manual. Exchanging a document could also be used to transfer information.

Box 4.3 provides an illustration of knowledge sharing.

KNOWLEDGE APPLICATION

Knowledge contributes most directly to organizational performance when it is used to make decisions and perform tasks. Of course, the process of **knowledge application** depends on the available knowledge, and knowledge itself depends on the processes of knowledge discovery, capture, and sharing, as shown in Figure 4.1. The better the

---

Box 4.3

Knowledge Sharing at the Veteran's Health Administration

Until 1997, the Veteran's Health Administration (VHA) did not have any systematic mechanism to enable its 219,000 employees to share their informal knowledge, innovations, and best practices. To address this need and also to serve as a place where any VHA employee can access knowledge capital of colleagues, the VHA Lessons Learned Project and its Web site, the Virtual Learning Center (VLC), were initiated in 1997. The VHA indicates that a major reason for initiating this project was a recognized need to transform the organization into a learning organization. In 1999, the VLC became available on the Internet. The site now has international participation from Korea, Canada, Spain, Pakistan, and elsewhere. By reducing red tape, cutting across organizational silos, partnering and benchmarking with others, and establishing best processing, the VHA is "saving countless hours of staff time by not having to reinvent the wheel at its 173 medical centers, more than 600 clinics, 31 nursing home care units, 206 counseling centers, and other federal and private healthcare institutions, Veterans Benefits and National Cemetery offices."

Source: Compiled from U.S. Department of Veterans Affairs, http://www.va.gov.

---

processes of knowledge discovery, capture, and sharing, the greater the likelihood that the knowledge needed is available for effective application in decision-making and task performance.

In applying knowledge, the party that makes use of it does not necessarily need to comprehend it. All that is needed is that somehow the knowledge be used to guide decisions and actions. Therefore, knowledge utilization benefits from two processes— routines and direction—that do not involve the actual transfer or exchange of knowledge between the concerned individuals but only the transfer of the recommendations that is applicable in a specific context (Grant 1996).

Direction refers to the process through which the individual possessing the knowledge directs the action of another individual without transferring to that individual the knowledge underlying the direction. Direction involves the transfer of instructions or decisions and not the transfer of the knowledge required to make those decisions, and hence it has been labeled as knowledge substitution (Conner and Prahalad 1996). This preserves the advantages of specialization and avoids the difficulties inherent in the transfer of tacit knowledge. Direction is the process used when a production worker calls an expert to ask her how to solve a particular problem with a machine and then proceeds to solve the problem based on the instructions given by the expert. He does this without himself acquiring the knowledge so that if a similar problem reoccurs in the future, he would be unable to identify it as such and would therefore be unable to solve it himself without calling an expert. Similarly a student taking a test who asks his fellow classmate for the answer to a question gets a direction (which of course could be wrong), and no knowledge is effectively shared between the two, which means the next time the student faces that question, posed perhaps in a slightly different form, he will not be able to discern the right answer. Note the difference between direction and socialization or exchange, where the knowledge is actually transferred to the other person in either tacit form (socialization) or explicit form (exchange).

Routines involve the utilization of knowledge embedded in procedures, rules, and norms that guide future behavior. Routines economize on communication more than directions as they are embedded in procedures or technologies. However, they take time to develop, relying on "constant repetition" (Grant 1996). Routines could be automated through the use of IT, such as in systems that provide help desk agents, field engineers, consultants, and customer endusers with specific and automated answers from a knowledge base (Sabherwal and Sabherwal, 2007). Similarly, an inventory management system utilizes considerable knowledge about the relationship between demand and supply, but neither the knowledge nor the directions are communicated through individuals. Also, enterprise systems are coded with routines that describe business process within industry segments.

Next, we examine KM systems that utilize KM mechanisms and technologies to support the KM processes. In this discussion, we also identify the roles of several specific KM technologies in enabling KM systems.

KNOWLEDGE MANAGEMENT SYSTEMS

Knowledge management systems are the integration of technologies and mechanisms that are developed to support the four KM processes. Knowledge management systems utilize a variety of KM mechanisms and technologies, discussed before, to support the KM processes discussed in Chapter 3. Each KM system utilizes a combination of multiple mechanisms and multiple technologies. Moreover, the same KM mechanism or technology could, under differing circumstances, support multiple KM systems.

Depending on the KM process most directly supported, KM systems can be classified into four kinds, which are discussed in detail in Part II: knowledge application systems (Chapter 6), knowledge capture systems (Chapter 7), knowledge sharing systems (Chapter 8), and knowledge discovery systems (Chapter 9). Here we provide a brief overview of these four kinds of systems and examine how they benefit from KM mechanisms and technologies.

KNOWLEDGE DISCOVERY SYSTEMS

As discussed in Chapter 3, **knowledge discovery systems** support the process of developing new tacit or explicit knowledge from data and information or from the synthesis of prior knowledge. These systems support two KM subprocesses associated with knowledge discovery: combination, enabling the discovery of new explicit knowledge; and socialization, enabling the discovery of new tacit knowledge.

Thus, mechanisms and technologies can support knowledge discovery systems by facilitating combination and/or socialization. Mechanisms that facilitate combination include collaborative problem-solving, joint decision-making, and collaborative creation of documents. For example, at the senior-management level, new explicit knowledge is created by sharing documents and information related to midrange concepts (e.g., product concepts) augmented with grand concepts (e.g., corporate vision) to produce new knowledge about both areas. This newly created knowledge could be, for example, a better understanding of products and a corporate vision (Nonaka and Takeuchi 1995). Mechanisms that facilitate socialization include apprenticeships, employee rotation across areas, conferences, brainstorming retreats, cooperative projects across departments, and initiation process for new employees. For example, Honda Motor Company, Ltd., "set up 'brainstorming camps' (*tama dashi kai*)—informal meetings for detailed discussions to solve difficult problems in development projects" (Nonaka and Takeuchi 1995, p. 63).

Technologies facilitating combination include knowledge discovery systems (see Chapter 9), databases, and Web-based access to data. According to Nonaka and Takeuchi (1995), "reconfiguration of existing information through sorting, adding, combining, and categorizing of explicit knowledge (as conducted in computer databases) can lead to new knowledge" (p. 67). Repositories of information, **best practice** databases, and lessons learned systems (see Chapter 8) also facilitate combination. Technologies can also facilitate socialization, albeit to a lesser extent than they can facilitate combination. Some of the technologies for facilitating socialization include videoconferencing and electronic support for communities of practice (see Chapter 10).

KNOWLEDGE CAPTURE SYSTEMS

Knowledge capture systems support the process of retrieving either explicit or tacit knowledge that resides within people, artifacts, or organizational entities. These systems can help capture knowledge that resides within or outside organizational boundaries including within consultants, competitors, customers, suppliers, and prior employers of the organization's new employees. Knowledge capture systems rely on mechanisms and technologies that support externalization and internalization.

KM mechanisms can enable knowledge capture by facilitating externalization—that is, the conversion of tacit knowledge into explicit form; or internalization—that is, the conversion of explicit knowledge into tacit form. The development of models or prototypes and the articulation of best practices or lessons learned are some examples of mechanisms that enable externalization. Box 4.2, presented earlier, illustrates the use of externalization to capture knowledge about projects in one organization.

Learning by doing, on-the-job training, learning by observation, and face-to-face meetings are some of the mechanisms that facilitate internalization. For example, at one firm, "the product divisions also frequently send their new-product development people to the Answer Center to chat with the telephone operators or the 12 specialists, thereby 're-experiencing' their experiences" (Nonaka and Takeuchi 1995, p. 69).

Technologies can also support knowledge capture systems by facilitating externalization and internalization. Externalization through **knowledge engineering**, which involves integrating knowledge into information systems to solve complex problems that normally require considerable human expertise" (Feigenbaum and McCorduck 1983), is necessary for the implementation of intelligent technologies such as expert systems, case-based reasoning systems (see Chapter 6), and knowledge capture systems (see Chapter 7). Technologies that facilitate internalization include computer-based training and communication technologies. Using such communication facilities, an individual can internalize knowledge from a message or attachment thereof sent by another expert, an AI-based knowledge capture systems, or computer-based simulations.

KNOWLEDGE SHARING SYSTEMS

Knowledge sharing systems support the process through which explicit or tacit knowledge is communicated to other individuals. They do so by supporting exchange (i.e., sharing of explicit knowledge) and socialization (which promotes sharing of tacit knowledge).

Mechanisms and technologies that were discussed as supporting socialization also play an important role in knowledge sharing systems. Discussion groups or chat groups facilitate knowledge sharing by enabling an individual to explain her knowledge to the rest of the group. In addition, knowledge sharing systems also utilize mechanisms and technologies that facilitate exchange. Some of the mechanisms that facilitate exchange are memos, manuals, progress reports, letters, and presentations. Technologies facilitating exchange include groupware and other team-collaboration mechanisms; Web-based access to data and databases; and repositories of information, including best practice databases, lessons learned systems, and expertise locator systems. Box 4.3 on Veteran's Health Administration (VHA), which was presented earlier, provides one illustration of the importance of knowledge sharing.

KNOWLEDGE APPLICATION SYSTEMS

Knowledge application systems support the process through which some individuals utilize knowledge possessed by other individuals without actually acquiring, or learning, that knowledge. Mechanisms and technologies support knowledge application systems by facilitating routines and direction.

Mechanisms facilitating direction include traditional hierarchical relationships in organizations, help desks, and support centers. On the other hand, mechanisms supporting routines include organizational policies, work practices, organizational procedures, and standards. In the case of both direction and routines, these mechanisms may be either within an organization (e.g., organizational procedures) or across organizations (e.g., industry best practices).

Technologies supporting direction include (experts' knowledge embedded in expert systems (see Chapter 8) and decision-support systems, as well as troubleshooting systems based on the use of technologies like case-based reasoning. On the other hand, some of the technologies that facilitate routines are expert systems (see Chapter 6), enterprise resource planning systems, and traditional management information systems. As mentioned for KM mechanisms, these technologies can also facilitate directions and routines within or across organizations. These are discussed in detail in Chapter 6.

Box 4.4 provides an illustration of a knowledge application.

Table 4.1 summarizes the discussion of KM processes and KM systems, and also

---

Box 4.4

Automated Knowledge Application at DeepGreen Financial

Based in Cleveland, Ohio, DeepGreen Financial (which was acquired in March 2004 by Light-year Capital, a New York-based private equity investment firm) has revolutionized the mortgage industry by providing low-rate, home equity products that are easy to apply for and obtain over the Internet. DeepGreen even offers to close the loan at the borrower's home. DeepGreen's efficient and innovative technology has reduced the cost of loan production, which they pass on to the consumer. An Internet-only home equity lender, DeepGreen originates loans in 47 states and makes them available through its Web site and through partners such as LendingTree, LLC, Priceline, and Costco Wholesale Corporation. DeepGreen originates home equity products at five times the industry average in terms of dollars per employee.

Right from its start in August 2000, DeepGreen has been based on efficient knowledge utilization. Right from the firm's creation, the vision for it was to rely on automated decision technology. DeepGreen created an Internet-based system that makes credit decisions within minutes by selecting the customers with the best credit. Efficient knowledge utilization through routines embedded as rules within an automated system, along with efficient use of online information, enabled only eight employees to process about 400 applications daily. Instead of competing on the basis of interest rates, DeepGreen competed in terms of ease of application (a customer could complete the application within five minutes) and by providing nearly instantaneous, unconditional decisions without requiring the borrowers to provide the usual appraisals or paperwork upfront. This quick decision is enabled through knowledge application and the computation of credit score and property valuation using online data. In about 80 percent of the cases, a final decision is provided to the customer within two minutes of the application being completed. *Online Banking Report* named DeepGreen's home equity lines of credit as the "Best of the Web."

Source: Compiled from Davenport and Harris 2005; Harris and Brooks 2004; http://www.home-equity-info.us/lenders_banks_deepgreen-bank.php; and http://www.deepgreenfinancial.com/.

---

indicates some of the mechanisms and technologies that might facilitate them. As may be seen from this table, the same tool or technology can be used to support more than one KM process.

MANAGING KNOWLEDGE MANAGEMENT SOLUTIONS

The management of KM systems will be discussed in Chapters 6 through 9, which will examine each of the four types of KM systems in greater detail. Moreover, the selection of KM processes and KM systems that would be most appropriate for the circumstances will be discussed in Chapter 11. Finally, the overall leadership of the KM function will be discussed in Chapter 12. Therefore, in this section, we focus on some overall recommendations regarding the management of KM processes and systems.

First, organizations should use a combination of the four types of **KM processes and systems**. Although different KM processes may be most appropriate in the light of the organization's business strategy, focusing exclusively on one type of KM processes (and the corresponding type of KM systems) would be inappropriate because they serve complementary objectives. More specifically, it is important to note the following:

Table 4.1

KM Processes and Systems, and Associated Mechanisms and Technologies

KM Processes	KM Systems	KM Subprocesses	Illustrative KM Mechanisms	Illustrative KM Technologies
Knowledge Discovery	Knowledge Discovery Systems	Combination	Meetings, telephone conversations, and documents, collaborative creation of documents	Databases, Web-based access to data, data mining, repositories of information, Web portals, best practices and lessons learned
		Socialization	Employee rotation across departments, conferences, brainstorming retreats, cooperative projects, initiation	Video-conferencing, electronic discussion groups, e-mail
Knowledge Capture	Knowledge Capture Systems	Externalization	Models, prototypes, best practices, lessons learned	Expert systems, chat groups, best practices, and lessons learned databases
		Internalization	Learning by doing, on-the-job training, learning by observation, and face-to-face meetings	Computer-based communication, AI-based knowledge acquisition, computer-based simulations
Knowledge Sharing	Knowledge Sharing Systems	Socialization	See above	See above
		Exchange	Memos, manuals, letters, presentations	Team collaboration tools, Web-based access to data, databases, and repositories of information, best practices databases, lessons learned systems, and expertise locator systems
Knowledge Application	Knowledge Application Systems	Direction	Traditional hierarchical relationships in organizations, help desks, and support centers	Capture and transfer of experts' knowledge, troubleshooting systems, and case-based reasoning systems; decision support systems
		Routines	Organizational policies, work practices, and standards	Expert systems, enterprise resource planning systems, management information systems

- Knowledge application enables efficiency. However, too much emphasis on knowledge application could reduce knowledge creation, which often benefits from individuals viewing the same problem from multiple different perspectives and thereby leads to reduced effectiveness and innovation.
- Knowledge capture enables knowledge to be converted from tacit form to explicit, or from explicit form to tacit, and thereby facilitates knowledge sharing. However, it might lead to reduced attention to knowledge creation. Moreover, knowledge capture could lead to some knowledge being lost in the conversion process; not all tacit knowledge is converted into explicit form during externalization, and not all explicit knowledge is converted into tacit form during internalization.
- Knowledge sharing enables efficiency by reducing redundancy. However, too much knowledge sharing could lead to knowledge leaking from the organization and becoming available to competitors, and consequently reduce the benefits to the focal organization.
- Knowledge discovery enables innovation. However, too much emphasis on knowledge discovery could lead to reduced efficiency. It is not always suitable to create new knowledge, just as it may not always be appropriate to reuse existing knowledge.

Second, each KM process could benefit from two different subprocesses, as depicted in Figure 4.1. The subprocesses are mutually complementary, and should be used depending on the circumstances as discussed in Chapter 11. For example, knowledge sharing could occur through socialization or exchange. If knowledge being shared is tacit in nature, socialization would be appropriate, whereas if knowledge being shared is explicit in nature, exchange would be suitable. However, when individuals need to share both tacit and explicit knowledge, the two subprocesses (socialization and exchange) could be integrated together, such as in a face-to-face meeting (i.e., using socialization to transfer tacit knowledge) where the participants are also sharing printed reports containing explicit knowledge (i.e., using exchange to transfer explicit knowledge). Overall, the seven KM subprocesses should be developed within a group such that they can complement each other in an efficient fashion.

Third, each of the seven KM subprocesses of the KM processes depends on the KM mechanisms and technologies, as discussed before. Moreover, the same mechanism could be used to support multiple different subprocesses. Development and acquisition of these mechanisms and technologies, respectively, should be done in the light of the KM processes that would be most appropriate for the organizational circumstances.

Finally, the KM processes and systems should be considered in the light of each other, so that the organization builds a portfolio of mutually complementary KM processes and systems over time. This requires involvement from senior executives, a long-term KM strategy for the organization, and an understanding of the synergies as well as common foundations (i.e., mechanisms and technologies that might support multiple KM systems and processes) across the various KM systems and processes.

Figure 4.2 **A Detailed View of Knowledge Management Solutions**

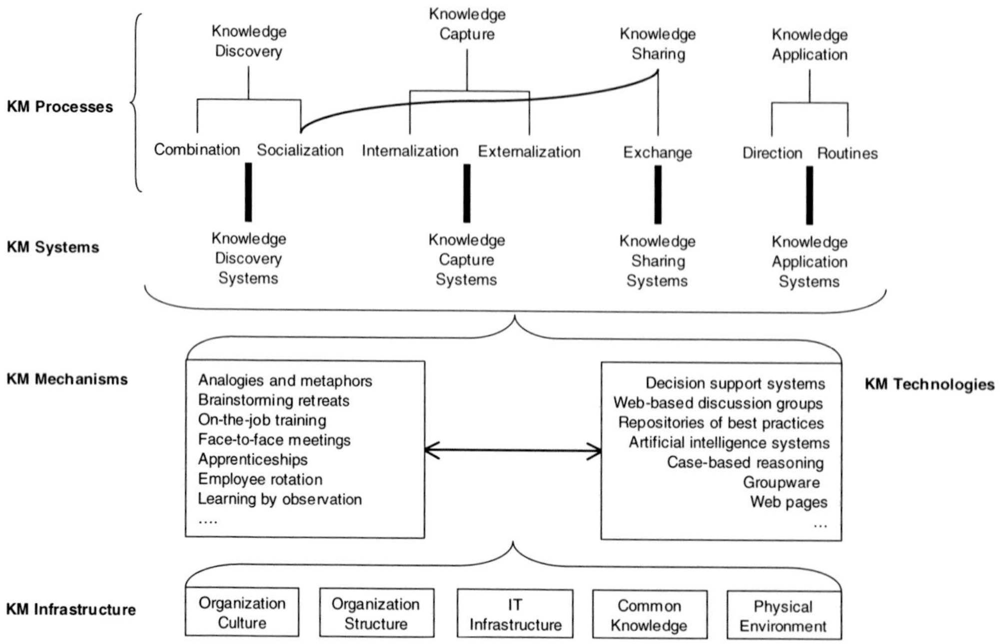

SUMMARY

Building on the discussion of knowledge management foundations in Chapter 3, we have examined KM solutions, including KM processes and systems, in this chapter. Figure 4.2 provides a summary of the various aspects of knowledge management, indicating the various aspects of KM processes (including the four overall processes as well as the seven specific processes that support them), KM systems, KM mechanisms and technologies, and KM infrastructure. The next chapter examines the value of knowledge and KM solutions, highlighting their importance for organizational performance.

KEY TERMS

Combination
Direction
Exchange
Externalization
Internalization
Knowledge application
Knowledge capture
Knowledge discovery
Knowledge management

Knowledge management foundations
Knowledge management mechanisms
Knowledge management processes
Knowledge management solutions
Knowledge management systems
Knowledge management technologies
Knowledge sharing
Routines
Socialization

REVIEW

1. Give an example of one knowledge management mechanism that could be used to facilitate each of the four knowledge management processes.
2. Give an example of one knowledge management technology that could be used to facilitate each of the four knowledge management processes.
3. Briefly explain the four kinds of classifications for knowledge management systems based on the process supported.
4. Distinguish between direction and routines.
5. Socialization could be used for knowledge discovery as well as knowledge sharing. Would the underlying process be any different depending on whether it is being used for knowledge discovery or knowledge sharing?
6. Tacit knowledge could be transferred from one person to another in two distinct ways. One possibility is to transfer it directly through socialization. The other possibility is to convert it into explicit form (through externalization), then transfer it in explicit form to the recipient (through exchange), who then converts it into tacit form (through internalization). What are the pros and cons of each approach? If the purpose is to transfer knowledge from one person to one other person, which approach would you recommend? If the purpose is to transfer knowledge from one person to 100 other individuals in different parts of the world, which approach would you recommend? Why?

APPLICATION EXERCISES

1. How would you, as a CEO of a manufacturing firm, facilitate the growth of knowledge management practices within your organization?
2. How would you utilize knowledge discovery systems and knowledge capture systems in an organization that is spread across the globe? Does geographic distance hamper the utilization of these systems?
3. Suggest reasons why a knowledge sharing system could be established between rival organizations (e.g., Mastercard Inc. and Visa Inc.) for the mutual benefit of both organizations.
4. Critique the following statement: "We have implemented several IT solutions: expert systems, chat groups, and best practices/lessons learned databases. These powerful solutions will surely induce our employees to internalize knowledge."
5. Consider the organization where you currently work or one with which you are familiar (either through your own prior experience or through interactions with someone who works there). What kind of knowledge management systems and processes does this organization use to manage knowledge? What are their effects on this organization's performance? In what order did the organization develop these KM systems and processes, and why?
6. Interview at least three managers from local organizations that have recently implemented a knowledge management system. How do these organizations differ in terms of the KM systems they have developed? What reasons led these organizations to develop these systems?

REFERENCES

Alavi, M., and D. Leidner. 2001. Knowledge management and knowledge management systems: Conceptual foundations and research issues. *MIS Quarterly,* 25(1), 107–136.

Brown, J.S. and Duguid, P. 2000. Balancing act: How to capture knowledge without killing it. *Harvard Business Review,* May–June, 73–80.

Conner, K.R. and Prahalad, C.K. 1996. A resource-based theory of the firm: Knowledge versus opportunism. *Organization Science,* 7(5), 477–501.

Davenport, T.H. and Harris, J.G. 2005. Automated decision making comes of age. *Sloan Management Review,* 46(4) (Summer), 83–89.

Davenport, T., and Prusak, L. 1998. *Working knowledge.* Boston, MA: Harvard Business School Press.

Feigenbaum, E. and McCorduck, P. 1983. *The fifth generation.* Reading, MA: Addison-Wesley.

Grant, R.M. 1996. Toward a knowledge-based theory of the firm. *Strategic Management Journal,* 17, 109–122.

Harris, J.G. and Brooks, J.D. 2004. In the mortgage industry, IT matters. *Mortgage Banking,* 65(3) (December), 62–66.

Jensen, M.C., and Meckling, W.H. 1996. Specific and general knowledge, and organizational structure. In *Knowledge Management & Organizational Design,* ed. P.S. Myers, 17–18. Newton, MA: Butterworth-Heinemann.

McKellar, Hugh. 2001. "The First Annual *KM*World Awards." The Fifth Annual KM World 2001 Conference and Exposition, October 29–November 1, http://www.infotoday.com/kmw01/kmawards.htm.

Nahapiet, J. and Ghoshal, S. 1998. Social capital, intellectual capital, and the organizational advantage. *Academy of Management Review,* 23(2), 242–266.

Nonaka, I. 1994. A dynamic theory of organizational knowledge creation. *Organization Science,* 5(1) (February), 14–37.

Nonaka, I. and Takeuchi, H. 1995. *The knowledge creating company: How Japanese companies create the dynamics of innovation.* New York: Oxford University Press.

Sabherwal, R. and Sabherwal, S. 2007. How do knowledge management announcements affect firm value? A study of firms pursuing different business strategies. *IEEE Transactions on Engineering Management,* 54(3) (August), 409–422.

Stewart, T.A. 2000. The house that knowledge built. *Fortune,* October 2.

5. Organizational Impacts of Knowledge Management

In the previous two chapters, we examined what we mean by knowledge management and discussed KM foundations including KM infrastructure, mechanisms, and technologies; and KM solutions including KM processes and solutions. In this chapter, we examine the impacts of knowledge management. Consistent with our emphasis on the use of KM in organizations, we focus our discussion on the impact of KM on companies and other private or public organizations.

The importance of knowledge (and KM processes) is well recognized. According to Benjamin Franklin, "An investment in knowledge pays the best interest" (NASA 2007). KM can impact organizations and organizational performance at several levels: people, processes, products, and the overall organizational performance (Becerra-Fernandez and Sabherwal 2008). KM processes can impact organizations at these four levels in two main ways. First, KM processes can help create knowledge, which can then contribute to improved performance of organizations along the above four dimensions. Second, KM processes can directly cause improvements along these four dimensions. These two ways in which KM processes can impact organizations is summarized in Figure 5.1.

Figure 5.2 depicts the impacts of KM on the four dimensions mentioned above and shows how the effect on one dimension can have an impact on another. The impact at three of these dimensions—individuals, products, and the organization—was clearly indicated in a joint survey by IDC[1] and *Knowledge Management Magazine* in May 2001 (Dyer and McDonough 2001). This survey examined the status of knowledge management practices in U.S. companies, and found three top reasons why U.S. firms adopt knowledge management: (1) retaining expertise of employees, (2) enhancing customers' satisfaction with the company's products, and (3) increasing profits or revenues. We will examine these issues closely in the next four sections.

IMPACT ON PEOPLE

Knowledge management can affect the organization's employees in several ways. First of all, it can facilitate their learning (from each other as well as from external sources). This learning by individual employees allows the organization to be constantly growing and changing in response to the market and the technology (Sabherwal 2008). Knowledge management also causes the employees to become more flexible

Figure 5.1 **How Knowledge Management Impacts Organizations**

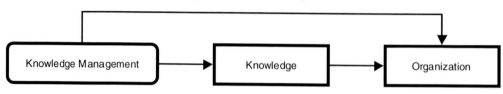

Figure 5.2 **Dimensions of Organizational Impacts of Knowledge Management**

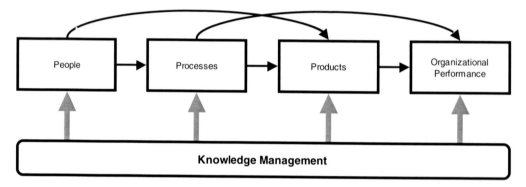

and enhances their job satisfaction. This is largely because of their enhanced ability to learn about solutions to business problems that worked in the past, as well as those solutions that did not work. These effects are now discussed.

IMPACT ON EMPLOYEE LEARNING

Knowledge management can help enhance the employee's learning and exposure to the latest knowledge in their fields. This can be accomplished in a variety of ways including externalization and internalization, socialization, and communities of practice, which were all discussed in Chapter 3.

We earlier described **externalization** as the process of converting tacit knowledge into explicit forms, and **internalization** as the conversion of explicit knowledge into tacit knowledge (Nonaka and Takeuchi 1995). Externalization and internalization work together in helping individuals learn. One possible example of externalization is preparing a report on lessons learned from a project. In preparing the report, the team members document, or externalize, the tacit knowledge they have acquired during the project. Individuals embarking on later projects can then use this report to acquire the knowledge gained by the earlier team. These individuals acquire tacit knowledge through internalization—that is, by reading the explicit report and thereby re-experiencing what others have gone through. Thus, an expert writing a book is externalizing her knowledge in that area, and a student reading the book is acquiring tacit knowledge from the knowledge explicated in the book.

Socialization also helps individuals acquire knowledge but usually through joint activities such as meetings, informal conversations, and so on. One specific, but im-

Box 5.1

Strategic Communities of Practice at Xerox

Xerox Corporation enabled individual learning through a strategic community of practice. Consistent with our definition of a community of practice, the groups at Xerox included geographically distributed individuals from the headquarters as well as business units. However, these groups were somewhat different from a traditional community of practice because they were not voluntarily formed by the individuals themselves but instead were deliberately established by the top management at Xerox with the goal of providing strategic benefits through knowledge sharing. This is the reason Storck and Hill (2000) characterized them as "strategic" communities. One of these strategic communities, which had been tasked to help in the management of technology infrastructure, consisted of a large group of information technology professionals who provided leading-edge solutions, addressed unstructured problems, and stayed in touch with the latest developments in hardware and software.

According to the group members surveyed by Storck and Hill, about two-thirds of the group's value resulted from face-to-face networking at the group's meetings. This attention to knowledge management by focusing on informal groups of employees has helped Xerox in its recent push in global services. Jim Joyce, a senior executive at Xerox remarked: "It is about understanding where knowledge is and how it is found. By working with human elements of this, there are real things you can do to help people embrace the technology and incorporate it into the workflow" (Moore 2001). Similarly, Tom Dolan, president, Xerox Global Services, recognized: "At the core of Xerox's heritage of innovation is a deep understanding of how people, processes and technology interact with each other in the creation of great work. As a result, our practical, results-oriented, knowledge management solutions can help businesses streamline work processes, enable better customer service, and grow revenue" (*Business Wire* 2002).

Xerox has continued the use of communities of practice, with about 15 learning communities, including more than 1,000 employees being launched in 2007 and 2008. According to Kent Purvis, a managing principal with Xerox's global services division: "We know there is a groundswell of knowledge among our managing principals, along all the lines of business. Now there is a structure in place for sharing it" (Kranz 2008).

Source: Compiled from *Business Wire* 2002; Kranz 2008.

portant, way in which learning through socialization can be facilitated involves the use of a **community of practice**, which we defined in Chapter 3 as an organic and self-organized group of individuals who may be dispersed geographically or organizationally but communicate regularly to discuss issues of mutual interest. In Box 5.1, we describe how one organization was able to enable individual learning via the implementation of communities of practice.

The experience of Xerox illustrates the way in which knowledge management can enable the organization's employees to learn from each other as well as from prior experiences of former employees. It is also indicative of how such processes for individual learning can lead to continued organizational success.

IMPACT ON EMPLOYEE ADAPTABILITY

When the knowledge management process at an organization encourages its employees to continually learn from each other, the employees are likely to possess the information and knowledge needed to adapt whenever organizational circumstances so require. Moreover, when they are aware of ongoing and potential future changes, they are less likely to be caught by surprise. Awareness of new ideas and involvement in free-flowing discussions not only prepare them to respond to changes, but they also make them more likely to accept change. Thus, knowledge management is likely to engender greater adaptability among employees.

When Buckman Laboratories International, Inc., a privately owned U.S. specialty chemicals firm with about 1,300 employees, was named "the 2000 Most Admired Knowledge Enterprise," its Chairman, Bob Buckman, remarked that the company's knowledge management efforts were intended to continually expose its employees to new ideas and enable them to learn from them (*Business Wire* 2000). He also emphasized that the employees were prepared for change as a result of being in touch with the latest ideas and developments, and they consequently embraced change rather than being afraid of it. The increased employee adaptability due to knowledge management enabled the company to become a very fast-changing organization around the needs of its customers. Buckman Laboratories has subsequently won the Most Admired Knowledge Enterprise award in 2001, 2003, 2004, 2005, and 2006, and been nominated Best Practice Partner by American Productivity and Quality Center (APQC) for their contributions to Leveraging Knowledge Across the Value Chain in 2006 (Buckman Laboratories International 2007).

IMPACT ON EMPLOYEE JOB SATISFACTION

Two benefits of knowledge management that accrue directly to individual employees have been discussed above: (a) They are able to learn better than employees in firms that are lacking in KM, and (b) they are better prepared for change. These impacts cause the employees to feel better because of the knowledge acquisition and skill enhancement and also the impacts enhance their market value relative to other organizations' employees. A recent study found that in organizations having more employees sharing knowledge with one another, turnover rates were reduced thereby positively affecting revenue and profit (Bontis 2003). Indeed, exit interview data in this study indicated that one of the major reasons many of the brightest knowledge workers changed jobs was because, "they felt their talent was not fully leveraged." Of course, it is possible to argue for the reverse causal direction; that is, more satisfied employees are likely to be more willing to share knowledge. The causal direction of the relationship between employee job satisfaction and knowledge sharing needs to be researched further.

In addition, knowledge management also provides employees with solutions to problems they face in case those same problems have been encountered earlier and effectively addressed. This provision of tried-and-tested solutions (for example, through the direction mechanism discussed in Chapter 3) amplifies employee's effectiveness in performing their jobs. This helps keep those employees motivated, for a successful employee would be highly motivated while an employee facing problems in performing his job would likely be demotivated.

Thus, as a result of their increased knowledge, improved market value, and greater on-the-job performance, knowledge management facilitates employees' job satisfaction. In addition, some approaches for knowledge management, such as mentoring

Figure 5.3 **How Knowledge Management Impacts People**

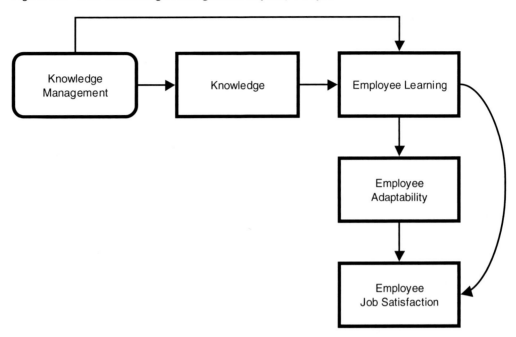

and training, are also directly useful in motivating employees and therefore increasing employee job satisfaction. Similarly, communities of practice provide the involved employees intimate and socially validated control over their own work practices (Brown and Duguid 1991).

Figure 5.3 summarizes the above impacts knowledge management and knowledge can have on employees of organizations.

IMPACT ON PROCESSES

Knowledge management also enables improvements in organizational processes such as marketing, manufacturing, accounting, engineering, public relations, and so forth. These impacts can be seen along three major dimensions: effectiveness, efficiency, and degree of innovation of the processes. These three dimensions can be characterized as follows:

- **Effectiveness:** Performing the most suitable processes and making the best possible decisions.
- **Efficiency:** Performing the processes quickly and in a low-cost fashion.
- **Innovation:** Performing the processes in a creative and novel fashion that improves effectiveness and efficiency—or at least marketability.

Knowledge management can improve the above interrelated aspects of organizational processes through several means, including better knowledge being imparted to individuals (through exchange, socialization, and so on) and the provision of workable solutions (through directions and routines), for employees to solve the problems faced in their tasks. The effects of KM on effectiveness, efficiency, and innovation are discussed in more detail below.

IMPACT ON PROCESS EFFECTIVENESS

Knowledge management can enable organizations to become more effective by helping them to select and perform the most appropriate processes. Effective knowledge management enables the organization's members to collect information needed to monitor external events. This results in fewer surprises for the leaders of the organization and consequently reduces the need to modify plans and settle for less effective approaches. In contrast, poor knowledge management can result in mistakes by the organization because they risk repeating past mistakes or not foreseeing otherwise obvious problems. For example, Ford Motor Company and Firestone (now part of Bridgestone Corporation) incurred numerous problems which may have been reduced through greater knowledge sharing, either by exchanging explicit knowledge and information or by using meetings (and other means of socialization) to share tacit knowledge. These firms did possess the necessary information to warn them about the mismatch of Ford Explorers and Firestone tires. However, the information was not integrated across the two companies, which might have inhibited either company from having the "full picture." It is interesting to note that although Ford had a good knowledge management process (the Best Practices Replication Process, discussed later in this chapter), it was not used to manage the information and knowledge relating to the Ford Explorer and the Firestone tires, or identify the potential risk of the tire's tread peeling off, leading to tire disintegration with the likelihood of accident in case the vehicle was then traveling at a high speed (Stewart 2000). The result was significant loss in lives for their customers and unprecedented legal liability.

Knowledge management enables organizations to quickly adapt their processes according to the current circumstances, thereby maintaining process effectiveness in changing times. On the other hand, organizations lacking in knowledge management find it difficult to maintain process effectiveness when faced with turnover of experienced and new employees. An illustrative example is from a large firm that reorganized its engineering department in 1996. This reorganization achieved a 75 percent reduction of the department's workforce. An external vendor subsequently absorbed many of the displaced engineers. However, like many organizations undergoing significant downsizing, this company failed to institutionalize any mechanisms to capture the knowledge of the employees that were leaving the department. A two-month review of the results following the reorganization effort showed that several key quality indicators were not met. This was a direct result of the loss of human knowledge with the displacement of the workforce. One important reason for the lack of attention to retaining knowledge is that the alternative approaches for capturing individual knowledge (which were discussed in Chapter 3) are not well understood. We will discuss some of these methods and technologies to capture knowledge in Chapter 7. Box 5.2 illustrates how one particular organization was able to significantly improve its processes in disaster management response through effective KM.

Box 5.2

Knowledge Management at Tearfund

Tearfund[1] is a large relief and development agency, based in the United Kingdom. It regularly responds to natural and humanitarian disasters such as floods, hurricanes, typhoons, famine, and displacement. Tearfund was introduced to knowledge management by Paul Whiffen, who was earlier a knowledge management champion at British Petroleum (Milton 2004). Its knowledge management efforts were founded on the recognition that learning from successes and failures during responses to disasters, both natural and man-made, should improve responses to later ones. It has proved this by identifying, consolidating, and then utilizing lessons learned in response to floods in Bangladesh, the Orissa Cyclone in India, the Balkan crisis, and other disasters. Its knowledge management efforts comprise of two main components. First, they utilize the learning opportunities that arise during and after any major activity by involving key participants in the activity to perform after-action reviews that describe lessons learned from the activity. In each project, the key project members participate in a structured, facilitated process to identify the key lessons learned and retrieve them again when they are next required. Second, Tearfund creates communities of practice to connect people with similar roles, issues, challenges, and knowledge needs. This enables Tearfund's employees to share their knowledge with its 350 United Kingdom and overseas partner organizations. Both these steps rely on cultural change and use of technology.

Through these KM efforts, Tearfund has been consciously learning different disaster responses, in each case identifying specific and actionable recommendations for future application. The explicit and conscious sharing of these recommendations provides Tearfund with the confidence and shared understanding needed to implement some of the lessons its many individuals had learned. The outcome has been a more proactive and integrated response to disasters that provides help to the beneficiaries more effectively. For example, Tearfund has modified its processes so that someone would be in the field no later than 48 hours after a disaster. It has also identified 300 specific and actionable recommendations. According to Whiffen (2001), "success relies on not just identifying the lessons, but actually implementing them the next time. It needs to be part of somebody 's job to make sure the learning happens and lessons are embedded in the processes we follow next time there's a disaster response."

Source: Compiled from Milton 2004; Whiffen 2001; Wilson 2002.
[1] Visit http://www.tearfund.org for more information on this organization.

IMPACT ON PROCESS EFFICIENCY

Managing knowledge effectively can also enable organizations to be more productive and efficient. Upon exploring the "black box" of knowledge sharing within Toyota Motor Corporation's network, Dyer and Nobeoka (2000, p. 364) found that "Toyota's ability to effectively create and manage network-level knowledge sharing processes, at least partially, explains the relative productivity advantages enjoyed by Toyota and its suppliers." Knowledge diffusion was found to occur more quickly within Toyota's production network than in competing automaker networks. This was because Toyota's network had solved three fundamental dilemmas with regard to knowledge sharing by devising methods to: (1) motivate members to participate and openly share valuable knowledge (while preventing undesirable spillovers to competitors); (2) prevent free riders—that is, individuals who learn from others without helping others learn; and

(3) reduce the costs associated with finding and accessing different types of valuable knowledge.

Another example of improved efficiency through knowledge management comes from British Petroleum (Echikson 2001). A BP exploration geologist located off the coast of Norway discovered a more efficient way of locating oil on the Atlantic seabed in 1999. This improved method involved a change in the position of the drill heads to better aim the equipment and thereby decrease the number of misses. The employee posted a description of the new process on BP's Intranet for everyone's benefit in the company. Within 24 hours, another engineer working on a BP well near Trinidad found the posting and e-mailed the Norwegian employee requesting necessary additional details. After a quick exchange of e-mail messages, the Caribbean team successfully saved five days of drilling and US$600,000. Of course, in utilizing this knowledge, the employees of the Caribbean unit needed to either trust their Norwegian colleagues or be able to somehow assess the reliability of that knowledge. Issues of trust, knowledge ownership, and knowledge hoarding are important and need to be examined in future research. This case study points to a real instance where knowledge sharing and taking advantage of information technology to quickly disseminate it resulted in a major cost savings to a company. Overall, the use of knowledge management and Internet technologies enabled BP to save US$300 million during the year 2001 while also enhancing innovation at every step of its value chain.

IMPACT ON PROCESS INNOVATION

Organizations can increasingly rely on knowledge shared across individuals to produce innovative solutions to problems as well as to develop more innovative organizational processes. Knowledge management has been found to enable riskier brainstorming (Storck and Hill 2000) and thereby enhance process innovation. In this context, Nonaka's (1998) concept of "ba"—which is equivalent to "place" in English and refers to a shared space (physical, virtual, or mental) for emerging relationships—is relevant. Unlike information, knowledge cannot be separated from the context. In other words, knowledge is embedded in ba, and therefore a foundation in ba is required to support the process of knowledge creation. J.P. Morgan Chase & Co., recognized the impact knowledge can have on process innovation when the following statement appeared in bold in their debut annual report: "The power of intellectual capital is the ability to breed ideas that ignite value" (Stewart 2001, p. 192).

Buckman Laboratories, discussed earlier in this chapter, linked their research and development personnel and technical specialists to their field-based marketing, sales, and technical support staffs to insure that new products were developed with the customers' needs in mind and that customer needs were quickly and accurately communicated to the product development group (Zack 1999). As a result, new knowledge and insights were effectively exploited in the marketplace leading to better products. In addition, the regular interactions with customers generated knowledge to guide future developments.

Another example of the impact of KM on process innovation (and efficiency), may

Figure 5.4 **How Knowledge Management Impacts Organizational Processes**

Knowledge Management → Knowledge →

Process Effectiveness
• Fewer mistakes
• Adaptation to changed circumstances

Process Efficiency
• Productivity improvement
• Cost savings

Process Innovation
• Improved brainstorming
• Better exploitation of new ideas

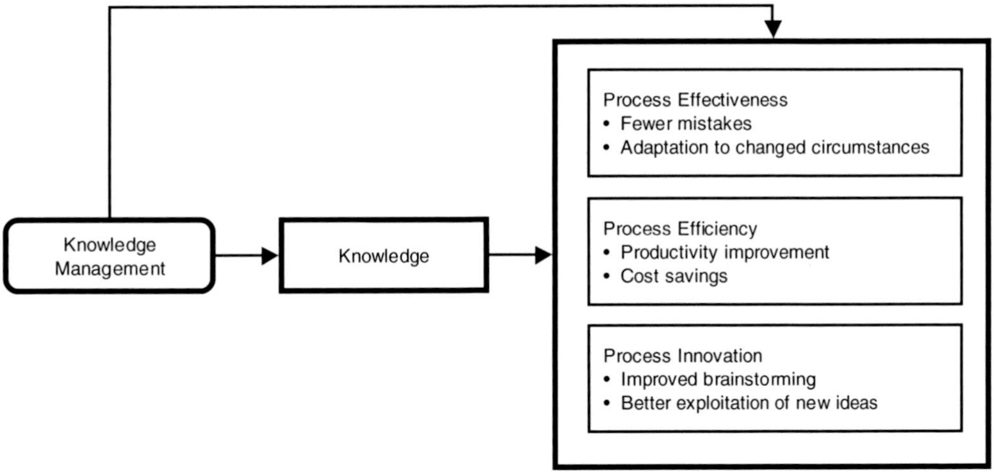

Figure 5.5 **How Knowledge Management Impacts Products**

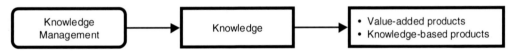

Knowledge Management → Knowledge →
• Value-added products
• Knowledge-based products

be seen in the case of the Office of Special Projects, Veteran's Health Administration (VHA), which was discussed in Box 4.3 in Chapter 4. VHA significantly enhanced innovation by reducing bureaucracy, breaking down organizational barriers, benchmarking and partnering with others, and institutionalizing best processes.

Through these process improvements, knowledge management also contributes to the organization's **dynamic capabilities**, which are viewed as identifiable and specific organizational processes such as strategic decision-making and product development that create value for organizations in dynamic environments (Eisenhardt and Martin 2000; Prieto and Easterby-Smith 2006). In one leading chemical company, knowledge management, especially technical training, word-of-mouth transfer of market knowledge, and informal exchanges between sales managers, seemed to facilitate dynamic capabilities (Prieto and Easterby-Smith 2006).

Figure 5.4 summarizes the above impacts of knowledge management and knowledge on organizational processes.

IMPACT ON PRODUCTS

Knowledge management also impacts the organization's products. These impacts can be seen in two respects: **value-added products** and **knowledge-based products**. Whereas the impacts on the above dimensions come either through knowledge or directly from KM, the impacts below arise primarily from knowledge created through KM. This is depicted in Figure 5.5.

IMPACT ON VALUE-ADDED PRODUCTS

Knowledge management processes can help organizations offer new products or improved products that provide a significant additional value as compared to earlier products. One such example is Ford's Best Practices Replication Process in manufacturing. Every year Ford headquarters provides a "task" to managers, requiring them to come up with a five percent, six percent, or seven percent improvement in key measures—for example, improvements in throughput or energy use. Upon receiving their task, the managers turn to the **best-practices** database to seek knowledge about prior successful efforts. Ford claims that its "best-practice replication" system, whose use Ford tracks in meticulous detail, saved the company $245 million from 1996 to 1997 (Anthes 1998). Over a four-and-a-half year period from 1996 to 2000, more than 2,800 proven superior practices were shared across Ford's manufacturing operations. The documented value of the shared knowledge in 2000 was US$850 million, with another $400 million of value anticipated from work in progress, for a total of $1.25 billion (Stewart 2000; Swarup 2005).

Value-added products also benefit from knowledge management due to the effect the latter has on organizational process innovation. For example, innovative processes resulting from knowledge management at Buckman Laboratories enables sales and support staff to feed customer problems into their computer network in order to access relevant expertise throughout the company and be able to develop innovative solutions for the customers. Similarly, Steelcase Inc., uses information obtained through video ethnography from its customers, the endusers of office furniture, to understand how its products are used and then to redesign the products to make them more attractive to customers (Skyrme 2000).

IMPACT ON KNOWLEDGE-BASED PRODUCTS

Knowledge management can also have a major impact on products that are inherently knowledge based—for example, in consulting and software development industries. For instance, consultants at ICL[2] can quickly access and combine the best available knowledge and bid on proposals that would otherwise be too costly or too time-consuming to put together. Indeed, in such industries, knowledge management is necessary for mere survival.

Knowledge-based products can also sometimes play an important role in traditional manufacturing firms. A classic example is Matsushita's (now Panasonic Corporation) development of an automatic breadmaking machine. In order to design the machine, Matsushita sought a master baker, observed the master baker's techniques, and then incorporated them into the machine's functionality (Nonaka and Takeuchi 1995). Similarly, companies such as Sun Microsystems have enhanced the level of customer service by placing solutions to customer problems in a shareable knowledge base. Moreover, customers can download software patches from the Internet based on their answers to an automated system that prompts customers with a series of questions aimed at diagnosing the customer needs.

IMPACT ON ORGANIZATIONAL PERFORMANCE

In addition to potentially impacting people, products, and processes, knowledge management may also affect the overall performance of the organization. The Deutsche Bank put it all in a nutshell when it took out a big advertisement in the *Wall Street Journal* (Stewart 2001, p. 192) that said: "Ideas are capital. The rest is just money." This advertisement reflects the belief that investments in knowledge management should be viewed as capital investments. This investment may be capable of producing long-term benefits to the entire organization rather than as assets that provide value only at the present time.

Knowledge management can impact overall organizational performance either directly or indirectly as discussed below.

DIRECT IMPACTS ON ORGANIZATIONAL PERFORMANCE

Direct impact of knowledge management on organizational performance occurs when knowledge is used to create innovative products that generate revenue and profit or when the knowledge management strategy is aligned with business strategy. Such a direct impact concerns revenues and/or costs and can be explicitly linked to the organization's vision or strategy. Consequently, measuring direct impact is relatively straightforward. It can be observed in terms of improvements in return on investment (ROI). For example, one account director at British Telecom (BT Groups plc) indicated that his sales team generated about US$1.5 million in new business based on briefings from a new knowledge management system (Compton 2001). Similarly, speaking to the Knowledge Management World Summit in San Francisco, California, on January 11, 1999, Kenneth T. Derr, the Chairman and CEO of Chevron Corporation stated:

> Of all the initiatives we've undertaken at Chevron during the 1990s, few have been as important or as rewarding as our efforts to build a learning organization by sharing and managing knowledge throughout our company. In fact, I believe this priority was one of the keys to reducing our operating costs by more than $2 billion per year—from about $9.4 billion to $7.4 billion—over the last seven years.

The experience of another large company—Shell—in computing the return on investment for its expenditure in KM communities of practice is described in Box 5.3.

INDIRECT IMPACTS ON ORGANIZATIONAL PERFORMANCE

Indirect impact of knowledge management on organizational performance comes about through activities that are not directly linked to the organization's vision, strategy, revenues, or costs. Such effects occur, for example, through the use of knowledge management to demonstrate intellectual leadership within the industry, which, in turn, might enhance customer loyalty. Alternatively, it could occur through the use of knowledge to gain an advantageous negotiating position with respect to competitors

Box 5.3

Evaluating Returns on Knowledge Management at Shell

Oil exploration often involves extrapolating from sketchy data and comparing exploration sites to known ones. This allows geoscientists to decide if enough reserves exist on a site to make developing it worthwhile. For example, one site contained layers of oil-bearing sand that were less than an inch think. A Shell exploration team needed to decide if thin sand beds could extend over a large enough area for the oil in them to be efficiently pumped out. This would normally require drilling and testing a number of exploratory wells. The team asked one of Shell's communities of practice, including geoscientists from several disciplines, for help. By comparing this site to others, the community helped in the team's analysis of where to drill more accurately, resulting in fewer exploratory wells.

   Community members estimated that the discussions of such comparisons enabled them to drill and test three fewer wells a year, saving US$20M in drilling and an additional US$20M in testing costs for each well, for an annual savings of US$120M. It is possible that they might have reached the same conclusions on where to drill, but the leader estimated that the community could claim 25 percent of the savings and was 80 percent sure of this estimate. So the community it may be argued had saved 25 percent of 80 percent of US$120M, or US$24M annually. Since it cost between US$300K and US$400K annually to run the community, this represented an annual return of 40 times the investment. This was not the only benefit, but it was sufficient to address the senior executives' need to know whether the community was worth the investment. Overall, Shell International Exploration and Production estimated that its use of KM resulted in more than $200 million in reduced costs and new income in 2000. (King 2001)

   Source: Compiled from King 2001; Wilson 2002.

or partner organizations. Unlike direct impact, however, indirect impact cannot be associated with transactions and, therefore, cannot be easily measured.

   One example of indirect benefits is the use of knowledge management to achieve economies of scale and scope. Before examining these effects, we briefly examine what we mean by economies of scale and scope.

   A company's output is said to exhibit **economy of scale** if the average cost of production per unit decreases with increase in output. Due to economy of scale, a smaller firm has higher costs than those of larger firms, which makes it difficult to compete with the larger firms in terms of price. Some of the reasons that result in economies of scale include: large setup cost makes low-scale production uneconomic, possibilities for specialization increase as production increases, and greater discounts from suppliers are likely when production is large scale.

   A company's output is said to exhibit **economy of scope** when the total cost of that same company producing two or more different products is less than the sum of the costs that would be incurred if each product was produced separately by a different company. Due to economy of scope, a firm producing multiple products has lower costs than those of its competitors focusing on fewer products. Some of the reasons that result in economies of scope include: incorporating new innovations into multiple products, joint use of production facilities, and joint marketing or administration. Economy of scope can also arise if the production of one good provides the other as a byproduct.

   Knowledge management can contribute to economies of scale and scope by improving the organization's ability to create and leverage knowledge related to products, customers, and managerial resources across businesses. Product designs, components, manufacturing processes, and expertise can be shared across businesses thereby reducing development and manufacturing costs, accelerating new product development, and supporting quick response to new market opportunities. Similarly, shared knowledge of customer preferences, needs, and buying behaviors can enable cross-selling of existing products or development of new products. Finally, economies of scope also result from the deployment of general marketing skills and sales forces across businesses. Although economies of scale and scope could, and usually do, lead to improvements in return on investments, the effect of knowledge management on scale and scope economies and their subsequent effect on return on investments cannot be directly linked to specific transactions and this is therefore considered as an "indirect" impact.

Another indirect impact of knowledge management is to provide a sustainable **competitive advantage**. Knowledge can enable the organization to develop and exploit other tangible and intangible resources better than the competitors can, even though the resources themselves might not be unique. Knowledge, especially context-specific tacit knowledge, tends to be unique and therefore difficult to imitate. Moreover, unlike most traditional resources, it cannot easily be purchased in a ready-to-use form. To obtain similar knowledge, the company's competitors have to engage in similar experiences, but obtaining knowledge through experience takes time. Therefore, competitors are limited in the extent to which they can accelerate their learning through greater investment.

LeaseCo, an industrial garment and small equipment leasing company described by Zack (1999), illustrates the use of knowledge management to gain a sustainable competitive advantage. LeaseCo's strategy involved occasionally bidding aggressively on complex, novel, or unpredictable lease opportunities. These bidding, and subsequent negotiation, experiences provided the company with unique and leverageable knowledge while reducing the opportunity for competitors to gain that same knowledge. LeaseCo realized two significant benefits over its competitors: first by investing in its strategic knowledge platform and second by learning enough about the particular client to competitively and profitably price leases for future opportunities with the same client. Sufficient mutual learning occurred between LeaseCo and their client for the client to contracted LeaseCo for future leases without even going out for competitive bids. In essence, LeaseCo created a sustainable (or renewable), knowledge-based barrier to competition.

Thus, sustainable competitive advantage may be generated through knowledge management by allowing the organization to know more than its competitors about certain things. Competitors, on the other hand, would need considerable time to acquire that same knowledge. Figure 5.6 summarizes the direct and indirect impacts KM and knowledge can potentially have on organizational performance.

SUMMARY

In Table 5.1, we summarize the various impacts of knowledge management examined in this chapter. The impact KM has on one level might lead to synergistic impacts

Figure 5.6 **How Knowledge Management Impacts Organizational Performance**

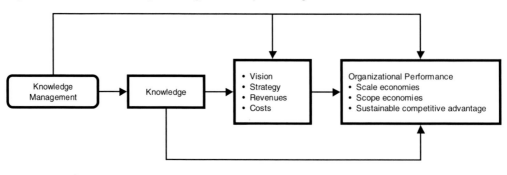

Table 5.1

A Summary of Organizational Impacts of Knowledge Management

Levels of Impact	Impacted Aspects
People	• Employee learning • Employee adaptability • Employee job satisfaction
Processes	• Process effectiveness • Process efficiency • Process innovativeness
Products	• Value-added products • Knowledge-based products
Organizational Performance	Direct Impacts • Return on investment • Indirect Impacts • Economies of scale and scope • Sustainable competitive advantage

on another level as well. For example, employee learning facilitates impacts on processes as well as on products. Thus, KM has the potential to produce several interrelated impacts on people, products, processes, and organizations as we have described in this chapter.

KEY TERMS

Communities of practice	Externalization
Dynamic capabilities	Innovation
Economy of scale	Internalization
Economy of scope	Knowledge-based products
Effectiveness	Socialization
Efficiency	Value-added products

REVIEW

1. Briefly enumerate the ways in which knowledge can impact an organization.
2. State the importance of knowledge management with specific reference to its impact on employee adaptability and job satisfaction.
3. Explain why poor knowledge management reduces the effectiveness of organizational processes.
4. What three dimensions are relevant for examining the impact of knowledge management on business processes?
5. Identify ways in which knowledge management helps improve process effectiveness, efficiency, and innovation.
6. Describe how knowledge management can contribute to an organization's products. Illustrate using the example of Xerox.
7. How can we assess: (a) the direct impacts and (b) the indirect impacts of knowledge management on organizational performance?
8. Knowledge management is an invaluable tool for the oil Industry. Justify this statement with suitable examples.

APPLICATION EXERCISES

1. Identify the possible ways in which knowledge management (or the lack thereof) in your organization (it could be your academic institution or your workplace) affects your learning and job satisfaction.
2. Identify the biggest positive impact on your organization (it could be your academic institution or your workplace) due to the implementation of knowledge management. Speculate on the possibilities if there were no knowledge management practices in place.
3. Now identify the biggest negative impact on your organization (it could be your academic institution or your workplace) due to improper/insufficient knowledge management practices and suggest ways of improvement.
4. Interview a friend or a family member who works at a different organization than you, and examine the overall effects of knowledge management on that organization.
5. You are a CEO who considers implementing a knowledge management system in your company. You have to decide one option out of two: (a) Our knowledge management system can be accessed by customers, or (b) Our knowledge management system cannot be accessed by customers. Describe your decision and provide the reason in terms of organizational performance.
6. Critique the following analysis: Our investment on knowledge management seems to be unsuccessful. The ROI decreased from 10 percent to 5 percent at the year of system implementation. Since direct measure of organizational performance decreased, we need to uninstall the knowledge management system right away.

Notes

1. IDC is one of the world's leading providers of technology intelligence, industry analysis, market data, and strategic and tactical guidance to builders, providers, and users of information technology. More information on it can be obtained from http://www.idc.com.

2. Formed in 1968, ICL was bought by STC in 1984. Fujitsu bought an 80 percent stake in ICL-UK from STC in 1990. In 2002, the consulting arm of ICL-UK was merged with DMR Consulting, and its service division became Fujitsu Services.

References

Anthes, G. 1998. Defending knowledge. *ComputerWorld,* 32(7) (February 16), 41–42.

Becerra-Fernandez, I. and Sabherwal, R. 2008. Individual, group, and organizational learning. In *Knowledge management: An evolutionary view,* ed. I. Becerra-Fernandez and D. Leidner, 13–39. Armonk, NY: M.E. Sharpe.

Bontis, N. 2003. HR's role in knowledge management. *Canadian HR Reporter,* 16(5) (March 10), G8.

Brown, J.S. and Duguid, P. 1991. Organizational learning and communities-of-practice: Toward a unified view of working, learning, and innovation. *Organization Science,* 2(1), 40–57.

Buckman Laboratories International. 2007. Awards and recognitions for Buckman Laboratories. *Knowledge nurture.* http://www.knowledge-nurture.com/recognitions.html (accessed February 12, 2009).

Business Wire. 2000. 2000 most admired knowledge enterprises announced. *Business Wire,* June 5.

———. 2002. Xerox ranked as one of North America's most admired knowledge enterprises: Winning practices available to customers through Xerox Global Services. *Business Wire,* May 6.

Compton, J. 2001. Dial K for knowledge. *CIO,* June 15.

Dyer, G. and McDonough, B. 2001. The state of KM. *Knowledge Management,* May, 21–36.

Dyer, J.H. and Nobeoka, K. 2000. Creating and managing a high-performance knowledge-sharing network: The Toyota case. *Strategic Management Journal,* 23(3), 345–367.

Echikson, W. 2001. When oil gets connected. *Business Week,* December 3.

Eisenhardt, K.M. and Martin, J.K. 2000. Dynamic capabilities: What are they? *Strategic Management Journal,* 21, 1005–1121.

King, J. 2001. Shell strikes knowledge gold. *ComputerWorld,* July 16.

Kranz, G. 2008. At Xerox, learning is a community activity. *Workforce Management Online,* December. http://www.workforce.com/section/11/feature/26/05/23/index.html (accessed February 12, 2009).

Milton, N. 2004. Knowledge management in the aid and development sector: A case study in implementation at Tearfund. In *Performance through learning: Knowledge management in practice,* ed. C. Gorelick, N. Milton, and K. April, 143–161. Boston: Elsevier Butterworth-Heinemann.

Moore, C. 2001. Xerox makes global services push. *InfoWorld,* November 19. *itWorldCanada,* http://www.itworldcanada.com/a/Daily-News/de565b27-f77d-4fd5–82ff-e861f4bbcfb9.html.

National Aeronautics and Space Administration (NASA). 2007. Quotes related to knowledge management or collaboration. http://km.nasa.gov/whatis/KM_Quotes.html (accessed February 12, 2009).

Nonaka, I. 1998. The concept of ba: Building a foundation for knowledge creation. *California Management Review,* 40(3) (Spring), 40–54.

Nonaka, I. and Takeuchi, H. 1995. *The knowledge creating company: How Japanese companies create the dynamics of innovation.* New York: Oxford University Press.

Prieto, I.M. and Easterby-Smith, M. 2006. Dynamic capabilities and the role of organizational knowledge: An exploration. *European Journal of Information Systems,* 15, 500–510.

Sabherwal, R. 2008. KM and BI: From mutual isolation to complementarity and synergy. *Cutter Consortium Executive Report,* 8(8), 1–18.

Skyrme, D.J. 2000. Developing a knowledge strategy: From management to leadership. In *Knowledge management: Classic and contemporary works,* ed. D. Morey, M. Maybury, and B. Thuraisingham, 61–84. Cambridge, MA: The MIT Press.

Stewart, T.A. 2000. Knowledge worth $1.25 billion. *Fortune,* November 27, 302–303.

———. 2001. Intellectual capital: Ten years later, how far we've come. *Fortune,* May 28, 192–193.

Storck, J. and Hill, P. 2000. Knowledge diffusion through strategic communities. *Sloan Management Review,* 41(2), 63–74.

Swarup, S. 2005. Applying KM to improve quality. *InsideKnowledge,* October 10.

Whiffen, P. 2001. Seizing learning opportunities at Tearfund. *Knowledge Management Review,* November/December.

Wilson, J. (Ed.). 2002. *Knowledge management review: The practitioner's guide to knowledge management.* Chicago: Melcrum Publishing Limited.

Zack, M.H. 1999. Developing a knowledge strategy. *California Management Review,* 41(3) (Spring), 125–145.

PART II

KNOWLEDGE MANAGEMENT TECHNOLOGIES AND SYSTEMS

6 Knowledge Application Systems: Systems that Utilize Knowledge

In the last chapter, we discussed the organizational impacts of knowledge management. In this chapter, we describe knowledge application systems, how they are developed, and relate experiences of how organizations have implemented such systems. As we discussed in Chapter 4, knowledge application systems support the process through which individuals utilize the knowledge possessed by other individuals without actually acquiring, or learning, that knowledge. Both mechanisms and technologies can support knowledge application systems by facilitating the knowledge management processes of routines and direction. Knowledge application systems are typically enabled by intelligent technologies. In this chapter, we introduce the reader to artificial intelligence (AI), its historical perspective, its relationship with knowledge, and why it is an important aspect of knowledge management. We also summarize the most relevant intelligent technologies that underlie most KM systems, from rule-based expert systems, to case-based reasoning (CBR), to traditional management information systems. Moreover, we discuss different types of knowledge application systems: expert systems, help desk systems, and fault diagnosis systems. The case studies in this chapter narrate the implementation of knowledge application systems. Each is based on different intelligent technologies and designed to accomplish different goals: provide advice, enhance fault detection, and facilitate creative reasoning. Finally, limitations of knowledge application systems are discussed.

You may recall, from Chapter 4, that knowledge application depends on direction and routines. Mechanisms facilitating **direction** include hierarchical relationships, help desks, and support centers; whereas mechanisms facilitating **routines** include organizational policies, work practices, and standards. Technologies supporting direction and routines include expert systems, decision support, advisor systems, fault diagnosis (or troubleshooting) systems, and help desk systems. These technologies may support direction, as in the case of a field service technician seeking to troubleshoot a particular product; or may support routines, as in the case of a customer service representative who may need to identify alternative product delivery mechanisms while preparing the shipment of an order. Moreover, mechanisms and technologies can facilitate knowledge application through direction and routines either within or across organizations.

For a quick overview of what knowledge application systems are and how they are used, let us look at a brief case study of how NEC Corporation redefined the way

---

Box 6.1

Applying Organizational Experiences to Produce Quality Software

NEC is a leading global company that manufactures cutting edge products for the broadband networking and mobile Internet market. In 1981, NEC recognized the need to extend their quality control (QC) activity to the domain of software development. In order to accomplish this goal, the company established a company-wide corporate structure to assist employees in applying the principles of software quality control (SWQC). QC activities typically resulted in a case report that outlined the problem analysis, its possible root cause, the corrective actions taken, and the results of the corrective actions.

By 1991, the company had collected over 25,000 such cases in an effort to apply the productivity improvements across the organization. Initially the case reports were stored in a book and later in a searchable database, but people found it difficult to search and apply the QC cases. NEC then decided to implement the software quality control advisor (SQUAD),[1] based on case-based reasoning methodology, to improve user access and application of the reported QC cases. The cases in SQUAD were nominated through a review committee that reviews each case and selects the best cases. Cases are selected on the basis of the quality of the analysis, significance of the results, and how generalizable the problem is.

Adequate incentives were established to encourage employee participation. Initially about 3,000 cases were submitted each year, and later new submissions decreased to about 1,000 cases a year. The significant drop in the rate of new cases submission came about because most typical cases were already reported in the system. By 1994, the system represented about 24,000 cases and served over 150,000 users.

Some of the success factors that marked the development of SQUAD included low development cost, since its development only required four person-months. Furthermore, the development of SQUAD supported incremental modifications, since it allowed for cases to incrementally be included in the case database. By 1991, it was estimated that SQUAD had already paid off to the organization over 100 million dollars per year.

[1]For further details about SQUAD, refer to Cheetham and Watson 2005; Kitano and Shimazu 1996.

---

the organization is able to apply their collective experience in order to better produce high-quality software—see Box 6.1.

TECHNOLOGIES FOR APPLYING KNOWLEDGE

ARTIFICIAL INTELLIGENCE

In this section we begin by describing the historical perspective of AI, the area of computer science that deals with the design and development of computer systems that exhibit human-like cognitive capabilities. **Artificial Intelligence (AI)** refers to enabling computers to perform tasks that resemble human thinking ability. Much like KM and human intelligence, AI is associated with knowledge. Definitions for AI range from: systems that act like humans, systems that think like humans, systems that think rationally, to systems that act rationally (Russell and Norvig 2002). Systems that act like humans refer to those that pass the Turing Test, which refers to a computer passing a test by a human interrogator, who cannot tell whether the responses came from a person or not. Systems that think like humans refer to a computer program whose input to output behavior matches those of humans, for example when solving problems, like playing chess or performing a medical diagnosis. Systems that think rationally refer to those that follow a specific logic to solve a problem. Finally, systems that act rationally refer to those computer agents that are expected to have specific characteristics that enable them to operate autonomously within their environments, and even adapt to change in the face of uncertainty.

Typically computers perform repetitive, logical tasks extremely well, such as complex arithmetic calculations and database retrieval and storage. One common characteristic of these conventional computer tasks is their **algorithmic** nature, which means that they engage precise and logically designed instructions to result in a distinct correct output. Humans, by contrast, excel at solving problems using symbols to which a specific meaning can be attached, such as understanding the meaning of a poem. Artificial intelligence deals with the manipulation of these symbols. Therefore, our own definition of AI (Becerra-Fernandez et al. 2004) in more specific terms is:

> The science that provides computers with the ability to represent and manipulate symbols so they can be used to solve problems not easily solved through algorithmic models.

Modern AI systems are based on the understanding that intelligence and knowledge are tightly intertwined. Knowledge is associated with the cognitive symbols we manipulate, while human intelligence refers to our ability to learn and communicate in order to solve problems. However, when we judge a student's performance in class or decide whom to hire, we generally focus on how much they know, not their intelligence. People are born with a certain degree of intelligence, which they use to learn and thus acquire new knowledge. Some AI systems (also known as knowledge-based systems or knowledge application systems) try to imitate the problem-solving capabilities of skillful problem-solvers in a particular domain. Intelligent systems offer us technologies to manage knowledge—that is, to apply, capture, share, and discover it.

The idea of creating computers that resemble the human intelligent abilities can be traced to the 1950s, when scientists predicted the development of such machines within a decade. Although those same scientists may have underestimated the complexities of the human mind, AI research made significant strides. The term "artificial intelligence" was coined by John McCarthy during a workshop he organized at Dartmouth College in 1956, where he convened the four pioneers of the field: John McCarthy, Marvin Minsky, Allan Newell, and Herbert Simon.

AI research first focused on games and **natural language** translation. In the area of gaming, scientists developed numerous chess programs including Greenblatt's "Mac Hack" and Slate and Atkin's "Chess 4.5" (Hsu et al. 1990). More recently, an AI program named Big Blue defeated Boris Kasparov, the reigning world champion in chess, in a widely publicized match in 1997. On the other hand, early efforts in machine translation of natural languages were not nearly as successful. Another seminal development in AI was the development of **General Problem Solver (GPS)** by Simon and Newell (Newell and Simon 1963). The importance of GPS was that it demonstrated the computer's ability to solve some problems by searching for an answer in a **solution space**, which represented a new trend for AI.

One of the areas in AI that has witnessed the greatest popularity is knowledge-based systems, which we refer to here as knowledge application systems. **Knowledge application systems** are the topic of this chapter, and they basically apply knowledge to solve specific problems. Other areas of research within AI include natural language understanding, **classification**, diagnostics, design, **machine learning**, planning and scheduling, robotics, and computer vision. Next we describe the two most relevant intelligent technologies that underpin the development of knowledge application systems: rule-based expert systems and case-based reasoning.

RULE-BASED SYSTEMS

Traditionally, the development of knowledge-based systems had been based on the use of rules or models to represent the **domain knowledge**. The development of such systems requires the collaboration of a subject matter expert with a knowledge engineer, the latter being responsible for the elicitation and representation of the expert's knowledge. We will see two examples of **rule-based expert systems** when we present cases on Westinghouse Electric Corporation's GenAID and the SBIR/STTR Online Advisor later in this chapter.

The process of developing knowledge application systems requires eliciting the knowledge from the expert and representing it a form that is usable by computers. This process is called **knowledge engineering**. Knowledge engineers typically build knowledge application systems by first interviewing in detail the **domain expert** and representing the knowledge more commonly in a set of heuristics, or rules-of-thumb. Experts develop these rules-of-thumb over years of practical experience at solving problems. In order for the computer to understand these rules-of-thumb, we represent them as *production rules* or *IF-THEN* statements. For example: *IF* the number of employees is less than 500, *THEN* the firm is a small business is one of the rules that the SOS Advisor checks to ensure the firm is eligible for the SBIR/STTR program. Rules are the most commonly used knowledge representation paradigm, perhaps due to their intuitive implementation. The IF portion is the *condition* (also *premise* or *antecedent*), which tests the truth-value of a set of assertions. If the statement is true, the THEN part of the rule (also *action, conclusion,* or *consequence*) is also inferred as a fact.

In addition to rules, other paradigms to represent knowledge include **frames**, predicates, associative networks, and objects. Rule-based systems have posed some disadvantages. One is that in many circumstances, the number of rules that may be needed to properly represent the domain may be quite large. For example, the GenAID system that we describe in the first case study below consisted of about 10,000 rules when it was first deployed. Although later developments of GenAID may have condensed the number of rules by about 3,000, it was still considered a large system. Expert systems with such a large number of rules offer many disadvantages, namely (1) difficulty in coding, verifying, validating, and maintaining the rules; and (2) reduction in the efficiency of the inference engine executing the rules. As an alternative, we consider the use of cases as a method to represent knowledge. For more details on a rule-based systems refer to Chapter 8 of the book *Knowledge Management: Challenges, Solutions, and Technologies* (Becerra-Fernandez et al. 2004).

CASE-BASED REASONING SYSTEMS

Although the rules approach to knowledge representation has produced many examples of successful knowledge application systems, many of these systems are increasingly based on the implementation of case-based reasoning (CBR) methodology.

Case-based reasoning is an artificial intelligence technique designed to mimic human problem solving. CBR is based on Schank's (1982) model of dynamic memory. Its goal is to mimic the way humans solve problems. When faced with a new problem, humans search their memories for past problems resembling the current problem and adapt the prior solution to "fit" the current problem. CBR is a method of analogical reasoning that utilizes old cases or experiences in an effort to solve problems, critique solutions, explain anomalous situations, or interpret situations (Aamodt and Plaza 1994; Kolodner 1991, 1993; Leake 1996; Watson 2003). A typical case-based knowledge application system will consist of the following processes:

1. *Search the case library for similar cases.* This implies utilizing a search engine that examines only the appropriate cases and not the entire case library, as it may be quite large.
2. *Select and retrieve the most similar case(s).* New problems are solved by first retrieving previously experienced cases. This implies having a means to compare each examined case to the current problem, quantifying their similarity, and somehow ranking them in decreasing order of similarity.
3. *Adapt the solution for the most similar case.* If the current problem and the most similar case are not similar enough, then the solution may have to be adapted to fit the needs of the current problem. The new problem will be solved with the aid of an old solution that has been adapted to the new problem.
4. *Apply the generated solution and obtain feedback.* Once a solution or classification is generated by the system, it must be applied to the problem. Its effect on the problem is fed back to the CBR system for classification of its solution (as success or failure).
5. *Add the newly solved problem to the case library.* The new experience is likely to be useful in future problem solving. This step requires identifying if the new case is worth adding to the library and placing it in the appropriate location in the case library.

There are several advantages to using CBR over rules or models for developing knowledge application systems. These advantages come to light when the relationship between the case attributes and the solution or outcome is not understood well enough to represent in rules. Alternatively, CBR systems are advantageous when the ratio of cases that are "exceptions to the rule" is high, as rule-based systems become impractical in such applications. CBR is especially useful in such situations because it incorporates the solution of a newly entered case. It is in such situations that methods for adaptation are used, providing the user with steps to combine and derive a solution from the collection of retrieved solutions.

There are several variants of CBR, such as exemplar-based reasoning, instance-based reasoning, and analogy-based reasoning. These different variations of CBR are described below (Aamodt and Plaza 1994; Leake 1996):

1. **Exemplar-based reasoning**—These systems seek to solve problems through classification, that is, finding the right class for the unclassified exemplar. Essentially the class of the most similar past case then becomes the solution to the classification problem, and the set of classes are the possible solutions to the problem (Kibler and Aha 1987).

2. **Instance-based reasoning**—These systems require a large number of instances (or cases) that are typically simple; that is, they're defined by a small set of attribute vectors. The major focus of study of these systems is automated learning, requiring no user involvement (Aha et al. 1991).

3. **Analogy-based reasoning**—These systems are typically used to solve new problems based on past cases from a different domain (Aamodt and Plaza 1994; Veloso and Carbonnell 1993). Analogy-based reasoning focuses on case reuse, also called the **mapping problem**, which is finding a way to map the solution of the analogue case to the present problem.

CBR, rules, and models are not the only type of intelligent technology underpinning the development of knowledge application systems. Other important technologies used to develop knowledge application systems are worth mentioning—namely, constraint-based reasoning, model-based reasoning, and diagrammatic reasoning. **Constraint-based reasoning** is an artificial intelligence technique that uses essentially "what cannot be done" to guide the process of finding a solution (Tsang 1994). This technique is useful in naturally constrained tasks such as planning and scheduling. For example, to schedule a meeting all the individuals that need to attend must be available at the same time, otherwise the "availability constraint" will be violated. **Model-based reasoning** is an intelligent reasoning technique that uses a model of an engineered system to simulate its normal behavior [Magnani et al. 1999]. The simulated operation is compared with the behavior of a real system and noted discrepancies can lead to a diagnosis; for example, a hurricane model can be designed and implemented to predict a hurricane's trajectory, given the set of current weather conditions such as wind speed, presence of a cold front, temperature, and so forth. Finally, **diagrammatic reasoning** is an artificial intelligence technique that aims to understand concepts and ideas using diagrams that represent knowledge (Chandrasekaran et al. 1993, Glasgow et al. 1995). These technologies are radically different from rule-based systems or CBR systems and have very specific application areas.

In summary, rule-based systems and case-based reasoning, as well as constraint-based reasoning, model-based reasoning, and diagrammatic reasoning are all technologies used to develop knowledge application systems. The applicability of each technology is dictated primarily by the characteristics of the domain as described above. Table 6.1 summarizes the technologies to develop knowledge application systems and the characteristics of the domain that define their applicability. The next sections describe specific types of knowledge application systems based on the aforementioned technologies.

As we previously mentioned, it has become increasingly clear that the most popular technique for the implementation of knowledge application systems in businesses

Table 6.1

Technologies for Knowledge Application Systems

Technology	Domain Characteristics
Rule-based systems	Applicable when the domain knowledge can be defined by a manageable set of rules or heuristics.
Case-based reasoning	Applicable in weak-theory domains, that is, where an expert either doesn't exist or does not fully understand the domain. Also applicable if the experience base spans an entire organization, rather than a single individual.
Constraint-based reasoning	Applicable in domains that are defined by constraints, or what cannot be done.
Model-based reasoning (MBR)	Applicable when designing a system based on the description of the internal workings of an engineered system. This knowledge is typically available from design specifications, drawings, and books, and can be used to recognize and diagnose its abnormal operation.
Diagrammatic reasoning	Applicable when the domain is best represented by diagrams and imagery, such as when solving geometric problems.

today is case-based reasoning. The reasons why CBR is more commonly used in the development of such systems include the fact that CBR implementations are, at least on the surface, more intuitive. In addition, CBR implementations take advantage of explicit knowledge that may already exist in the organization, for example in problem reports. We will see two examples of CBR systems: National Semiconductor Corporation's Total Recall and NASA's Out-of-Family-Disposition prototype later in this chapter. In the next section, we describe how to implement knowledge applications systems. For the reasons mentioned here, we will assume that the underpinning technology for the knowledge application system will be CBR, although the methodology applies to any of the aforementioned technologies.

DEVELOPING KNOWLEDGE APPLICATION SYSTEMS

Here we describe how to build a knowledge application system. We make extensive use of examples and boxes in order to enhance the learning experience. The next section discusses the different types of knowledge application systems, and specific examples are presented in subsequent sections.

The effective implementation of the knowledge application system requires a carefully thought-out methodology. The **Case-Method Cycle** (Kitano 1993; Kitano and Shimazu 1996) is a methodology that describes an iterative approach to effectively develop CBR and knowledge application systems in general. The Case-Method Cycle describes the following six processes:

1. **System development process**—This process is based on standard software engineering approaches, and its goal is to develop a knowledge application system that will store new cases and retrieve relevant cases.

2. **Case library development process**—The goal of this process is to develop and maintain a large-scale **case library** that will adequately support the domain in question.
3. **System operation process**—This process is based on standard software engineering and relational database management procedures. Its goal is to define the installation, deployment, and user support of the knowledge application system.
4. **Database mining process**—This process uses rule-inferencing techniques and statistical analysis to analyze the case library. This step could help infer new relationships between the data, which could be articulated to enhance the knowledge application system.
5. **Management process**—This process describes how the project task force will be formed and what organizational support will be provided to the project.
6. **Knowledge transfer process**—This process describes the incentive systems that will be implemented to encourage user acceptance and support of the knowledge application system. This step will ensure that users will feel compelled to augment the case library with new cases.

In terms of actually developing the case library (step 2 above), the process can also be described in terms of the following subprocesses (Kitano and Shimazu 1996):

1. **Case Collection**—This process entails the collection of seed cases, which provide an initial view of the application. For example, for the SQUAD system described in Box 6.1, the developers started with 100 seed cases. These seed cases were used to define a format for the collection of future cases and for the design of the database structure. Seed cases typically do not follow a predefined structure, while the subsequent collection of cases will follow the defined format. The number of seed cases may vary according to the application, as we will see in this chapter, and may even be generated artificially by creating permutations of the cases available, as discussed in the case study later in the chapter.
2. **Attribute-Value Extraction** and **Hierarchy Formation**—This step is essential for indexing and organizing the case library. The goal of this phase is to extract the attributes that define the case representation and indexing. This phase will seek to create a list of attributes that define each case, a list of values for each attribute, and a possible grouping of such attributes. In addition, the relationships among the attributes must also be defined. After the hierarchy is defined, the relative importance of each attribute is determined. This decision is typically reflective of the implementation domain. This phase results in a concept hierarchy created for each attribute, assigned with similarities between values. Also, this step will require mapping a hierarchy into a relational database or **flat case library**.
3. **Feedback**—This phase will provide necessary feedback to those supplying the cases to the CBR system, so the quality of the cases can be improved.

The use of the Case Method Cycle has been shown to result in significant reduction in system development workload and costs (Kitano and Shimazu 1996). For example, use of the Case method during the development of SQUAD resulted in a savings of six person-months from the expected development time for the entire system. Furthermore, the workload required for the system maintenance was reduced to less than 10 percent of the initial workload.

Knowledge application systems not only apply a solution to a similar problem but can also serve as a framework for **creative reasoning** (Leake 1996). For example analogy-based reasoning could provide the initial ideas in solving new problems. Case memories can provide humans with the experience base they may lack. Faced with a problem, experts may recall experiences from the case library, and perform the adaptation and evaluation of the solutions that is sometimes relegated to the knowledge application systems. This is the emphasis of the SQUAD system presented in Box 6.1.

Knowledge application systems have enabled the implementation of decision support systems to support design tasks in diverse domains such as architecture, engineering, and lesson planning (Domeshek and Kolodner 1991, 1992, 1993; Griffith and Domeshek 1996). These decision-support systems, also called **case-based design aids** or CBDAs, help human designers by making available a broad range of commentated designs. CBDAs can serve to illustrate critical design issues, explain design guidelines, and provide suggestions or warnings regarding specific design solutions. One of the critical components in the development of such systems is the supporting indexing system used to perform the relevant case search.

Finally, case libraries can serve to accumulate organizational experiences and can often be viewed as a corporate memory. For example, the case library for a help desk system could be considered a corporate memory of organizational experiences related to customer support. The same thing can be said of a rule-base supporting an expert system. For more details on a case-based reasoning systems, refer to Chapter 9 of the book *Knowledge Management: Challenges, Solutions, and Technologies* (Becerra-Fernandez et al. 2004).

TYPES OF KNOWLEDGE APPLICATION SYSTEMS

Recall that knowledge application systems include advisor systems, fault diagnosis or troubleshooting systems, expert systems, help desk systems, and decision-support systems in general.

One area where knowledge application systems are specifically important is in the implementation of **help desk technologies**. For example Compaq Computer Corporation implemented a help desk support technology named SMART (Acorn and Walden 1992), to assist help desk employees track calls and resolve customer service problems. Compaq's SMART system was developed to support its Customer Service Department when handling user calls through its toll-free number. SMART is an integrated call-tracking and problem-solving system, supported by hundreds of cases that help resolve diagnostic problems resulting from the use of Compaq products (Allen 1994). The system automatically retrieves from the case library historical cases similar to the one currently faced by the customer. The customer service representative then uses that solution to help customers solve the problem at hand. SMART developers reported an increase from 50 percent to 87 percent of the problems that could be resolved directly by the first level of customer support. The implementation of SMART at Compaq paid for itself in one year with the productivity improvements it brought to the company.

Fault diagnosis is increasingly becoming a major emphasis for the development of knowledge applications systems, as we will discuss below. Fault diagnosis has been one of the main focuses of intelligent systems implementation (Davis 1984; de Kleer 1976; Genesereth 1984; Patton et al. 2000). One of the earliest successful implementations of knowledge application systems for the diagnosis and recovery of faults in large multistation machine tools was CABER at Lockheed Martin Corporation (Mark et al. 1996). Although these milling machines are equipped with self-diagnostic capabilities, typically they resolved only 20 percent to 40 percent of the systems faults. The expectation for the CABER system is that it must help identify how the equipment experienced the fault and how to safely exit the faulted state. Typically, an equipment fault results in a call to the field-service engineer. For the creation of the case library that supports this system, Lockheed counted on over 10,000 records collected by the field service engineers. CABER augmented the self-diagnostic capabilities of the milling machine, which provided junior field-service engineers with the necessary tools to resolve the fault and reduce machine downtime.

In addition, Compaq also developed a fault diagnosis system early on for its Page-Marq printer line known as QuickSource (Nguyen et al. 1993). A case base of over 500 diagnostic cases supported the QuickSource knowledge applications system. This system, designed to run in a Windows environment, was shipped with printers to enable customers to do their own diagnosis.

Finally, another prominent CBR system is FormTool, the system developed at General Electric (GE) in order to determine the correct formulas to color plastics according to the customers' specifications (Cheetham 2005). What is difficult about the process of determining the colorants and levels to be added to the plastics is that the possible number of colorants is very large, the amounts of each colorant also need to be determined, there's no exact algorithm for predicting the color produced by a set of colorants, a given formula can appear different due to lighting conditions, and different base plastics have different starting colors. FormTools was originally developed in 1994 and continued to be used ten years later, saving GE millions of dollars in productivity and colorant costs. The benefits from this development included improved color matcher productivity, pigment cost reduction, global color consistency, improved color-match speed, and served as the basis of development for other tools, such as a tool to control the color produced by the manufacturing line. Also, the technology developed in this knowledge application system was used to create an online color-selection for GE's customers, and a customer innovation center developed around the system's software. Other successful CBR implementations at GE include automation of an appliance call center via the Support the Customer (STC) tool, which helps call takers solve customers' problems by suggesting questions that could help with the problem diagnosis (Cheetham and Goebel 2007). This implementation improved the accuracy of the diagnostic process and the speed of resolution, ultimately improving customer satisfaction. The STC knowledge application system also has been in use for around ten years, saving the company more than $50M.

In the following five sections, we discuss the development and implementation details for five knowledge application systems. The first system, **GenAID**, is one of the earliest diagnostic knowledge application systems. GenAID is based on the use of rules and is still operational today. Later, we describe the development of SOS Advisor, a Web-based expert system built using a set of rules. The reason heuristics were used for the implementation of this system is that a small number of rules can define the domain—that is, defining the eligibility potential for companies interested in applying for a specific federal program. Following that, we describe the development of a knowledge application system based on CBR technology, which was designed with the goal of reusing the solutions to software quality problems, as these problems recur throughout the organization. The system deployed at Darty, described in the following section is also based on CBR technology and it's in use at call centers to help resolve problems at tier support and minimize the deployment of technicians to the field. CLAIM, the CBR-based system developed at GE Healthcare presented later in this chapter, is improving the process of healthcare services reimbursement. The knowledge application system described is somewhat different in the sense that it's designed to assist in the solution of new problems as they occur, by identifying similar problems that may have happened in the past and their corresponding solutions.

We begin by describing the development of GenAID.

CASE STUDIES

GenAID—A Knowledge Application System for Early Fault Detection at Westinghouse[1]

By the year 1990, there were over 3,000 AI-based systems in use around the world for a variety of purposes including Ace (telephone cable maintenance advisory system), XCON (computer configuration system), Dispatcher (printed-wire, board assembly, work-dispatching system), APES (electronic design), CDS (configuration-dependent part sourcing), National Dispatcher (transportation sourcing and routing), XFL (floor layout assistance), XSEL (sales assistance), Compass (network management), Cooker (food-processing control), ESP (facility analysis), Ocean (computer configuration), Opgen (process planning), Trinity Mills Scheduler (scheduling), VT (elevator configuration), CDS (flexible manufacturing system cell control), GenAID (generator diagnosis), Intellect (natural language database interfacing), Mudman (drilling mud analysis), and Telestream (telemarketing assistance); (Fox 1990).

In the early 1980s, Westinghouse Electric Corporation, a manufacturer of large power generation equipment (now Siemens Power Generation), started the development of Process Diagnosis System (PDS) also known as GenAID (Gonzalez et al. 1986). The goal of GenAID was to enable the early detection of abnormal operating conditions of their turbine generators, which could cause them to eventually malfunction. For Westinghouse's customers, electrical power utilities that operate generation plants, a plant outage could represent costs that range from $60,000 to $250,000 *per day,* depending on the size and the type of the plant. A generator malfunction could cause unplanned outages to repair the broken unit that could last up to six months. Clearly, anticipating a generator outage when it's a minor fault and before it's completely inoperative and becomes a major incident can result in corrective actions that could reduce the magnitude of the problem and thus reduce the downtime from months to perhaps days.

GenAID was one of the first real-time, sensor-based diagnosis systems. Before the development of GenAID, sensor data from the power generation equipment which is transmitted to the data acquisition system would be periodically inspected by a technician who traveled to the site. Typically power plant personnel at the site lacked the expertise to analyze the sensor measurements. The goal behind GenAID was to continuously analyze the generator sensor data; therefore anticipating major destructive incidents.

The early attempts at performing this analysis date from the 1970s, when Westinghouse developed a computer-based system that used probabilistic analysis. The system performed well for a limited number of malfunctions, but posed serious limitations which forced the research attention to shift to intelligent systems. In 1980, a collaboration between Westinghouse's Research and Development Laboratories in Pittsburgh and the Robotics Institute at Carnegie-Mellon University resulted in the development of the Process Diagnostic System (PDS). The combination of PDS and the diagnostic knowledge was called GenAID, which stands for Generator Artificial Intelligence Diagnostics. Originally, GenAID was located in Orlando, Florida, where it processed data on a semicontinuous basis from each of the power plant sites across the United States to produce a diagnosis of potential malfunctions in real time. GenAID would later on be colocated with each power plant generator to produce a malfunction diagnosis for each power plant operator.

GenAID went into production use in 1985, and in 1986 it was recognized as one of the top 100 engineering achievements of the year. By 1990, about 14 generators were connected to the system. Since the time of its development, the PDS shell was modified to run on general-purpose personal computers and its user interface was completely revamped. The system contains in the neighborhood of 2,500 rules. GenAID has successfully diagnosed numerous malfunctions that otherwise could have resulted in serious outages. As a result, Siemens extended this concept to other pieces of equipment, including steam turbines and gas turbines. GenAID is a prototypical knowledge application system. Its development required the elicitation of important knowledge possessed by human experts, capturing this knowledge electronically in a knowledge base, and the ability to apply this knowledge in a way that multiplied manifold the original utility of that knowledge by placing it in an automatic monitoring and diagnostic system.

To this date, the GenAID system is still sold as a site-based monitor for power plants. In the late 1990s, Siemens began a research and development project to expand the system to cover other power generation equipment. The new expanded product is similar in features but is run remotely in the Siemens Power Diagnostics Center, which monitors nearly 300 power plants worldwide. The new version covers not only the generator but the gas turbine, steam turbine, and balance of plant equipment as well and has saved Siemens' customers millions of dollars in the last decade.[2]

Next we describe the development of SOS Advisor, a simple system based on a small set of heuristics.

The SBIR/STTR Online System (SOS) Advisor: A Web-based Expert System to Profile Organizations

The **SBIR/STTR Online System (SOS) Advisor**, a Web-based expert system, was developed to assist potential applicants to the Small Business Innovation Research (SBIR) and Small Business Technology Transfer Research (STTR) programs. Established by Congress in 1982, the SBIR and STTR programs help federal agencies develop innovative technologies by providing competitive research contracts to U.S.-owned small business companies with fewer than 500 employees. These programs also help by providing seed capital to increase private sector commercialization of innovations resulting from federal research and development (see, for example, NASA 2008 and USDOD 2009). The goal of the SOS Advisor was to optimize the time required to examine the potential eligibility for companies seeking SBIR/STTR funding by prompting users through an interactive questionnaire that was used to evaluate the company's potential eligibility to be a grant recipient. The user only needed to click on *Yes* or *No* to answer the 10 questions that frame the eligibility criteria.

Once the user submitted the registration information to the Web-based system, the SOS Advisor Questionnaire page was launched. The questionnaire consists of 10 questions used to determine the eligibility of the company. The profile questions are listed in Table 6.2, to which users could respond by selecting the radio button next to the *Yes, No,* or *Not Sure*. Answering Not Sure will prompt users for more information, necessary in order to define the potential candidate's eligibility for funding. In order to match the SBIR winners' profile, users were expected to answer according to the responses specified in Table 6.2. Question 6 was for information purposes only, since it does not constitute a necessary criterion for eligibility. Each question had a *Tip* icon that allowed the user to obtain additional information related to the corresponding question through the use of a pop-up window. In this manner, users could learn about SBIR/STTR requirements and the reasoning for each question. The one-page questionnaire format allowed users to spend minimum time when answering the profile questions. Furthermore, the user had the opportunity to see at once all the questions and answers in order to review and modify the answers before submission. The *suggestions* field provided users with the option of providing feedback to the development team. Figure 6.1 describes the architecture of the SOS Advisor.

The user information provided and the corresponding answers to the questionnaire were stored in the SOS Advisor database and evaluated automatically by the system. Using a set of rules that evaluate the user responses, the system identified if the user profile matched the profile of an SBIR/STTR candidate. SOS Advisor then would automatically send an e-mail to the user with the results of the evaluation. At the same time, if the user profiles match was positive the system automatically notified via e-mail the corresponding agency program personnel, with the user point-of-contact.

Table 6.2

SBIR/STTR Profile Framing Questions

Question	SBIR winners' profile
1. I would like to know if your company is independently owned and operated.	Yes
2. Is this company located in the United States?	Yes
3. Is this company owned by at least 51% U.S. citizens or permanent U.S. residents?	Yes
4. Regarding your company size, does it have less than 500 employees?	Yes
5. What about your proposed innovation? Has it been patented or does it have any patents pending?	No
6. Could it be patented, copyrighted, or otherwise protected?	Don't care

7. Are you planning on using SBIR/STTR funding to conduct any of the following:
  a. Systems studies
  b. Market research
  c. Commercial development of existing products or proven concepts
  d. Studies
  e. Laboratory evaluations
  f. Modifications of existing products without innovative changes
	No

8. Does your technology area align with any of the following research areas of interest to NASA?	Yes
9. Is there a likelihood of your proposed technology having a commercial application?	Yes
10. Has your firm been paid or is currently being paid for equivalent work by any agency of the federal government?	No

The rules used to evaluate the user profiles were developed using a scripting code. The scripts were used to evaluate the answers given and based on predefined rules to generate the user profiles. Based on the user's answers to the questionnaire, the SOS Advisor was able to determine whether the user profile indeed matched that of an SBIR/STTR recipient and provided sufficient information to educate potential applicants about related funding opportunities.

In summary, the SOS Advisor is an example of a knowledge application system that was used to identify those companies whose profiles matched that of an SBIR/STTR candidate and, therefore, helped focus the resources of federally funded assistance programs. The system prompts users to answer a set of questions that describe if the company meets the stipulated criteria defined for companies interested in the SBIR/STTR program. The system then used a set of **heuristics** or rules to quickly examine each company's qualifications rather than attempting to transfer the knowledge about the program requirements to each of the companies interested in applying for the program (although that option is available through launching the *Tip* section). For those companies with matching profiles, the SOS Advisor automatically sent the company's contact information to a federal agency employee who then identified appropriate assistance resources available for the benefit of the inquiring company. In this way, the SOS Advisor helped minimize distractions to the federal program representative caused by casual cyber surfers, since it would only forward the information for the companies that matched the qualification criteria. In addition, a byproduct of this effort was the creation of a database with point-of-contact information for each

Figure 6.1 **SOS Advisor Architecture**

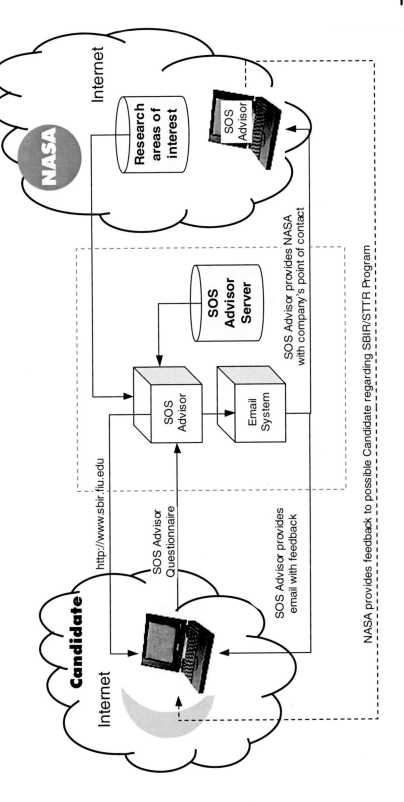

company that completed the survey, which could be used to generate mailings and announcements of upcoming SBIR/STTR informative events.

The key importance of SOS Advisor is that it enabled federal agency personnel to apply the knowledge about qualification requirements for the SBIR/STTTR program without tying up the time of the program representative. Prior to the development of the SOS Advisor, a federal employee provided this information and performed the initial assessment of companies interested in the program. The federal agency representative repeatedly used her tacit knowledge base to perform the analysis. The SOS Advisor helped to apply this knowledge, freeing up the employee to use her time so she can provide more personalized advice to those companies that meet the program's stipulated criteria.

Now we will discuss how knowledge technologies can be used to reuse organizational knowledge about software quality.

Product Quality Analysis for National Semiconductor

National Semiconductor[3] was established in 1959 in Santa Clara, California. Since that time, with manufacturing sites around the world, the company has been a leader in the semiconductor industry. National Semiconductor had annual sales of $1.5 billion in fiscal 2002 and approximately 10,100 employees worldwide. National Semiconductor has set the pace for revolutionary electronics technologies. With 2,170 patents and over 10,000 products, this company's achievements range from the design and manufacture of early discrete transistors to the introduction of sophisticated integrated circuit product lines.

National Semiconductor's product quality record represents about a 22-parts per million defect rate. Although this is an extraordinary quality record, today's environment requires semiconductor component deliveries with zero defects, enabling manufacturers to achieve lower costs and **just-in-time manufacturing** schemes. Therefore, a rare failure is a cause of immediate concern for both National and the customer, as it is imperative to quickly determine and take corrective action; in particular, if the failure indicates that a manufacturing process is moving out of statistical control. National's customers demand rapid and complete failure analysis, as well as the adoption of corrective actions that will ensure the accurate identification and solution for the root cause of the failure. The advanced technology and high degree of complexity in today's semiconductors make this analysis a major challenge. For this purpose, National depends on its Worldwide Quality Network, a centralized manufacturing quality assurance (QA) group. This group consists of engineers who use the **Product Quality Analysis** (PQA) process to focus on root cause determination and finding solutions to each of these failures.

In order to support the engineers involved in the PQA and other quality-related business processes, an in-house team at National developed the Advanced Quality and Reliability Information System (AQUARIS) in 1995, a tracking system that provided a searchable repository of PQAs. Some of the limitations of AQUARIS related to its inefficient ability to query similar past failures. The workflow associated with the PQA process is quite elaborate and can involve many analysis steps to determine the true causes of a device's failure or, in some cases, just a cursory analysis revealing that there is no problem with the part at all. In any event, these steps taken to analyze parts are carefully and methodically accomplished and the interim and final results are captured and stored in the AQUARIS system. Many times, engineers engaged in the various stages of analysis make "hunch" decisions based on prior experiences or anecdotal information, which can significantly shorten the analysis cycle.

By 1999, it was recognized that AQUARIS did not provide an effective means of recalling information that could prevent unnecessary work from being performed, while at the same time promoting learning from prior failures. Engineers would typically spend hours attempting to search on AQUARIS for similar past PQAs that they distantly remembered, based on some similarity to their current analysis. Typically since their search centered on retrieving recalled PQAs, it only focused on those with which they were previously involved and didn't include the work of others. Soon National recognized the need to better collect these experiences in a way that could be adequately applied by others, because written reports collected in AQUARIS did not provide an efficient means to extract and apply this knowledge when needed.

To respond to this challenge, National developed a knowledge application system based on the use of CBR technology. The development team adapted and expanded the back-end relational database that had driven AQUARIS to provide integration with the CBR system. The overall application, titled **Total Recall**, can be viewed as consisting of four components and the Web client.

Figure 6.2 illustrates the Total Recall System Architecture. Users typically enter PQAs into the Application Server, and the users' workflow is illustrated with the dark arrows labeled as *User operation* in the figure. The Total Recall Database is used to collect the results from the testing performed in the different PQA activities. Data from the Total Recall Database are used to create the CBR case library. Note that not all PQAs produce new cases for the case library. A **nomination process** to the case library administrator is used to denote *potential* cases for the case library, illustrated by the arrows labeled as *Admin. only* in the figure.

The case library stores the experience gained from the PQA process as a collection of cases. During an active analysis, the Total Recall system relays queries to the CBR server by gathering information entered up to that point. The CBR server will respond to the query with an ordered set of cases sorted by declining similarity. The footprint number identifies the cases in the CBR server, and the Total Recall application performs an additional search to translate these footprint numbers into the original PQA and device serial numbers that are more meaningful to the user. This information then allows the engineers to retrieve, online, the corresponding PQA reports. Engineers can then study the reports identified as similar to the case at hand and decide if the failure mechanism and corrective actions described for these earlier failures apply to their current situation. The engineer makes the final decision to adopt or adapt these findings.

Each basic component of Total Recall is described as follows:

1. *Application Server:* The main server for the Total Recall application. This server performs data manipulation and user presentation. This component is the result of the system development process, described on page 97.

Figure 6.2 **Total Recall System Architecture**

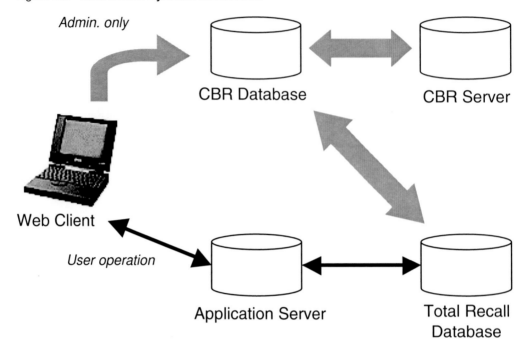

2. *Total Recall Database:* Maintains all the information related to the testing results of the PQA process.
3. *Case Library:* A separate database containing CBR representation of cases, including mapping information that relates the case footprint numbers to specific devices analyzed during PQA processing. This component is the result of the case library development process, which is described later.
4. *CBR Server:* The final case library and CBR engine.

When a CBR query is made, it is made from the Application Server to the CBR engine. The CBR engine responds with a set of **footprint numbers** that represent the set of cases that are similar to the case in the query. Other devices on other PQAs may have failed in a similar way. Rather than treat these as separate cases, they are considered reference cases. The same *footprint number* is also used to identify these reference cases.

As mentioned before, when the engineer completes a new PQA analysis, she decides if she will nominate the PQA for possible inclusion in the case base. The Total Recall System at this point attempts to take advantage of her current knowledge of the failure by allowing a thorough refinement of the case description. At this point the case-base administrator performs the final evaluation of the nominated case by searching the case library to identify if similar cases already exist in the library. In general, it's preferred not to have numerous similar cases in the case library in order to provide users with manageable search results. If multiple cases reflecting the same

Figure 6.3 **CBR Database Detail**

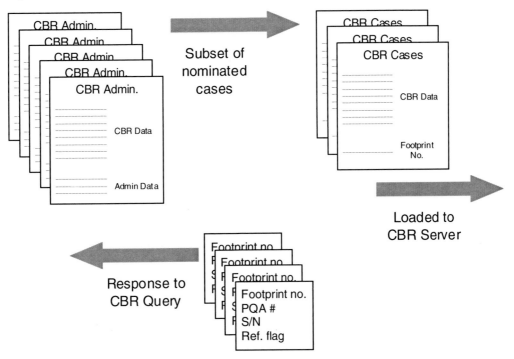

Source: Courtesy of National Semiconductor.

type of failure and analysis are to be included in the case library, one is designated as the footprint case while the others are designated as **reference cases**. Figure 6.3 presents the details of how the CBR database is populated. The case library administrator can make the decision to treat newly nominated cases as a new footprint or as a reference case to an existing case. Also, this decision may be left to an engineering technical review board.

One of the most time-consuming tasks required for the implementation of Total Recall was the initial population of the case library. A subset of PQAs from AQUARIS was evaluated, and the corresponding test data had to be cleansed and augmented prior to manually representing them as cases in the new system. This task also presented significant cultural challenges, since it required the involvement of failure analysis engineers to review each potential case at a technical level. This task represented significant additional work requirement from this group, so only limited success could be claimed. In addition, lack of adequate CBR training and commitment from the users could also be attributed to the low level of support from this group. The initial case library represented approximately 200 cases, which was barely enough to perform the initial testing. The size of the case library was expected to grow substantially during the implementation of Total Recall. This was not expected to impact the application adversely, given the system's structured architecture.

In terms of its user interface, Total Recall mimics much of the AQUARIS workflow, with Web-based functionality and options required to capture new information such as activities and the explicit, related observations. Testing included the analysis of prior solved cases through Total Recall. Engineers familiar with these cases then correlated these results with prior results. The testing process confirmed that the results of using Total Recall were consistent with the prior cases' solution.

Although the team at National is still faced with the evaluation of the usefulness of Total Recall, the benefits it offers are already prompting other developments at the company. For example, other organizational subunits are considering the use of CBR to support the company's external Web site in helping customers select devices that most closely meet their circuit needs. Systems like Total Recall are not intended to eliminate the analysis engineer. The Total Recall system acts as a cognitive prosthesis for the engineer, who is able to make a faster and perhaps more accurate prognosis of the failure case on hand.

The key importance of Total Recall is that it enables the application of knowledge gained from completed failure analyses performed throughout the worldwide quality organization. Prior to the development of Total Recall, only some of this information was kept in the AQUARIS database. The AQUARIS database wasn't a useful platform for knowledge application, since it was hard to identify and apply prior relevant knowledge. The Total Recall system helps to apply knowledge resulting from the software-enabled quality process. This knowledge can be applied to prevent unnecessary work from being performed while promoting learning from prior failures. For more details on the Total Recall system, refer to Watson (2003).

In the next section, we describe the implementation of a CBR-based call center application at Darty, the European retailer of electronic products.

DARTY IMPROVES CUSTOMER SATISFACTION THROUGH EFFECTIVE CALL CENTER PROBLEM RESOLUTION

Darty, a consumer electronic retailer, was established in 1957 and since then has become one of the largest retailers in Europe, with operations originally in France, but now extending to Turkey, Italy, and Switzerland. Darty currently has revenues of over $2.9 billion, over 200 stores, 11,000 employees, a fleet of over 400 trucks, and 1,000 field technicians.[4] Darty counts on seven call centers that handle over 4 million calls a year concerning 1.3 million home repairs. The company was facing increasing productivity losses as first-level agents lacked the required technical background to resolve the majority of the call center calls, 95 percent of which resulted in calls that escalated to the next level of more experienced and expensive technicians. In order to improve the efficiency of the level 1 call center technicians, the retailer implemented a knowledge application system to support **call center operations**. The system was developed over a three-month period and initially covered approximately 1,500 cases, or problem-resolution pairs. Three months into the implementation of the knowledge application solution, the number of calls that required escalation to level 2 went down to 20 percent, and more products were being fixed remotely without the need to dispatch a technician to the trouble site.

The user interface for the knowledge application system implemented at Darty

Figure 6.4 **Technology Architecture for the Darty Knowledge Application System**

Technologies

Functions				
Interact (UI)	Free Text Search	Guided Search	Expert Search	Browse Search
Interpret	Domain Model (Ontology)			
Retrieve & Refine	Retrieval Engine— Case-based Reasoning (CBR)		Questioning Engine— Dynamic Induction (DI)	
Manage	Structured Knowledge Base (Solutions)			

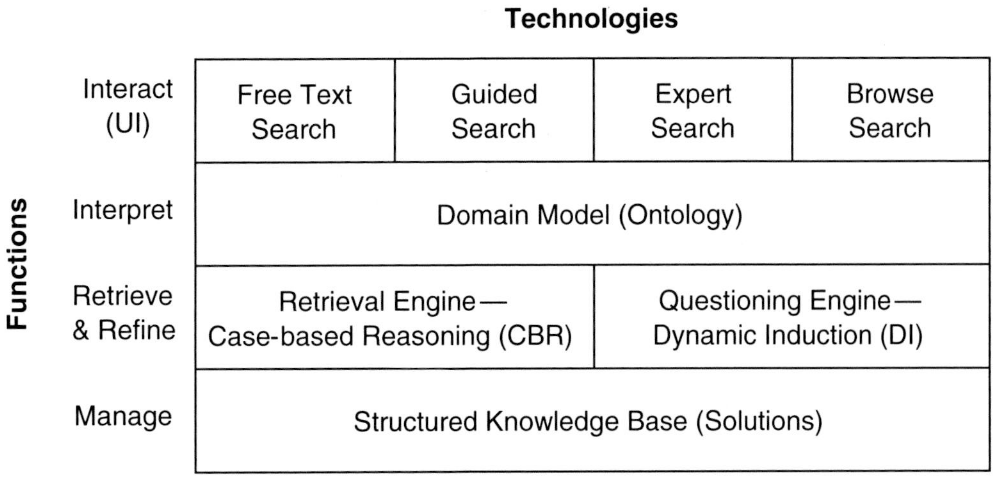

allowed users to access the system via a combination of search methods as depicted in Figure 6.4. Users can query the system by entering any of the following:

1. Free text search—such as "washing machine has a leak during the rinse cycle."
2. Guided search—when the system poses a set of questions for the user in order to further refine the search such as "are there any error lights on the panel?"
3. Expert search—where all possible questions are presented to the user, who in this case is likely to be a more experienced technician.
4. Browse—enables users to review all the problem/solutions pairs for a particular product or model.

The Domain Model layer enables to interpret and translate the user's request into the common vocabulary of the knowledge base. The Retrieve layer is built on a CBR engine, but in addition the question engine helps refine the resulting set of solutions if too many are presented to the user at this level. Finally the Manage layer enables to build reports as well as support the administrative modules. Figure 6.5 describes in details the search operations of the Darty knowledge application system.

Today, Darty's call centers receive an average of 10,000 calls per day and provide assistance to about 120 concurrent users. Customer satisfaction data show that 95 percent of the callers are satisfied with the support they receive. The system also includes a sensory search engine that allows users to include complex data that may be hard to explain. For example, Figure 6.6 presents the user interface for the Darty knowledge application system, including the sensory search engine that in this case is used to explain the problem that the user entered as "laundry white marks" in the wash, which the system allows the user to select the picture that best depicts the discolored material.

Figure 6.5   **Darty Knowledge Application System Search Example**

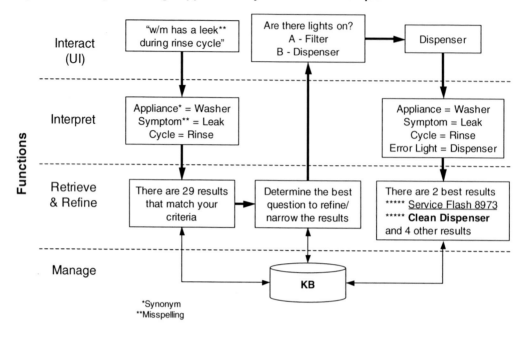

Figure 6.6   **Darty Knowledge Application System User Interface**

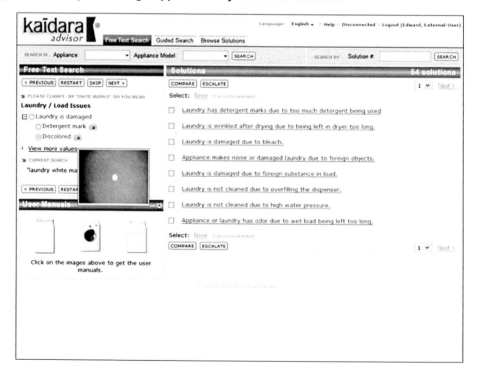

Next steps for the Darty knowledge application system include the provision of incentives to level 2 agents to promote the authoring of new cases that will continue to enrich the case database and thus facilitate the system's continued learning.

We have seen how knowledge application systems can help resolve recurring problems at Darty. The next section describes in detail an innovative application of CBR: to improve the process of claim reimbursement in healthcare.

AUTOMATING IDENTIFICATION OF ATTACHMENTS FOR HEALTHCARE CLAIMS

In 2006, healthcare costs in the United States were $2.2 trillion.[5] Thirty percent of these costs ($660 billion) were spent processing claims for reimbursement of healthcare services. Efficient processing of these claims could greatly reduce the overall cost of healthcare. General Electric provides automation tools and outsourcing services for processing claims. This case study describes a project aimed at making those tools and services more efficient.

There is a shift under way in the healthcare industry: a focus on quality and results. As such, health insurance providers (or "payers") want more information to determine the appropriateness of care as well as documentation on outcomes, setting up a new shift in paying for performance versus paying by procedure. This results in providers being required to send more and more clinical documentation to payers as part of the claim process. A claim that is not sent with the documentation deemed necessary by a payer is typically denied. This stretches out the reimbursement process, as the healthcare provider needs to then locate the right information to be included and then has to resubmit the claim over again. This added delay can cost the healthcare provider in lost payments and interest. Unfortunately, it is hard to know at claim submission time what additional documentation the payer requires. There are over 500 payers in the United States. Each payer has different requirements for what clinical documentation needs to be submitted with a claim. There are 30,000 documented medical procedures and 20,000 unique diagnoses, all of which can be associated with documentation needs by a payer. The attachments requested by one payer may not be the same documentation that was requested by another. This makes for an astronomical amount of knowledge that both healthcare and related software providers need to be aware of when submitting claims.

To make matters more complex, the relevant knowledge constantly changes. Payers' requirements for additional documentation are not static but are continually evolving as new procedures become widespread or experimental procedures become accepted. Many payers do not publish their policies on attachment requirements, leaving healthcare providers to determine the corresponding rules by trial and error. For those payers that do publish their policies, the material may be in nonstandard formats. Even within a single payer's documentation it may be hard to locate the required information, resulting in a significant manual effort for the provider to unveil the relevant knowledge for each payer.

The goal for the **Clinical Artificial Intelligence Manager** (**CLAIM**) project was to automate the identification of attachments for healthcare claims by creating tools that can maintain and use the knowledge of the payers "needs for attachments." Then that knowledge can be used to determine if additional documentation is required for a specific claim prior to submission to a payer. GE Healthcare is already in the business of facilitating the submission of medical claims and has a database with over 300 million past claims and remittances (responses from the payer as to whether or not the claim is rejected, approved, or partially approved). Selected data from this database were used as a case base for a case-based reasoning (CBR) system. For this research, in order to preserve patient confidentiality, the data used were scrubbed to remove any information that could identify any specific person. In the CBR system a new claim is compared to similar past claims to determine if an attachment was needed. The claim is similar to a past claim if it is for the same payer, procedure, diagnosis, and procedure modifiers. Additional factors can make the claim more or less similar. The set of similar claims is then analyzed to determine if an attachment is needed. Because of variability within payers, policy changes, and other factors, these similar past claims will often not all have required the same attachment. When discrepancies arise between similar claims in CLAIM, the system uses a confidence algorithm to determine which attachments are needed. The algorithm takes information such as the *date of the claim, degree of similarity* match, and *claim quality* in performing this calculation. After the new claim is paid or rejected it is added to the database for use on future claims.

Since there's a great deal of similarity in claims that are submitted, it is necessary to create a single prototypical case that represents the entire set of similar cases, called a *protocol.* Payers could have their own set of protocols. An automated learning algorithm was created to look through historical claims and remittance data on a periodic basis, searching for cases where a claim was denied and the denial reason was that it required "additional documentation not submitted." From this set of cases, the learning algorithm clusters like claims/remittances based on common characteristics. Then the number of remittances denied for "needing attachment" are grouped and tallied for each unique value found for that field. For each of the field values, count of denials for "needing attachment" can then be compared against all other claims/remittances with that same field value that were not denied. If the number of denials versus acceptances is significant, then the value can be used to define a protocol. CLAIM identifies if a protocol with similar criteria already exists, and if not it creates a new protocol for that field/value. The field and value are captured as a "condition" of the protocol.

The learning algorithm is as automated as possible. However, there still exists the benefit of having a person in the loop to review and approve a newly discovered protocol before making it available for use when processing claims. This review and approval process has been implemented as part of a prototype **graphical user interface (GUI)** tool that allows users to manually approve, create, and maintain protocols. Once protocols are approved they are stored in a repository where they can be accessed by algorithms for processing claims and predicting additional documentation needs. A high-level picture of this toolset is shown in Figure 6.7.

The graphical user interface can also be used to create protocols that are based on documented or tacit knowledge. A person, acting as the protocol manager can browse or search for protocols, select a protocol, and view the details of a protocol. They can also modify existing protocols to add new conditions, references to additional

Figure 6.7 **Process Flow for the CLAIM Knowledge Application System**

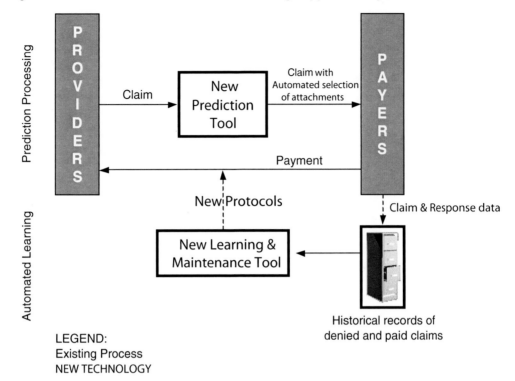

LEGEND:
Existing Process
NEW TECHNOLOGY

information and so forth, or delete protocols that no longer are necessary. In this way the repository is always kept up to date.

GE Healthcare processes over 10 million claims per month. Pilot studies of the CLAIM system using a subset of these new claims has shown the accuracy in selecting the correct attachments for an initial claim to be over 90 percent. This is better than currently exists because many providers just send claims without the proper attachments knowing that when the claim is rejected by the payer, information will be provided on the documentation that was needed.

Next, we see how knowledge application systems can assist the problem-solving process, even when these are new problems.

OUT-OF-FAMILY DISPOSITION SYSTEM FOR SHUTTLE PROCESSING

The Shuttle Processing Directorate of the Kennedy Space Center provides preflight, launch, landing, and recovery services for KSC. Within the directorate, the Shuttle Vehicle Engineering department is responsible for the engineering management and technical direction of preflight, launch, landing, and recovery activities for all Space Shuttle vehicles and integration of payloads. An important function of this group is to perform the **out-of-family disposition (OFD)** process, which deals with any operation or performance outside the expected range or which has not been previously experienced. These anomalies are described as out-of-family in the sense that they are new anomalies and differentiated from in-family anomalies that have previously occurred. In the OFD process, new problems (which we'll reference as cases) are referenced, solved, and documented. Just like in problem-solving, drawing analogies to similar prior cases helps to solve new problems. Therefore, this process lends itself to the adoption of knowledge application technologies and to documenting these anomalies in a way that makes the solutions to these problems available to the rest of the organization. As more unfamiliar cases get documented within the knowledge application system, the case database grows and becomes more comprehensive.

In order to build the OFD prototype, a sample set of twelve OFD **Problem Reports (PR)** were collected, each describing an anomaly identified during the processing of the Space Shuttle, together with the anomaly resolution. The OFD PRs comprise a cover page with 36 entries that describe details for the OFD anomaly. Part of the report also details the description and requirement of the troubleshooting plan, damaged parts' specifications, and alternative replacement parts. PRs are typically from 10 to 70 pages in length and do not follow a prescribed format. The final pages of the report include the most reasonable rationale, which details the most likely reason for the failure, as well as the most reasonable repair plan and justification. Also, the PR includes engineering orders for replacement parts as well as related part specifications. Finally, the OFD PR includes a problem summary and conclusion. Each of the twelve OFD PRs were used to build a case in the case library.

The twelve OFD PRs were very different from one another. The steps in the creation of the case library were:

1. Identify and establish a set of categories or clusters to stratify them through analysis of their similarities and differences. In our example, we found the PRs grouped into four categories. This resulted in a 4th order **distribution tree** (see Figure 6.8). The most appropriate problem categories identified were Computer, Electrical, Mechanical, and Materials. Given that this was only a prototype based on a total of only 12 PRs, there was only an average of two to three cases corresponding to each problem category.

2. Analyze each PR to identify a case title, a description, a set of characterizing questions and answers, and a resulting action. Building the case library required combining information from the sections of the PR, since the reporting format of the PR is different from the way cases are stored in the case library. For example, for each case in the library, the description of the action taken was deduced from a combination of the PR sections describing the most reasonable rationale, summary, and conclusion.

3. Develop a set of descriptive questions for each case, which need to be in natural-language format. Some CBR software packages require that the set of descriptive questions for each case must be normalized to ensure that the similarity function will work properly. The objective of the similarity function is to identify from the case database those cases that are similar to the case under analysis by the **enduser**. Consider for example the Electrical category in Figure 6.8. Normalization means that cases 4, 7, and 11 should be described by a similar number of <question, answer> pairs. However, cases that are considerably different from other cases (like those catalogued in different clusters) can be defined with fewer questions because retrieval conflicts are less likely to occur.

Figure 6.8 **Distribution Order Tree for the OFD Problem Reports**

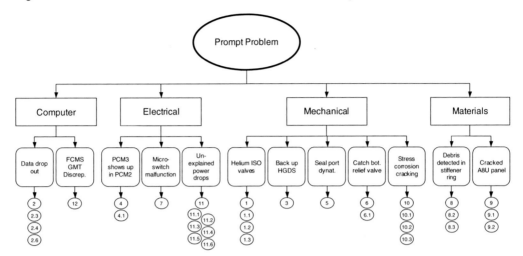

4. Just as an expert draws upon her wide experience in order to infer solutions to new problems, case-based systems work best when the case library is large enough to be representative of the total set of possible anomalies. As such, in order to develop a working prototype, the application developers were compelled to add permutations of the OFD Problem Reports to the case library, so that the additional cases improved the system's ability of finding a relevant solution. With a total of 12 cases, permutations of these original reports were developed to allow the library to represent a larger subset of possible anomalies. These permutations were created through the definition of variations for each <question, answer> pair that didn't correspond to the PR in question. Referring back to Figure 6.4, each PR corresponds to case numbers 1 through 12. In this example, the case corresponding to the **Data Drop Out** PR appears as case 2, and the permutations corresponding to this case appear as 2.3, 2.4, and 2.6. The diagnosing solution for case 2 is found after answering *yes* or *no* to the set questions that accurately describe the Data Drop Out problem. The permutations for case 2 correspond to a differing answer to the questions that essentially describe the case. This process of adding permuted cases resulted in a total set of 34 cases in the case library.

5. Following the development of the case library, the case library must be validated to ensure the proper execution of the application. The validation process requires that none of the following conditions exist in the case library, which essentially diminishes the accuracy of the application:

    a. **Disjunctions** (i.e., otherwise identical cases with separate solutions): Disjunctive cases must be combined into a single case.
    b. **Internal disjunctions:** These are characterized by situations in which a single case in a cluster contains multiple questions that are not answered in any other case in the same cluster. To resolve internal disjunctions, combine these questions into a single question with multiple answers, which allows

Figure 6.9 **Search Results**

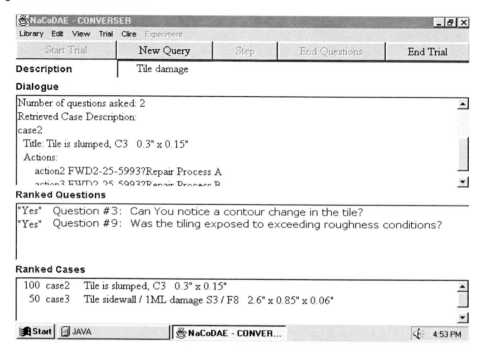

the system to match a conversation's query containing either answer and also reduces the number of questions in the cases.

c. **Subsumed cases:** These are characterized by one case being a logical specialization of another and having the same solution. In these circumstances, eliminate the more specific case.

d. **Validation:** some case-authoring tools provides the ability to validate the case library through an automated testing functionality. This functionality allows for verification if the retrieval precision for the case library is acceptable.

The user inputs the topic of trouble in the description box. After this is done, the software will output all relevant cases in a ranked order inside the Ranked Cases box. Cases are given a rank score according to their relevance to the description topic. The application also outputs all relevant questions that are to be answered by the user in order to further constrain the search to the most relevant topic. These questions are also ranked according to their relevance to the topic. Once the user has answered the questions, a single most relevant case is identified. Figure 6.9 presents the screen with the dialogue box which shows the output of the search, the title, and description of the most relevant case (the highest ranking case) and the steps and actions needed to solve the case. More information about this case study can be found in Becerra-Fernandez and Aha (1998).

The key importance of the OFD system is that it enables one to apply the knowledge gained through solving prior problems when solving new anomalies experienced during the Shuttle Processing process. The OFD system helps to apply knowledge to prevent unnecessary work from being performed, while promoting learning from prior failures.

Prior to the development of the OFD system, this information remained in the tacit knowledge base of the engineer in charge of the process. Since NASA enjoys the advantage of having a relatively stable workforce, engineers use their own knowledge base to identify similar cases that they have solved in the past. But as downsizing continues to be part of the federal landscape, systems like the OFD will be essential as a platform for knowledge application in order to identify and apply prior relevant knowledge.

In the next section, we discuss how rule-based systems can be instrumental to the design of troubleshooting systems that have stood the test of time.

LIMITATIONS OF KNOWLEDGE APPLICATION SYSTEMS

There are some practical limitations to the development of knowledge application systems. These relate to the fact that most of these systems are developed to serve a task-specific domain problem and are typically not integrated with the organization's enterprise systems. Other limitations also exist—for example, for knowledge application systems based on CBR technologies, the following limitations apply (Kitano and Shimazu 1996):

1. *Security:* Cases may include sensitive information. Knowledge application systems must consider the incorporation of security measures, including access control according to the user's organizational role. If knowledge application systems do not incorporate security measures, systems may not realize their maximum value.

2. *Scalability:* Knowledge application systems must represent a large enough number of cases so that the majority of the new experiences are represented in the case-based system. This means the knowledge application system must reach saturation prior to its deployment. Reaching system saturation means that most typical cases would have already been reported in the system. The number of cases necessary to reach the saturation point changes according to the domain. For SQUAD, discussed earlier, reaching this point required the inclusion of about 3,000 cases each year, a number that later was reduced to 1,000 per year. The more complex the domain, the higher the importance of keeping the growth of the case base viable. Clearly, the continual growth of the case library will also require the use of complex indexing schemes, which may result in decreased system stability.

3. *Speed:* As the size of the case library grows to a more comprehensive representation of real environments, computing and searching costs will also increase. Therefore, developers of knowledge application systems must consider the use of complex indexing schemes that will guarantee acceptable case-retrieval times and performance levels.

In addition, knowledge application systems may not be able to solve all the problems that they encounter. In particular, diagnosing problems may be increasingly difficult in complex environments, as evidenced by the Space Shuttle Columbia tragedy. Diagnosing everything that went wrong or may go wrong in such environments may not be possible with systems like the ones already described. New technologies will need to be developed in order to prevent incidents in complex engineering environments.

Some rule-based systems could suffer from other limitations, namely the lack of scalability. Other technologies offer a different set of limitations. But in essence, the benefits that the implementation of knowledge application systems brings to the organization outweigh their limitations, and they will continue to provide competitive advantages to those organizations that continue to implement them.

SUMMARY

In this chapter we discussed what knowledge application systems are, along with design considerations and specific types of intelligent technologies that enable such systems. The Case-Method Cycle, a methodology to effectively develop knowledge application systems is presented. Also the chapter discusses different types of knowledge application systems: expert systems, help desk systems, and fault diagnosis systems. Six case studies that describe the implementation of knowledge application systems are presented, each based on different intelligent technologies and designed to accomplish different goals: provide advice, recognize fault detection, and spur creative reasoning. The first system uses rules to troubleshoot electrical generators in real time. The second system is based on rules to advise potential applicants to the SBIR/STTR program if they meet the program's criteria. The third system, based on CBR technology, helps engineers diagnose faulty chips. The fourth system, also based on CBR technology, helps improve customer service at Darty. The fifth system, also CBR-based, is improving the reimbursement of claims for healthcare services. Finally, the sixth system helps NASA engineers find solutions to new problems faced while processing the Shuttle, assuming that new problems could be related or be a combination of old problems. Finally, limitations of knowledge application systems are discussed.

KEY TERMS

Artificial intelligence (AI)
Analogy-based reasoning
Attribute-value extraction
Call center operations
Case-based design aids (CBDA)
Case-based reasoning (CBR)
Case library
Case-Method cycle
CLAIM
Constraint-based reasoning
Creative reasoning
Data drop out
Diagrammatic reasoning
Direction
Disjunctions
Distribution order tree
Domain knowledge
Enduser
Exemplar-based reasoning

Fault diagnosis
Footprint number
Hierarchy formation
Instance-based reasoning
Internal disjunctions
Knowledge application systems
Mapping problem
Model-based reasoning (MBR)
Nomination process
Out-of-family disposition (OFD) process
Problem reports (PR)
Product quality analysis (PQA)
Reference cases
Routines
Rule-based systems
SBIR/STTR Online System (SOS) Advisor
Subsumed cases
Total Recall System

REVIEW

1. What are some of the intelligent technologies that provide the foundation for the creation of knowledge application systems?
2. Describe in your own words when you should use rules as opposed to CBR when developing a knowledge application system.
3. Describe the four steps in the CBR process.
4. Describe the steps and the importance of the Case-Method Cycle.
5. Explain the case library development process.
6. What are some of the limitations of knowledge application systems?

APPLICATION EXERCISES

1. Identify examples of knowledge application systems in use in your organization. What are some of the intelligent technologies that enable those systems?
2. Describe five knowledge application scenarios that could be supported via CBR systems and explain why. For example, one such scenario is a system that will identify the most likely resolution of a court case based on the outcome of prior legal cases.
3. Design a knowledge application system to support your business needs. Describe the type of system and the foundation technologies that you would use to develop such a system.
4. Design the system architecture for the system described in question 2 above.
5. Identify three recent examples in the literature of knowledge application systems.

NOTES

1. We acknowledge Avelino Gonzalez of the University of Central Florida for this case study.
2. We acknowledge Monica Wood, Sheila Oliva, and Carolyn Joiner all of Siemens for contributing the current status of the GenAID system.
3. We acknowledge National Semiconductor, in particular Art Hamilton, Mike Glynn, Mike Meltzer, and Amir Razavi, for their support in creating this section.
4. We acknowledge Glenn Gardner and Greg Leary of Kaidara Software, Inc. (www.kaidara.com) for contributing this material.
5. We acknowledge William Cheetham, Bernhard Scholz, and Deborah Belcher of General Electric Research for this Box.

REFERENCES

Aamodt, A. and Plaza, E. 1994. Case-based reasoning: Foundational issues, methodological variations, and system approaches. *AI Communications,* 7(1), 39–52.

Acorn, T. and Walden, S. 1992. SMART: Support management automated reasoning technology for Compaq customer service. In *Proceedings of the 4th Innovative Applications of Artificial Intelligence Conference*, San Jose, California, July 12–16, 1992.

Aha, D., Kibbler, D. , and Albert, M. 1991. Instance-based learning algorithms. *Machine Learning,* 6 (1).

Allen, B. 1994. Case-based reasoning: Business applications. *Communications of the ACM,* 37(3), 40–42.

Becerra-Fernandez, I. and Aha, D. 1998. Case-based problem solving for knowledge management systems. In *Proceedings of the 12th Annual International Florida Artificial Intelligence Research Symposium* (FLAIRS): Knowledge Management Track, Orlando, Florida, May 1999.

Becerra-Fernandez, I., Gonzalez, A., and Sabherwal, R. 2004. *Knowledge management: Challenges, solutions, and technologies.* Upper Saddle River, NJ: Prentice Hall.

Chandrasekaran, B., Narayanan, H., and Iwasaki, Y. 1993. Reasoning with diagrammatic representations. *Artificial Intelligence Magazine,* 14(2), 49–56.

Cheetham, W. 2005. Tenth anniversary of plastics color matching. *Artificial Intelligence Magazine,* 26(3), 51–61.

Cheetham, W. and Goebel, K. 2007. Appliance call center: A successful mixed-initiative case study. *Artificial Intelligence Magazine,* 28(2), 89–100.

Cheetham, W. and Watson, I. 2005. Fielded applications of case-based reasoning. *The Knowledge Engineering Review,* 20(3), 321–323.

Davis, R. 1984. Diagnostic reasoning based on structure and behavior. *Artificial Intelligence,* 24(1–3), 347–410.

de Kleer, J. 1976. *Local methods for localizing faults in electronic circuits.* Memo 394, MIT Artificial Intelligence Laboratory, Cambridge, MA, 154.

Domeshek, E. and Kolodner, J. 1991. Toward a case-based aid for architecture; toward a case-based aid for conceptual design. *International Journal of Expert Systems,* 4(2), 201–220.

———. 1992. A case-based design aid for architecture. In *Artificial Intelligence in Design* 92, ed. J.S. Gero, 487–516. Norwell, MA: Kluwer.

———. 1993. Using the points of large cases. *Artificial Intelligence for Engineering Design, Analysis, and Manufacturing,* 7(2), 87–96.

Fox, M. 1990. AI and expert system myths, legends, and facts. *Intelligent Systems and Their Applications,* 5(1), 8–20.

Genesereth, M. 1984. The use of design descriptions in automated diagnosis. *Artificial Intelligence,* 24(1), 411–436.

Glasgow, J., Narayanan, H., and Chadrasekaran, B. (Eds.). 1995. *Diagrammatic reasoning: Cognitive and computational perspectives.* Cambridge, MA: MIT Press, p. 148.

Gonzalez, A.J., Osborne, R.L., Kemper, C., and Lowenfeld, S. 1986. On-line diagnosis of turbine generators using artificial intelligence. *IEEE Trans. on Energy Conversion,* EC-1(2), June, 68–74.

Griffith, A. and Domeshek, E. 1996. Indexing evaluations of buildings to aid conceptual design. In *Case-based reasoning experiences, lessons, and future directions,* ed. D. Leake, 68–80. Menlo Park, CA: AAAI Press.

Hsu, F., Anantharaman, T., Campbell, M., and Nowatzyk, A. 1990. A grandmaster chess machine. *Scientific American,* 263(4) (October), 44–50.

Kibler, D. and Aha, D. 1987. Learning representative exemplars of concepts: An initial study. In *Proceedings of the Fourth International Workshop on Machine Learning,* UC-Irvine, June, 24–29.

Kitano, K. 1993. Challenges for massive parallelism. In *Proceeding of the 13th Annual Conference on Artificial Intelligence* (IJCAI-93), Chabery, France, 813–834.

Kitano, H. and Shimazu, H. 1996. The experience-sharing architecture: A case study in corporate-wide case-based software quality control. In *Case-based reasoning: experiences, lessons, and future directions,* ed. D. Leake, 235–268. Menlo Park, CA: AAAI Press.

Kolodner, J. 1991. Improving human decision making through case-based decision aiding. *AI Magazine,* 12(2), 52–68.

———. 1993. *Case-based reasoning.* San Mateo, CA: Morgan Kaufmann.

Leake, D. 1996. CBR in context: The present and future. In *Case-based reasoning: Experiences, lessons, and future directions,* ed. D. Leake, 3–30. Menlo Park, CA: AAAI Press.

Magnani, L., Nersessian, N.J., and Thagard, P. (Eds.). 1999. *Model-based reasoning in scientific discovery.* New York: Kluwer Academic Press, p. 148.

Mark, W., Simoudis, E., and Hinkle, D. 1996. CBR: Expectations and results. In *Case-based reasoning: Experiences, lessons, and future directions,* ed. D. Leake, 269–294. Menlo Park, CA: AAAI Press.

National Aeronautics and Space Administration (NASA). 2008. *SBIR and STTR solutions.* http://sbir.nasa.gov/SBIR/solicit.htm.

Newell, A. and Simon, H.A. 1963. GPS, a program that simulates human thought. In *Computers and thought,* ed. E.A. Fiegenbaum and J. Feldman, 279–296. New York: McGraw-Hill.

Ngyen, T., Czerwishki, M., and Lee, D. 1993. COMPAQ QuickSource: Providing the consumer with the power of artificial intelligence. In *Proceedings of the 5th Innovative Applications of Artificial Intelligence Conference,* Washington, D.C., July 11–15, 1993.

Patton, R.J., Frank, P.M. and Clark, R.N. (Eds.). 2000. *Issues of fault diagnosis for dynamic systems.* Berlin: Springer-Verlag, p. 154.

Russell, S. and Norvig, P. 2002. *Artificial intelligence.* Upper Saddle River, NJ: Pearson Education.

Schank, R. 1982. *Dynamic memory: A theory of learning in computers and people.* New York: Cambridge University Press.

Tsang, E. 1994. *Foundations of constraint satisfaction.* London: Academic Press. p. 148.

U.S. Department of Defense. 2009. *The DoD SBIR & STTR programs.* http://www.acq.osd.mil/osbp/sbir/.

Velloso, M. and Carbonnell, J. 1993. Derivational analogy in PRODIGY. *Machine Learning,* 10(3), 249–278.

Watson, I. 2003. *Applying case-based reasoning techniques for enterprise systems.* San Francisco: Morgan Kauffmann Publishers.

7 Knowledge Capture Systems: Systems that Preserve and Formalize Knowledge

In the previous chapter, we discussed knowledge application systems. In this chapter, we discuss what knowledge capture systems are about and how they serve to elicit and store organizational and individual knowledge. Knowledge capture systems are designed to help elicit and store knowledge, both tacit and explicit. Knowledge can be captured using mechanisms or technologies so that the captured knowledge can then be shared and used by others. Perhaps the earliest mechanisms for knowledge capture dates to the anthropological use of stories—the earliest form of art, education, and entertainment. **Storytelling** is the mechanism by which early civilizations passed on their values and their wisdom from one generation to the next.

In this chapter, we first discuss issues about organizational storytelling and how this mechanism can support knowledge capture. We then discuss how technology can enable the knowledge capture process. We also describe issues related to how to design the knowledge capture system, including the use of intelligent technologies in support of this process. In particular, the role of RFID technologies in knowledge capture is discussed. We discuss two types of knowledge capture systems: one that serves best to support educational settings; and a second system that serves best to capture tactical knowledge. Recall from Chapter 2 that tactical knowledge is defined as knowledge that pertains to the short-term positioning of the organization.

For a quick overview of how organizations can utilize strategic stories, let us look at a brief case study and how 3M Corporation uses stories to embody their innovative culture in Box 7.1.

WHAT ARE KNOWLEDGE CAPTURE SYSTEMS?

As discussed in Chapter 4, **knowledge capture systems** support the process of eliciting either explicit or tacit knowledge that may reside in people, artifacts, or organizational entities. These systems can help capture knowledge existing either within or outside organizational boundaries, among employees, consultants, competitors, customers, suppliers, and even prior employers of the organization's new employees. Knowledge capture systems rely on mechanisms and technologies that support externalization and internalization. Both mechanisms and technologies can support knowledge capture systems by facilitating the knowledge management processes of externalization and internalization.

Box 7.1

Using Stories to Build Effective Business Plans at 3M

Few companies rival 3M's 100 record years of innovation. From the invention of sandpaper in 1904 to the invention of masking tape in 1925 and Post-it Notes in 1980, 3M's culture is noted by its use of stories. Stories are part of 3M's sales representatives' training, award ceremonies, and in short a "habit-of-mind." At 3M, the power of stories is recognized as a means to "see ourselves and our business operations in complex, multidimensional forms—that we're able to discover opportunities for strategic change. Stories give us ways to form ideas about winning" (Shaw et al. 1998, p. 41.)

Recently, recognition about the power of stories reached 3M's boardroom. Traditionally at 3M, business plans were presented through bulleted lists. Cognitive psychologists have proven that lists are ineffective learning artifacts since item recognition decreases with the length of the list (Sternberg 1975), and typically only items at the beginning or end of the list are remembered (Tulving 1983). As a contrast, a good story can better represent a business plan, since it includes a definition of the relationships, a sequence of events, and a subsequent priority among the items which in turn causes the strategic plan to be remembered. Therefore, stories are currently used as the basic building blocks for business plans at 3M.

Shaw et al. (1998) defines an effective business plan to be a lot like a good story, and appropriately illustrates this with a narrative example. The strategic business plan must first set the stage or define the current situation. For example:

> Global Feet Graphics (a 3M division that makes durable graphic-marking systems for buildings, signs, and vehicles) was facing increasing demand from customers at the same time that they were experiencing eroding market share due to diminishing patent advantages and competitors' low-cost strategies.

Next, the strategic story must introduce the dramatic conflict. Continuing with the same example:

> The 3M division had to effect a quantum change in the production system that enabled the quick and competitive delivery of products. The solution included the development of innovative technologies that enabled this group's product offerings to differentiate from its competitors. In addition, sales and marketing skills had to appropriately match the new strategy.

Finally, the strategic narrative must reach a resolution. In other words, it must summarize how the organization will win through effectively drawing upon the diverse technological skills required to transform the business.

Studies at 3M have shown that the adequate use of narrative business plans have resulted in an improved understanding of the requirements for the plan to succeed. In addition, narrative strategy spurs excitement among 3M employees as well as generating commitment about the plan. As summarized by Shaw et al. (1998)

> When people can locate themselves in the story, their sense of commitment and involvement is enhanced. By conveying a powerful impression of the process of winning, narrative plans can motivate and mobilize an entire organization.

You may recall from Chapter 4 that **knowledge capture mechanisms** facilitate **externalization** (i.e., the conversion of tacit knowledge into explicit form) or **internalization** (i.e., the conversion of explicit knowledge into tacit form). The development of models or **prototypes**, and the articulation of stories are some examples of mechanisms that enable externalization. Learning by observation and face-to-face meetings are some of the mechanisms that facilitate internalization.

Technologies can also support knowledge capture by facilitating externalization and internalization. Externalization through **knowledge engineering**, described earlier in Chapter 6, is necessary for the implementation of intelligent technologies such as expert systems and case-based reasoning systems, also described in Chapter 6. Technologies that facilitate internalization include computer-based communication and computer-based simulations. For example, an individual can use communication facilities to internalize knowledge from a message sent by another expert or an AI-based knowledge-acquisition system. Furthermore, computer-based simulations can also support individual learning. Both knowledge capture mechanisms and technologies can facilitate externalization and internalization within or across organizations.

Knowledge Management Mechanisms For Capturing Tacit Knowledge: Using Organizational Stories

The importance of using metaphors and stories as a mechanism for capturing and transferring tacit knowledge is increasingly drawing the attention of organizations. For example as illustrated in Box 7.1, 3M currently uses stories as part of its business planning to set the stage, introduce dramatic conflict, reach a resolution to the challenges the company is facing, and generate excitement and commitment from all the members of the organization (Shaw et al. 1998). Storytelling at 3M is currently expected to take a center stage, as it seeks to develop a culture of problem preventers rather than "an eleventh-hour problem-solver." In order to reinforce this paradigm shift, 3M leaders turn to telling pet stories that describe "what not to do" (Clark 2004). Storytelling is now considered of strategic importance as organizations recognize the need to develop their company's next generation leaders and has been recognized as one of the most effective means to develop high-potential managers in a firm (Ready 2002).

Stories are considered to play a significant role in organizations characterized by a strong need for collaboration. **Organizational stories** are defined as

> a detailed narrative of past management actions, employee interactions, or other intra- or extraorganizational events that are communicated informally within organizations (Swap et al. 2001).

Organizational stories typically include a plot, major characters, an outcome, and an implied moral. Stories originate within the organization and typically reflect organizational norms, values, and culture. Because stories make information more vivid, engaging, entertaining, and easily related to personal experience and because of the rich contextual details encoded in stories, they are the ideal mechanism to capture tacit knowledge (Swap et al. 2001). Stories have been observed to be useful to capture and communicate organizational managerial systems (how things are done), norms, and values.

Dave Snowden (1999), a long time proponent of storytelling at IBM, identifies the following set of guidelines for organizational storytelling:

1. Stimulate the natural telling and writing of stories.
2. Stories must be rooted in anecdotal material reflective of the community in question.
3. Stories should not represent idealized behavior.
4. An organizational program to support storytelling should not depend on external experts for its sustenance.
5. Organizational stories are about achieving a purpose, not entertainment.
6. Be cautious of overgeneralizing and forgetting the particulars. What has worked in one organization may not necessarily work in others.
7. Adhere to the highest ethical standards and rules.

According to Phoel (2006), the following eight steps to successful storytelling will help work magic in the organization:

1. Have a clear purpose.
2. Identify and example of successful change.
3. Tell the truth.
4. Say who, what, when.
5. Trim detail.
6. Underscore the cost of failure.
7. End on a positive note.
8. Invite your audience to dream.

But Phoel also emphasizes that to tell the story right, it is not just what you say but how you say it, that will determine its success. In this regard, stories should speak as one person to another, they should present the truth as one sees it, should seem spontaneous but must be rehearsed, and one should relive the story as one tells it. Perhaps the one theme that all storytelling experts agree on is the "crucial importance of truth as an attribute of both the powerful story and the effective storyteller" (Guber 2007). In fact, according to Guber, there are four kinds of truth in each effective story:

1. Truth to the teller—the storyteller must be congruent to her story.
2. Truth to the audience—the story must fulfill the listeners' expectations by understanding what the listeners know about, meeting their emotional needs, and telling the story in an interactive fashion.
3. Truth to the moment—since great storytellers prepare obsessively and never tell a story the same way twice.
4. Truth to the mission—since great storytellers are devoted to the cause, which is embodied in the story, capturing and expressing the values that she believes in and wants others to adopt as their own.

Other important considerations in the design of an effective organizational storytelling program include (Post 2002):

1. People must agree with the idea that this could be an effective means of capturing and transferring tacit organizational knowledge.
2. Identify people in the organization willing to share how they learned from others about how to do their jobs.
3. Metaphors are a way to confront difficult organizational issues.
4. Stories can only transfer knowledge if the listener is interested in learning from them.

In fact, one of the strengths of stories is that they are clearly episodic in nature, which means related to events directly experienced. To the extent that the storyteller is able to provide a sufficiently vivid account for the listener to vicariously experience the story, many features of the story will be encoded in the listener's memory and later available for retrieval (Swap et al. 2001). In fact, the relatively recent emphasis on the use of case studies at most business schools is related to the effectiveness of stories as a pedagogical tool. Much like case studies, Steve Denning (2000), who is best known for his efforts to implement communities of practice and storytelling at the World Bank, describes the importance of **springboard stories**. Springboard stories enable a leap in understanding by the audience in order to grasp how an organization may change by visualizing from a story in one context what is involved in large-scale organizational transformations. Springboard stories are told from the perspective of a protagonist who was in a predicament, which may resemble the predicament currently faced by the organization. As an example of a springboard story, consider the story used by Denning to convince his colleagues at the World Bank about the importance of knowledge management:

> In June of last year, a health worker in a tiny town in Zambia went to the Web site of the Centers for Disease Control and got an answer to a question about the treatment of malaria. Remember that this was in Zambia, one of the poorest countries in the world, and it was in a tiny place six hundred kilometers from the capital city. But the most striking thing about this picture, at least for us, is that the World Bank isn't in it. Despite our know-how on all kinds of poverty-related issues, that knowledge isn't available to the millions of people who could use it. Imagine if it were. Think what an organization we would become (Denning 2005, p. 4).

An interesting question is the role storytelling plays with respect to analytical thinking. Denning (2000) supports the argument that storytelling supplements analytical thinking by enabling us to imagine new perspectives and new worlds. He sees storytelling as ideally suited to communicating change and stimulating innovation, because abstract analysis is easier to understand when seen through the lens of a well-chosen story and can of course be used to make explicit the implications of a story.

Finally, Denning (2000) describes the organizational areas where storytelling can be effective, including:

1. *Igniting action in knowledge-era organizations:* Storytelling can help managers and employees actively think about the implications of change and the opportunities for the future of their organization. Listeners actively understand

what it would be like if things were done a different way, re-creating the idea of change as an exciting and living opportunity for growth.

2. *Bridging the knowing-doing gap:* This view proposes that storytelling can exploit the interactive nature of communication by encouraging the listener to imagine the story and to live it vicariously as a participant. The listener perceives and acts on the story as part of their identity.

3. *Capturing tacit knowledge:* Probably this line of reasoning is best captured in Denning's (2000) words: "Storytelling provides a vehicle for conveying tacit knowledge, drawing on the deep-flowing streams of meaning, and of patterns of primal narratives of which the listeners are barely aware, and so catalyzes visions of a different and renewed future."

4. *To embody and transfer knowledge:* A simple story can communicate a complex multidimensional idea by actively involving the listeners in the creation of the idea in the context of their own organization.

5. *To foster innovation:* Innovation is triggered by the inter-relatedness of ideas. Storytelling enables to easily absorb and relate knowledge, the same spark that triggers innovation.

6. *Launching and nurturing communities:* In many large organizations, the formation of communities of practice enables the grouping of professionals who come together voluntarily together to share similar interests and learn from each other. These communities of practice may be known under different names: *thematic groups* (World Bank), *learning communities* or *learning networks* (Hewlett-Packard Company), *best practice teams* (Chevron), and *family groups* (Xerox). Denning (2000) explains how a storytelling program provides a natural methodology for nurturing communities and integrating them to the organization's strategy and structure because:

   a. Storytelling builds trust—enabling knowledge seekers in a community to learn from knowledge providers through the sharing of candid dialogue.
   b. Storytelling unlocks passion—because they enable the members of the community to commit "passionately" to a common purpose, being the engineering design of a new artifact, or sharing the discovery of a new medical remedy.
   c. Storytelling is nonhierarchical—because storytelling is collaborative, with the members of the community pooling resources to jointly create the story.

7. *Enhancing technology:* Most people agree that e-mail has made increasing demands in our lives, resulting in the expectation that we're available 24/7 to answer electronic requests that span from office memos to virtual garbage mail. Communities of practice and storytelling can enable us to interact with our neighbors and remain connected when we want to, providing us with "tranquility yet connectedness."

8. *Individual growth:* The world of storytelling is one that proposes avoiding adversarial contests and win-win for all sides: the knowledge seeker and the knowledge-provider.

TECHNIQUES FOR ORGANIZING AND USING STORIES IN THE ORGANIZATION

The power of narratives or stories as a knowledge capture mechanism in an organization lies in the fact that **narratives** capture the knowledge content as well as its context and the social networks that define the way "things are done around here." In order to capture organizational knowledge through narratives, it is best to encourage storytelling in a work context. In addition to the knowledge-elicitation techniques described in Chapter 6, here we present **knowledge-elicitation** techniques pertaining specifically to stories.

One technique described by Snowden (2000) for narrative knowledge capture is **anthropological observation**, or the use of naïve interviewers, citing an example where they used a group of school children to understand the knowledge flows in an organization. The children were naïve, therefore they asked innocent and unexpected questions which caused the subjects to naturally volunteer their anecdotes. They were also curious, which resulted in a higher level of knowledge elicitation.

He also describes a second technique, **storytelling circles**, formed by groups having a certain degree of coherence and identity such as a common experience in a project. Story circles are best recorded in video. Certain methods can be used for eliciting anecdotes such as:

1. **Dit-spinning**—or *fish tales*—represents human tendencies to escalate or better the stories shared previously.
2. **Alternative histories**—are fictional anecdotes which could have different turning points, based for example on a particular project's outcome.
3. **Shifting character or context**—are fictional anecdotes where the characters may be shifted to study the new perspective of the story.
4. **Indirect stories**—allow disclosing the story with respect to fictional characters, so that any character similarities with the real-life character are considered to be pure coincidence.
5. **Metaphor**—provides a common reference for the group to a commonly known story, cartoon, or movie.

Once a number of stories has been elicited and captured, the next problem is how to store the narratives so people will find them. **Narrative databases** can be indexed by the theme of the story, by the **stakeholders** of the story, or by **archetypal characters**. The theme could be, for example, innovative stories. The stakeholders could be the scientists, the marketing group, or the customers. The archetypal characters represent well-known characters that represent a virtue, for example, the good father archetype represented by Bill Cosby in his TV role as Dr. Cliff Huxtable.

DESIGNING THE KNOWLEDGE CAPTURE SYSTEM

Typically the documentation available in organizations is the result of applying expertise rather than expertise itself. For example, a radiologist interpreting high-precision functional images of the heart will have the results of his diagnosis captured in a document, but the reasoning process by which he reaches the diagnosis is not usually captured. In addition, consider the process of engineering for complex systems. Traditional methods for documenting and representing the engineered designs include creating engineering drawings, specifications, and **computer-aided design (CAD)** models. But often the decisions leading to the design choices including the assumptions, constraints, and considerations, are not captured. Capturing these decisions is not only important but may lead to a more useful representation of the design, specifically when designing complex systems in an environment characterized by high uncertainty.

Knowledge-elicitation techniques have been studied and used extensively in AI for the development of expert systems (Chapter 6). The purpose of these techniques is to assist the knowledge-elicitation process based on interview sessions between a knowledge engineer and the domain expert, with the goal of jointly constructing an expertise model. Although computers may understand the resulting expertise models, these models may not directly meet the objective of capturing and preserving the expert's knowledge so it can be transferred to others, or in other words, so others can learn from it.

Next, we discuss how technology can facilitate capturing the knowledge of experts. We will describe two such systems based on different methodologies and intelligent technologies. The first system is based on the use of concept maps as a knowledge-modeling tool. The second system is based on the use of context-based reasoning (CxBR) to simulate human behavior. Each of these systems is best suited for certain specific situations. For example, the use of concept maps may be best suited to capture the knowledge of experts when supporting educational settings. On the other hand, CxBR is best suited to capture the tactical knowledge of experts, which requires assessment of the situation, selecting a plan of action, and acting on the plan. Both of these knowledge capture systems can then be used to construct simulation models of human behavior.

CONCEPT MAPS

KNOWLEDGE REPRESENTATION THROUGH THE USE OF CONCEPT MAPS

One type of knowledge capture system that we describe in this chapter is based on the use of **concept maps** as a knowledge-modeling tool. Concept maps, developed by Novak (Novak 1998; Novak and Cañas 2008; Novak and Gowin 1984), aim to represent knowledge through *concepts* enclosed in circles or boxes of some types, which are related via connecting lines or *propositions*. Concepts are perceived regularities in events or objects that are designated by a label.

In the simplest form, a concept map contains just two concepts connected by a linking word to form a single *proposition,* also called a **semantic unit** or *unit of meaning.* For example, Figure 7.1 is a concept map that describes the structure of concept maps. Based on the concept map represented in Figure 7.1, the two concepts—concept maps and organized knowledge—are linked together to form the proposition: "Concept maps represent organized knowledge." Additional propositions expand the meaning of concept maps, such as "Concepts are hierarchically structured."

In a concept map, the vertical axis expresses a hierarchical framework for organizing the concepts. More general, inclusive concepts are found at the top of the map with progressively more specific, less inclusive concepts arranged below them. These maps emphasize the most general concepts by linking them to supporting ideas with **propositions**. Concept maps represent meaningful relationships between concepts in the form of propositions. In addition relationships between concepts (propositions) in different domains of the concept map are defined as *cross-links*. These cross-links help to visualize how different knowledge domains are related to each other.

Sometimes the difference between concept maps and semantic networks could be a source of confusion. **Semantic networks**, also called *associative networks,* are typically represented as a directed graph connecting the nodes (representing concepts) to show a relationship or association between them. This type of associative network can be useful in describing, for example, traffic flow in that the connections between concepts indicate direction, but directed graphs do not connect concepts through propositions. Furthermore, in a directed graph there's no assumption about the progression of generality to more specific concepts as the nodes are traversed from the top of the network. The same holds true for associative networks in general.

Concept maps were developed based on Ausubel's (1963) learning psychology theory. Ausabel's cognitive psychology research provides us with the understanding that learning takes place through the assimilation of new concepts and propositions into existing concept frameworks by the learner. Ausubel's studies uncovered the conditions for meaningful learning to include (1) a clear presentation of the material, (2) the learner's relevant prior knowledge, and (3) the learner's motivation to integrate new meanings into their prior knowledge. Concept maps can be useful in meeting the conditions for learning by identifying concepts prior to instruction, building new concept frameworks, and integrating concept maps through cross-links.

In educational settings, concept-mapping techniques have been applied to many fields of knowledge. Their rich expressive power derives from each map's ability to allow its creator the use of a virtually unlimited set of linking words to show how meanings have been developed. Consequently, maps having similar concepts can vary from one context to another. Also, concept maps may be used to measure a particular person's knowledge about a given topic in a specific context. Concept maps can help formalize and capture an expert's domain knowledge in an easy to understand representation of an expert's domain knowledge. Figure 7.2 shows a segment of a concept map from the domain of nuclear cardiology.

KNOWLEDGE CAPTURE SYSTEMS BASED ON CONCEPT MAPS

The goal of **CmapTools** (Cañas et al. 2004),[1] a concept map-based browser, is to capture the knowledge of experts. The navigation problem, an important concern in hypermedia systems, is alleviated by the use of concept maps, which serve as guides in the traversing of logical linkages among clusters of related objects. The Cmap-Tools extend the use of concept maps beyond knowledge representation to serve as the browsing interface to a domain of knowledge.

Figure 7.3 shows the concept map-based browser as the interface for the expla-

Figure 7.1   **Concept Map about Concept Maps**

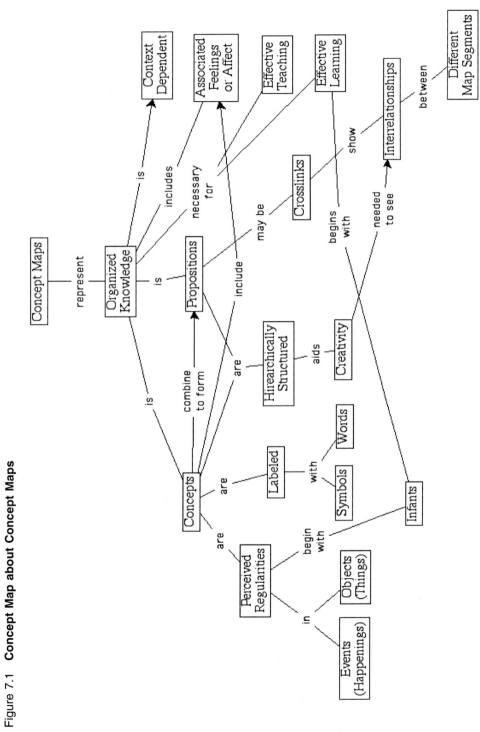

Source: Novak and Cañas 2008.

134

Figure 7.2   **A Segment of a Concept Map from the Domain of Nuclear Cardiology**

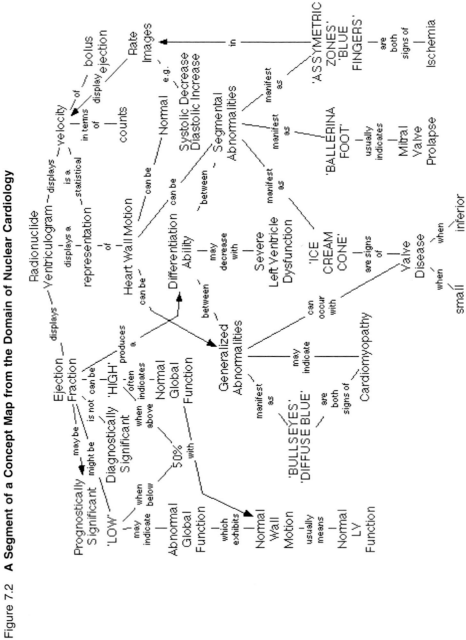

Source: Ford et al. 1996.

Figure 7.3 **Segment of a Concept Map from the Domain of Nuclear Cardiology, Represented using CmapTools**

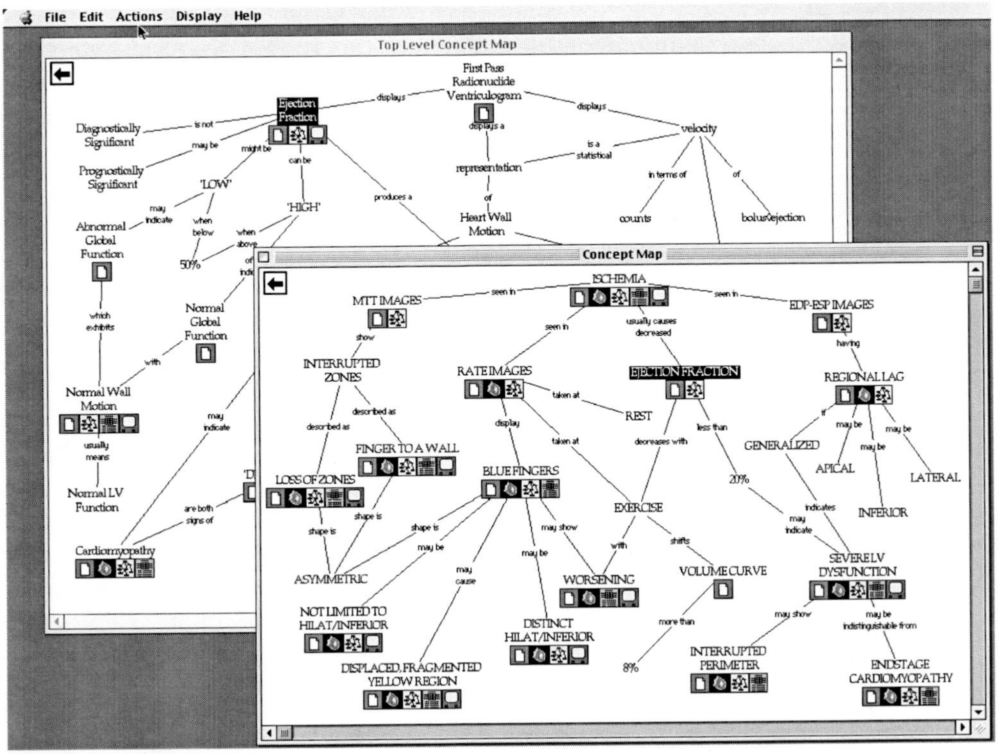

Source: Ford et al. 1996.

nation subsystem of a nuclear cardiology expert system (Cañas et al. 1997, 2001, 2003, 2004; Cañas and Novak 2005; Ford et a1. 1996). Each of the concept nodes represents an abstraction for a specific cardiology pathology, which is fully described by the icons at the concept node. For the cardiologist, the image results of a Nuclear Medicine Radionuclide Ventriculogram[2] scan resembling a picture of "asymmetric blue fingers" (later depicted in Figure 7.4) is a sign of myocardial ischemia or chronic heart failure. An image resembling a "ballerina foot" is usually a representation of a mitral valve prolapse. Clearly the first patient will quickly need to be rushed to a hospital for emergency surgery, while the second may be given medication and a diet to relieve him of his symptoms.

The icons below the concept nodes provide access to auxiliary information that helps explain the concepts in the form of pictures, images, audio-video clips, text, Internet links, or other concept maps related to the topic. These linked media resources and concept maps can be located anywhere accessible via the Internet (Cañas et al. 2001).

The browser provides a window showing the hierarchical ordering of maps, highlights the current location of the user in the hierarchy, and permits movement to any other map by clicking on the desired map in the hierarchy. This concept map-based interface provides a unique way of organizing and browsing knowledge about any domain.

CmapTools provides a practical application of the idea of utilizing concept maps to capture and formalize knowledge resulting in context-rich knowledge representation models that can be viewed and shared through the Internet. CmapTools takes advantage of the richness provided by multimedia, providing an effective platform for aspiring students to learn from subject-matter experts.

Concept maps provide an effective methodology to organize and structure the concepts representing the expert's domain knowledge. During the knowledge capture process, the knowledge engineer and domain expert interact to collaboratively construct a shared conceptual model of the domain which eventually becomes the concept map for the multimedia system. Users later browse this conceptual model through the CmapTools. Browsing enables the learner to implicitly gain the expert's view of the domain. In general, this model for knowledge representation provides a broad view of the domain as understood by that particular domain expert.

Links in concept maps are explicitly labeled arcs, and usually connect two concepts to form a concept-link-concept relation that may be read as a simple proposition. CmapTools users learn about the domain by clicking on the small icons depicted at the nodes in the concept map and directly navigate to other contexts (or subcontexts) through hyperlinks where other concepts are described. Figure 7.4 shows some of the different media windows opened from the windows in Figure 7.3.

Another advantage of using concept maps for knowledge representation is that, because of their hierarchical organization, concept maps can easily scale to large quantities of information. This particular characteristic can then enable the easy integration of domain concepts together.

CmapTools has been showed to facilitate virtual collaboration and the creation of concept maps at a distance (Cañas et al. 2003), which are stored on public servers that can be accessed via the Internet. Concept maps are the ideal mechanism to make explicit and capture ideas so they can later be shared to collaboratively create new knowledge.

In summary, concept-mapping tools like CmapTools can be an effective way to capture and represent the knowledge of domain experts in representation models that can later be used by potential students of the domain (Cañas and Novak 2005). Practically speaking, the knowledge representation models illustrated in the aforementioned Figures 7.2, 7.3, and 7.4 could be used by students in the field of cardiology to effectively learn the practical aspects of the domain from one of the best experts in the field.

CONTEXT-BASED REASONING

KNOWLEDGE REPRESENTATION THROUGH THE USE OF CONTEXT-BASED REASONING

Recall from Chapter 2 that tactical knowledge is defined as pertaining to the short-term positioning of the organization relative to its markets, competitors, and suppliers;

Figure 7.4 **The Explanation Subsystem Based on the Concept Map**

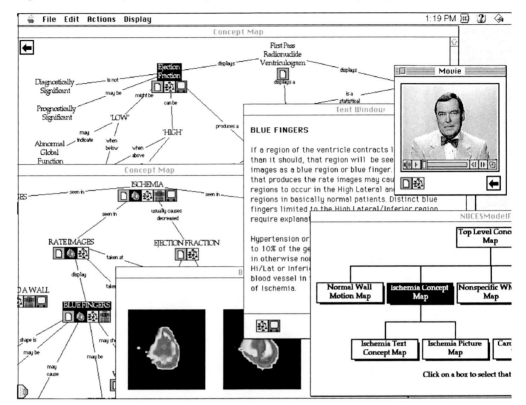

Source: Ford et al. 1996.

and is contrasted to **strategic knowledge**, which pertains to the long-term positioning of the organization in terms of its corporate vision and strategies for achieving that vision. In the context of this example **tactical knowledge** refers to the human ability that enables domain experts to assess the situation at hand (therefore short-term) among a myriad of inputs, select a plan that best addresses the current situation, and execute that plan (Gonzalez and Ahlers 1998; Thorndike and Wescort 1984). Consider the following scenario:

> The commanding officer of the submarine is generally bombarded with a multitude of inputs when performing his job. He receives audio inputs such as engine noise, electronic noise, and conversations with others around him. He likewise receives visual inputs such as the radar and sonar screens, possibly the periscope and so forth, and tactile inputs such as vibrations of the submarine. He is able to cognitively handle these inputs rather easily when they are all in the normal expected range. However, if one of these should deviate from normal, such as abnormal noise and vibrations, the officer will immediately focus only on these inputs in order to recognize the present situation as, for instance, a potential grounding, collision, or engine malfunction. All other inputs being received, meanwhile, are generally ignored during the crisis.

Alternatively, consider an example more relevant to our daily lives:

> The daily routine drive to and from work is marked by a myriad of inputs while performing the task. A Dad driving to work with his children receives audio inputs such as the noise from babies, siblings vying for attention, pop music, their spouse's conversation, and who could forget the cellular phone. In addition, he receives visual inputs like the gas gauge level (typically empty at this time), traffic signals (including those marking school zones), and the all-too-familiar police strobe lights. He's able to cognitively handle these inputs (even in the absence of coffee) when they're in the normal (albeit borderline chaotic) range. However, if any of these should deviate from normal—for example, the strobe signal from police following the car will signal to the driver that perhaps he has committed an infraction and needs to immediately pull over. At this point all other signals, including the screaming children, will be ignored during the crisis at hand.

Context-based Reasoning (CxBR) helps to model this behavioral phenomenon. Context-based Reasoning is a human behavior representation paradigm specifically designed to effectively represent human tactical behavior (Gonzalez et al. 2008). Tactical behavior is defined as: "the continuous and dynamic process of decision making by a performing agent (human or otherwise) who interacts with his/its environment while attempting to carry out a mission in that environment" (Gonzalez et al. 1998, 2002, 2008). In this sense tactical knowledge is associated with assessing a current situation, selecting a plan to address the current situation, and executing that plan. Tactical experts recognize and treat only the salient features of the situation and thus are able to abstract a small, but important portion of the available inputs for general knowledge. Just like the nuclear cardiologist in Figure 7.3 is able to abstract a heart pathology that he describes as "blue fingers," the commanding officer is able to abstract and treat the key features of the situation at hand and act based on these features. CxBR is based on the following basic tenets (Gonzalez and Ahlers 1993):

1. A tactical situation calls for a set of actions and procedures that properly address the current situation. In the case of a driver, for example, these actions could include maintaining the car in its proper lane, stopping at a stop sign, and not exceeding the speed limit (by much). The set of actions and procedures is described as the context.
2. As the situation evolves, a transition to another context or set of actions and procedures may be required to address the new situation. For example, when a driver exits an interstate highway onto a city street, a different set of functions and procedures will be necessary to manage this new situation. In addition, one must be aware of cross traffic, traffic lights, and so forth that would not have to be considered when driving on an interstate highway.
3. What is likely to happen in a context or current situation is limited by the context itself. Continuing with the same example, one would not have to worry about operating the cruise control while waiting at a traffic light. However, that could be a potential action while driving on the interstate.

Figure 7.5 **Context Hierarchy**

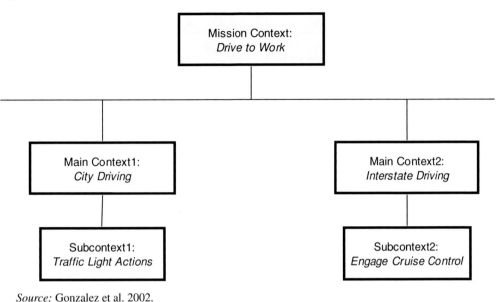

Source: Gonzalez et al. 2002.

CxBR encapsulates knowledge about appropriate actions and/or procedures, as well as compatible new situations, into hierarchically organized contexts. Tactical behavior is action-based at low levels (e.g., keeping the car on the traffic lane), decision-and-action based at middle levels (stop or go at a traffic light), and decision-based at high levels (take the freeway or the back roads). In this sense, CxBR is hierarchical and modular and a sample hierarchy is depicted in Figure 7.5.

The **mission context** defines the scope of the mission, its goals, the plan, and the constraints imposed (time, weather, etc). The **main context** contains functions, rules, and a list of compatible subsequent main contexts. Identification of a new situation can now be simplified because only a limited number of all situations are possible under the currently active context. **Subcontexts** are abstractions of functions performed by the main context, which may be too complex for one function or that may be employed by other main contexts. This encourages re-usability. Subcontexts are activated by rules in the active main context. They will deactivate themselves upon completion of their actions.

Decisions are heavily influenced by a sequence of main contexts, each of which, when active, controls behavior of an autonomous vehicle agent (either real or simulated) with an expectation for the future. Active main contexts change not only in response to external events or circumstances but also because of actions taken by the agent itself. One example of a main context could be driving in city traffic, called *City Driving*. Such a context would contain functions to maintain the vehicle on the road at a speed not to exceed the speed limit, the know-how to handle intersections, pedestrians, school zones, and so forth. It could call subcontexts to help it deal with traffic lights, school zones, and emergency vehicles.

One and only one specific main context is always active for each agent, making it the sole controller of the agent. When the situation changes, a transition to another main context may be required to properly address the emerging situation. For example, the automobile may enter an interstate highway requiring a transition to another main context, called *Interstate Driving*. Transitions between contexts are triggered by events in the environment—some planned, others unplanned. Expert performers are able to recognize and identify the transition points quickly and effectively.

Any situation, by its very nature, will limit the number of other situations that can realistically follow. Therefore, only a limited number of things can be expected to happen within any one context. Using the domain of driving an automobile, a tire blowout is typically not expected while idling at a traffic light. However, getting rear-ended is a definite possibility. The converse is true when driving on an interstate highway. This can be used as an advantage in pruning the search space of the problem, since there is no need to monitor the simulation for blowouts when the driver is in the traffic light subcontext. If unexpected occurrences do take place, they introduce the element of surprise into the agent's behavior, which is highly consistent with actual human behavior.

CxBR has proven to be a very intuitive, efficient, and effective representation technique for human behavior. As such, it provides the important hierarchical organization of contexts. Additionally, it has the ability to incorporate any programming paradigm within the control activity (e.g., neural networks, a knowledge discovery technique described in Chapter 9, have been used as subcontexts). The presence of a mission context to define the mission and provide global performance modifiers is also a notable difference. CxBR provides the ability to perform complex reasoning to dictate the transitions between main contexts if necessary for the application. Transitions can be coded through the use of rules (described in Chapter 6). This flexibility and representational richness distinguishes CxBR not only from the traditional state transition paradigms but also from other commonly used modeling paradigms for human behavior. CxBR can be used to adequately capture and represent tactical knowledge. Potential applications include the capture and representation of the knowledge of airline pilots and of air traffic controllers. In addition, it can serve to capture and represent the knowledge of commercial pilots and bus drivers as well as of subway and train engineers. Finally, CxBR can serve to represent knowledge related to military affairs (Gonzalez and Ahlers 1998) and even poker playing (Stensrud 2005). A full description of CxBR can be found in (Gonzalez et al. 2008).

KNOWLEDGE CAPTURE SYSTEMS BASED ON CONTEXT-BASED REASONING

As we discussed briefly in Chapter 6, knowledge engineers elicit the knowledge of experts primarily through detailed interview sessions with the subject-matter expert. Furthermore, the success of the knowledge elicitation process depends on many nontechnical factors such as the expert's personality, the knowledge engineer's experience, and her preparation. Ultimately, one of the goals of the field of artificial intelligence, which still remains unachieved, is to be able to build an expert's cognitive model directly via a query session between the expert and the intelligent system. Clearly, the advantages of accomplishing this would be many, the most important being the dramatic reduction in manpower required to capture the knowledge of experts and a significant reduction in the logical errors coded in the system.

Because of its hierarchical and modular nature, context-based reasoning lends itself well to automating the knowledge capture process. Here we describe a knowledge capture system based on CxBR known as **Context-based Intelligent Tactical Knowledge Acquisition (CITKA)** (Gonzalez et al. 2002). CITKA uses its own knowledge base to compose a set of intelligent queries to elicit the tactical knowledge of the expert.

CITKA composes questions and presents them to the expert. The questions are designed to elicit tactical knowledge and represent it in the underlying CxBR paradigm. Upon responding to the questions, the result is a nearly complete context base which, when used with a CxBR reasoning engine, can be used to control someone performing the mission of interest in a typical environment (e.g., driving from New York to Boston, flying an airplane from Houston to Dallas). CITKA can be used by the expert or by the knowledge engineer. It is likely that both will need to use it to complete the context base. The query sessions only take place with the expert. The knowledge engineer is given direct edit access to the context base. Let us now look at how CITKA works.

The CITKA system consists of four modules of independent but cooperating subsystems. These modules are:

1. Knowledge engineering database back-end (KEDB)—A data structure that holds the evolving context base as it gradually becomes developed, either by the knowledge engineer or by the **subject matter expert (SME)**. The KEDB is subject to the hierarchical structure of mission, main, and subcontexts imposed by CxBR. To implement these data structures, a table is created for each context type.
2. Knowledge engineering interface (KEI)—Maps into the KEDB module. Data entry in the KEI is provided by eight interacting dialogs: Mission Context, Main Contexts, Subcontexts, Entity Objects, Helping Functions, Memory Variables, Transition Criteria, and Action Definitions. The KEI is designed in a table-driven fashion.
3. Query rule-base back-end (QRB)—A rule-based system containing the rules for executing the intelligent dialog with the subject matter expert (SME). A rule is provided for each SME interface input screen. These query rules have to be mapped to buttons, checkboxes, and menus by the SME Interface.
4. Subject matter expert interface (SMEI)—the graphical user interface (GUI) for the QRB. This environment allows a great deal of flexibility: The SMEI dynamically produces interfaces that correspond to the questions and rules that are put forth in the QRB.

The CITKA system was evaluated for its effectiveness. There were two main issues here: (1) estimating the reduction in person-hour effort to develop a context-based model for a particular mission, and (2) estimating the percentage of a context-based model that could conceivably be automatically developed through CITKA. The proto-type was tested on a nontrivial mission for a submarine to monitor a port and protect surface assets against underwater threats emanating from the monitored port. This context base was first developed through the traditional interview methods, and the hours spent developing it were carefully documented. It was then estimated how long it would take to develop the same model with the CITKA tool. Its developers report that there could be as much as an 80 percent reduction in person-hour effort to build with a context-based system as compared to the current manual means (Gonzalez et al. 2002). Furthermore, they estimate that 50 percent to 80 percent of the context-based model could be developed directly through a query session in CITKA.

BARRIERS TO THE USE OF KNOWLEDGE CAPTURE SYSTEMS

This section discusses the barriers to the deployment of knowledge capture systems from two perspectives. The first perspective describes that of the knowledge engineer who seeks to build such systems. The second perspective is that of the subject matter expert, who would interact with an automated knowledge capture system to preserve his knowledge. First let's consider the barriers to the development of knowledge capture systems.

As discussed at the beginning of this chapter, there are two possible mechanisms to capture the knowledge of experts. The first mechanism is to simply ask the ex-pert, through a knowledge-elicitation process (described in Chapter 10), that must be properly managed in order to maximize the results of the process. This is the es-sence of the externalization process. The second mechanism is to observe a person's behavior or performance while they're executing their tasks. This method, learning by observation, is essentially the internalization process. Perhaps in the not too far future, we may be able to connect a device to a person's brain that could sense and capture the neural firings of the brain that constitutes expertise, but clearly this is not yet a possibility. Undoubtedly, this futuristic possibility raises a host of ethical considerations as well. In fact, this possibility would clearly contradict the essence of KM that we described in Chapter 1—that is, KM should not distance itself from the knowledge owners but instead celebrate and recognize their position as experts in the organization.

One of the largest barriers to the automatic elicitation of expert's knowledge is that in order to effectively accomplish this task, the knowledge engineer requires developing some idea of the nature and structure of the knowledge very early in the process. In this chapter, we have discussed how knowledge engineers must attempt to become versed in the subject matter, or the nature of knowledge, prior to the interview process. Familiarization with the structure of knowledge is an additional requirement, often a fairly difficult proposition, in the sense that the interviewer must quickly de-velop some idea of which paradigm would best represent the knowledge at hand. For example, while conducting the expert interviews, the knowledge engineer observes that the expert's knowledge is very conditional. In other words, the expert describes it as "if A then B," this would be a good indication that his knowledge would best be represented as rules. If the expert describes the knowledge in terms of connections, in other words "A is related to B, B is related to C" as in describing an architecture, then perhaps the most adequate representation is the concept map paradigm. Furthermore, if the expert's knowledge is based on recollections "I remember when one such instance happened" then case-based reasoning is the most likely alternative. If the expert describes his knowledge in base of a schedule of events, "this happens on A after B event," then a constraint-based paradigm may be the best alternative. Finally, if the expert's knowledge is described in tactical terms such as "how to drive a car," then context-based reasoning would be the best representation.

Only if the interviewer is able to develop an idea of the **type or nature of knowledge** early in the process, will she be able to adequately represent it. In theory, we could replace the knowledge engineer by an intelligent knowledge capture system that would develop a set of questions to adequately elicit the knowledge of the subject matter expert. The system would need to know the nature and structure of the knowledge and how to ask such questions accordingly. In other words, the intelligent knowledge capture system and the expert would need to be "in tune" with each other. This is several generations ahead of the CmapTools and CITKA systems described before. On the other hand, if the end result is only to elicit the expert's knowledge to capture it in a document or a story, the structure requirement may not be necessary.

In summary, developing an automated system for knowledge capture without *a priori* knowledge of the nature and structure of the knowledge in question is essentially not possible. Furthermore, developing a multiparadigm tool that could essentially define the appropriate knowledge capture technique is almost impossible. The knowledge acquisition process must be tailored to the specific type of knowledge, and making that assessment ahead of time could be difficult.

From the point of view of the expert who will be faced with the task of interacting with the knowledge capture system, this may pose additional barriers. The first one is that the expert will need to take the initiative of learning how to interact with the system, and he may need to be coached through the first few sessions until he's reached a certain comfort level with the technology. Naturally some people may be resistant to trying new things, and the proposition of interacting with a machine may be one that many experts may not necessarily look forward to. This barrier can be overcome with adequate training and the utilization of user-friendly interfaces. In the area of **graphical user interfaces** current research examines the impact that "talking heads," even those that could portray emotion, could play on the user's feeling of ease with the technology.

RESEARCH TRENDS

USING LEARNING BY OBSERVATION TO CAPTURE KNOWLEDGE

This section discusses some research trends about how learning by observation could be used to capture knowledge. Without a doubt, humans and many animals learn first by observation. Infants learn their language, what foods to eat and avoid, and the signs of danger including distinguishing prey from predators. Many animals have been shown to learn by observation including chimpanzees, dolphins, and some bird species. Research on how humans and animals learn through observation has been one important area of study in artificial intelligence. Learning by observation refers to a computing agent's ability to improve how it will act in the future, as the agent observes its interactions with the world and its own decision-making process (Russell and Norvig 2002).

Just like humans can learn by observing others perform a task, robots could improve their effectiveness by doing the same thing. Providing robots with such ability implies they would need to be equipped with vision. In addition, the movements required for a specific task would need to be encoded to "train" the robot. Exact emulation of human movement has been occurring since the 1970s. For example, a human could take a robot that paints automobile parts through his motions, and it could easily replicate exactly the same exact motions thereafter. What is much harder for the robot is to "understand" why the human is doing what he does so that it can extrapolate the learned tasks to slightly different situations. For example if a robot has to paint only the doorknob in a door forthcoming on the assembly line, as long as the doorknob is in exactly the same location every time, learning dumb moves suffices. But if the location of the doorknob varies with each door, and the robotic painting arm must look for it and paint it wherever it is that's more difficult. Even more difficult is to understand when a door comes along that doesn't have doorknobs, which means the robot should not paint anything at all. Clearly the benefits for the robot arm to learn by observation would be significant, since it would allow shortening its learning time while decreasing the required programming effort.

Learning through observation has been used successfully to automate the knowledge acquisition task. For example Sammut et al. (1992) used learning by observation (which they term as *behavioral cloning*) to learn the knowledge required to fly a Cessna through observation of a human using a flight simulator to fly a predefined flight plan. In their research, observation logs were kept from a large set of training examples that recorded the sensor inputs and appropriate actions, which were used to create decision trees describing the pilot's behavior. Also Pomerleau et al. (1994) developed an autonomous vehicle-driving system that he entitled Autonomous Land Vehicle in a neural network (ALVINN), using neural networks that were trained by observing how human drivers responded to diverse driving environments. ALVINN was trained to drive in a variety of conditions, including single-lane paved and unpaved roads, multilane roads, obstacle ridden on-road and off-road environments, and even under adverse environmental conditions like rain and snow, at speeds up to 55 miles an hour. Wang (1995) also described another system that learned to produce machine parts through observation. OBSERVER recorded each step the expert performed to generate the machine part and had the ability to learn operator preconditions and the corresponding actions for each step, even refining its actions through practice. Sidani and Gonzalez (1995) also captured the behavior of an expert automobile driver by observing his actions in a simulated task. In their work, they built a system based on neural networks and symbolic reasoning that learned by observing the expert driver's behavior. The system successfully operated a car at a traffic light as well as in the presence of a pedestrian crossing in front of the vehicle. Later van Lent and Laird (1999) defined a system they called OBSERVO-SOAR, which combined behavioral cloning with OBSERVER's behavioral representation in order to learn effectively in complex and dynamic domains such as a flight simulator domain.

More recently the term *cognitive imitation,* first introduced by Subiaul et al. (2004), is being used to denote "a type of observational learning in which a naïve student copies an expert's use of a rule." In this sense, cognitive imitation involves imitation with observational learning. Observational learning is not the same as cognitive imitation, because observational learning does not always involve imitation. For example, a student may learn via observation *what not to do,* which implies observational learning without imitation. But the reverse does hold in the sense that imitation requires observational learning.

The modern approach to learning by observation is "to design agents that already know something and are trying to learn some more" (Russell and Norvig 2002). In this sense, the agent must have some way to obtain the background knowledge that it will use to learn new episodes via incremental development. Although systems that learn by observation may still be in their infancy, the early success of these systems has proven the possibility of capturing knowledge from experts through nonintrusive interaction and observation of the behavior of the human expert. Perhaps the science fiction idea of plugging in expertise through an electronic socket behind our ears is not such a remote possibility after all. Do you want to be a rocket scientist? Just put on your rocket scientist eyeglasses, and voilá!

The next section discusses the role of radio-frequency identification (RFID) technology in knowledge capture.

RADIO FREQUENCY IDENTIFICATION

Consider the following scenarios:

> On a snowy slope in Norway, a skier glides to the lift and goes right through the turnstile without slowing to show a ticket. In a Danish suburb, a woman's blood pressure is monitored as she weeds her garden. And during a safety drill at a Canadian oil refinery, over 200 workers are rapidly evacuated and instantly accounted for (IBM 2007).

All of these scenarios have one thing in common: **radio frequency identification** or, in short, **RFID**. In the last ten years RFID, a technology that was originally developed for radio and radar applications, has taken center stage in capturing information for the purpose of identification via radio waves. The first paper that explored RFID technology was the seminal paper by Harry Stockman in which he describes that "point-to-point communication, with the carrier power generated at the receiving end and the transmitter replaced by a modulated reflector, represents a transmission system which possesses new and different characteristics. Radio, light, or soundwaves (essentially microwaves, infrared, and ultrasonic waves) may be used for the transmission under approximate conditions of specular reflection" (1948, p. 1196). Even though Stockman states in that same paper that "considerable research and development work has to be done before the remaining basic problems in reflected-power communication are solved, and before the field of useful applications is explored"

(1948, p. 1204), the field of RFID has seen a dramatic surge of useful applications just in the last couple of years. Even though commercial activities would start in the 1960s, the 1980s saw the first significant implementations of RFID in the United States primarily for transportation interests such as toll collection (Landt 2001). RFID is the combination of radio broadcast with radar technology, and consists of two parts: an RFID tag which is an integrated circuit that modulates and demodulates a radio frequency signal and processes and stores information. The second part is an antenna that receives and transmits the signal. There are three kinds of RFID tags: passive (which have no battery and the power is supplied by the reader[3]), active (which have a power supply[4]), and semi-passive (which have a power supply that powers the tag). The difference among the three lies in that for passive tags, the power level to power up the RFID circuitry must be 100 times stronger than with active or semi-active tag. In addition, condition-sensing tags include a battery and the electronic circuitry to read and transmit diagnostics back to the reader. The tags monitor the environmental conditions and communicate and collect data that are later transmitted to back-end systems using network software (IBM 2007).

Applications of RFID technology today help improve inventory tracking and supply chain management. Since 2005, Wal-Mart mandated the use of RFID on all shipments in order to improve their supply chain and recently Sam's Club, a Wal-Mart division, announced that companies that supply them with goods that didn't meet their RFID tagging requirements would need to pay a service fee (Bachelor 2008). Manufacturers are increasingly looking to include RFID tags in their products in order to better manage their inventories and their work in progress, and as many as 40 percent of U.S. manufacturers are expecting to deploy RFID by 2010 (Kharif 2005). One area where RFID is making a big impact is in asset management. For example, hospitals are increasingly using RFID technology to locate expensive equipment using real-time location systems (RTLS), in addition to using RFID to improve their surgical room throughput and patient flow. In short, RFID tags and services in healthcare are expected to grow into a US$2.1 billion industry by 2016 (Raths 2008).

From the KM perspective, the promise of RFID will continue to generate huge returns in better inventory management for manufacturers, hospitals, and retail stores. RFID tags have also been implanted in animals, for example, to track livestock such as cattle (Gumpert and Pentland 2007) and also humans who are wary about abductions (Haines 2004). But the use of RFID implants in humans is also meeting great criticism as the debate grows about the privacy implications that this technology could pose in the hands of authoritarian governments that could use them to remove individuals' freedom (Monahan and Wall 2007). Should we then get a chip on our shoulders?

SUMMARY

In this chapter, you learned the definitions and characteristics of knowledge capture systems and design considerations and various types of such systems. Specific attention was placed on the two knowledge capture systems based on different methodologies and intelligent technologies. The first system is based on the use of concept maps as a knowledge-modeling tool and is best suited to capture the knowledge of experts when supporting educational settings. The second system is based on the use of context-based reasoning to simulate human behavior and is best suited to capture the tactical knowledge of experts. Finally, the use of stories in organizational settings was discussed as a mechanism that can support knowledge capture.

KEY TERMS

Alternative histories
Anthropological observation
Archetypal character
Concept maps
CmapTools
Context-based Intelligent Tactical
   Knowledge Acquisition (CITKA)
Context-based reasoning (CxBR)
Dit-spinning
Indirect stories
Knowledge capture mechanisms
Knowledge capture systems
Main context
Metaphor
Mission context

Narrative databases
Organizational stories
Radio frequency identification
   (RFID)
Semantic unit or propositions
Shifting character or context
Springboard stories
Stakeholders
Storytelling
Storytelling circles
Strategic knowledge
Subcontexts
Subject matter expert (SME)
Tactical knowledge

REVIEW

1. What is a concept map?
2. What is context-based reasoning?
3. How would you describe the domains that are best suited to be captured by concept maps versus context-based reasoning?
4. Describe the two techniques for knowledge elicitation via the use of stories.
5. What types of knowledge can be acquired through automated knowledge by observation?

APPLICATION EXERCISES

1. Pick a sample domain in which you're knowledgeable and build a concept map to represent that domain.
2. Define, using context-based hierarchy, the main contexts and subcontexts of the mission context that describes your particular driving pattern from home to work each day.
3. Define the rules that will cause the switch between main contexts and subcontexts in the aforementioned context hierarchy.

4. Describe a story that adequately embodies your organization's corporate culture.
5. Describe a specific type of knowledge that could adequately be captured through automated knowledge by observation.

Notes

1. CmapTools can be downloaded for free at http://cmap.ihmc.us.
2. A medical procedure to assess how well the heart is beating when at rest and also when exercising. Also known as MUGA test. During the test, a small amount of radioactive material is injected into the patient so pictures can be taken of the blood in the heart. Experienced cardiologists are able to detect pathological conditions by abstracting a familiar shape from this image, which may resemble *asymmetric blue fingers,* a *ballerina's foot,* or an *ice cream cone.*
3. When the passive tag encounters radio waves from the reader, the coiled antenna within the tag forms a magnetic field that draws power to the tag, energizing the circuits in the tag. The tag then sends the data stored in the tag's memory (IBM 2007).
4. Active RFID tags are outfitted with a battery, which can serve as a partial or complete power source for the tag's circuitry and antenna. Some active tags are equipped with replaceable batteries for years of use while others are sealed (IBM 2007).

References

Ausubel, D.P. 1963. *The psychology of meaningful verbal learning.* New York: Grune and Stratton.
Bachelor, B. 2008. Sam's Club tells suppliers to tag or pay. *RFID Journal,* January 11.
Cañas, A.J., Coffey, J., Reichherzer, T., Suri, N., and Carff, R. 1997. El-Tech: A performance support system with embedded training for electronics technicians. *Eleventh Florida Artificial Intelligence Research Symposium,* Sanibel Island, FL, May.
Cañas, A.J., Ford, Novak, J., Hayes, P., Reichherzer, T., and Suri, N. 2001. Online concept maps: Enhancing collaborative learning by using technology with concept maps. *The Science Teacher,* 68(4), 49–51.
Cañas, A., Hill, G., Carff, R., Suri, N., Lott, J., and Eskridge, T. 2004. CmapTools: A knowledge modeling and sharing environment. In *Concept maps: Theory, methodology, technology: Proceedings of the First International Conference on Concept Mapping,* vol. I, ed. A.J. Cañas, J.D. Novak, and F. M. Gonzalez, 125–133. Pamplona, Spain: Unversidad Publica de Navarra.
Cañas, A., Hill, G., Granados, A., Perez, C., and Perez, J. 2003. *The network architechture of Cmap tools.* Technical Report No. IHMC CmapTools 2003–01. Pensacola, FL: Institute for Human and Machine Cognition.
Cañas, A. and Novak, J. 2005. *A concept map-centered learning environment.* Paper presented at the Symposium at the 11th Biennial Conference of the European Association for Research in Learning and Instruction (EARLI), Cyprus, August 24.
Clark, E. 2004. *Around the corporate campfire: How great leaders use stories to inspire success.* Sevierville, TN: Insight Publishing Co.
Denning, S. 2000. *The springboard: How storytelling ignites action in knowledge-era organizations.* Boston: Butterworth-Heinemann.
———. 2005. *The leader's guide to storytelling: Mastering the art and discipline of business narrative.* San Francisco: Jossey-Bass/Wiley.
Ford, K.M., Cañas, A.J., Jones, J., Stahl, H., Novak, J., and Adams-Weber, J. 1991. ICONKAT: An integrated constructivist knowledge acquisition tool. *Knowledge Acquisition,* 3, 215–236.
Ford, K.M., Coffey, J.W., Cañas, A.J., Andrews, E.J., and Turner, C.W. 1996. Diagnosis and explanation by a nuclear cardiology expert system. *International Journal of Expert Systems,* 9, 499–506.
Gonzalez, A.J. and Ahlers, R.H. 1993. Concise representation of autonomous intelligent platforms in

a simulation through the use of scripts. In *Proceedings of the Sixth Annual Florida Artificial Intelligence Research Symposium,* Ft. Lauderdale, FL, April.

———. 1998. Context based representation of intelligent behavior in training simulations. *Transactions of the Society of Computer Simulation,* 15(4), 153–166.

Gonzalez, A.J., Georgiopoulos, M., DeMara, R.F., Henninger, A.E., and Gerber, W. 1998. Automating the CGF model development and refinement process by observing expert behavior in a simulation. In *Proceedings of the 1998 Computer Generated Forces Conference,* Orlando, FL, May.

Gonzalez, A.J., Gerber, W.J., and Castro, J. 2002. Automated acquisition of tactical knowledge through contextualization. In *Proceedings of the Conference on Computer Generated Forces and Behavior Representation,* Orlando, FL, May.

Gonzalez, A., Stensrud, B., and Barret, G. 2008. Formalizing context based reasoning-A modeling paradigm for representing tactical human behavior. *Journal of Intelligent Systems,* 23(7), 822–847.

Guber, P. 2007. The four truths of the storyteller. *Harvard Business Review,* 85(12), 55–56.

Gumpert, D. and Pentland, W. 2007. USDA bets the farm on animal ID program. *The Nation,* December 14.

Haines, L. 2004. Kidnap-wary Mexicans get chipped—shot in the arm for RFID? *The Register,* July 14.

International Business Machines (IBM). 2007. Keeping tabs on RFID—It's way more than barcodes and it's changing the way the world works. *Ideas from IBM,* June 12. http://www.ibm.com/ibm/ideasfromibm/us/rfid/061207/images/RFID_061207.pdf (accessed August 24, 2008).

Kharif, O. 2005. RFID's second wave. *Business Week,* August 9.

Landt, J. 2001. Shrouds of time: The history of RFID. *Association for Automatic Identification and Data Capture Technologies (AIM) Publications.* http://www.aimglobal.orgon (accessed August 16, 2008).

Monahan, T. and Wall, T. 2007. Somatic surveillance: Corporeal control through information networks. *Surveillance and Society,* 4(3), 154–173.

Novak, J.D. 1998. *Learning, creating, and using knowledge: Concept maps as facilitative tools in schools and corporations.* Mahwah, NJ: Lawrence Erlbaum Associates.

Novak, J.D. and Cañas, A. 2008. *The theory underlying concept maps and how to construct them.* Technical Report IHMC CmapTools 2006–01 Rev 01–2008, Florida Institute for Human and Machine Cognition. http://cmap.ihmc.us/Publications/ResearchPapers/TheoryUnderlyingConceptMaps.pdf.

Novak, J.D. and Gowin, D.B. 1984. *Learning how to learn.* New York: Cambridge University Press.

Phoel, C.M. 2006. Leading words: How to use stories to change minds and ignite action. *Harvard Management Communication Letter,* Spring, 3–5.

Pomerleau, D., Thorpe, D., Longer, J., Rosenblatt, K., and Sukthankar, R. 1994. AVCS Research at Carnegie-Mellon University. *Proceedings of the Intelligent Vehicle Highway Systems America 1994, Annual Meeting,* 257–262.

Post, T. 2002. The impact of storytelling on NASA and EduTech. *Knowledge Management Review,* March/April.

Raths, D. 2008. Hospitals play tag—RFID finds a niche in healthcare. *KM World,* July 11.

Ready, D. 2002. How storytelling builds next-generation leaders. *Sloan Management Review,* 43(4), 63–69.

Russell, S. and Norvig, P. 2002. *Artificial intelligence: A modern approach.* Upper Saddle River, NJ: Pearson Education.

Sammut, C., Hurst, S., Kedzier, D., and Michie, D. 1992. Learning to fly. In *Proceedings of the Ninth International Conference on Machine Learning,* ed. D. Sleeman, 385–393. San Francisco: Morgan Kauffmann.

Shaw, G., Brown, R., and Bromiley, P. 1998. Strategic stories: How 3M is rewriting business planning. *Harvard Business Review,* May–June, 41–50.

Sidani, T.A. and Gonzalez, A.J. 1995. IASKNOT: A simulation-based, object-oriented framework for the acquisition of implicit expert knowledge. In *Proceedings of the IEEE International Conference on System, Man and Cybernetics,* Vancouver, Canada, October.

Snowden, D. 1999. Three metaphors, two stories, and a picture. *Knowledge Management Review,* March/April.

———. 2000. The art and science of story or are you sitting uncomfortably? Part 1: Gathering and harvesting the raw material. *Business Information Review,* 17(3), 147–156.

Stensrud, B.S. 2005. *FAMTILE: An algorithm for learning high-level tactical behavior from observation.* Doctoral Dissertation, Department of Electrical and Computer Engineering, University of Central Florida, May.

Sternberg, S. 1975. Memory scanning: New findings and current controversies. *Quarterly Journal of Experimental Psychology,* 27, 1–32.

Stockman, H. 1948. Communication by means of reflected power. *Proceedings of the Institute of Radio Engineers,* 36(10), 1196–1204.

Subiaul, F., Cantlon, J., Holloway, R.L., and Terrace, H.S. 2004. Cognitive imitation in Rhesus Macaques. *Science,* 305(5682), 407–410.

Swap, W., Leonard, D., Shields, M., and Abrams, L. 2001. Using mentoring and storytelling to transfer knowledge in the workplace. *Journal of Management Information Systems,* 18(1), 95–114.

Thorndike, P.W. and Wescort, K.T. 1984. *Modeling time-stressed situation assessment and planning for intelligent opponent simulation.* Final Technical Report PPAFTR-1124–84–1, Office of Naval Research, July.

Tulving, E. 1983. *Elements of episodic memory.* New York: Oxford University Press.

van Lent M. and Laird, J. 1999. Learning hierarchical performance knowledge by observation. In *Proceedings of the Sixteenth International Conference on Machine Learning,* ed. I. Bratko and S. Dzeroski. San Francisco: Morgan Kaufmann.

Wang, X. 1995. Learning by observation and practice: An incremental approach for planning operator acquisition. In *Proceedings of the Twelfth International Conference on Machine Learning,* ed. A. Prieditis and S.J. Russell. San Francisco: Morgan Kauffman.

8 Knowledge Sharing Systems: Systems that Organize and Distribute Knowledge

In the last chapter, we discussed knowledge capture systems. In this chapter, we discuss what knowledge sharing systems are about, how they serve to organize and distribute organizational and individual knowledge, what constitutes their makeup, and provide examples of such systems. Knowledge sharing systems are designed to help users share their knowledge, both tacit and explicit. Most of the knowledge management systems in place at organizations are designed to share the explicit knowledge of individuals and organizations, and these are the focus of this chapter. These systems are also referred to as *knowledge repositories*. In this chapter we also discuss some guidelines on how to design knowledge sharing systems for practical use. The two types of explicit knowledge sharing systems most widely discussed in the KM literature are lessons learned systems and expertise locator systems; therefore this chapter concentrates on those. Systems that support tacit knowledge sharing are those typically utilized by communities of practice, particularly those that meet virtually. Finally, we discuss issues about communities of practice and how KM systems can support tacit knowledge sharing.

Corporate memory (also known as an organizational memory) is made up of the aggregate intellectual assets of an organization. It is the combination of both explicit and tacit knowledge that may or may not be explicitly documented but which is specifically referenced and crucial to the operation and competitiveness of an organization. Knowledge management is concerned with developing applications that will prevent the loss of corporate memory. Such loss often results from a lack of appropriate technologies for the organization and exchange of documents, lack of adequate support for communication, and the proliferation of disparate sources of information. Often this results in the loss of explicit **organizational knowledge**. Another contributing factor to the loss of corporate memory is the departure of employees because of either turnover or retirement. The lost knowledge is typically the organization's tacit knowledge. A knowledge sharing system helps to organize and distribute an organization's corporate memory so that it can be accessed even after the original sources of knowledge no longer remain within the organization.

The standard communications medium upon which KM applications are based is the World Wide Web, a medium that facilitates the exchange of information, data, multimedia, and even applications among multiple distinct computer platforms. This characteristic of the Web is referred to as *platform independence*. Because the

Web is pervasive and can interface with different computer platforms through a common user interface, it is often the base upon which knowledge sharing systems are created.

For a quick overview of what knowledge sharing systems are and how they are used, let us look at how two organizations view knowledge sharing. The following boxes explain how Ernest & Young, a professional services organization, and the Center for Advancing Microbial Risk Assessment (CAMRA), funded by the Environmental Protection Agency and Department of Homeland Security successfully introduced knowledge sharing systems to share important knowledge. Box 8.1 discusses some of the KM experiences at a professional services organization in the business of providing its clients with the knowledge they require to effectively compete and succeed.

Ernst & Young's KM initiatives specifically support knowledge sharing. These initiatives earned the firm many accolades for their leadership in KM in addition to a competitive advantage. In Box 8.2, we review how a group of diverse researchers share knowledge across different federal agencies.

What Are Knowledge Sharing Systems?

Knowledge sharing systems can be described as systems that enable members of an organization to acquire tacit and explicit knowledge from each other. Knowledge sharing systems may also be viewed as *knowledge markets*: just as markets require adequate liquidity[1] to guarantee a fair exchange of products, knowledge sharing systems must attract a critical volume of knowledge seekers and knowledge owners in order to be effective (Dignum 2002). In a knowledge sharing system, knowledge owners will:

1. want to share their knowledge with a controllable and trusted group,
2. decide when to share and the conditions for sharing, and
3. seek a fair exchange, or reward, for sharing their knowledge.

By the same token, knowledge seekers may:

1. not be aware of all the possibilities for sharing, thus the knowledge repository will typically help them through searching and ranking, and
2. want to decide on the conditions for knowledge acquisition.

A knowledge sharing system is said to define a learning organization, supporting the sharing and reuse of individual and organizational knowledge. One tool frequently emphasized under the auspices of knowledge sharing systems is document management. At the core of a document management system is a repository, an electronic storage medium with a primary storage location that affords multiple access points. The document management system essentially stores information. This repository can be centralized or it can be distributed. Document management builds upon the repository by adding support to the classification and organization of information, unifying the actions of storage and retrieval of documents over a platform-independent system. A

Box 8.1

Ernst & Young: The Development of a Knowledge Organization

In 1995, Ernst & Young[1] underwent an important restructuring of their business strategy. This restructuring was designed to facilitate a move towards knowledge management. It included capturing and leveraging knowledge from consulting engagements. Another aspect of the revised strategy was to use knowledge to accelerate the process of providing consulting solutions for clients. This strategy led to the creation of several different KM initiatives within the company.

One such KM initiative was the establishment of the Center for Business Knowledge (CBK) and its network of local centers, with the goal of harvesting the knowledge of the firm's employees and enabling firm-wide knowledge sharing practices to meet their client needs and support their employees. The CBK served as a library for consulting methods and techniques as well as documents resulting from client engagements. Moreover, this center was created with the idea of distributing and integrating the knowledge of all the projects. The North American CBK employs 200 staff members that work to ensure that North American professionals have the required resources necessary to apply the experience and thought leadership of their colleagues throughout the world.

Ernst & Young's CBK uses many tools and methods to assist their client-serving professionals. The firm's Global Knowledge Steering group recognized early on that the key to leveraging knowledge capital is through the way people work together across business units and geographic boundaries, and the group focused its efforts on developing a knowledge sharing culture underpinned by a robust information and knowledge management infrastructure that included (Dellow 2004):

1. A collection of 22 standardized computer-mediated tools that support both synchronous as well as asynchronous collaboration. The KM infrastructure pivots on the firm's award-winning KnowledgeWeb (KWeb) which is home to more than 4,600 databases and Web sites that provide employees with access to internal and external resources including business knowledge, intelligence, global news, and information.
2. A strong sociotechnical support system to help people effectively engage with these tools in practice. In fact, to better connect Ernst & Young professionals the firm is renovating its people directories and experimenting with social network resources like for example using blogs as collaboration tools.
3. Knowledge centers in 10 countries supported by over 400 staff support employees.

At Ernst & Young the investments made in the development of the right collaborative infrastructure included more than the investment on the right technology, and the support provided by the CBK is what enabled the business to succeed. Knowledge management is a visible leadership priority and an integral part of the organization's business strategy. Ernst & Young's success is based on the successful development of the shared technology platforms coupled with the knowledge management function of the CBK (Dellow 2004). For its innovative workplace initiatives, Ernst & Young was named global Most Admired Knowledge Enterprises (MAKE) for the past ten years, was recognized by *Fortune* magazine as one of "100 Best Companies to Work For" for the past nine years, and won the "Best Information/Knowledge Team in a Business Environment" by the International Information Industry for the past two years.

[1]We acknowledge Maria Thomas of Ernst & Young Center for Business Knowledge for contributing to this box.

---

document management system aggregates relevant information through a common typically Web-based interface. The document management collaborative application increases communication, thus allowing the sharing of organizational knowledge.

The document management application increases the sharing of documentation across the organization, which helps in the sharing of organizational knowledge.

Box 8.2

Sharing Scientific Knowledge at CAMRA

Following the anthrax attacks in Washington, DC, and Florida in 2001, the Environmental Protection Agency and Department of Homeland Security jointly funded the Center for Advancing Microbial Risk Assessment (CAMRA) to broaden and consolidate knowledge of Bacterial Agents of Concern.[1] The CAMRA team is composed of researchers with diverse backgrounds: engineers, epidemiologists, and health, computer, and information scientists, working on five different projects and spread across seven different universities.

The CAMRA Knowledge Repository (KR) is a repository-based KM system built to meet the needs of this multidisciplinary user-base. Its design was based on knowledge engineering principles, lessons learned and best practices systems, and KM studies on failure prevention. The CAMRA KM approach is aimed at supporting the tasks of knowledge sharing and leveraging, collaboration, and integration (Weber et al. 2006). First, the CAMRA KR adopts a representation for knowledge artifacts that is both minimal and sufficient, which facilitates the transparency of research activities and encourages knowledge sharing and reuse among the community. Second, human intermediation is provided by knowledge facilitators who fill technological gaps by educating users on the importance of the approach, helping to build a culture of sharing and collaboration. Finally, users are asked to identify connections between their contributions and existing contributions by creating associations between knowledge artifacts.

Version 1.0 of the CAMRA KR was released in 2006. In the first two years of use, researchers contributed 177 knowledge artifacts and made 93 associations. As an indication that the CAMRA KR is successfully supporting the task of knowledge sharing and leveraging, 76 percent of associations were between artifacts contributed by different authors and 22 percent were between artifacts across different projects. Version 2.0 is expected to be released by early 2009 and will support the tasks of collaboration and integration by generating knowledge maps to demonstrate how researchers' contributions are connected to the rest of the community and to allow researchers to discover potential collaborators. The new version will also include automatically generated reports to compensate researchers for the time and effort needed to share research activities.

[1] We acknowledge Sid Gunawardena, Rosina Weber, and Craig MacDonald for authoring this box.

Documents are typically organized or indexed following a standard hierarchical structure or classification taxonomy, much like the index catalog is used to organize the books in a library. Frequently, *portal* technologies are used to build a common entry into multiple distributed repositories, using the analogy of a "door" as a common entry into the organization's knowledge resources. Portals provide a common user interface, which can often be customized to the user's preferences such as local news, weather, and so forth.

In its purest sense, workflow represents the automation of a business process. A workflow management system (WfMS) is a set of tools that support defining, creating, and managing the execution of workflow processes (Workflow Management Coalition 1999); in other words, they provide a method of capturing the steps that lead to the completion of a project within a fixed time frame. In doing so, it provides a method for illustrating such steps. WfMS have been around on factory assembly lines for some time. By automating many of their routine business processes, companies are able to save time and valuable human resources. Workflow systems can be useful for projects by enacting its elemental tasks, as well as by providing a mechanism for the analysis and optimization of the entire process detailing the project. Also, workflow systems provide a mechanism for the analysis and optimization of the entire process that make up a project. One benefit of using a WfMS is that it provides the user with an audit of necessary skills and resources prior to project initiation. Workflow systems also provide a platform for the replication and reuse of stored processes. Finally, WfMS can also serve as a training tool since they provide a broad overview with detailed operations of tasks as well as an identification of possible "weak links" in a process.

WfMS can serve as the basis for **collaborative computing**, as evidenced by their growing popularity. A collaborative environment (which allows the informal exchange of ideas) combined with a detailed workflow (which captures process steps) is an efficient method for streamlining business practices. A document management system unifies an aggregate of relevant information conveniently in one location through a common interface. Categorizing and processing information for search purposes provides a detailed knowledge warehouse. The collaborative application increases communication, thus allowing the sharing of organizational knowledge. Information technology tools like document management systems, groupware, e-mail, databases, chat groups, discussion forums, videoconferencing technologies, and workflow management systems, which historically were used for singular unrelated purposes are now typically integrated into knowledge sharing systems. Although there are benefits of using these tools independently of each other, their integration in a knowledge sharing system augments their individual contributions. The document management system essentially stores information. The electronic documents are usually organized and relevant to its hierarchical structure. The workflow, which details the steps involved in completing a project, combined with a central repository that contains information relevant to a project, provides added benefits. The most important benefits, according KM theory, are the elicitation and capturing of organizational know-how that typically is not captured by most information systems, as well as an obvious user interface to access and reuse this organizational know-how. Collaborative computing provides a common communication space, improves sharing of knowledge, provides a mechanism for real-time feedback on the tasks being performed, helps to optimize processes, and results in a centralized knowledge warehouse.

Collaborative environments support the work of teams, which may not necessarily be present at the same time or same place. Groupware allows the informal exchange of ideas, increasing organizational communication and thus allowing the sharing of knowledge. Knowledge management mechanisms, discussed in Chapter 3, facilitate the use of knowledge sharing systems. For example, meetings and communities of practice facilitate knowledge sharing, as illustrated in Box 8.1 earlier in the chapter. This part of the chapter also examines the use of knowledge management mechanisms such as communities of practice for sharing tacit knowledge.

Traditional information systems are based on a consented interpretation based on the company's business culture and management's needs. Computer-generated information typically does not lend itself to interpretation that produces action, and knowledge implies action based on the information. Today's fast-paced highly competitive business world forces the need for variety and complexity in the interpretation of information generated by computer systems. Group decision-making tools can help companies make better decisions by capturing the knowledge from groups of experts. Furthermore, companies that capture their customers' preferences can improve their customer service, which translates to larger profits (Becerra-Fernandez 1998). In short, knowledge sharing systems integrate the capabilities of document management and collaborative systems along with knowledge management mechanisms. A document management system unifies an aggregate of relevant information through a common, typically Web-based, interface. Categorizing and processing organizational information for search and distribution purposes provides a detailed knowledge warehouse. A collaborative environment that includes workflow is an effective complement to a platform for sharing knowledge across the organization. These systems can later be used as the basis for organizations to further focus their efforts not only in gathering documentation, but also in discovering new knowledge, by mining the knowledge and experiences of their employees, customers, and competitors.

Next, we describe how information and computer technology enable knowledge sharing.

THE COMPUTER AS A MEDIUM FOR SHARING KNOWLEDGE

Much of knowledge management is about communicating knowledge among people. Certainly, knowledge must be applied in order to be useful. However, the wider the application of knowledge is, the more beneficial it is for the organization fostering that interchange of knowledge. Such widespread application comes from communicating the knowledge in its natural or electronically represented form. Furthermore, knowledge bases benefit from widespread contributions which are only possible through wide-ranging communications. In several previous chapters, we discussed some of the leading technologies for capturing and applying knowledge. Now let's look at some of the communications technologies that permit and enhance this sharing of knowledge.

Prior to the information age, two-way communication relied on the telephone's synchronous capability which enabled parties to exchange information much like they did via face-to-face communications. Prior to the telephone, knowledge sharing required asynchronous communication via telegraph and written artifacts. Asynchronous communications allowed communicants to exchange ideas without the need to both be present at the same time, which is one of the limitations offered by the telephone. In addition, the telephone did not facilitate communication of nonverbal multimedia information such as documents, photos, drawings, videos, and others. But the emergence of the Internet and the **World Wide Web** (WWW) would later revolutionize the concept of communications.

The Internet is the underpinning infrastructure that allows the information exchange between computers in remote and heterogeneous networks. The Internet enables the secure transport of information packets. The WWW provides the required format so that a large-scale storage of documents may be accessed by a specialized software package called the *browser*. WWW servers are computers whose main objectives are to serve as repositories of multimedia information. The **Client** refers to that computer that requests information from the WWW server, while servers share their contents to their clients through Web pages. Web pages are hypermedia documents that express, in an organized and often highly artistic and dynamic fashion, the contents of the server. Web pages are files expressed in **Hypertext Markup Language (HTML).** HTML is a standard representation that enables the browser to interpret both text and graphics stored on the Web page. Client browsers process the request for information via the **Uniform Resource Locator (URL)** of a server to be accessed. The URL is of the form

protocol://computer_name:port/document name

where computer name refers to the address of the computer acting as the server, and protocol is the format used by the Web page (typically http, which stands for hypertext transfer protocol). This request causes the file to be displayed to the client. In short, the function of the server is to send the requested file to the client. The browser displays the files received. One important aspect of Web pages is to provide the ability for the client to download documents. This is a critical aspect of knowledge management where documents can be easily shared among a knowledge community.

DESIGNING THE KNOWLEDGE SHARING SYSTEM

The main function of a knowledge sharing system is "to enhance the organization's competitiveness by improving the way it manages its knowledge" (Abecker et al. 1998). The creation of a knowledge sharing system is based on the organization of digital media, including documents, Web-links, and the like, which represent the explicit organizational knowledge. Khun and Abecker (1997) identify the crucial requirements for the success of a knowledge sharing system in industrial practice:

1. *Collection and systematic organization of information from various sources.* Most organizational business processes require information and data including CAD drawings, e-mails, electronic documents such as specifications, and even paper documents. This requisite information may be dispersed through the organization. This first step requires the organization and collection of this information throughout the organization.

2. *Minimization of up-front knowledge engineering.* Knowledge sharing systems must take advantage of explicit organizational information and data such that these systems can be built quickly, generate returns on investment, and adapt to new requirements. This information and data is mostly found in databases and documents.

3. *Exploiting user feedback for maintenance and evolution.* Knowledge sharing systems should concentrate on capturing the knowledge of the organization's members. This includes options for maintenance and user feedback so the knowledge can be kept fresh and relevant. Furthermore, knowledge sharing systems should be designed to support user's needs and their business process workflows.

4. *Integration into existing environment.* Knowledge sharing systems must be integrated into an organization's information flow by integrating with the IT tools currently used to perform the business tasks. Humans, by nature, will tend to avoid efforts to formalize knowledge (ever met a computer programmer that enjoys adding

comments to her code?). In fact, as a rule-of-thumb, if the effort required in formalizing knowledge is too high, it should be left informal to be described by humans and not attempt to be made explicit. For instance, consider the possibility of capturing the "how-to" knowledge, of how to ride a bicycle. Clearly an understanding of the laws of physics can help explain why a person stays on the bicycle while it's moving, but few of us recall these laws while we ride. Other than the proverbial "keep your feet on the pedals" which doesn't explicate much about the riding process, most of us learned to ride a bicycle through hours of practice, and many falls, when we were kids. It would be impractical to try to codify this knowledge and make it explicit. On the other hand, it might be useful to know who's a good bicycle rider, in particular if one is locking to put together a cycling team.

5. *Active presentation of relevant information.* Finally, the goal of an active knowledge sharing system is to present its users with the required information when and wherever it's needed. These systems are envisioned as intelligent assistants, automatically eliciting and providing knowledge that may be useful in solving the current task whenever and wherever it's needed.

BARRIERS TO THE USE OF KNOWLEDGE SHARING SYSTEMS

Many organizations, specifically science- and engineering-oriented firms, are characterized by a culture known as the **not-invented-here syndrome (NIH)**. In other words, solutions that are not invented at the organizational subunit are considered worthless. Organizations suffering from this syndrome tend to essentially reward employees for "inventing" new solutions, rather than reusing solutions developed within and outside the organization. Organizations that foster the not-invented-here syndrome discourage knowledge seekers from participating in the knowledge market, since the organizational rewards are tied to creating knowledge and not necessarily to sharing and applying existing knowledge. Furthermore, organizations that do not reward their experts for sharing their knowledge or that try to disassociate the knowledge from those that create it will also discourage knowledge owners from participating in the knowledge market. The necessary critical volume can only be accomplished through adequate rewards to both knowledge creators and knowledge seekers to participate in the sharing of knowledge.

One of the impediments to nurturing the human component of KM is the lack of institutionalized reward systems for knowledge sharing in most organizations. Typically, rewards exist at the individual level. When a group is rewarded, the reward is usually tied to contributions in *strong tie networks,* such as when people collaborate as a team to develop a new product. It is much more difficult to reward people who contribute in *weak tie networks;* for example, someone who pops into one discussion group and says something that makes people think a bit differently but who is not working in those groups on a long-term basis. Thus, organizations with significant intellectual capital recognize the importance of not only capturing knowledge for later reuse, but also ensuring that adequate reward systems are in place to encourage the sharing of ideas and the life-long learning by their employees.

Recent research has also pointed out some of the other reasons why knowledge sharing systems may fail (Weber 2007). They may fail:

1. If they don't integrate humans, processes, and technology—since technology alone will not achieve acceptance if both people and processes, the main component in delivering organizational goals, are not adequately associated with the knowledge sharing systems (Abecker et al. 2000). In fact, KM approaches are likely to fail if they are designed as stand-alone solutions outside of the process context (Weber and Aha 2003).
2. If they attempt to target a monolithic organizational memory—memories to be useful must be both an artifact that holds its state and an artifact embedded in organizational and individual processes. Furthermore, to be useful memory objects must be decontextualized by the creator and recontextualized by the user. Finally, to be useful memories must tag an authenticity marker (Ackerman and Halverson 2000).
3. If they don't measure and state their benefits—this is a requirement of any successful business initiative which we discussed at length in Chapter 5.
4. If they store knowledge in textual representations—knowledge artifacts that are stored in textual format may lack the adequate representation structure, including long texts that are hard to review, read, and interpret—therefore, almost guaranteeing their lack of reusability and vital contents due to their difficulty in comprehension (Weber and Aha 2003).
5. If users are afraid of the consequences of their contributions—in addition to the importance of the organization to provide incentives for the employees' contributions to the knowledge repository, there may be some organizational barriers that actively act against knowledge sharing. For example, employees may be afraid that their contributions may be taken out of context, may aid competitors, may cause an information security breach, and may lack the necessary validation to be useful to others (Weber et al. 2001).
6. If users perceive a lack of leadership support, lack an understanding of the generalities that would make their knowledge useful, or just don't feel it's worth their time to make a contribution (Disterer 2002).

SPECIFIC TYPES OF KNOWLEDGE SHARING SYSTEMS

Knowledge sharing systems are classified according to their attributes. These specific types of knowledge sharing systems include:

1. Incident report databases
2. Alert systems
3. Best practices databases
4. Lessons learned systems
5. Expertise locator systems

In this section, we briefly describe the differences among the first four systems. Specific attention is placed on the two knowledge sharing systems most frequently discussed in the knowledge management literature: lessons learned systems and expertise locator systems.

INCIDENT REPORT DATABASES

Incident report databases are used to disseminate information related to incidents or malfunctions, for example, of field equipment (like sensing equipment outages) or software (like bug reports). Incident reports typically describe the incident together with explanations of the incident, although they may not suggest any recommendations. Incident reports are typically used in the context of safety and accident investigations. As an example, the U.S. Department of Energy (DOE) disseminates chemical mishaps through their Chemical Occurrences Web page (U.S. DOE 2009).

ALERT SYSTEMS

Alert systems were originally intended to disseminate information about a negative experience that has occurred or is expected to occur. However, recent applications also include increasing exposure to positive experiences. Alert systems could be used to report problems experienced with a technology, such as an alert system that issues recalls for consumer products. Alert systems could also be used to share more positive experiences, such as Grants.gov, which offers registered users alerts to funding opportunities that match a set of user-specified keywords. Alert systems could be applicable to a single organization or to a set of related organizations that share the same technology and suppliers.

BEST PRACTICES DATABASES

Best practices databases describe successful efforts, typically from the re-engineering of **business processes** (O'Leary 1999) that could be applicable to organizational processes. Best practices differ from lessons learned in that they capture only successful events, which may not be derived from experience. Best practices are expected to represent business practices that are applicable to multiple organizations in the same sector and are sometimes used to benchmark organizational processes. For example, Microsoft Corporation offers a Web page that describes best practices for developers using their products (Microsoft Developer Network 2009), which provides helpful tips including how-to and reference documentation, sample code, and technical articles, for instance, on how to prevent database corruption. Also, the Federal Transit Administration publishes a *Best Practices Procurement Manual* on the Web (U.S. DOT 2009). This manual describes procedures and practices for organizations wishing to pursue procurement opportunities with this agency.

LESSONS LEARNED SYSTEMS (LLS)

The goal of lessons learned systems is "to capture and provide lessons that can benefit employees who encounter situations that closely resemble a previous experience in a similar situation" (Weber et al. 2001). LLS could be pure repositories of lessons or be sometimes intermixed with other sources of information (e.g., reports). LLS are

Table 8.1

Types of Knowledge Repositories

Knowledge Sharing System	Originates from experiences?	Describes a complete process?	Describes failures?	Describes successes?	Orientation
Incident Reports	Yes	No	Yes	No	Organization
Alerts	Yes	No	Yes	No	Industry
Lessons Learned System	Yes	No	Yes	Yes	Organization
Best Practices Databases	Possibly	Yes	No	Yes	Industry

Source: Weber et al. 2001.

typically not focused on a single task, for example, pure knowledge representations. In many instances, enhanced document management systems are supporting distributed project collaborations and their knowledge sources while actively seeking to capture and reuse lessons from project report archives.

The differences among these types of knowledge sharing systems are based upon:

- *Content Origin*—Does the content originate from experience like in lessons learned systems or from industry standards and technical documentation as in best practice databases?
- *Application*—Do they describe a complete process or perhaps a task or a decision?
- *Results*—Do they describe failures, as in incident report databases or alert systems, or successes, as in best practices databases?
- *Orientation*—Do they support an organization or a whole industry?

Table 8.1 contrasts these knowledge sharing systems based on these attributes.

In Box 8.3, we describe how a small government contractor was able to achieve a competitive advantage through a business strategy that emphasizes knowledge sharing of its best practices. This box is important in that it proves that KM is not only important to large knowledge-intensive organizations but can also help small organizations gain a competitive advantage and succeed.

LESSONS LEARNED SYSTEMS

Lessons learned systems[2] have become commonplace in organizations and on the Web. The most complete definition of what constitutes a lesson learned is currently used by the American, European, and Japanese space agencies (Weber et al. 2001):

A lesson learned is knowledge or understanding gained by experience. The experience may be positive, as in a successful test or mission, or negative, as in a mishap or failure. Successes are also considered sources of lessons learned. A lesson must be significant in that it has a real or assumed impact on operations; valid in that is factually and technically correct; and applicable in that it identifies a specific design,

Box 8.3

Small Business Knowledge Management Success Story

In January 1999, RS Information Systems, Inc. (RSIS) in McLean, Virginia, was a minority-owned 8(a)[1] small business with annual revenues of $15 million and a total staff numbering 120[2] (Frey 2002). There were no institutional or even *ad hoc* processes in place to identify, audit, collect, archive, and leverage key business and technical knowledge within the company. In other words, it was just like the thousands of other small businesses that provided support services in the federal government market space. The practice of knowledge management was initiated within the company that same year. By the end of CY2001, RSIS closed its financial books with $142 million in revenues and 1,200 staff members nationwide. Six years later, those numbers had rocketed to $364 million in revenue and 1,965 people.

Were KM initiatives integral to the tangible success that RSIS enjoyed? Absolutely!

Their impact was important both at the business development and operations levels. For example, the company was able to develop more high-impact, client-focused winning proposals than ever before and do multiple proposals concurrently. Importantly, the company's bid and proposal (B&P) costs were also contained. By leveraging the business development knowledge base in a process called rapid proposal prototyping, RSIS proposal managers were able to generate first-draft proposal documents quickly with minimal B&P expenditure and little impact on billable technical staff. Direct-charge operations (technical) staff were able to stay focused on their client-support activities rather than be required to spend days at corporate headquarters writing proposals. This practice translated to enhanced customer satisfaction because RSIS' technical professionals stayed on their primary job.

Through knowledge management initiatives, RSIS' operations staff were able to harness best practices and lessons learned from across the company's contractual portfolio and apply these proven solutions quickly to address their specific client's technical and programmatic requirements. This knowledge sharing program facilitated near-real-time solutions and was conducted through a firewalled Intranet and e-mail system. Significantly, knowledge sharing was incentivized and also built into each person's annual performance evaluation.

There were four key ingredients in the RSIS KM success story: (1) a KM champion, an individual who understood and articulated the tangible benefits of knowledge management to executive management as well as business development and operations staff; (2) executive leadership, support, and vision necessary to grasp the value of KM and then fund the processes and clear the internal organizational impediments to knowledge sharing in order to institutionalize this critical business enabler; (3) disciplined and repeatable processes put into place enterprisewide within the company to leverage information and knowledge in near real time; (4) Web-based knowledge management tools, which included infoRouter by Active Innovations, Inc.

Experience has demonstrated the significant business value of launching your company's KM initiative as soon as possible within the corporate life of your firm. This approach does two things. First, there will be less explicit data and information as well as tacit knowledge to collect, review, and categorize. Second, the sooner that your staff develop and hone knowledge-sharing behaviors and skills, the more quickly your firm will emerge as a learning organization—one that adapts and prospers in a high-velocity business environment of unpredictable change.

[1]The Small Business Administration (SBA) 8(a) Business Development Program assists in the development of small businesses owned and operated by individuals who are socially and economically disadvantaged. To be SBA 8a certified, the firm must be a small business (less than 500 employees); must be unconditionally owned and controlled by one or more socially and economically disadvantaged individuals (women or minority) who are of good character and citizens of the United States; and must demonstrate potential for success. Federal acquisition policies encourage federal agencies to award a certain percentage of their contracts to small and disadvantaged (8a) businesses.

[2]We acknowledge Robert S. Frey, author of *Successful Proposal Strategies for Small Businesses: Using Knowledge Management to Win Government, Private-sector, and International Contracts* (Boston: Artech House, 2008), for this box.

Figure 8.1 **Lesson Learned Process**

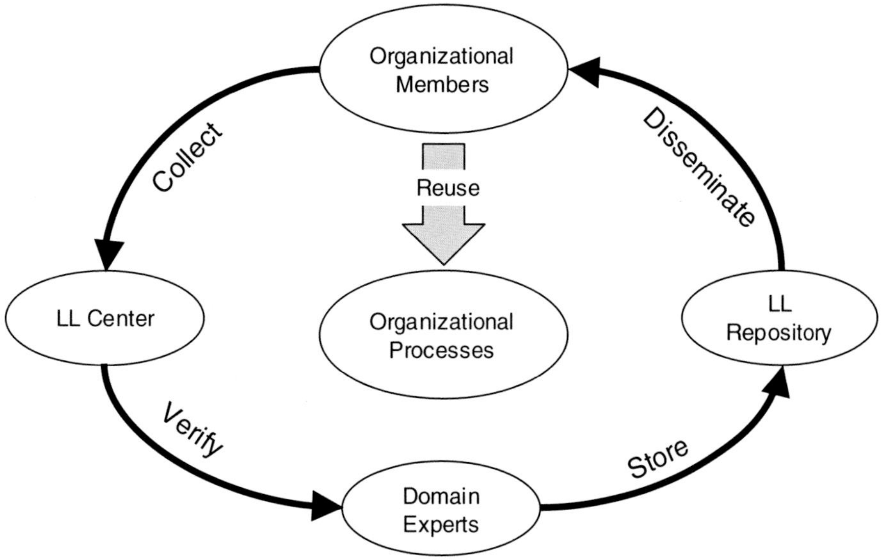

Source: Weber et al. 2001.

process, or decision that reduces or eliminates the potential for failures and mishaps, or reinforces a positive result. (Secchi et al. 1999)

A second definition for LLS and what constitutes a lesson learned follows (Weber and Aha 2003, p. 34):

> Lessons learned systems (LLS) are knowledge management (KM) initiatives structured over a repository of lessons learned (LL). Lessons learned are knowledge artifacts that convey experiential knowledge that is applicable to a task, decision, or process such that, when reused, this knowledge positively impacts an organization's results. For this reason, LLS are ubiquitous in governmental organizations that need to leverage knowledge, such as the Department of Defense (DOD), where military operations may risk human lives, the Department of Energy (DOE), where accident prevention is a major concern, and space agencies (e.g., American space agency [NASA], European Space Agency [ESA], Japanese Space Agencies [NASDA] due to their potential for incurring costly mission failures.

The purpose of LLS is to support organizational processes. Figure 8.1 describes the essential tasks of LLS as *collect, verify, store, disseminate,* and *reuse* (Weber et al. 2001):

1. COLLECT THE LESSONS

This task involves the collecting the lessons (or content) that will be incorporated into the LLS. There are six possible lesson content collection methods:

a. Passive—the most common form of collection. Contributors submit lessons through a paper or Web-based form.

b. Reactive—where contributors are interviewed by a third party for lessons. The third party will submit the lesson on behalf of the contributor.

c. After-action collection—where lessons are collected during a mission debriefing, as for example, in military organizations.

d. Proactive collection—where lessons are automatically collected by an expert system, which may suggest that a lesson exists based on analysis of a specific content. For example, an expert system could monitor an individual's e-mail and prompt him/her when it understands that a lesson is described.

e. Active collection—where a computer-based system may scan documents to identify lessons in the presence of specific keywords or phrases.

f. Interactive collection—where a computer-based system collaborates with the lesson's author to generate clear and relevant lessons.

2. VERIFY THE LESSONS

Typically a team of **domain experts** performs the task required by this component, which requires the verification of lessons for correctness, redundancy, consistency, and relevance. The verification task is critically important, but sometimes introduces a significant bottleneck in the inclusion of lessons into the LLS, since it's a time-consuming process. Some systems, for example Xerox's Eureka LLS, provide a two-stage process. The Eureka LLS, described later in Box 8.4, supports field engineers in solving hard-to-fix repair problems with the company's printers. Contributors can enter fixes into the Eureka LLS. At that point, a team charged with the verification task receives an alert prompting their test of the solution to ensure that it works. If everything checks out, the fix is made available to the rest of the field engineers.

3. STORE THE LESSON

This task relates to the representation of the lessons in a computer-based system. Typical steps in this task include the indexing of lessons, formatting, and incorporating into the repository. In terms of the technology required to support this task, LLS could be based on structured relational or object-oriented databases as well as case libraries (case-based reasoning) or semistructured document management systems. LLS can also incorporate relevant multimedia such as audio and video, which may help illustrate important lessons.

4. DISSEMINATE THE LESSON

This task relates to how the information is shared to promote its reuse. Six different dissemination methods have been identified:

a. Passive dissemination—where users look for lessons using a search engine.
b. Active casting—where lessons are transmitted to users that have specified relevant profiles to that particular lesson.
c. Broadcasting—where lessons are disseminated throughout an organization.
d. Active dissemination—where users are alerted to relevant lessons in the context of their work (for example by a software help-wizard that alerts a user of related automated assistance).
e. Proactive dissemination—where a system anticipates events used to predict when the user will require the assistance provided by the lesson.
f. Reactive dissemination—when a user launches the LLS in response to a specific knowledge need, for example when he launches a Help system in the context of specific software.

5. APPLY THE LESSON

This task relates to whether the user has the ability to decide how to reuse the lesson. There are three categories of reuse:

a. Browsable—where the system displays a list of lessons that match the search criteria.
b. Executable—where users might have the option to execute the lesson's recommendation (as when the word processor suggests a specific spelling for a word).
c. Outcome reuse—when the system prompts users to enter the outcome of reusing a lesson in order to assess if the lesson can be replicated.

Today, many commercial as well as government organizations maintain LLS. Future LLS are expected to integrate advanced intelligent technologies that will alert the decisionmaker of available support in the form of explicit lessons in the context of the decision-making process. Furthermore, LLS are expected to integrate e-mail systems. E-mail messages could be a source for lesson extraction, as many contain historical archives of communications often comprised of specific-case problems, and their solutions that could be mined for organizational lessons. Now we'll see how Xerox successfully developed LLS to support the work of its technicians, with a return on investment of about $15M to the company.

EXPERTISE LOCATOR KNOWLEDGE SHARING SYSTEMS

Several different business organizations have identified the need to develop **expertise locator systems (ELS)** to help locate intellectual capital (Becerra-Fernandez 2006). The main motives for seeking an expert are as a source of information and as someone who can perform a given organizational or social function (Yiman-Seid and Kobsa 2003). The intent when developing these systems is to catalog knowledge competencies, including information not typically captured by human resources systems, in a way that could later be queried across the organization. Box 8.5 illustrates a sample ELS developed across different industries (Becerra-Fernandez 2006).

Box 8.4

Eureka: A Lessons Learned System for Xerox

In the mid-1990s, Xerox's customers reported the lowest customer satisfaction in the company's history. This prompted the company to look at the way the more than 20,000 copier field technicians serviced the machines. Xerox researchers realized field technicians would frequently share fixes over company-provided radios originating from a set of notes that each technician carried.

Researchers developed Eureka in 1996, the first LLS designed to help service technicians detect and solve problems on the road, by integrating each of these original sets of notes. Eureka allows Xerox technicians to share the knowledge about how to better fix Xerox's copy machines. Each service technician is provided with a notebook computer that contains the subset of the Eureka database that is pertinent to his area of expertise. Eureka has an alert system that delivers new fixes according to the subscriber's profile. When a technician uncovers a problem that is not addressed by Eureka, he will submit the fix to the system, including their point of contact. At this point the fix will be sent to a team tasked with verifying the solution to ensure it works. The team then rates and publishes the solution in Eureka. Useless tips were discarded; others were certified as valuable or edited as necessary.

It was agreed that tips would be validated within a few days, and the submitter's name would appear alongside the tip as both reward and incentive (Mitchell 2001). By 2002, the system supported field technicians in 71 countries and stored about 50,000 fixes, which have helped solve about 350,000 problems and has saved Xerox approximately $15M in parts and labor to date (Roberts-Witt 2002).

One interesting outcome of Eureka is that seven years after its development, the outcome of the development and deployment of a system for sharing knowledge from the front lines became a vehicle for organizational change (Bobrow and Whalen 2002). Even though in the beginning of the project, few people in the management ranks at Xerox believed there would be much value in what technicians could learn on their own in the field differently from other suggestions systems, local champions were able to assemble sufficient resources to make the system a go. As the system grew into a major corporate program it faced other challenges, namely that moving to a central organization required a uniform, worldwide approach which was opposite to the original paradigm that tried to adapt to local needs and practices. But one of the most significant outcomes of this system is that Xerox may have become a better learning organization as a result of the Eureka project (Bobrow and Whalen 2002). Other Eureka-like knowledge systems were created at other operational units. For example, LinkLite was developed to support the sales organization. And perhaps this learning organization "spirit" is the most important legacy of Eureka at Xerox (Bobrow and Whalen 2002).

Although ELS across organizations serve a similar purpose, a number of characteristics differentiate these systems:

1. *Purpose of the system:* An ELS may serve a different purpose across organizations. For example the purpose could be to identify experts to help solve technical problems or staff project teams, to match employee competencies with positions within the company, or to perform gap analyses that point to intellectual capital inadequacies within the organization. For instance, if a specific expertise domain is a critical knowledge area for an organization and the ELS points to only three experts, it may serve to identify the need to hire or internally train additional experts in that area.

2. *Access Method:* Most company ELS are accessed via a company's Intranet. However interorganizational systems such as SAGE (Searchable Answer Generating Environment, described later) are accessed via the Web. Systems accessed via the Web

Box 8.5

Examples of Industry Expertise Locator Systems

Hewlett-Packard developed CONNEX, an expertise-locator KMS (Davenport and Prusak 1998). The goal of the project was to build a network of experts, available online, to provide a guide to human knowledge within HP. CONNEX consisted of a centralized database of user knowledge profiles with a Web-browser interface that allowed users to find profiles in multiple ways. User's profiles contained a summary of their knowledge and skills, affiliations, education and interests, as well as contact information. CONNEX users could easily find experts within Hewlett-Packard by searching the database using any combination of profile fields or by browsing through the different areas of knowledge, geographies, and/or names.

   The National Security Agency (NSA) also took steps early on towards the implementation of a system to locate experts (Wright and Spencer 1999). The NSA is part of the "Intelligence Community," and their two missions are Foreign Signals Intelligence and National Information System Security. The goal of the implementation of the Knowledge and Skills Management System (KSMS) ELS was to catalog the talent pool within the agency to allow the precise identification of knowledge and skills and to take advantage of information technology. The NSA went through the development of the system by applying "database engineering" in order to solve the complexities of implementing an adequate, workable, and successful KMS. They also divided the execution of this project into several "Work Tasks" including the development of knowledge taxonomy applicable to their workforce.

   The goal of Microsoft's Skills Planning und (and) development, known as SpuD, was to develop a database containing job profiles available online across the IT group and to help match employee's competency with jobs and work teams. The following are the five major components of the SPuD project (Davenport and Prusak 1998): (1) developing a structure of competency types and levels, (2) defining the competencies required for particular jobs, (3) rating the employees' performance in particular jobs by the supervisors, (4) implementing the knowledge competencies in an online system, and (5) linking the competency models to learning offerings. Note that the validation of the data in this model rested with the supervisor who essentially assigned the competency criteria to each of the employees under his/her supervision.

provide experts with an increased level of visibility, but organizations may fear that such increased visibility may be luring their experts to outside job opportunities.

3. *Self-assessment:* Most of the expertise locator KMS in place today rely on each employee completing a self-assessment of competencies, which is later used when searching for specific knowledge areas. Clearly there're some advantages to this approach, mainly that it allows building a repository of organization-wide competencies quickly. On the other hand, using self-assessment as the way to identify expertise presents an inherent shortcoming, in that the results are based on each person's self-perception and thus could be hard to normalize. Furthermore, employees' speculation about the possible use of this information could skew the results. Employees have been known to either exaggerate their competencies for fear of losing their position or downplay their duties so as not to have increasing responsibilities. For example, one particular organization conducted a skills self-assessment study during a period of downsizing. This resulted in employees' exaggeration of their competencies for fear they might be laid off if they did not appear maximally competent. On the other hand, another organization made it clear the self-assessment would be used to contact people with specific competencies to answer related questions. This resulted in employees downplaying their abilities in order to avoid serving as consultants for the

organization. Microsoft's SPuD system addressed this problem by requiring supervisors to ratify their subordinates' self-perceptions and to assign a quantifiable value to it. Though this can be successful if adhered to, many organizations would find this requirement too taxing on their supervisors.

4. *Participation:* Defines whether the system represents expertise across the organization like at the National Security Agency (NSA), a department at Microsoft, or merely volunteer experts willing to share their knowledge with others.

5. *Taxonomy:* Refers to the specific taxonomy used to index knowledge competencies within the organization. Some organizations like Microsoft developed their own knowledge taxonomy—NSA's was based on O*NET, a standard published by the U.S. Department of Labor, and HP based their taxonomy of an existing standard published by the U.S. Library of Congress augmented by their own knowledge competencies.

6. *Levels of Competencies:* Refers to expressing expertise as capability levels. Levels of competencies could be defined according to Wiig's (1993) levels of proficiency classifications

- Ignorant—Totally unaware
- Beginner—Vaguely aware, no experience
- Advanced beginner—Aware, relatively unskilled
- Competent—Narrowly skilled
- Proficient—Knowledgeable in selected areas
- Expert—Highly proficient in a particular area, generally knowledgeable
- Master—Highly expert in many areas, broadly knowledgeable
- Grand Master—World-class expert in all areas of domain

Other differentiating characteristics for ELS may include technological differences, for example, the type of underlying database, the programming language used to develop the system, or the specifics about how the data are maintained current. Table 8.2 summarizes some of the major characteristics that differentiate the ELS described in Box 8.5 and in the case studies to follow.

THE ROLE OF ONTOLOGIES AND KNOWLEDGE TAXONOMIES IN THE DEVELOPMENT OF EXPERTISE LOCATOR SYSTEMS

A significant challenge in the development of expertise locator KMS is the accurate development of a **knowledge taxonomy** or ontology. Taxonomy is the study of the general principles of scientific classification. **Ontology** is an explicit formal specification of how to represent the objects, concepts, and other entities that are assumed to exist in some area of interest and the relationships that hold among them. Taxonomies, also called classification or categorization schemes, are considered to be knowledge organization systems that serve to group objects together based on a particular characteristic. Knowledge taxonomies allow organizing knowledge or competency areas in the organization. In the case of ELS, the taxonomy is used to identify the critical knowledge areas used to describe and catalog people's knowledge, an important design consideration.

Table 8.2

Summary of Characteristics of Expertise Locator Knowledge Management Systems

ELS Categorization Dimensions	ELS Name				
	CONNEX (HP)	KSMS (NSA)	SPuD (Microsoft)	SAGE (FL Universities)	Expert Seeker (NASA)
Purpose of the System	To share knowledge for consulting and to search for experts	To staff projects and match positions with skills	To compile the knowledge and competency of each employee	To identify expert researchers within FL universities for possible research opportunities	To identify experts in the organization to staff projects and match positions with skills
Self-Assessment	Yes	Yes, supervisors also participate in data gathering	No, supervisors rate employee's performance	No, uses funded research data as the proxy for expertise	Both, self-assessment using competency assessment and database and Web content mining as proxy for expertise
Participation	Only those who are willing to share	Whole personnel	Whole personnel in the IT group	Profiles all researchers at universities (public and private) who are active in funded research in FL	Whole personnel
Knowledge Taxonomy	U.S. Library of Congress; INSPEC Index; Own	Department of Labor (O*NET)	Own	None required	Own for competency assessment, none required for database and Web content mining
Levels of Competencies	No	Yes	Yes	No	Yes
Data Maintenance	User (nagging)	User and Supervisor	Supervisor	Fusion of universities' funded research databases	Optional user maintenance for career summary and competency management, none required for database and Web content mining
Company Culture	Sharing, Open	Technology, Expertise	Technology, Open	Expertise	Technology, Expertise
Platform	HP-9000 Unix, Sybase, and Verity	OS/2, VMS, and Programming Bourne shell	SQL and MS Access	Coldfusion and MS Access	Coldfusion, MS Access, and multiple existing DB platforms

Source: Becerra-Fernandez 2006.

The development of adequate knowledge taxonomies and ontologies could be an expensive, time-consuming, and complex process. Typically, this exercise will require the collaboration of a cross-functional group tasked with defining the organization's most significant knowledge areas. In fact, this development requires consensus across a community whose members may have radically different visions of the domains under consideration (Gruninger and Lee 2002). In practice, organizations typically opt to create small lightweight ontologies that are later merged or seek to reuse formal ontologies developed by consortia and standards organizations (Gruninger and Lee 2002). But the latter solution also faces severe limitations in that it is difficult for users to understand the implicit assumptions and the distinctions between elements in the ontology, thus resulting in inappropriate modeling choices (Guarino and Welty 2002).

In addition, the process of developing knowledge taxonomies is complex because these decisions could play on organizational politics, since lack of representation in the knowledge taxonomy could be considered threatening to organizational subunits. Many ELS systems in place have addressed this consideration keeping in mind that taxonomies should easily describe a knowledge area, provide minimal descriptive text, facilitate browsing, and have the appropriate level of granularity and abstraction. If the level of granularity is too high then the knowledge taxonomy will be too difficult to use, but if the level is too low it will not properly describe the knowledge areas. Figure 8.2 depicts an excerpt from the competence taxonomy developed for NASA Goddard Space Flight Center. The complete taxonomy includes 57 competency areas, many of them with up to 12 additional subareas specified.

As we saw in the previous section, there exist a number of work classification standards that could be used to organize knowledge areas, such as the U.S. Library of Congress, INSPEC database, or the U.S. Department of Labor's O*NET. Using these standards may aid the development of knowledge taxonomies, but it may not be simple to apply any of these standards directly without some thought and further development of the taxonomy.

Taxonomies and ontologies are related to other knowledge organization systems, including semantic networks and authority files. **Semantic networks** serve to structure concepts and terms in networks or webs versus the hierarchies typically used to represent taxonomies. Ontologies are relevant to knowledge management in that they are used to represent complex relationships between objects as rules and axioms, which are not included in semantic networks. **Authority files** are lists of terms used to control the variant names in a particular field, and link preferred terms to nonpreferred terms. Authority files are used to control the taxonomy vocabulary, in particular within an organization. In other words, authority files are used to ensure that everyone in the organization uses the same terms to organize similar concepts.

The use of **Web text data mining** can mitigate some of the problems inherent to relying on biased self-reporting required to keep employee profiles up to date, or the need to develop an accurate knowledge taxonomy *a priori*. This technique draws from an existing pool of information that provides a detailed picture of what the employee knows based on what she already publishes as part of her job, including her Web pages. Web data mining makes use of data mining techniques to extract information from Web-related data. An approach based upon Web data mining re-

Figure 8.2 **Competence Taxonomy for NASA Goddard Space Flight Center**

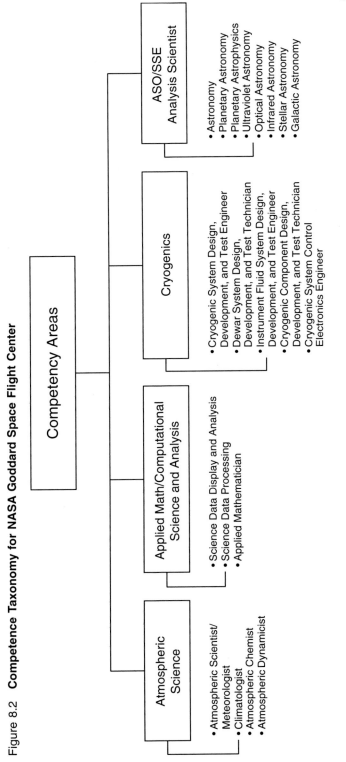

Source: Becerra-Fernandez 2006.

quires minimal user effort to maintain the accuracy of the records, eliminating the need for "nagging" systems that prompt users to maintain their profiles up-to-date. Through Web data mining the collection of expertise data is based on published documents, eliminating the need for possibly biased self-reporting. Using Web data mining this information can be collected automatically, and employee skill information can be kept up-to-date through periodic reprocessing of the document body for documents that are new or have been updated. Chapter 9 discusses Web data mining in more detail.

In the next four case studies, we explore how one premier knowledge organization successfully launched their first Web-based collaboration infrastructure to support teams working at a distance. Then the next three cases explore the development of innovative systems to identify experts either across organizations—in this case across universities in Florida—or within a large organization—in this case NASA and IBM respectively. We first look at the evolution of e-collaboration at NASA.

CASE STUDIES

THE LAUNCH OF VIRTUAL COLLABORATIVE DECISION SUPPORT AT NASA

This section presents how one of the best-known knowledge intensive organizations, the National Aeronautics and Space Administration (NASA), was able to successfully develop a Web-based collaboration system, Postdoc, in order to be able to coordinate complex projects (Becerra-Fernandez et al. 2006, 2007b).

The pioneering research to develop Remote Agent,[3] the innovative software that operated the Deep Space 1 (DS-1) spacecraft and its futuristic ion engine, involved three teams of artificial intelligence experts (from Carnegie Mellon University in Pittsburgh, the Jet Propulsion Lab [JPL] in Pasadena, California, and the NASA Ames Research Center [ARC] in Silicon Valley) who together developed the intelligent software that operated the DS-1 spacecraft more than 60 million miles away from Earth.

Remote Agent required innovations that were considered at that time as highly risky intelligent technologies for systems execution, fault tolerance and recovery, and autonomous planning systems. The Remote Agent design team could not work at the same location due to budget constraints. It was quickly recognized that e-mail would not provide an adequate infrastructure for group work at a distance, so in order to support the team's need for distributed collaboration the Postdoc Web-based collaborative document management system was developed. The first version of Postdoc supported the collaboration and project management needs of the 25-researcher team. As summarized by Kanna Rajan, a computer scientist who participated in the Remote Agent research project:

> Postdoc enabled the team to develop a common language that we used to share our design ideas and start talking about them. We created a token dictionary that enabled the defined team to establish clear semantics that were used to exchange comments among the team members (Becerra-Fernandez et al. 2006, 2007b).

The Postdoc collaborative system was developed by a team comprised of employees at NASA ARC and JPL as well as partners from Stanford University's Center for Design Research and from private industry. The design team recognized the following guiding principles for the collaborative structure: (1) It had to use the emerging Web infrastructure for document uploading, archiving, visualization, and integration; (2) it had to support agency-wide implementation with access controls and authentication capabilities, (3) it had to provide a portable application source; and (4) it had to provide users with features that allowed full control of their information anytime and anywhere. The Postdoc development effort required five-person-years of software coding and testing and became the collaborative infrastructure of choice to support teams throughout NASA in their cooperative research efforts with other NASA facilities, private industry, and academia.

NASA's use of the Postdoc software created agency-wide awareness about how virtual workspaces could be shared among geographically distributed teams. It was estimated that during the period of 1995 to 2004, the use of Postdoc as a collaboration infrastructure resulted in savings to the agency of over US$4M a year. NASA programs across the organization estimated that the use of Web-based collaboration translated in savings in annual travel expenditures of at least $100K and up to $200K. This did not consider the intangible efficiency gains achieved such as eliminating the hardships associated with attaching large documents to e-mails as well as increased document security and integrity.

Postdoc's use grew to support approximately 30 NASA programs, which even included partnerships across the federal government including programs at the Department of Defense, National Institutes of Standards and Technology, Naval Research Laboratories, and the National Imagery and Mapping Agency. Today Postdoc has been successfully migrated into NX, a new KM based technology that leveraged Postdoc's foundation of lessons learned and user requirements (Becerra-Fernandez et al. 2006, 2007b).

OVERVIEW OF THE SEARCHABLE ANSWER GENERATING ENVIRONMENT (SAGE) EXPERT FINDER: LOCATING UNIVERSITY EXPERTISE

This section presents insights and lessons learned from the development of the **Searchable Answer Generating Environment (SAGE) Expert Finder**, which is in the category of ELS (Becerra-Fernandez 1999, 2000a, 2006). The motivation to develop SAGE was based on the National Aeronautics and Space Administration (NASA)–Kennedy Space Center (KSC)'s requirement to partner with Florida experts, as the agency looks to develop new technologies necessary for the continuation of their space exploration missions. The purpose of SAGE was to create a searchable repository of university experts in the state of Florida. Each university in Florida keeps a database of funded research for internal use, but these databases are disparate and dissimilar. The SAGE Expert Finder created a single funded research data warehouse by incorporating a distributed database scheme that could be searched by a variety of fields including research topic, investigator name, funding agency, or university. Figure 8.3 represents the SAGE architecture. In this figure, the canisters in the Florida map represent each of disparate databases at each of the Florida universities.

Figure 8.3 **SAGE Architecture**

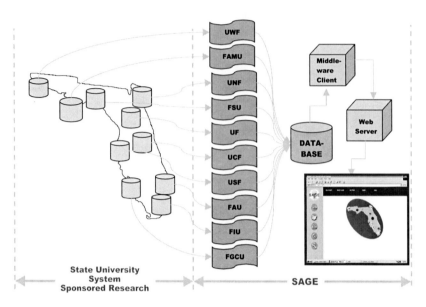

Source: Becerra-Fernandez 2006.

The content of each database was pulled by a file transfer protocol (FTP) client application that automatically obtained and transferred the database contents of each participating university. The file transfer took place according to a prescheduled transfer rule to the SAGE database server, represented by the canister DATABASE. The FTP client was customized to each university, and it is marked by the abbreviations that represent each university: University of West Florida (UWF), Florida Agricultural and Mechanical University (FAMU), University of North Florida (UNF), Florida State University (FSU), University of Florida (UF), University of Central Florida (UCF), Florida Atlantic University (FAU), Florida International University (FIU), and Florida Gulf Coast University (FGCU). After the information is in the SAGE server, the next steps involved the migration of the data to the SQL server format, followed by cleansing and transforming the data to a relational format.

The SAGE system combined the unified database by masking multiple databases as if they were one. This methodology provided flexibility to users and the database administrator, regardless of the type of program used to collect the information at the source. One of the advantages of SAGE was that it provided a single user a point of entry at the Web-enabled interface. The main interfaces developed on the query engine used text fields to search the processed data for key words, fields of expertise, names, or other applicable search fields. The application processed the enduser's query and returned the pertinent information. The SAGE Expert Finder also included an interactive data dictionary or thesaurus and, upon user request, launched a query for similar words.

The development of SAGE was marked by two design requirements: a need to minimize the impact on each of the universities' offices of sponsored research that collect most of the required data and the need to validate the data used to identify experts. For this reason, the system was designed to receive the content in its native form, which made necessary data cleansing at the SAGE server site. SAGE's strength lies in the fact that it validated the data at the source, using the assumption that researchers who successfully obtained funded-research grants were indeed experts in their fields. At that point, a number of database systems existed on the Web that claimed to help the locate experts with a defined profile, such as Community of Science. However, most of these tools relied on people assessing their own skills against a predefined taxonomy, which is inherently unreliable and hard to keep up-to-date. Figure 8.4 illustrates the technologies used to implement SAGE.

One of the technical challenges faced during the design and implementation of this project was that the source databases of funded research from the various universities were dissimilar in design and file format. The manipulation of the source data was one of the most important issues, because the credibility of the system would ultimately depend on the consistency and accuracy of the information. Manipulating the data included the process of cleansing the data, followed by the data transformation into the relational model, and ultimately the databases' migration to a consistent format. One of the most important research contributions of SAGE was the merging of interorganizational database systems.

SAGE made its online debut on August 16, 1999. A demo of SAGE can be viewed at www.kmlab.fiu.edu. NASA personnel have used SAGE to target university researchers for conferences and requests for proposals. SAGE has also been used by small businesses that need to identify research collaborators when pursuing contracts, businesses that need to identify experts who could assist in solving technical problems, and researchers who need to identify potential collaborators.

The SAGE system design required participating institutions to forward the most recent funded research data to a human agent. Then, this human agent uploaded the new data to keep the data repository current. Even though a file transfer protocol utility was developed to facilitate the maintenance of SAGE in a more automated fashion, using funded research as a proxy for expertise limited the SAGE system's ability to identify expertise using only a limited criterion: funded research projects. To overcome this limitation, SAGE could be integrated with other Web-based tools that could expand the criteria for defining domain expertise and thus generate a more complete list of experts. For example, SAGE could be integrated with CiteSeer (Giles et al. 1998), an autonomous citation-indexing system, which indexes academic literature published on the Web. This functionality would allow SAGE to also consider expertise through publications in specific high-quality journals and number of citations. Although, there are inherent limitations to this idea (e.g., CiteSeer is limited to only some scientific fields), it proposes to take advantage of other resources available on the Web to improve the scale of the search. In the future, SAGE could be redesigned to take advantage of intelligent agent techniques, which will increase the scope of researchers that SAGE is able to identify (Becerra-Fernandez et al. 2005). In addition, many data source owners are resistant to providing their data to a "data broker" due to potential privacy issues. An agent approach could serve to overcome this crucial shortcoming by allowing a searching agent locating for an expert to negotiate with

Figure 8.4 **Technologies to Implement SAGE**

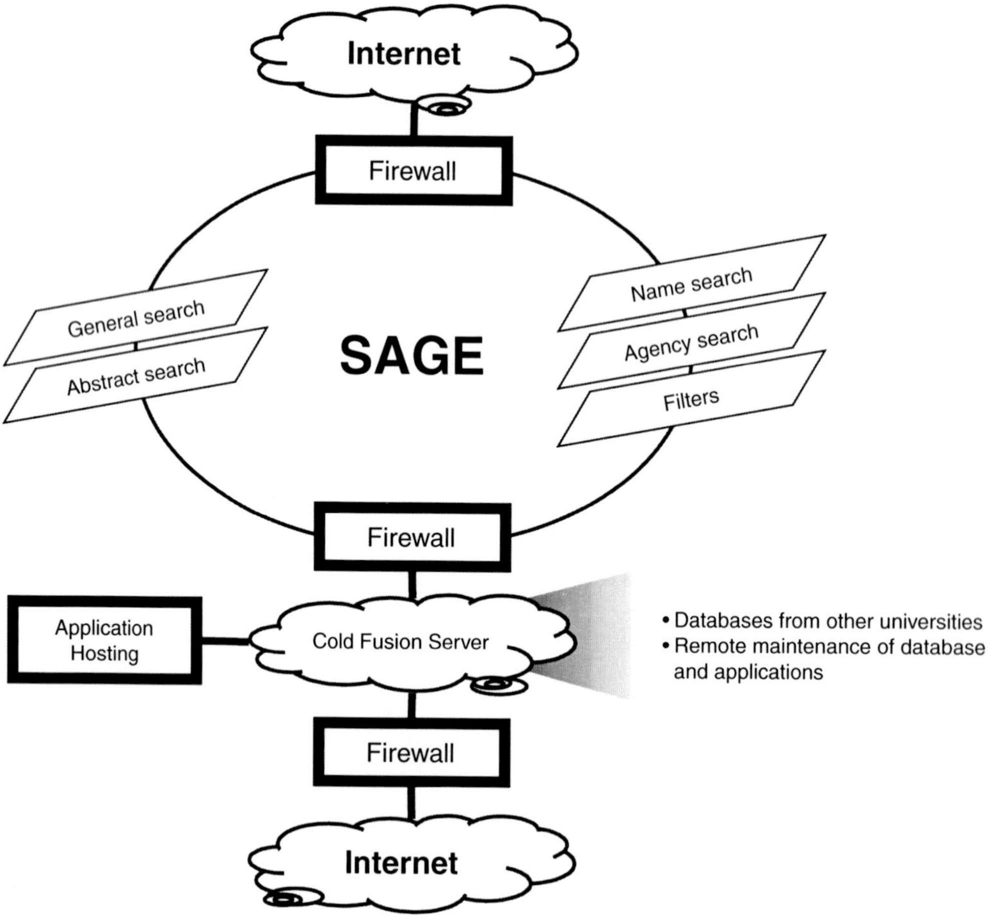

Source: Becerra-Fernandez 1999.

a gatekeeper agent, guarding the data source. The gatekeeper would evaluate the request from the searching agent and only provide the necessary information to build the expert profile, eliminating the need for consolidating data from different sources in an overarching database. This enhancement would make it possible to represent data from a larger number of data sources, enabling the formulation of ELS that could search for experts at a national and even international level. Figure 8.5 depicts the agent-based approach to expertise location (Becerra-Fernandez et al. 2005).

OVERVIEW OF EXPERT SEEKER: LOCATING EXPERTS AT THE NATIONAL AERONAUTICS AND SPACE ADMINISTRATION

What follows presents insights and lessons learned from the development of **Expert Seeker** (Becerra-Fernandez 2000b, 2001, 2006; Becerra-Fernandez and Sabherwal

Figure 8.5 **Event Diagram for an Actor Model-based ELS**

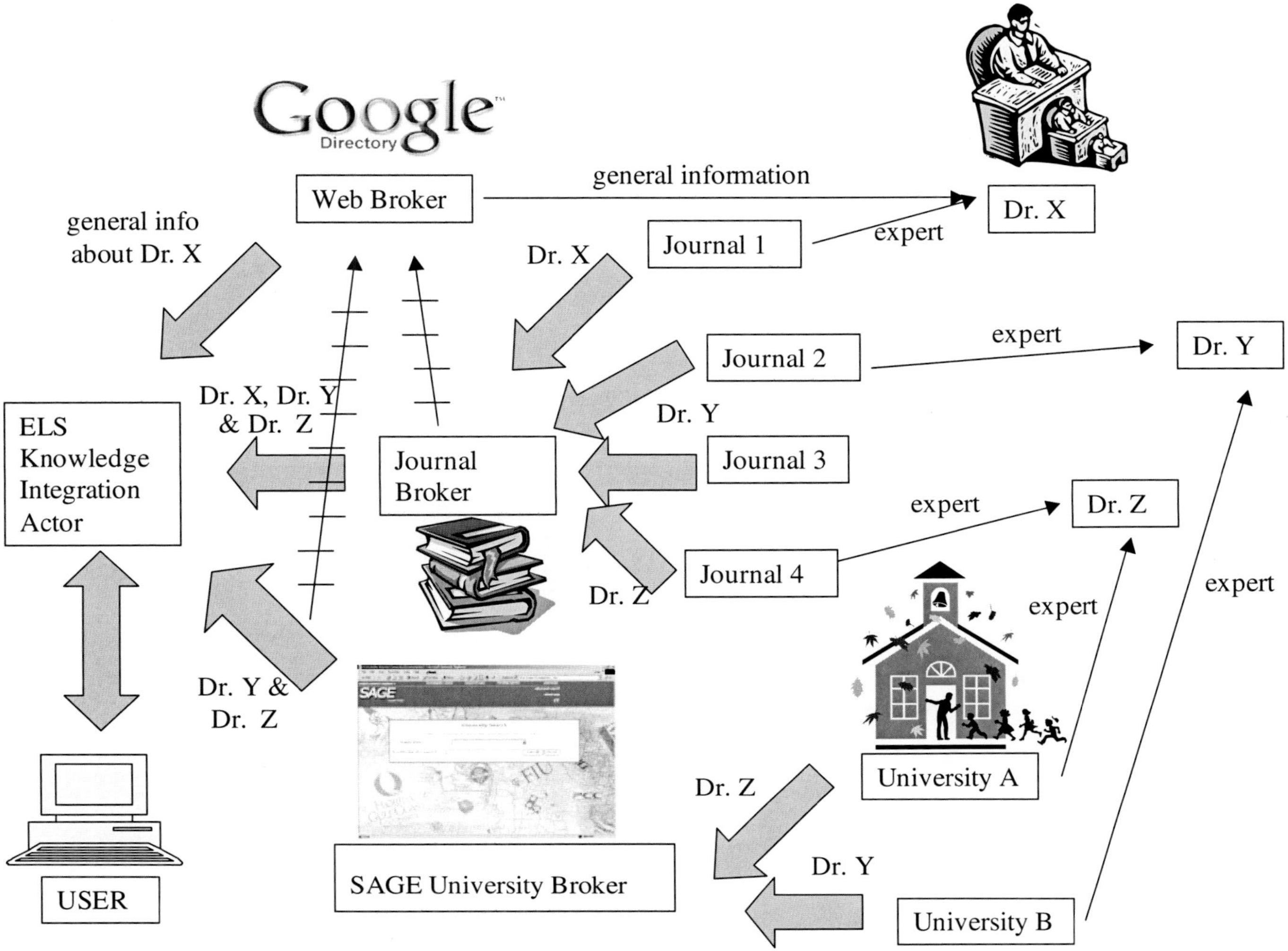

Source: Becerra-Fernandez et al., 2005.

2005), an organizational expertise locator KMS used to locate experts at NASA. The main difference between Expert Seeker and SAGE is that the former searched for expertise at NASA (KSC and GSFC—Goddard Space Flight Center), while the latter is on the Web and sought for expertise at various universities. Expert Seeker included an interface to SAGE, which allowed for specifying a search scope that was not bounded by the organization but included the base of researchers who work at different universities. Another important difference between SAGE and Expert Seeker is that the latter enables the user to search for much more detailed information regarding the experts' achievements including information, skills, and competencies as well as the proficiency level for each of the skills and competencies.

Previous knowledge management studies at Kennedy Space Center (KSC) affirmed the need for a centerwide repository that would provide KSC employees with Intranet-based access to experts with specific backgrounds (Becerra-Fernandez 1998; Becerra-Fernandez and Sabherwal 2005). To further create **synergies** between the efforts to develop Expert Seeker at KSC, a similar effort was funded to prototype Expert Seeker at GSFC. It was expected that the knowledge taxonomy for GSFC would differ from the one for KSC. However, this requirement did not pose a concern as Expert Seeker could be developed so the software could be "configured" with a customizable knowledge taxonomy. Expert Seeker offered NASA experts more visibility and at the same time allowed interested parties to identify available expertise within NASA, and this is especially useful when organizing cross-functional teams.

The Expert Seeker ELS was accessed via NASA's Intranet and provided a Web-based unified interface to access experts with specific competencies within the organization. The main interfaces on the query engine in Expert Seeker used text fields to search the repository by fields of expertise, names, or other applicable search fields. Expert Seeker unified a myriad of structured, semistructured, and unstructured data collections to create an expert's profile repository that could easily be searched via a Web-based interface facilitating communication via a point of contact. The development of Expert Seeker required the utilization of existing structured data as well as semistructured and unstructured Web-based information as much as possible. It used the data in existing human resources databases for information such as employee's formal educational background, the X.500 directory for point-of-contact information, a skills database that profiles each employee's competency areas, and the Goal Performance Evaluation System (GPES). Information regarding skills and competencies as well as proficiency levels for the skills and competencies needed to be collected, to a large extent, through self-assessment. Figure 8.6 depicts the architecture of Expert Seeker, and Table 8.3 describes the data sources for Expert Seeker. Furthermore, other related information deemed important in the generation of an expert profile not currently stored in an in-house database system can be user-supplied such as employee's picture, project participation data, hobbies, and volunteer or civic activities.

Recognizing that there are significant shortcomings of self-assessment, the system relied on other systems' information in order to update employees' profiles, and thus was less dependent on self-assessed data. For example, Expert Seeker used the Global Performance Evaluation System an in-house performance evaluation tool, to

Figure 8.6 **Expert Seeker Architecture**

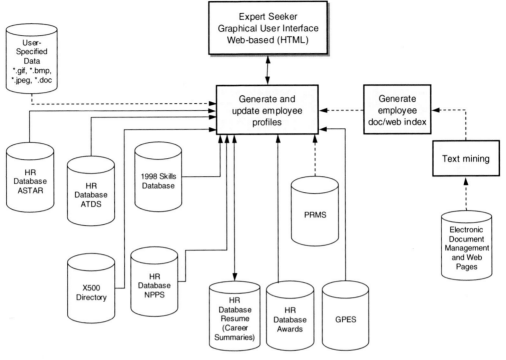

Source: Becerra-Fernandez 2006.

mine employees' accomplishments and automatically update their profiles. Typically, employees find it difficult to make time to keep their resumes updated. Performance evaluations, on the other hand, are without a doubt, part of everybody's job. Therefore, it makes perfect sense to use this tool to unobtrusively keep the employees profiles up to date. Future developments for expertise locator systems will incorporate advanced technologies, such as data mining and intelligent agent technologies, to automatically identify experts within as well as outside the organization.

Recent developments for expertise location at NASA include the use of Semantic Web technologies (Grove and Schain 2008). The recent deployment of the POPS ELS (People, Organizations, Projects, and Skills) combines Expert Seeker's original approach of reusing existing information sources with their integration via Resource Description Framework (RDF), a metadata data model, and other aggregation technologies. The system displays the social network between the user and the people who work on the same projects and people with the same skill sets and competencies. In addition, the system includes a know-who function that given the current user and target person will return an intermediate person related to both the user and the target person (see Figure 8.7). This functionality allows project managers to find intermediaries with whom to talk about potential project members, their abilities, interests, qualifications, and so forth. More information on social networks is presented in Chapter 10.

Table 8.3

Description of the Data Sources for Expert Seeker

User-Specified Data	This information is optionally user-supplied. For example, experts can opt to provide career summaries that will be used by Expert Seeker to augment the expertise search. A database table to hold this information was created and linked to the system, initially populated from the NPPS human resources database. Other user-supplied data could include pictures, publications, patents, hobbies, civic activities, etc.
ASTAR	This human resources database view provides the experts' in-house training courses.
ATDS	This human resources database view provides the experts' workshops and academic classes employees are planning to take.
X.500	This database view provides the experts' general employee data such as first name, last name, work address, phone, organization, fax, and e-mail. X.500's unique identifier is also used to cross reference employees in different databases.
Skills Database	This database view provides a set of skills and subskills that are used by Expert Seeker to index the expertise search. The KSC Core Competency team defined this set of skills and subskills as a refinement to a previous Center-wide skills-assessment.
NPPS Database	This human resources database view provides the experts' formal education, including professional degrees and the corresponding academic institutions. NPPS is also the source of the employee's department used for the directorate search. The contents of this database were also used to initially populate the career summary section table.
KPro	This database view will be populated with project participation information through a new project management system under development at NASA/KSC.
GPES	The Goal Performance Evaluation System (GPES) is a system developed at KSC. This database view serves as the data source for profile information such as employees' achievements. GPES will replace the Skills Database since GPES will also be populated with KSC's strategic competencies and levels of expertise.
Data Mining	Expert Seeker expertise search is augmented through the use of data-mining algorithms, which build an expert's profile based on information published by employees on their WebPages. Similarly a document repository could be mined for expertise using these algorithms.
SAGE	The Searchable Answer Generating Environment (SAGE) is an expertise locator system developed and hosted at the Florida International University Knowledge Management Laboratory to identify experts within Florida's universities. Expert Seeker user's can define the search scope to be within KSC or to expand it to universities in Florida. The latter means that Expert Seeker would launch an expert search to SAGE, and the results of this search will be integrated into one output at the Expert Seeker GUI.

Source: Becerra-Fernandez 2006.

Figure 8.7 **The POPS Expertise Locator System**

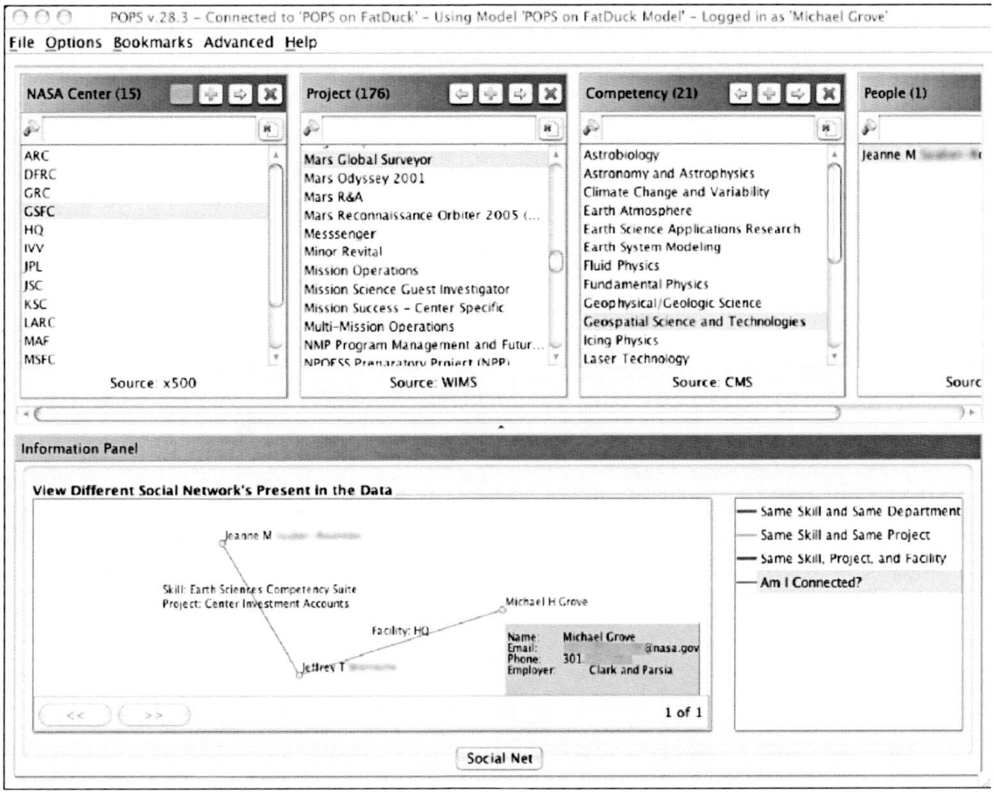

Source: Grove and Schain 2008.

OVERVIEW OF BLUEREACH: A SYSTEM TO FACILITATE REAL-TIME KNOWLEDGE SHARING, CAPTURE, AND REUSE

Large globally distributed organizations like IBM[4] continue the quest of how to adequately enable the sharing of expertise across organizational, geographic, and time boundaries. The motivation to develop and implement the BlueReach solution emerged initially from the immense growth in the global SAP consulting practice. A survey of SAP consultants in India revealed substantial shortcomings in terms of timely access to information for junior consultants. For example, of the 227 SAP respondents around 73 percent expressed they had to wait at least one day or longer for a typical question to be resolved, and 93 percent felt this wait was too long (Singley et al. 2008)

In order to respond to this need, the BlueReach Web-based system was built on the Lotus Sametime enterprise system. The goal of BlueReach is to provide the infrastructure for real-time expertise sharing and capture, to connect information-seekers (i.e., people with questions) to people with the expertise to answer them, while placing safeguards around the experts' time. The system was designed with two constraints in

Figure 8.8   **IBM's BlueReach User Interface**

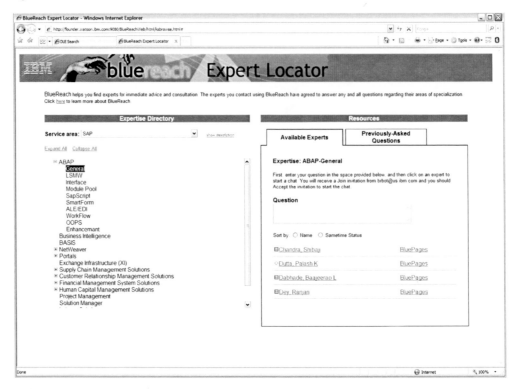

Source: Singley et al. 2008.

mind, the first being to provide sufficient controls for the experts regarding their visibility in the system to ensure that they are not overwhelmed by questions thus causing them to immediately drop out of the system. This first constraint must be balanced with the second requirement, which is to make the experts sufficiently accessible to information-seekers so as to create the vital "critical mass," that we described earlier as liquidity, necessary for collaborative systems. BlueReach gives users direct access to experts, by topic, in real time.

When a user selects a topic of interest, the application displays a taxonomy of expertise (with subtopics) for that topic area which the user can browse. The taxonomy is displayed as a simple tree structure that only goes a few levels deep. Once the question-asker has selected a subtopic, BlueReach does a real-time lookup of registered experts for that subtopic and displays only those who are available (see Figure 8.8). Some of the features of BlueReach include:

1. Multiple ways for the expert to control when they are "visible" in the system.
2. Ability for a question-asker to indicate if their question is urgent or can be deferred up to 90 minutes.

3. Logging of all chats and their associated ratings.
4. Browsable topic taxonomies for each of the supported service areas.
5. Support for composing a question before initiating chat with an expert, which can then be reused with other experts if immediate satisfaction is not obtained.
6. Full text search and browsing of stored questions with their associated answers.

Additionally, various types of export enrollment are supported by the tool. Enrollment can be specified as either: (a) open-enrollment model—anybody can volunteer, and it is up to the expert to designate his/her areas of expertise; (b) administrator-controlled model—only designated users can enroll experts in each of the topics; or (c) closed enrollment—when areas are saturated with experts, and no additional experts are accepted. A chat-harvesting tool allows experts to review and manage all the chats s/he has engaged in, quickly harvest and store important questions and answers that have value for reuse, and associate key words with the answers. One of the most valuable features of the tool is the reporting aspect. At any time BlueReach can report on the number of experts registered for a given topic, how many questions being asked (by topic, by country, by expert, by practitioner), average ratings for each expert, and so on. This feature allows for companies to understand where they have concentrations of expertise and also to monitor emerging hot areas of interest as well as problem areas.

Load-balancing features in BlueReach enable the ability to view the number of experts visible in the system with a status of either available or idle. This can also used for stress testing the system.

As part of the BlueReach initiative, the team of developers is looking to understand the motivational aspects around this activity. Some of the findings show that many junior practitioners are reluctant to ask a question of experts for fear of disturbing them at an inopportune time. This concern resulted in a feature to indicate the urgency of the question, allowing information-seekers to make their question less disruptive to the expert and thus making them more comfortable asking.

BlueReach was initially piloted with SAP consultants in India in the first quarter of 2007 and then rolled out to other global delivery centers around the world during the third quarter of 2007. More than 1,000 BlueReach experts are currently registered in 16 different service areas supporting over 30,000 practitioners. Studies show that 60 percent of BlueReach users are getting their questions answered in less than an hour (as compared to 27 percent in the initial survey), and that half of the usage of BlueReach consisted of questions that would have normally been asked of a Team Lead. Additionally, 88 percent of practitioners said they would use it again, 85 percent found it easy to use, and 96 percent of experts said they would enroll again (Singley et al. 2008).

SHORTCOMINGS OF KNOWLEDGE SHARING SYSTEMS

Perhaps one of the biggest challenges for knowledge management systems is to make this knowledge meaningful across the organization (Becerra-Fernandez and Sabherwal

2008). For example, lessons learned systems were one of the first types of KMS that gained acceptance in organizations and many consulting agencies quickly adopted the implementation of such systems, which later they proposed to their clients. As the volume of information represented in these knowledge bases increased, information and knowledge overload coupled with a lack of awareness about the lessons' context became a significant problem (Davenport and Hansen 1998).

> One of the problems was that many documents failed to provide much information about the context in which the insight and experience embodied in the document was generated . . . Imagine . . . you start reusing the drawings for the development of an office building and notice that the elevators in the previous drawings were constructed to be very deep. You later discover that the previous drawings were for a hospital where elevators need to be deep to hold beds. Wouldn't it have been helpful if the document had stated up front that the drawings were only relevant for hospital elevators? Contextualizing . . . would involve . . . describing the context in which the knowledge was generated and used, where it may be useful, and where it should—and should not—be used. (Davenport and Hansen 1998, p. 9)

The lack of contextual components for most of the lessons learned systems severely limited the recipient's ability to realize the environment in which the knowledge was generated and furthermore restricted its reuse. In order to overcome this limitation, at the time of collection, lessons learned could be augmented with those attributes describing the identity, sensory, informational, and positioning components could be detected in the background aided by the sensor network. These attributes could then be combined with the user's cognitive model, which could be used to stamp the lesson learned. This stamp could effectively describe where the lesson originated and under what physical and logical conditions. Subsequently, when lessons are being retrieved in order to ascertain their relevance to the current context, the system could match the stamp of the retrieved lessons to the user's current contextual components. Thus, using the example above, the system could proactively inform the user that the retrieved elevator design originated from the hospital architecture group and may not be applicable to an office building design (Becerra-Fernandez et al. 2007a).

In addition, organizations are still challenged by how to get more value from their own knowledge, in particular since it's estimated that 70 percent of the organizations with more than 10,000 employees have more than 100 separate information repositories (Weiss et al. 2004). This proliferation of repositories translates to lost productivity as employees often fall short at finding the knowledge they need. In order to improve the success of their knowledge sharing activities, organizations are encouraged to:

1. Develop one-stop access to content that emulates Google's one-stop search functionality. This requires companies to integrate their repositories, including effective back-end design. In addition, search functionality should be designed with content metadata or tags for each document including keywords, abstracts, author name, and document date.
2. Design dynamic classification systems and consistent formats that emulate eBay's classification system, which was developed based on what its customers want to buy and sell. Improving the browsing experience also requires

consistency of formats of the information presented to the user, which allows people to spend less time analyzing the results.

3. Entice employees to find what they need much like Amazon helps people identify needed products based on their relevance to the user. Furthermore, Amazon's ability to support shoppers in assessing the quality of their products via customer-supplied reviews significantly improves the buyer's experience. More information on how Web 2.0 technologies supports user-generated reviews is presented in Chapter 10. Additional attributes for the relevance and quality of knowledge could include an excerpt of the abstract, a snapshot of the content including who to contact for additional information, and a link to the author profiles.

KNOWLEDGE MANAGEMENT SYSTEMS THAT SHARE TACIT KNOWLEDGE

The systems discussed so far assist organizations in sharing explicit knowledge. In order to create a cultural environment that encourages the sharing of knowledge, some organizations are creating knowledge communities (Dignum 2002). As we discussed in Chapter 3, a community of practice, also known as a *knowledge network,* is an organic and self-organized group of individuals who are dispersed geographically or organizationally but communicate regularly to discuss issues of mutual interest. Two examples of communities of practice mentioned in that chapter are a tech club at Daimler Chrysler, which includes a group of engineers who don't work in the same unit but meet regularly to discuss problems related to their area of expertise, and a strategic community of IT professionals at Xerox, who frequently meet to promote knowledge sharing among them.

Many studies have demonstrated that any technological support for knowledge exchange requires users to feel they know and can trust each other. One company that has already taken steps in this direction is Achmea Holding N.V., one of the top insurance and financial services companies in the Netherlands. The company encourages direct contacts among participants in their knowledge community through formalized workshops. Through these workshops the company assures the creation, maintenance, and uniformity of domain knowledge and at the same time enables members to appreciate other colleagues, thus contributing to a feeling of community. In Box 8.6 we describe how the World Bank developed a knowledge sharing culture through the development of communities of practice, which they called *thematic groups.* As we see, KM plays a significant role at the World Bank, an international organization funded by the governments of 184 countries.

Communities are groups of people who come together to share and learn from one another and who are held together by a common interest in a body of knowledge. Communities come together either face-to-face or virtually and are driven by a desire and need to share problems, experiences, insights, templates, tools, and best practices (McDermott 2000). This section concentrates on systems used to share tacit knowledge, specifically to support **communities of practice (CoPs)**. According to McDermott, people come together in communities of practice because they're passionately interested in the topic and will receive direct value from participating in the community, or because they're emotionally connected to the community, or to learn new tools and techniques. Communities grow out of its members' natural networks, and follow five stages of development: planning, start-up, growth, sustenance, and closure. Although

Box 8.6

Sharing Knowledge at the World Bank

In 1996 James Wolfensohn, then president of the World Bank, outlined his vision for the Knowledge Bank, a partnership for creating and sharing knowledge, and making it a major driver of development. At the World Bank, KM is synonymous with sharing the experiences gained from staff, clients, and development partners and creating linkages between groups and communities. The World Bank recognizes that "fighting poverty requires a global strategy to share knowledge effectively and to ensure that people who need that knowledge get it on time, whether from the World Bank or others." The World Bank has concentrated its KM efforts in becoming a global development partner enabling the necessary knowledge exchange within and outside Bank. Early on, the World Bank developed a matrix structure to combine local country knowledge with world-class technical expertise along communities of practice that they called *Thematic Groups* (TGs). TGs refer to voluntary groups of people who are passionate about a common subject. Leadership and membership in any Thematic Group is open to all staff and may also include external partners enabling knowledge sharing seamlessly across the group via e-mail distribution lists and Web sites. The role of TGs has been to bring together, online and face-to-face, experts from within and outside the Bank and across all its regions. TGs receive funding from their sector board(s) based on work program agreements which tie their work to the sector strategy. The activities of the thematic groups include:

1. Production of knowledge collections (good practices, knowhow, sector statistics, etc.).
2. Dissemination and outreach to staff and partners (brown bag lunches, clinics, workshops, study tours, Web sites, newsletters, etc.).
3. Support to task teams, thus enabling staff to apply and adapt the global knowledge to the local situation.
4. Raising additional funds for specific work program activities.

Currently, there are 79 TGs at the World Bank, and a list of these groups and their leaders can be accessed via the World Bank Web site.

The Bank also implemented a number of advisory services that functioned as help desks, as an interface for connecting people and answers. The Bank also launched a knowledge management system for the purpose of sharing lessons and best practices. Other KM initiatives at the World Bank included starting a Global Knowledge Partnership conference, linking all its local offices to global communications and establishing an innovation marketplace to share ideas, talents, and resources that address development challenges. This level of success would not have been accomplished if the organization had not rewarded knowledge sharing, which in 1998 became part of their annual performance evaluation system. In 2000, the bank launched the Global Development Learning Network, which provided 17 countries with simultaneous videoconferencing and Internet facilities for distance learning. Also the World Bank established the Knowledge for Development program, to help developing countries better understand how to exploit the knowledge revolution to help reduce poverty. For all its KM efforts, the American Productivity and Quality Center recognized the World Bank as a best practice partner.

Current efforts at the World Bank include increased awareness about the role of metrics in the implementation of KM programs (Carayannis and Laporte 2002), and the importance of knowledge for long-term economic growth (Chen and Dahlman 2006).

Knowledge sharing at the World Bank is now a mainstream activity that has required significant investments in infrastructure, communities of practice, global networks, training, and in understanding the role of knowledge in development. As a result, the role of the World Bank is now considered to be catalytic, ensuring effective integration of internal and client knowledge. The World Bank now understands that capacity building is about creating environments in which local and global knowledge can inform action and influence the change necessary to end poverty.

communities of practice are not new phenomena, the Internet has enabled the proliferation of virtual communities facilitated through the same collaborative technologies. In 1995, IBM started supporting the growth and development of communities of practice focused on the competencies of the organization. By the year 2000 at IBM the number of CoPs numbered around 60, and more than 20,000 employees had participated in a community (Gongla and Rizzuto 2001).

While knowledge repositories support primarily codified and explicitly captured knowledge, virtual communities of practice are supported through technology that enables interaction and conversations amongst its members. Interaction technology can support structured (and perhaps more explicated) communication such as in discussion groups and Web-based forums to unstructured (and perhaps more tacit) communication such as in videoconferencing.

For example, in Box 8.6 presented in this section, we mentioned the World Bank's initiative to establish CoPs, as a powerful venue for sharing global experiences while at the same time adapting them to meet local challenges. For example, the Knowledge for Development (K4D) Community combines experts from across sectors, networks, and regions of the Bank to share knowledge related to capacity development in each of the different regions of the world. At the World Bank, technology is considered a critical building block for CoPs but only as support for the social aspects of sharing knowledge which are building trust, personal communication, and face-to-face meetings. At the World Bank, technology is adapted to the needs of the community and the tools that support their CoPs include: document repositories, debriefings to identify lessons learned, an Internet-based broadcasting station, newsletters and printed publications, and Web sites. Specifically, the World Bank developed a Web site that supports virtual discussions called The Development Forum (DevForum), an electronic venue for dialogue and knowledge sharing on issues of sustainable development. Participants of this forum must adhere to a set of rules, namely:

1. *Personal Identification:* Participants should include their name in all messages posted to the discussion and never represent themselves as another person.
2. *Conduct:* Participants may not post libelous or defamatory messages or materials or links to such materials. They may not post messages or materials that are obscene, violent, abusive, threatening, or designed to harass or intimidate another person.
3. *Liability and Responsibility:* Participants are legally responsible, and solely responsible, for any content posted to a discussion. They may only post materials that they have the right or permission to distribute electronically. The sponsors of the Development Forum are not responsible for any liability arising from users' posting of any materials to the Forum Dialogues.
4. *Accuracy:* The World Bank, as sponsor of the Development Forum, cannot and does not guarantee the accuracy of any statements made in or materials posted to the Forum by participants.
5. *Attribution:* Participants in the Development Forum, including participants in the Development Dialogues and the authors of contributions to the Speakers' Corner, are assumed to be speaking in their personal capacity, unless they

explicitly state that their contribution represents the views of their organization. For this reason, participants in the Forum should not quote the postings of other participants as representing the views of the organizations to which those other participants belong.

6. *Copyright and Fair Use:* As a participant in the Development Forum, participants retain copyright of any materials that is their own creation that is posted to the Forum. However, users authorize other participants in the Forum to make personal and customary use of that work, including creating links to or reposting such materials to other Internet discussion sites but not otherwise to reproduce or disseminate those materials unless you give permission. Participants must always identify the source and author of materials downloaded from the Forum if it's reposted elsewhere.

CoPs have been observed to impact organizational performance (Lesser and Storck 2001) in four areas:

1. Decreasing new employee's learning curves—CoPs can help new employees identify subject matter experts in the organization who can guide them to the proper resources and thus foster relationships with more senior employees. CoPs can help develop mentor-protégé relationships that can help employees with career development and to understand the larger organizational context of their individual tasks.
2. Enabling the organization to respond faster to customer needs and inquiries—CoPs can help identify experts that can address customer issues. Furthermore since many communities maintain electronic document repositories, relevant codified knowledge can often be reused.
3. Reducing rework and preventing to "reinvent the wheel"—CoPs are able to locate, access, and apply existing knowledge in new situations. Repositories serve as common virtual workspace to store, organize, and download presentations, tools, and other valuable materials. Metadata is used to identify authors and subject matter experts. Most repositories include human moderation. For example the sponsors of World Bank's Development Forum retain the right to refuse to post any message that they consider to be in violation of the rules, and may opt to publish the messages posted to the Forum in whole or in part. CoPs help create trust within the organization by helping individuals build reputations both as experts and for their willingness to help others.
4. Spawning new ideas for products and services—CoPs serve as a forum in which employees are able to share perspectives about a topic. Discussing diverse views within the community can often spark innovation. Furthermore, CoPs provide a safe environment where people feel comfortable about sharing their experiences.

In short, CoPs are effective mechanisms for tacit knowledge sharing that can provide significant value to organizations. The role of management is to carefully craft interventions that are likely to support the formation and development of CoPs.

SUMMARY

In this chapter, we discussed what knowledge sharing systems are including design considerations and specific types of such systems. Specific attention was placed on the two systems most frequently discussed in the KM literature: lessons learned systems (LLS) and expertise locator systems (ELS). The lessons learned process was discussed. Also we discussed LLS and ELS in further detail, including design considerations and three representative case studies. The experience gained from the development of four such systems was presented: Postdoc—a collaborative system to support dispersed teams at NASA; SAGE Expert Finder—an ELS to locate experts in universities in Florida; Expert Seeker—an ELS used to identify experts at NASA; and BlueReach—a system to locate and share expertise at IBM. The chapter concludes with a discussion of systems used to share tacit knowledge through communities of practice.

KEY TERMS

Alert systems
Authority files
Collaborative computing
Communities of practice (CoPs)
Corporate memory
Expertise locator systems (ELS)
Expert Seeker
Incident report databases
Knowledge repositories
Knowledge sharing systems

Knowledge taxonomies
Lessons learned systems (LLS)
Not-invented-here (NIH) syndrome
Ontologies
Organizational knowledge
Searchable Answer Generating
    Environment (SAGE)
Semantic networks
Web text data mining

REVIEW

1. Describe the crucial requirements for the successful implementation of knowledge sharing systems.
2. Discuss the different types of knowledge sharing systems.
3. Explain the lessons learned process.
4. Explain the role that taxonomies play in knowledge sharing systems.
5. Explain the differentiating characteristics of the ELS developed at HP, NSA, Microsoft, state of Florida universities, and NASA.
6. Discuss the role that communities of practice play in sharing tacit knowledge.

APPLICATION EXERCISES

1. Identify examples of knowledge sharing systems in use in your organization. What are some of the intelligent technologies that enable those systems?
2. Design a knowledge sharing system to support your business needs. Describe

the type of system and the foundation technologies that you would use to develop such a system.
3. Describe the nontechnical issues that you will face during the implementation of the system designed in the previous question.
4. Design the system architecture for the system described in question 2 above.
5. Identify three recent examples in the literature of knowledge sharing systems.

NOTES

1. Liquidity refers to the number of trades made in the market: The greater the volume of trades, the greater liquidity.
2. For a comprehensive survey of lessons learned systems including capabilities, limitations, design issues, and the role of artificial intelligence in the creation of these systems, please refer to Weber et al. (2001).
3. Remote Agent was a complex software system for controlling and monitoring of autonomous spacecraft.
4. We acknowledge IBM, in particular Jennifer Lai of the IBM T.J. Watson Research Center, for the support in creating this section.

REFERENCES

Abecker, A., Bernardi, A., Hinkerlmann, K., Kuhn, O., and Sintek, M. 1998. Towards a technology for organizational memories. *IEEE Intelligent Systems and Their Applications,* 13(3) (May/June).
Abecker, A., Decker, S., and Maurer, F. 2000. Organizational memory and knowledge management. *Information Systems Frontiers,* 2(3–4), 251, 252.
Ackerman, M. and Halverson, C. 2000. Reexamining organizational memory. *Communications of the ACM,* 43(1), 59–64.
Becerra-Fernandez, I. 1998. *Corporate memory project.* Final Report, NASA grant No. NAG10–0232, 12–25.
———. 1999. Searchable answer generating environment (SAGE): A knowledge management system for searching for experts in Florida. In *Proceedings of the Twelfth Annual International Florida Artificial Intelligence Research Symposium,* ed. A.N. Kumar and I. Russell. Orlando, Florida, May.
———. 2000a. The role of artificial intelligence technologies in the implementation of people-finder knowledge management systems. *Knowledge-Based Systems,* 13(5) (October).
———. 2000b. Facilitating the online search of experts at NASA using Expert Seeker People-Finder. In *Proceedings of the Third International Conference on Practical Aspects of Knowledge Management,* ed. U. Reimer. Basel, Switzerland.
———. 2001. Locating expertise at NASA—developing a tool to leverage human capital. *Knowledge Management Review,* 4(4), 34–37.
———. 2006. Searching for experts on the Web: A review of contemporary expertise locator systems. *ACM Transactions on Internet Technology,* 6(4), 333–355.
Becerra-Fernandez, I., Cousins, K., and Weber, R. 2007a. Nomadic context-aware knowledge management systems: Applications, challenges, and research problems. *International Journal of Mobile Learning and Organisation,* 1(2), 103–121.
Becerra-Fernandez, I., Del Alto, M., and Stewart, H. 2006. A case study of Web-based collaborative decision support at NASA. *International Journal of e-Collaboration,* 2(3), 49–63.

———. 2007b. The launch of Web-based collaborative decision support at NASA. In *E-collaboration in modern organizations: Initiating and managing distributed projects,* ed. Ned Kock, Hershey, PA: Information Science Reference, 113–125.

Becerra-Fernandez, I. and Sabherwal R. 2005. Knowledge management at NASA–Kennedy Space Center. *International Journal of Knowledge and Learning,* 1(1/2), 159–170.

———. 2008. Individual, group, and organizational learning: A knowledge management perspective. In *Knowledge management: An evolutionary view,* Advances in Management Information Systems, vol. 12, ed. I. Becerra-Fernandez and D. Leidner, 13–39. Armonk, NY: M.E. Sharpe.

Becerra-Fernandez, I., Wang, T., Agha, G., and PSP Sin, T. 2005. Actor model and knowledge management systems: Social interaction as a framework for knowledge integration. *Lecture Notes in Computer Science,* 3782, 19–31.

Bobrow, D. and Whalen, J. 2002. Community knowledge sharing in practice: The Eureka story. *Journal of the Society for Organizational Learning,* 4(2), 47–59.

Carayannis, E. and Laporte, B. 2002. *By decree or by choice?* A Case Study-Implementing Knowledge Management and Sharing at the Education Sector of the World Bank Group. Stock No. 37206. http://www.worldbank.org/reference/ (accessed August 19, 2008).

Chen, D. and Dahlman, C. 2006. *The knowledge economy, the KAM Methodology, and World Bank operations.* Stock No. 37256. http://www.worldbank.org/reference/ (accessed August 19, 2008).

Davenport, T. and Hansen, M. 1998. *Knowledge management at Andersen Consulting.* Case No. 9–499–032. Boston: Harvard Business School Press.

Davenport, T. and Prusak, L. 1998. *Working knowledge: How organizations manage what they know.* Boston: Harvard Business School Press.

Dellow, J. 2004. Success at Ernst & Young's center for business knowledge: Online collaboration tools, knowledge managers, and a Cooperative Culture. In *Knowledge management tools and techniques,* ed. Madanmohan Rao. London: Elsevier.

Dignum, V. 2002. A knowledge sharing model for peer collaboration in the non-life insurance domain. In *Proceedings of the 1st German Workshop on Experience Management,* ed. M. Minor and S. Staab. Berlin, Germany.

Disterer, G. 2002. Management of project knowledge and experiences. *Journal of Knowledge Management,* 6(5), 512–520.

Frey, R.S. 2002. Small business knowledge management success story—This stuff really works! *Knowledge and Process Management,* 9(3), 172–177.

Giles, C., Bollacker, K., and Lawrence, S. 1998. CiteSeer: An automatic citation indexing system. In *Proceedings of the ACM Conference on Digital Libraries.* New York: Association for Computing Machinery.

Gongla, P. and Rizutto, C. 2001. Evolving communities of practice: IBM global services experience. *IBM Systems Journal,* 4(4), 842–862.

Grove, M. and Schain, A. 2008. *Semantic Web use cases and case studies.* W3C Semantic Web. http://www.w3.0rg/2001/sw/sweo/public/UseCases/ (accessed September 12, 2008).

Gruninger, M. and Lee, J. 2002. Ontology applications and design. *Communications of the ACM,* 45(2), 39–41.

Guarino, N. and Welty, C. 2002. Evaluating ontological decisions with Ontoclean. *Communications of the ACM,* 45(2), 61–65.

Khun, O. and Abecker, A. 1997. Corporate memories for knowledge management in industrial practice: Prospects and challenges. *Journal of Universal Computer Science,* 3(8), 929–954.

Lesser, E. and Storck, J. 2001. Communities of practice and organizational performance. *IBM Systems Journal,* 40(4), 831–841.

McDermott, R. 2000. Community development as a natural step. *Knowledge Management Review,* November/December.

Microsoft Developer Network. 2009. MSDN library. http://msdn.microsoft.com/en-us/library/default.aspx.

Mitchell, M. 2001. Share and share alike. *Darwin Magazine,* February.

O'Leary, D.E. 1999. Knowledge Management for best practices. *Intelligence,* 10(4), 12–24.

Roberts-Witt, S. 2002. A "eureka!" moment at Xerox. *PC Magazine,* March.

Secchi, P., Ciaschi, R., and Spence, D. 1999. A concept for an ESA lessons learned system. In *Proceedings of Alerts and LL: An effective way to prevent failures and problems* (Technical Report WPP-167), ed. P. Secchi. Noordwijk, The Netherlands: ESTEC.

Singley, K., Lai, J., Kuang, L., and Tang, J. 2008. *Blue reach: Harnessing synchronous chat to support expertise sharing in a large organization.* Conference on Human Factors in Computing Systems (CHI), Florence, Italy, April.

U.S. Department of Energy. 2009. *Chemical occurrences.* Office of Health, Safety, and Security Web site. http://www.hss.energy.gov/HealthSafety/WSHP/chem_safety/chemstart.html.

U.S. Department of Transportation. 2009. *Best practices procurement manual.* Grants and Financing, Federal Transit Administration website. http://www.fta.dot.gov/funding/thirdpartyprocurement/grants_financing_6037.html.

Weber, R. 2007. Addressing failure factors in knowledge management. *Electronic Journal of Knowledge Management,* 5(3), 333–346.

Weber, R. and Aha, D. 2003. Intelligent delivery of military lessons learned. *Decision Support Systems,* 34(3), 287–304.

Weber, R., Aha, D.W., and Becerra-Fernandez, I. 2001. Intelligent lessons learned systems. *International Journal of Expert Systems Research and Applications,* 20(1), 17–34.

Weber, R.O., Morelli, M.L., Atwood, M.E., and Proctor, J.M. 2006. Designing a knowledge management approach for the CAMRA community of science. In *Proceedings of the Sixth International Conference on Practical Aspects of Knowledge Management,* LNAI vol. 4333, ed. U. Reimer and D. Karagiannis, 315–325. Heidelberg: Springer-Berlin.

Weiss, L., Capozzi, M., and Prusak, L. 2004. Learning from the Internet giants. *MIT Sloan Management Review,* 45(4), 79–84.

WFMC-TC-1011, Issue 2: Workflow Management Coalition. 1999. Terminology and Glossary. http://www.huihoo.org/jfox/jfowfbw/specfication/03.Terminology.glossary.pdf.

Wiig, K. 1993. *Thinking about thinking—How people and organizations create, represent, and use knowledge.* Arlington, TX: Schema Press.

Wright, A. and Spencer, W. 1999. *The National Security Agency (NSA) Networked Knowledge and Skills Management System.* Presentation at Delphi's International Knowledge Management Summit (IKMS), San Diego, CA.

Yiman-Seid, D. and Kobsa, A. 2003. Expert finding systems for organizations: Problem and domain analysis and the DEMOIR approach. *Journal of Organizational Computing and Electronic Commerce,* 13(1), 1–24.

9 Knowledge Discovery Systems: Systems that Create Knowledge

In the last chapter, we discussed knowledge sharing systems. In this chapter we introduce **knowledge discovery systems**. Knowledge discovery dates back to the time before the existence of the word "researcher." Certainly, popular lore contends that Galileo discovered knowledge while dropping objects from the Tower of Pisa and observing the time each took to reach the ground. The Wright brothers, Alexander Graham Bell, Thomas Edison, and thousands of other less well-known researchers and inventors throughout history have discovered knowledge that has helped our understanding of how things work in nature. Cumulatively, their contributions have shaped our present lives in many ways. But how is knowledge discovered? For the purposes of this chapter, we focus on two significant ways:

1. Synthesis of new knowledge through socialization with other knowledgeable persons; and
2. Discovery by finding interesting patterns in observations, typically embodied in explicit data.

As we saw in Chapter 4, knowledge discovery systems support the development of new tacit or explicit knowledge from data and information or from the synthesis of prior knowledge. Knowledge discovery systems rely on mechanisms and technologies that can support the combination and the socialization processes. For the purpose of the discussions in this chapter we don't distinguish between knowledge creation and knowledge discovery, and we consider both to describe the same thing: the innovation and advancement of knowledge. We do distinguish knowledge creation from knowledge capture, the latter activity presumes that knowledge has already been created and may exist tacitly in the minds of experts, which was the topic of Chapter 7. Knowledge creation assumes knowledge didn't exist before the activity that catalyzed the innovation.

You may recall from Chapter 4 that **knowledge discovery mechanisms** involve socialization processes. In the case of tacit knowledge, **socialization** facilitates the synthesis of tacit knowledge across individuals and the integration of multiple streams for the creation of new knowledge, usually through joint activities rather than written or verbal instructions. For example one mechanism for socialization is research conferences, which enable researchers to develop new insights through sharing their own findings. Also, when friends brainstorm and do **"back-of-the-napkin" diagrams**, leading to the discovery of new knowledge that didn't exist individually before the group activity, knowledge is created or discovered by the team. We expand on the topic of socialization as a mechanism for knowledge discovery in the next section.

On the other hand technologies can support knowledge discovery systems by facilitating combination processes. New explicit knowledge is discovered through **combination,** wherein the multiple bodies of explicit knowledge (and/or data and/or information) are synthesized to create new, more complex sets of explicit knowledge. Existing explicit knowledge may be **re-contextualized** to produce new explicit knowledge, for example during the creation of a new proposal to a client that is based upon existing prior client proposals. Knowledge discovery mechanisms and **technologies** can facilitate socialization and combination within or across organizations. **Knowledge creation systems** can be enabled by the use of data mining technologies, such as those discussed later in this chapter. These may be used to uncover new relationships among explicit data, which in turn can serve to develop models that can predict or categorize highly valuable assets in business intelligence.

MECHANISMS TO DISCOVER KNOWLEDGE: USING SOCIALIZATION TO CREATE NEW TACIT KNOWLEDGE

Socialization, as defined in Chapter 4, is the synthesis of tacit knowledge across individuals, usually through joint activities rather than written or verbal instructions. Socialization enables the discovery of tacit knowledge through joint activities between masters and apprentices, or between researchers at an academic conference. Many Japanese companies, for example Honda, encourage socialization through **"brainstorming camps"** to resolve problems faced in R&D projects (Nonaka and Takeuchi 1995). The format for these meetings is outside the workplace, much like the one spearheaded at Westinghouse and presented in Box 9.1. The idea is to encourage participants to meet outside their normal work environment, perhaps at a resort, where they are able to discuss their problems in an informal and relaxed environment. These meetings serve not only as a medium for creativity to flourish but also to share knowledge and build trust amongst the group members. Socialization as a means of knowledge discovery is a common practice at many organizations, pursued either by accident or on purpose.

Simple discussions over lunch among friends discussing their daily problems often lead to knowledge discovery. Cocktail napkins have been known to contain descriptions of critical new ideas. Organizations interested in fostering discovery of knowledge take steps to formalize this socialization among their employees. This process promotes innovation and creativity, which in turn leads to advances in knowledge. The following box describes a formal mechanism instituted by a major U.S. corporation back before knowledge management had become a household word.

Box 9.2 describes the use of the **creative brainstorming** process, which involves a customer (the person with the problem or need), a **facilitator** (the person controlling the process), and the **innovators** (who will brainstorm solutions to the customer's

Box 9.1

The Westinghouse Innovation Group

George Westinghouse, considered by many as one of the world's leading inventor-engineers, founded Westinghouse Electric Corporation in 1886 and eventually 59 other companies, receiving over 100 patents for his work.[1] Westinghouse Electric Corporation established one of the nation's first industrial research laboratories in 1886 with the invention of the transformer, which enabled the transmission of electricity over large distances by increasing the voltage of alternating current electricity.

The company had established a reputation for developing advanced technology products. Its Transmission and Distribution (T&D) business unit was a relatively small segment of the corporation's product range and sales volume and was comprised of several product divisions. These divisions were fairly independent. They manufactured products for electric utilities and large industrial complexes, and each division addressed different (noncompeting) product lines within the same industries. The products ranged from the world's largest power transformers, power circuit breakers, and electronic voltage regulators for large electrical generators all the way to the more mundane pole-mounted transformers and standard house meters.

In 1979, the Westinghouse T&D Business Unit (comprising all the divisions that built and marketed products for the T&D market segment) realized that its product offerings were rather mature and in serious need of upgrading. The president of the T&D Business Unit, in cooperation with the Westinghouse Headquarters technical staff, instituted and sponsored the T&D Innovation Group to foster innovation and creativity in its technical offerings. Its mission was to creatively apply new ideas to solve old problems, and more specifically, to inject a measure of high technology into its product line. Furthermore, through this group, it sought to "upgrade the competence" (that is, enhance the knowledge) of the technical staff at their home divisions. One senior engineer from each T&D division was selected to participate in this twelve-member group. In addition, the sponsoring manager from corporate headquarters, who arranged the meetings, suggested the agenda and provided guidance to the group and also served as the communication link to the T&D president and his staff. Each selected engineer would communicate directly with his own division general manager, bypassing the three or four hierarchical levels in the chain of command. This communication involved briefing the general manager on the proceedings of the group, as well as obtaining from him any problems that he would like to have addressed by the group.

The T&D Innovation Group meetings took place once per quarter and lasted for two-and-a-half days (and three nights), typically in a resort hotel near one of the participating division headquarters or factories that served as the host for that meeting. This location ensured freedom from interruptions from the members' daily responsibilities. While some of the problems to be addressed were defined by the business unit staff or the division general managers, others originated within the group itself. In the early meetings, most of the problems addressed were of a technical nature. As the group matured and the operating procedures became more streamlined, the discussions shifted to problems of an organizational nature. The group always addressed each problem using the technique of creative brainstorming (described below), until a consensus was reached on a set of recommendations for the individual presenting the problem, typically during the same two- or three-hour meeting.

The T&D Innovation Group continued to meet for three years before reorganizations, divestitures, promotions, transfers, retirements, and such took a toll on those individuals who had a vested interest in this concept. Nevertheless, in its relatively short existence, the group succeeded in generating a few dozen patent disclosures many of which later became valuable corporate patents. In addition, several products were upgraded as a direct result of the group's work. Moreover, several recommendations were made to senior management, which were either implemented, or at the very least, seriously considered. Lastly, the T&D Innovation Group had some success in injecting advanced technology into the technical staff of the divisions.

[1] We acknowledge Avelino Gonzalez of the University of Central Florida for this box.

Box 9.2

Creative Brainstorming

Westinghouse Electric Corporation was a major manufacturer of home appliances before White Consolidated Industries acquired the product line in 1974 (now called White-Westinghouse).[1] Once upon a time, they built washing machines that stood on four small metal legs on each corner at the bottom of the box-like structure that we commonly recognize as a washing machine. The legs were fitted with built-in screws to stabilize the machine during operation and avoid vibrations. These small legs protruded from the basic box-like design of the washing machine. Unfortunately when these appliances were shipped in boxes, their movement (and often dropping of the boxes from trucks) caused these small legs to bend. Bent legs destabilized the washing machine and caused annoying as well as damaging vibrations when the machine was in operation. This resulted in significant warranty expenses to Westinghouse when a serviceman had to be called to fix the bent legs.

   The manager of engineering at the product division that built the washing machines was told to solve the problem. He assembled his best design engineers and told them to go into a room and not come out until they had solved the problem. The lore goes that the engineers labored night and day for three days and finally emerged from the room proudly with a new design that greatly strengthened the legs by adding steel thickness and additional bracing. The manager looked at the solution and saw that this would add significant cost to the product, which was deemed unacceptable. The leader of the group, angry that their three days of captivity had gone for naught screamed, "What do you want us to do, stand on our heads?" Immediately, another member of the group, one who apparently had gotten some sleep the night before, immediately said "I've got it! We ship the washing machines upside down." They proceeded to do an analysis of whether the top of the box could withstand the shocks and whether there were any components that would be damaged by the upside-down shipment. They found out there were none. The problem was solved without adding any cost to the product.

[1]We acknowledge Avelino Gonzalez of the University of Central Florida for this box.

problem or need). The process begins by having the facilitator establish the ground rules, which are not many. The main one is that one person speaks at a time and there are no such things as crazy, dumb, wild, or silly ideas. The latter ensures the creative freedom of the innovators to generate solutions, which may at first glance appear silly or wild. The customer then takes her turn explaining the problem briefly, without discussing what has already been tried. Then the main part of the process begins. The innovators voice ideas out loud to the facilitator. These ideas are described in one or two sentences. The facilitator displays them each in a way that is visible to the participants (a flipchart, a whiteboard, a computer with a projection device, etc.). This process runs unabated until the ideas cease to flow (typically, 30 to 45 minutes depending on the size of the group and the complexity of the problem). The customer is then once again given the floor and asked to select a few (three to five) ideas that appeal to her. The appealing ideas are then further examined in order to make them viable. Lastly, those ideas showing the greatest potential are even further examined and the potential drawbacks are identified. The process ends at this point, and the customer departs with some innovative potential solutions to her problem. It should be mentioned that the problem does not need to be technical or scientific in nature. Any kind of problem is eligible for this approach.

The process addresses two important aspects of problem-solving and decision-making. One is to identify the real problem. In many situations, problem-solvers are not addressing the real problem but a perceived one. Even if the perceived problem is solved, it does not address the real problem. Group thinking may be able to identify the real problem and address it. The second aspect is what is referred to as **lateral thinking**. This is when an entirely different approach is taken to solve a problem. Identifying wild, crazy, or silly ideas may trigger ideas (new knowledge) in the other innovators that may be not be wild, crazy, or silly and which may actually solve the problem. Box 9.2 describes an anecdotal experience of the successful application of the collaboration process fostered in creative brainstorming.

This box shows that the engineering task force was solving the wrong problem. The problem was in the shipment of the washing machines, not in their design. The legs were well designed for their purpose. There was no need to design them for anything else. Furthermore, it shows how seemingly silly ideas can become realistic and provide a way to solve the problem in unintended ways. This, of course, is new knowledge!

Box 9.3 illustrates how modern innovation teams are structured to create new products. One important aspect of innovation teams is the importance of diversity in backgrounds and expertise of the members, as well as being loosely coupled to other expertise networks as the most significant factors for teams to come up with their aha! moment.

Next, Box 9.4 illustrates how technology can improve the process of brainstorming and knowledge discovery. In the next section, we describe how technologies can support the discovery of new knowledge.

TECHNOLOGIES TO DISCOVER KNOWLEDGE: USING DATA MINING TO CREATE NEW EXPLICIT KNOWLEDGE

The technologies that enable the discovery of new knowledge uncover the relationships from explicit information. Knowledge discovery technologies can be very powerful for organizations wishing to obtain an advantage over their competition. Recall that **knowledge discovery in databases (KDD)** is the process of finding and interpreting patterns from data, involving the application of algorithms to interpret the patterns generated by these algorithms (Fayyad et al. 1996). Another name for KDD is **data mining (DM)**. Although the majority of the practitioners use KDD and DM interchangeably, for some KDD is defined to involve the whole process of knowledge discovery including the application of DM techniques.

Although data mining systems have made a significant contribution in scientific fields for years, for example in breast cancer diagnosis (Kovalerchuk et al. 2000), perhaps the recent proliferation of e-commerce applications providing reams of hard data ready for analysis presents us with an excellent opportunity to make profitable use of these techniques. The increasing availability of computing power and integrated DM software tools, which are easier than ever to use, have contributed to the increasing popularity of DM applications to businesses. Many success stories have been published in the literature

---

Box 9.3

Creativity and Learning in New Product Development Teams

What happens at the Eureka moment in the creative process is what we call insight. In that split second we grasp the real problem, a pathway to the solution, and/or a concrete answer, and we transition from not knowing to knowing. We may, for example, discover that despite differences in appearance, fractions and decimals are inherently the same thing.

Solving complex real-world problems requires insight through creativity and learning. Sometimes insight happens in the mind of an individual or it could occur through the dynamics of a team effort. Consider the "Hyena Pack," a carefully selected innovation team in one of the largest pharmaceutical companies. This particular team was charged with developing new products in a market that the company had not yet entered—a doubly difficult problem. Suffice to say that the team was immensely successful, but how did their success come about?

First, they were wonderfully diverse. Besides gender and the cross-functional diversity of their professional specialties, their backgrounds were remarkably different. The team leader was a pharmacist who had been a military pilot. One young scientist spent his evenings playing in a rock-and-roll band. One researcher had grown up in Ireland; another chemist had grown up in Hong Kong. The facilitator was an outside consultant with a mixed background in military special warfare and cognitive science. The information specialist was an Internet librarian with an undergraduate degree in science and extensive travel experience in India. In organizing this team, R&D management knew how important learning would be to the creative process. For that reason, the information specialist was a full member of the team and participated in all team efforts including idea generation. In addition, the team had two adjunct members on call: a Ph.D. in psychology, who provided market research information and an intellectual property (IP) specialist with a strong background in both science and the IP process.

As this team had to both explore a new market and create the next generation of products, they divided their time between explicit creative problem-solving (opportunity finding, problem definition, idea generation, etc.) and just-in-time learning. For example, after the team narrowed the focus to four or five promising product areas they engaged in jigsaw learning, which meant engaging in exploration outside of the team by separately reading research articles provided by the information specialist and then coming back together to share new insights, redefine their problem, make new connections, generate new ideas, and evaluate new possibilities. The team did follow a systematic process, the Problem Solving Model, IDEATECTS strategy for both creative and diagnostic problem-solving depicted in Figure 9.1. Each team moves through the Problem Solving Model in a unique manner illustrated by the numbered arrows in the figure.

This team was able to deliver on their mandate in just in twelve workdays. They combined just-in-time learning, a strong knowledge generation process, and free-flowing communication with systematic creative problem-solving to produce four patent proposals and two recommendations for acquisition or licensing of outside resources. Of special interest from this case is the importance of adequately selecting team members for a high-value initiative with a wide range of diversity (in gender, age, educational experience, professional expertise, ethnic background, international experience, etc.). Further, it is important to choose people not just for *what they know* but also for *whom they may know*, that is, for those outside resources they may be able to tap. Team members that are *loosely coupled*, to other experts and resources outside the team and the organization, can be extraordinarily valuable (Le Storti 2003).

Note: We acknowledge Anthony Le Storti and IDEATECTS for this box.

---

describing how data mining techniques have been used to create new knowledge. Here we briefly describe some of the more mature and/or specifically relevant applications of data mining to knowledge management for business.

Over the last decade, data mining techniques have been applied across business problems.[1] Examples of such applications are as follows:

Box 9.4

Solving Problems via Electronic Brainstorming

The conventional brainstorming process described in Box 9.1 typically requires a moderator to record ideas on flipcharts and whiteboards and then use Post-it notes and sticky notes to prioritize these ideas. But at the Executive Decision Centre at Queens University, facilitators use Group Decision Support Software (GDSS) as a means to develop new ideas and reach consensus. The process requires that after the facilitator poses a question, meeting participants enter their ideas on laptops. Once all the ideas are shared via a big screen, the facilitator together with the group of participants, clarifies, merges, and reorganizes them as needed. Following a clarification discussion, each participant individually votes via the computer on the top ideas. The system then collects and ranks the results, at which point the group can then further discuss and further develop the top ideas and their corresponding action plans. One of the benefits of this virtual brainstorming process is that people tend to feel empowered and committed, and it minimizes the impact that strong personalities could have on the team dynamics. Other benefits include:

- Time savings by getting to the key issues more quickly;
- Simultaneous input allows each panel expert to participate equally generating richer ideas;
- More focused discussions with greater participation;
- More structured, disciplined decision-making; and
- Much more enjoyable brainstorming sessions because a varied approach creates a focused, energetic group.

The team at Queens Executive Decision Centre has facilitated the work of over 400 groups in the past five years who have used the GDSS to innovate and reach decisions related to strategic direction and thinking, team building, resource allocation, new product development, planning and review, SWOT analysis, training and development, policy formulation, focus groups, conflict resolution, process improvement, sales account planning, employee satisfaction surveys, expert panels, action planning, and vision and mission goal setting. More recently, the group used a GDSS to assist in the facilitation of over 4,000 people engaged in the monumental task of facilitating the rebuilding of New Orleans after Hurricane Katrina. At this meeting, each facilitator used a GDSS to discuss with fifteen current and former residents of New Orleans the most important issues facing these residents—namely, education, crime and policing, health care, neighborhoods, and resettlement. In this environment, no issue was too contentious and no idea was too extreme. The outcome of this meeting was integral to the creation of the Unified New Orleans Plan. The 10-site, coast-to-coast meeting included a cast of more than 100 facilitators who shared group dynamics skills and a passion for computer-based meeting support. In the end, the technology helped the participants to focus on difficult and sometimes controversial community and corporate issues.

Note: We acknowledge Erick Lockhart <elockhart@business.queensu.ca> for this information.

1. *Marketing*—**Predictive DM techniques**, like **artificial neural networks (ANN)**, have been used for target marketing including market segmentation. This allows the marketing departments using this approach to segment customers according to basic demographic characteristics such as gender, age group, and so forth, as well as their purchasing patterns. They have also been used to improve direct marketing campaigns through an understanding of which customers are likely to respond to new products based on their previous consumer behavior.

Figure 9.1 **IDEATECTS Problem Solving Model**

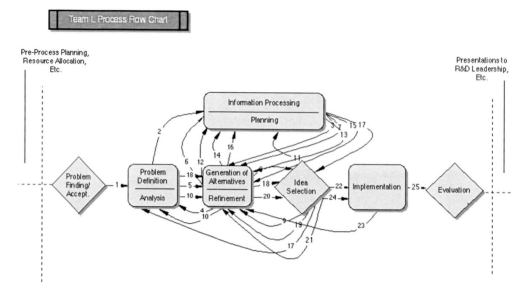

2. *Retail*—DM methods have likewise been used for sales forecasting. These take into consideration multiple market variables, such as customer profiling based on their purchasing habits. Techniques like **market basket analysis** also help uncover which products are likely to be purchased together.
3. *Banking*—Trading and financial forecasting have also proven to be excellent applications for DM techniques. These are used to determine derivative securities pricing, futures price forecasting, and stock performance. Inferential DM techniques have also been successful in developing scoring systems to identify credit risk and fraud. An area of recent interest is attempting to model the relationships among corporate strategy, financial health, and corporate performance.
4. *Insurance*—DM techniques have been used for segmenting customer groups to determine premium pricing and to predict claim frequencies. **Clustering techniques** have also been applied to detecting claim fraud and to aid in customer retention.
5. *Telecommunications*—Predictive DM techniques, like artificial neural networks, have been used mostly to attempt to reduce **churn**, that is, to predict when customers will attrition to a competitor. In addition, predictive techniques like neural networks can be used to predict the conditions that may cause a customer to return. Finally, market basket analysis has been used to identify which telecommunication products are customers likely to purchase together.
6. *Operations management*—Neural networks have been used for planning and scheduling, project management, and quality control.

Diagnosis is a fertile ground for mining knowledge. Diagnostic examples typically abound in large companies with many installed systems and a wide network of service representatives. The incidents are typically documented well, and often in a highly structured form. Mining the incident database for common aspects in the behavior of particularly troublesome devices can be useful in predicting when they are likely to fail. Having this knowledge, the devices can be preventatively maintained in the short-range and designed or manufactured in a way to avoid the problem altogether in the long-term. Witten (2000) mentions a specific example where diagnostic rules were mined from 600 documented faults in rotating machinery (e.g., motors, generators) and compared to the same rules elicited from a diagnostic expert. It was found that the learned rules provided slightly better performance than the ones elicited from the expert.

In the electric utility business, neural networks have been used routinely to predict the energy consumption load in power systems. The load on a power system depends mostly on the weather. In hot weather areas, air conditioners during the summer represent the biggest load. In cold regions, it is the heating load in the winters. Knowing the weather forecast and how that maps to the expected load can help forecast the load for the next 24, 48, and 72 hours, and thereby place the appropriate generating capacity in readiness to provide the required energy. This is particularly important because efficient power stations cannot be turned on and off within minutes if the load is greater than expected. Nuclear power stations (the most efficient) take several days or weeks to place online from a cold state. Coal- or oil-fired stations (the next most efficient) take the better part of one day to do the same. Although other types of generating equipment can be turned quickly on and off, they are highly inefficient and costly to operate. Therefore, utilities greatly benefit if they can bring their efficient units online in anticipation of energy load increases, yet running them unnecessarily can also be expensive.

All major electric utilities have entire departments expressly dedicated to this load-forecasting function. The expected temperature is the most influential factor. However, other attributes such as the day of the week, the humidity, and wind speed have some influence as well. Data mining in this context consists of training neural networks to predict the energy load in a certain area for a specified period of time. This is considered supervised training. The relations are embedded in the weights computed by the training algorithm, typically the **back-propagation algorithm.** By mining a database containing actual recorded data on ambient temperatures, wind speed, humidity, day of the week (among others), and the actual power consumed per hour, the network can be trained. Then, the forecast values can be fed for the same attributes and it can predict the load on a per hour basis for 24, 48, and 72 hours. Results have been very promising, leading the Electric Power Research Institute to offer neural network-based tools to perform this specific function.

Witten (2000) describes a use of data mining for credit applications. In this project, a credit institution undertook a project in data mining to learn the characteristics of borrowers who defaulted in their loans in order to better identify those customers who are likely to default on their loans. Using 1,000 examples and 20 attributes, a set of rules was mined from the data, which resulted in a 66 percent successful prediction rate.

By 1996, 95 percent of the top banks in the United States were utilizing data mining techniques (Smith and Gupta 2000). For example in the mid-1990s, Bank of Montreal was facing increased competition and the need to **target-sell** to its large customer base. Earlier telemarketing attempts had proven unsuccessful, therefore the bank embarked on an attempt to develop a knowledge discovery system to determine a customer's likelihood of purchasing new products. As a result, the bank can now segment its customers for a more targeted product marketing campaign (Stevens 2001).

Nevertheless, the most common and useful applications are in product marketing and sales and in business operations. Every time someone purchases a product, a sales record is kept. Often, these records contain demographic information on the buyer and other times not. In any case, obtaining a **personal profile** of the purchasers of the product can serve to better direct the product to this cross-section of consumers or expand its appeal to other cross-sections not currently purchasing the product. This is true for not only hard products but also for services such as long distance, Internet service providers, banking and financial services, and others.

For example, Proflowers is a Web-based flower retailer. Flowers perish quickly; therefore, Proflowers must level its inventory as the day progresses in order to adequately serve its customers. Proflowers has achieved better management of its customer traffic via inventory optimization that downplays the better-selling products on their Web-storefront while highlighting the slower-selling ones. Based on their analysis of Web purchases, Proflowers is able to change their Web site throughout the day and therefore effectively attract attention to lower-selling items through their Web site (Stevens 2001).

Another example is eBags a Web-based retailer of suitcases, wallets, and related products. Through the use of **Web content mining**, the company is able to determine which Web pages result in higher customer purchases. This information is used to adequately determine how Web content can drive the sales process. Finally eBags uses the results from their Web content mining to help them personalize their retailing Web pages on the fly, based on customer's buying preferences and even geographic location. For example, capturing the Web visitor's zip code could be used to infer how affluent the online shopper is. If she comes from an affluent neighborhood, the Web site may feature designer items. If the online shopper comes from a zip code marked by a large number of apartments, discounted offers would be made prominent in the user's view of the Web store (Stevens 2001).

Data mining techniques have also been used in areas as diverse as facilitating the classification of a country's investing risk based on a variety of factors and identifying the factors associated with a country's competitiveness (Becerra-Fernandez et al. 2002). For a quick overview of what knowledge discovery systems are and how they are used, let us look at Box 9.5, which shows how Britain's Safeway supermarkets (now Wm Morrison Supermarkets) have used data mining techniques to recommend products to shoppers and thus increase sales. In Box 9.6, we describe the role that data mining can play in detecting money laundering and terrorist financing.

The KDD process is viewed as both an interactive and iterative process that turns data into information and information into business knowledge. Next, we discuss the steps in the KDD process.

Box 9.5

Filling up the Grocery Cart at Safeway

Safeway Stores is one of the Britain's leading food grocers, employing around 90,000 staff and owning more than 500 stores across the country. Since the penetration of personal computers (PCs) in Britain is lower than in the United States, IBM developed an application for Britain's Safeway Stores that enables customers to prepare their shopping lists on a personal digital assistant (PDA) and transmit their order to the store for subsequent pickup without having to walk the aisles of the market. Shoppers quickly jumped on the convenience, which removes the marketer from the opportunity to suggest via attractive displays the spontaneous purchase of additional products that invariably fill up the shopping cart (IBM 2004).

In order to provide for a means to suggest the purchase of additional products, Safeway turned to the use of data mining as a means to recommend additional purchases to its clients. The idea of personalizing the recommendations was based on the prior successful implementations of such systems, which work by *filtering* a set of *items* (for example, grocery products) through a *personal profile*. This filtering may be *content-based,* which recommends items based on what a person has liked in the past. Alternatively, the filtering may be collaborative, which recommends items that other people, similar to the one at hand, have liked in the past (Lawrence et al. 2001). Safeway shoppers construct a shopping list via the PDA and e-mail it to the grocer's server. Shoppers select products from lists residing in the personal catalog, the store's recommendations, and special promotions. Safeway customers are clustered based on their prior purchasing behavior, and a list of most popular products is generated to represent the preferred product purchases for the customers in each cluster. The *recommender* system at Safeway then ranks this list of products, according to computed affinities with each customer, to produce a list of 10 to 20 of the highest-ranking products. When customers synchronize with the store server they are presented with the recommended list, which in fact contains products that were not previously purchased by the customer.

Results demonstrated that using the recommender resulted in 25 percent of the orders including something from the recommendation list and a 1.8 percent increase in revenue. The study demonstrates that data mining can help improve the understanding of customer preferences and thereby boost the business revenue. For more information on this study, see Lawrence et al. (2001).

Recent developments at Safeway include testing of new in-store shopping cart technology to flash personalized ads to customers while they shop through the store (Gilbert 2002). As customers walk down the store aisles, the shopping cart screen flashes promotions and coupons based on prior purchasing patterns which remain stored in their loyalty Club Cards.

DESIGNING THE KNOWLEDGE DISCOVERY SYSTEM

Discovering knowledge can be different things for different organizations. Some organizations have large databases, while others may have small ones. The problems faced by the users of data mining systems may also be quite different. Therefore, the developers of DM software face a difficult process when attempting to build tools that are considered generalizable across the entire spectrum of applications and corporate cultures. Early efforts to apply data mining in business operations faced the need to learn, primarily via trial and error, how to develop an effective approach to DM. In fact, as early adopters of DM observed an exploding interest in the application of techniques, the need to develop a standard process model for KDD became apparent. This standard should be well-reasoned, nonproprietary, and freely available to all DM practitioners.

Box 9.6

Using Data Mining to Detect Money Laundering and Terrorist Financing

In the past, U.S. intelligence agencies have prevented money laundering and terrorist financing via focused attention on transactions in the financial service sectors, such as banks and other financial service institutions. But a more significant and largely overlooked mechanism for money laundering is via abnormal international trade pricing. Overvaluing imports or undervaluing exports is perhaps the oldest technique used to elude the government's attention. Paying a higher value for an imported product means the money is shifted to the foreign exporter who could be an operative of a terrorist organization. Similarly, undervalued exports, preferred by terrorists and money launderers because they avoid the use of financial institutions, involves purchasing products at market price for cash and then exporting to a colluding importer at below market prices who resells them for their true value. All of these activities can translate to customs fraud, income tax evasion, and money laundering (Zdanowicz 2004).

   A data mining study of the 2001 U.S. import and export transactions produced by the U.S. Department of Commerce reported suspicious prices that translated to overvalued imports and undervalued exports to the tune of US$156.22 billion in 2001. Money laundered from the United States to countries appearing in the U.S. State Department Al Qaeda watch list was estimated to be around $4.27 billion that same year (Zdanowicz 2004). Thus, data mining is without a doubt critical in order to win the war against terrorism.

In 1999, a consortium of vendors and early adopters of DM applications for business operations—consisting of Daimler-Chrysler (then Daimler-Benz AG, Germany), NCR Systems Engineering Copenhagen (Denmark), SPSS/Integral Solutions Ltd. (England), and OHRA Verzegeringen en Bank Groep B.V. (The Netherlands)—developed a set of specifications called **Cross-Industry Standard Process for Data Mining (CRISP-DM)** (Brachman and Anand 1996; Chapman et al. 2000; Edelstein 1999). CRISP-DM is an industry consortium that developed an industry-neutral and tool-neutral process for data mining. CRISP-DM defines a hierarchical process model that defines the basic steps of data mining for knowledge discovery as follows:

BUSINESS UNDERSTANDING

The first requirement for knowledge discovery is to **understand the business** problem. In other words to obtain the highest benefit from data mining, there must be a clear statement of the business objectives. For example, a business goal could be "to increase the response rate of direct mail marketing." An economic justification based on the return of investment of a more effective direct mail marketing may be necessary to justify the expense of the data mining study. This step also involves an assessment of the current situation, for example:

> the current response rate to direct mail is 1 percent. Results of the study showed that using 35 percent of the current sample population for direct mail (the one that is likely to buy the product), a marketing campaign could reach 80 percent of the prospective buyers.

In other words, the majority of the people in a marketing campaign who receive a target mail do not purchase the product. This example illustrates how you could effectively isolate 80 percent of the prospective buyers by mailing only to 35 percent of the customers in a sample marketing campaign database. Identifying the most likely prospective buyers from the sample and targeting the direct mail to those customers could save the organization significant costs, mainly those associated with mailing a piece to 65 percent of the customers who are the least likely to buy the new product offering. The maximum profit occurs from mailing to the 35 percent of the customers that are most likely to buy the new product. Finally, this step also includes the specification of a project plan for the DM study.

DATA UNDERSTANDING

One of the most important tenets in data engineering is "know thy data." Knowing the data well can permit the designers to tailor the algorithm or tools used for data mining to their specific problem. This maximizes the chances for success as well as the efficiency and effectiveness of the knowledge discovery system. This step, together with preparation and modeling, consumes most of the resources required for the study. In fact, data understanding and preparation may take from 50 percent to 80 percent of the time and effort required for the entire knowledge discovery process. Typically, data collection for the data mining project requires the creation of a database, although a spreadsheet may be just as adequate. Data mining doesn't require data collection in a **data warehouse** and in the case the organization is equipped with a data warehouse, its best not to attempt to manipulate the data warehouse directly for the purpose of the DM study. Furthermore, the structure of the data warehouse may not lend itself for the type of data manipulation required. Finally, the construction of a data warehouse that integrates data from multiple sources into a single database is typically a huge endeavor that could extend a number of years and cost millions of dollars (Gray and Watson 1998). Most data mining tools enable the input data to take many possible formats, and the data transformation is transparent to the user. The steps required for the data understanding process are as follows:

1. Data Collection

This step defines the data sources for the study, including the use of external public data (e.g., real estate tax folio) and proprietary databases (e.g., contact information for businesses in a particular zip code). The **data collection** report typically includes the following: a description of the data source, data owner, who (organization and person) maintains the data, cost (if purchased), storage format and structure, size (e.g., in records, rows, etc.), physical storage characteristics, security requirements, restrictions on use, and privacy requirements.

2. Data Description

This step describes the contents of each file or table. Some of the important items in this report are number of fields (columns) and percent of records missing. Also for each field or column: data type, definition, description, source, unit of measure, number of unique values, list and range of values. Also some other valuable specifics are about how the data were collected and the time frame when the data were collected. Finally, in the case of relational databases, it is important to know which attributes are the primary or foreign keys.

3. Data Quality and Verification

In general, good models require good data; therefore, the data must be correct and consistent. This step determines whether any data can be eliminated because of irrelevance or lack of quality. In addition, many data mining packages allow specifying which columns in a table will be ignored (for the same reasons) during the modeling phase. Furthermore, missing data can cause significant problems. Some data mining algorithms (e.g., C5.0) can handle the missing data problem by automatically massaging the data and using **surrogates** for the missing data points. Other algorithms may be sensitive to missing values. In that case, one approach would be to discard the data sample if some of the attributes or fields are missing which could cause a substantial loss of data. A better approach is to calculate a substitute value for the missing values. Substitute values could consist of the mode, median, or mean of the attribute variable depending on the data type.

4. Exploratory Analysis of the Data

Techniques such as visualization and online analytical processing (OLAP) enable preliminary data analysis. This step is necessary to develop a hypothesis of the problem to be studied and to identify the fields that are likely to be the best predictors. In addition, some values may need to be derived from the raw data, for example factors such as per capita income may be a more relevant factor to the model than the factor income.

DATA PREPARATION

The steps for this task are:

1. Selection

This step requires the selection of the predictor variables and the **sample set**. Selecting the predictor variables is necessary because typically data mining algorithms don't work well if all the variables (fields or database columns) are considered as **potential predictors**. In essence, that's why data mining requires an understanding of the domain and the potential variables influencing the outcome in question. As a rule-of-thumb, the number of predictors (columns) must be smaller than the number of samples (rows) in the data set. In fact, the number of simple observations should be at least 10 to 25 times the number of predictors. As the number of predictors increases, the computational requirement to build the model also increases. Selecting the sample set is necessary because when the data set is large, a sample of the data set can be selected to represent the complete data set. In selecting the sample, attention must be paid to the constraints imposed by sampling theory in order for the sample to be representative of the complete data set.

2. Construction and Transformation of Variables

Often, new variables must be constructed to build effective models. Examples include ratios and combination of various fields. Furthermore, some algorithms, like market basket analysis, may require data to be transformed to categorical format (integer) when in fact the raw data exist in continuous form. This may require transformations that group values in ranges like *low, medium,* and *high.*

3. Data Integration

The data set for the data mining study may reside on multiple databases, which would need to be consolidated into one database. Data consolidation may require redefinition of some of the data fields to allow for consistency. For example, different databases may relate to the same customer with different names; for instance, one database may refer to the *National Aeronautics and Space Administration* while other database fields may just use *NASA.* These incompatibilities must be reconciled prior to data integration.

4. Formatting

This step involves the reordering and reformatting of the data fields as required by the DM model.

MODEL BUILDING AND VALIDATION

Building an accurate model is a trial-and-error process. The process often requires the data mining specialist to iteratively try several options until the best model emerges. Furthermore, different algorithms could be tried with the same data set and the results then compared to see which model yields the best results. For example, both neural network and **rule induction algorithms** could be applied to the same data set to develop a predictive model. The results from each algorithm could be compared for accuracy in their respective predictive quality. Following the model development, the models must be evaluated or validated. In constructing a model, a subset of the data is usually set aside for validation purposes. This means that the validation data set is not used to develop or train the model but to calculate the accuracy of predictive qualities of the model. The most popular validation technique is n-fold cross-validation, specifically ten-fold validation. The **tenfold validation** divides the population of the validation data set into ten approximately equal-sized data sets and then uses each of the ten holdout sets a single time to evaluate the models developed with the remaining nine training sets. For each of the ten models (the last model includes using the whole data set) the accuracy is determined, and the overall model accuracy is determined as the average of each of the model samples.

EVALUATION AND INTERPRETATION

Once the model is determined, the validation data set is fed through the model. Because the outcome for this data set is known, the predicted results are compared with the actual results in the validation data set. This comparison yields the accuracy of the model. As a rule-of-thumb, a model accuracy of around 50 percent would be insignificant because that would be the same accuracy as for a random occurrence.

DEPLOYMENT

This step involves implementing the "live" model within an organization to aid the decision-making process. A valid model must also make sense in the real world, and a pilot implementation is always warranted prior to deployment. Also, following implementation it's important to continue to monitor how well the model predicts the outcomes and the benefits that this brings to the organization. For example, a clustering model may be deployed to identify fraudulent Medicare claims. When the model identifies potential instances of fraud, and these instances are validated as indeed fraudulent, the savings to the organization from the deployment of the model should be captured. These early successes will then act as champions and will result in continued implementation of knowledge discovery models within the organization.

Figure 9.2 summarizes the CRISP-DM process methodology. Figure 9.3 illustrates the iterative nature of the CRISP-DM process.

CRISP-DM is only one of the institutions that have ongoing efforts towards streamlining the KDD process. Other similar efforts include:

1. **Customer Profile Exchange (CPEX)**: offers a vendor-neutral, XML-based open standard for facilitating the privacy-enabled interchange of customer information across disparate **enterprise** applications and systems.
2. **Data Mining Group (DMG)**: is an independent, vendor led group, which develops data mining standards, such as the Predictive Model Markup Language (PMML).

In general, the goal that these standards pursue is to facilitate the planning, documentation, and communication in data mining projects and to serve as a common reference framework for the DM industry. Many of these standards were developed based on practical experience resulting from the implementation of DM projects. In fact, the purpose of these standards is to help people involved in the process to communicate.

The next section describes in detail step four in the KDD process, which is building and validating the data mining predictive model.

GUIDELINES FOR EMPLOYING DATA MINING TECHNIQUES

Once the goal of the data mining system is understood (step 1 of the CRISP-DM process) and the data have been collected (step 2) and prepared (step 3), the next step involves building and validating the data mining model (step 4). In terms of defining

Figure 9.2 **CRISP-DM Data Mining Process Methodology**

Business Understanding	Data Understanding	Data Preparation	Modelling	Evaluation	Deployment
Determine Business Objectives • Background • Business objectives • Business success criteria	Initial Data Collection • Initial data collection report	• Data set • Data set description	Generate Test Design • Test design	Evaluate Results • Approved models • Assessment of data mining results w.r.t. business success criteria	Plan Deployment • Deployment plan
Situation Assessment • Inventory of resources • Requirements • Assumptions • Constraints • Risks and contingencies • Terminology • Costs and benefits	Data Description • Data description report	Selection • Rationale for inclusion/exclusion	Build Model • Parameter settings • Models	Review Process • Review of process	Produce Final Report • Final report • Final presentation
Determine Data Mining Goal • Data mining goals • Data mining success criteria	Data Quality Verification • Data quality report	Cleaning • Data cleaning report	Model Evaluation • Model description • Assessment	Determine Next Steps • List of possible actions • Decision	Plan Monitoring and Maintenance • Maintenance plan
Produce Project Plan • Project plan	Exploratory Analysis • Exploratory analysis report	Construction • Derived variables • Generated records • Transformation			Review Project • Experience documentation
		Integration • Merging • Aggregation			
		Formatting • Rearranging attributes • Reordering records • Within-value reformatting			

Figure 9.3 **The Iterative Nature of the KDD Process**

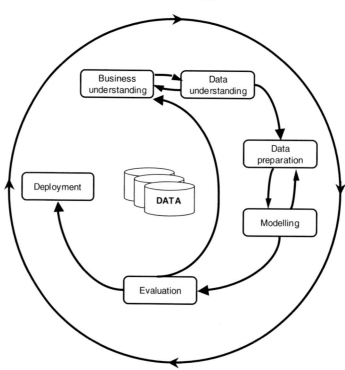

Source: SPSS 2000.

the adequate data mining techniques to be used, the nature of the data will play the deciding role as to which technique is most appropriate. Input variables (also called predictors) and output variables (also called outcomes), could be continuous or discrete (also called categorical). In addition, the data could also be textual, which command a different set of data mining techniques.

In general the first step in defining the data mining technique to be used involves defining if the study is of a predictive nature, meaning there is an outcome in mind. For example, to build a model to predict credit risk for customers seeking a loan from a bank, a data set must exist that includes for each customer their corresponding characteristics (such as credit score, salary, years of education, etc.), which will serve as the predictors or inputs to the model as well as the outcome variable credit risk. In this example, there is an outcome in mind: credit risk. This is also called **inferential techniques** or supervised learning. In unsupervised learning, there is not a previously known outcome in mind, and we describe these methods later as the descriptive techniques that appear in Table 9.4.

Data mining techniques include both statistical as well as nonstatistical techniques. Statistical techniques are known as traditional data mining methods including regression, logistic regression, and multivariate methods. Nonstatistical techniques, also known as intelligent techniques or data-adaptive methods, include memory-based reasoning, decision trees, and neural networks.

Table 9.1

Summary of Applicability of Inferential Statistical Techniques

Goal	Input Variables (Predictors)	Output Variables (Outcomes)	Statistical Technique	Examples (SPSS, 2000)
Find linear combination of predictors that best separate the population	Continuous	Discrete	Discriminant Analysis	• Predict instances of fraud • Predict whether customers will remain or leave (churners or not) • Predict which customers will respond to a new product or offer • Predict outcomes of various medical procedures
Predict the probability of outcome being in a particular category	Continuous	Discrete	Logistic and Multinomial Regression	• Predicting insurance policy renewal • Predicting fraud • Predicting which product a customer will buy • Predicting that a product is likely to fail
Output is a linear combination of input variables	Continuous	Continuous	Linear Regression	• Predict expected revenue in dollars from a new customer • Predict sales revenue for a store • Predict waiting time on hold for callers to an 800 number • Predict length of stay in a hospital based on patient characteristics and medical condition
For experiments and repeated measures of the same sample	Most inputs must be discrete	Continuous	Analysis of Variance (ANOVA)	• Predict which environmental factors are likely to cause cancer
To predict future events whose history has been collected at regular intervals	Continuous	Continuous	Time Series Analysis	• Predict future sales data from past sales records

Table 9.1 summarizes the different inferential statistic techniques and their applicability pertaining to the characteristics of the input and output variables. Inferential statistical techniques are differentiated from descriptive statistics. Inferential statistics are used to generalize from data and thus develop models that generalize from the observations. Descriptive statistics (which appear in Table 9.4) are used to find patterns or define classes of similar objects in the data collected.

The key difference between using statistical techniques and nonstatistical techniques is that the statistical techniques require a hypothesis to be specified beforehand. In addition, statistical techniques often are subject to stringent assumptions such as normality of the sample data, uncorrelated error, or homogeneity of variance. In particular when the number of explanatory variables is large, model specification and selection is increasingly difficult, making it harder to work with statistical techniques. However, statistical techniques provide for a more rigorous test of hypotheses. Table 9.2 summarizes the predictive nonstatistical techniques and their applicability pertaining to the characteristics of the input and output variables. Memory-based reasoning (MBR) is a DM technique that looks for the nearest neighbors of known data samples and combines their values to assign classification or prediction values for new data samples. It is very similar to Case-based Reasoning as described in Chapter 6. Like CBR, MBR uses a distance function to find the nearest element to a new data sample, and a combination function to combine the values at the nearest neighbors to make a prediction. For more information on MBR refer to Berry and Linoff (1997).

Among the techniques described in Table 9.2, decision trees (or rule induction methods) are used to predict the outcome by splitting data into subgroups. Different decision tree and rule induction methods are applicable depending on the characteristics of the data. Table 9.3 summarizes the various methods.

Table 9.4 summarizes the different descriptive techniques, including both association and clustering methods, and their applicability pertaining to the characteristics of the input variables. Note that for all these techniques, the outcome or output variable is not defined. Market basket or association analysis can include the use of two techniques: Apriori is an association rule algorithm that requires the input fields to be discrete. Apriori is generally faster to train than Generalized Rule Induction (GRI). Apriori allows only the specification of logical (or dichotomies) for the input variables, such as (True, False) or (1,0) to indicate the presence (or absence) of the item in the market basket. Generalized rule induction is an association rule algorithm, capable of producing rules that describe associations between attributes to a symbolic target and is capable of using continuous or logical data as its input.

Typically, several methods could be applied to any problem with similar results. The knowledge discovery process is an **iterative** process as we will describe in the next section. Once the model has been developed, the results must be evaluated. The potential for errors and their consequences must be carefully considered when performing a data mining exercise. An intelligent computer system can make two types of errors when trying to solve a problem. To simplify the argument, let's assume that the possible solutions can only be "yes" or "no." One instance of this could be in a medical diagnosis of a serious disease, such as cancer. The two possible errors are: (1) an indication of "no" when the true answer is "yes," and (2) an indication of "yes" when the true answer is "no." The former is called the user's risk, while the latter is called the developer's risk. Depending on the application of the system, one type of error may be tolerable while the other may not be. For example, in the case of medical diagnosis such as cancer, a false positive ("no" when the answer is truly "yes") can be very costly in terms of the seriousness of the error. On the other hand, a system designed to select a type of wine for a meal may tolerate such an error quite acceptably.

The cost of errors must be carefully evaluated when the model is examined. For example, Table 9.5 presents the results of a study to predict the diagnosis of patients with heart disease based on a set of input variables. In the table, the columns represent predicted values for the diagnostic and the rows represent actual values for diagnostics of patients undergoing a heart disease examination. Actual values are coded in

Table 9.2

Summary of Applicability of Non-Inferential Predictive Techniques

Goal	Input (Predictor) Variables	Output (Outcome) Variables	Statistical Technique	Examples (SPSS, 2000)
Predict outcome based on values of nearest neighbors	Continuous, Discrete, and Text	Continuous or Discrete	Memory-based Reasoning (MBR)	• Predicting medical outcomes
Predict by splitting data into subgroups (branches)	Continuous or Discrete (Different techniques used based on data characteristics)	Continuous or Discrete (Different techniques used based on data characteristics)	Decision Trees	• Predicting which customers will leave • Predicting instances of fraud
Predict outcome in complex nonlinear environments	Continuous or Discrete	Continuous or Discrete	Neural Networks	• Predicting expected revenue • Predicting credit risk

Table 9.3

Summary of Applicability of Decision Tree Techniques

Goal	Input (Predictor) Variables	Output (Outcome) Variables	Statistical Technique	Examples (SPSS, 2000)
Predict by splitting data into more than two subgroups (branches)	Continuous, Discrete, or Ordinal	Discrete	Chi-square Automatic Interaction Detection (CHAID)	• Predict which demographic combinations of predictors yield the highest probability of a sale • Predict which factors are causing product defects in manufacturing
Predict by splitting data into more than two subgroups (branches)	Continuous	Discrete	C5.0	• Predict which loan customers are considered a "good" risk • Predict which factors are associated with a country's investment risk
Predict by splitting data into binary subgroups (branches)	Continuous	Continuous	Classification and Regression Trees (CART)	• Predict which factors are associated with a country's competitiveness • Discover which variables are predictors of increased customer profitability
Predict by splitting data into binary subgroups (branches)	Continuous	Discrete	Quick, Unbiased, Efficient, Statistical Tree (QUEST)	• Predict who needs additional care after heart surgery

the cells, with percentages coded in parentheses along the actual values. In this table, the predictions made along the quadrant (*Actual No disease/Predicted No disease*) represent patients that were correctly predicted as being healthy. That means that 118 patients (or 72 percent of a total of 164 patients) were diagnosed with *No disease* and they were indeed healthy. On the other hand, looking at the quadrant (*Actual Presence of disease/Predicted Presence of disease*) 96 patients (or 69.1 percent of a total of 139 patients) were diagnosed with *Presence of disease* and they were indeed sick. So for the patients in these two quadrants the classification algorithm correctly predicted their heart disease diagnosis. But the patients whose diagnosis falls off this diagonal were incorrectly classified. In this example, 46 patients (or 28 percent of a total of 164 patients) were diagnosed with the disease when if fact they were healthy. Furthermore, 43 patients (or 30.9 percent of a total of 139 patients) were incorrectly diagnosed with no disease when in fact they were sick.

In summary, 70.6 percent of the patients in this example were correctly classified with the prediction algorithm. Note that in this example, the cost of incorrectly giving a patient a sound bill of health, when in fact she is sick, is considered much higher than incorrectly predicting the patient to be sick, when in fact he is healthy. The former may cause the patient to die without the proper care, while the latter will give the patient a jolt but further tests are likely to exonerate him.

Table 9.4

Summary of Applicability of Clustering and Association Techniques

Goal	Input Variables (Predictor)	Output Variables (Outcome)	Statistical Technique	Examples (SPSS 2000)
Find large groups of cases in large data files that are similar on a small set of input characteristics	Continuous or Discrete	No outcome variable	K-means Cluster Analysis	• Customer segments for marketing • Groups of similar insurance claims
To create large cluster memberships			Kohonen Neural Networks	• Cluster customers into segments based on demo-graphics and buying patterns
Create small set associations and look for patterns between many categories	Logical	No outcome variable	Market Basket or Association Analysis with Apriori	• Identify which products are likely to be purchased together • Identify which courses students are likely to take together
Create small set associations and look for patterns between many categories	Logical or numeric	No outcome variable	Market Basket or Association Analysis with GRI	• Identify which courses students are likely to take together
To create linkages between sets of items to display complex relationships	Continuous or Discrete	No outcome variable	Link Analysis	• To identify a relationship between a network of physicians and their prescriptions

Table 9.5

Classification Table Results

Heart Disease Diagnostic	Predicted No Disease	Predicted Presence of Disease
Actual No Disease	**118 (72%)**	46 (28%)
Actual Presence of Disease	43 (30.9%)	**96 (69.1%)**

Source: SPSS 2000.

DISCOVERING KNOWLEDGE ON THE WEB

Business organizations can profit greatly from mining the Web. The business need for Web DM is clear:

> Companies venturing in e-commerce have a dream. By analyzing the tracks people make through their Web site, they'll be able to optimize its design to maximize sales. Information about customers and their purchasing habits will let companies initiate e-mail campaigns and other activities that result in sales. Good models of customers' preferences, needs, desires, and behaviors will let companies simulate the personal relationship that businesses and their clientele had in the good old days (Edelstein 2001).

Web-based companies are expecting to discover all this knowledge in the logs maintained by their Web servers. The expectation is that a customer's path through the data may enable companies to customize their Web pages, increase the average purchase amount per customer visit to the site, and in a nutshell increased profitability.

Certainly, e-business provides a fertile ground for learning market trends as well as what the competitors are up to. Therefore, learning to mine the Web can lead to a tremendous amount of new knowledge. Web pages and documents found on the Web can provide important information at a minimal cost to develop or maintain. Text mining refers to automatically "reading" large documents (called *corpora*) of text written in natural language and being able to derive knowledge from the process. Web mining is "Web crawling with on-line text mining" (Zanasi 2000). Zanasi reports about Online Analyst, a system that can mine the Web to provide competitive intelligence—a term that indicates knowledge leading to competitive advantages for a business organization. This system provides the user with an intelligent agent that surfs the Web in an intelligent fashion, and reads and quickly analyzes documents that are retrievable online. This system has the advantage that it can review many more documents than a human analyst can, even working 24 hours per day. Some of the documents may be well hidden (unintentionally or otherwise), and often times the relevant information can be found deeply buried within one document. Zanasi does not describe the techniques behind Online Analyst, probably to protect its own secrets. The system was developed by IBM-Bologna in Italy and is used as a tool for consulting.

Unfortunately, the information and data in the Web are unstructured. This can lead to difficulties when mining the Web. Conventional data mining techniques described earlier are not all applicable to Web mining, because by their nature they are limited to highly structured data. There are several differences between traditional data mining and Web mining. One significant difference is that Web mining requires linguistic analysis or natural language processing (NLP) abilities. It is estimated that 80 percent of the world's online content is based on text (Chen 2001). Web mining requires techniques from both information retrieval and artificial intelligence domains. Therefore, Web text mining techniques are rather different from the DM techniques described previously.

Web pages are indexed by the words they contain. Gerald Salton (1989) is generally considered the father of **information retrieval** (IR). IR indexing techniques consist of calculating the function **term frequency inverse document frequency (TFIDF)**. The function consists of the product of a term frequency and its inverse document frequency, which depends on the frequency of occurrence of a specific keyword-term in the text and the number of documents it appears in. The term frequency (TF) refers to how frequently a term occurs in the text, which represents the importance of the term. The inverse document frequency (IDF) increases the significance of terms that appear in fewer documents, while downplaying terms that occur in many documents. TFIDF then highlights terms that are frequently used in one document but infrequently used across the collection of documents. The net effect is that terms like cryogenics which may occur frequently in a scientist's Web page, but infrequently across the whole domain of Web pages, will result in a good indexing term.

WEB MINING TECHNIQUES

Web mining techniques can be classified into four main layers (Chen 2001):

1. Linguistic Analysis/NLP

Linguistic Analysis/NLP is used to identify key concept descriptors (the *who, what, when,* or *where*), which are embedded in the textual documents. In NLP the unit of analysis is the word. These functions can be combined with other linguistic techniques such as *stemming, morphological analysis, Boolean, proximity, range,* and *fuzzy search.* For example, a **stemming algorithm** is used to remove the suffix of a word. **Stoplists** are used to eliminate words that are not good concept descriptions, such as prepositions (e.g., *and, but,* etc.). Linguistic techniques can be combined with statistical techniques, for example to represent grammatically correct sentences. Also **semantic analysis** is used to represent meaning in stories and sentences.

2. Statistical and Co-occurrence Analysis

Statistical and co-occurrence analysis is similar to the TFIDF function mentioned before. For example, **link analysis** is used to create conceptual associations and automatic thesauri for keyword concepts. Also **similarity functions** are used to compute co-occurrence probabilities between concept pairs.

3. Statistical and Neural Networks Clustering and Categorization

Like those discussed previously in "Designing the Knowledge Discovery System" section, statistical and neural networks clustering and categorization are used to group similar documents together as well as communities into domain categories. Kohonen NN techniques work well for large-scale Web text mining tasks and its results can be graphically visualized and intuitive.

4. Visualization and Human Computer Interfaces

Visualization and **human computer interfaces (HCI)** can reveal conceptual associations, which can be represented in various dimensions (one-, two-, and three-dimensional views). Furthermore, interaction techniques, such as zooming, can be incorporated to infer new knowledge.

USES FOR WEB DATA MINING

There are three types of uses for Web data mining. They are as follows:

1. Web Structure Mining

Mining the Web structure examines how the Web documents are structured and attempts to discover the model underlying the link structures of the Web. **Intra-page**

structure mining evaluates the arrangement of the various HTML or XML tags within a page; **inter-page structure** refers to hyperlinks connecting one page to another. Web structure mining can be useful to categorize Web pages, and to generate relationships and similarities among Web sites (Jackson 2002).

2. Web Usage Mining

Web usage mining, also known as **clickstream analysis**, involves the identification of patterns in user navigation through Web pages in a domain. Web usage mining tries to discover knowledge about the Web surfer's behaviors through analysis of his/her interactions with the Web site including the mouse clicks, user queries, and transactions. Web usage mining includes three main tasks: *preprocessing, pattern discovery,* and *pattern analysis* (Jackson 2002):

   a. Preprocessing—converts usage, content, and structure from different data sources into data sets ready for pattern discovery. This step is the most challenging in the data mining process, since it may involve data collection from multiple servers (including **proxy servers**), cleansing of extraneous information, and using data collected by cookies for identification purposes.
   b. Pattern analysis—This step takes advantage of visualization and **Online Analytical Processing (OLAP)** techniques, like the ones discussed earlier, to aid understanding of the data, notice unusual values, and identify possible relationships between the **variables**.
   c. Pattern discovery—based on the different DM techniques discussed earlier except that certain variations may be considered. For example in a market basket analysis of items purchased through a Web storefront, the click-order for the items added to the shopping cart may be significant, which is not typically studied in brick-and-mortar settings.

3. Web Content Mining

Web content mining is used to discover what a Web page is about and how to uncover new knowledge from it. Web content data include what is used to create the Web page including the text, images, audio, video, hyperlinks, and metadata. Web content mining is based on text mining and IR techniques, which consist of the organization of large amounts of textual data for most efficient retrieval—an important consideration in handling text documents. IR techniques have become increasingly important, as the amount of semistructured as well as unstructured textual data present in organizations has increased dramatically. IR techniques provide a method to efficiently access these large amounts of information.

Mining Web data is by all means a challenging task, but the rewards can be great including aiding the development of a more personalized relationship with the virtual customer, improving the virtual storefront selling process, and increasing Web-site revenues.

DATA MINING AND CUSTOMER RELATIONSHIP MANAGEMENT

Customer relationship management (CRM) is the mechanisms and technologies used to manage the interactions between a company and its customers. Database marketers were the early adopters of CRM software, in order to automate the process of customer interaction. CRM implementations can be characterized as being operational and/or analytical. **Operational CRM** includes sales force automation and call centers. Most global companies have implemented such systems. The goal of operational CRM is to provide a single view and point of contact for each customer. On the other hand, **analytical CRM** uses data mining techniques to uncover customer intelligence that serves to better understand and serve the customer.

In particular, the financial services, retailing, and telecommunications industry, facing increasing competitive markets, are turning to analytical CRM in order to (Schwenk 2002):

a. Integrate the customer viewpoint across all touchpoints—since many CRM solutions combine infrastructure components such as **enterprise application integration (EAI)** technology and data warehouses, as well as OLAP and data mining. The CRM promise is to build an integrated view of the customer, to understand the customer touchpoints, and resulting customer intelligence that will enable organizations to better recognize and service the needs of the customer.

b. Respond to customer demands in "Web time"—because the Web has changed the dynamics of decision making, and competitive environments require organizations to react to increasingly complex customer requests at faster speeds. Also the analysis and interpretation of Web data can be used to enhance and personalize customer offerings. Analysis of Web data can uncover new knowledge about customer behavior and preferences, which can be used to improve Web site design and content.

c. Derive more value from CRM investments—since data mining analysis can be used to perform market segmentation studies that determine what customers could be targeted for certain products, to **narrowcast** (send out target e-mails) customers, and to perform other related studies such as market basket analysis.

For example Redecard, a company that captures and transmits MasterCard, Diners Club, and other credit and debit card transactions in Brazil, uses CRM to analyze transaction and customer data. The company performs market segmentation analysis to determine which customers to target for certain products (Lamont 2002). Also Soriana, a Mexican grocery retailer, uses the market basket analysis capability of its CRM product to study promotion effectiveness and the impact of price changes on purchasing behavior (Lamont 2002).

The first step in the CRM process involves identifying customer market segments with the potential of yielding the highest profit. This step requires sifting through large amounts of data in order to find the "gold nuggets"—the mining promise. CRM software automates the DM process to find predictors of purchasing behaviors. In addition, CRM technology will typically integrate the solution of the DM study into **campaign management software** used to manage the targeted marketing campaign. The goal of campaign management software is to effectively manage the planning, execution, assessment, and refinement of myriad marketing campaigns at an organization. Campaign management software is used to manage and monitor a company's communications with its customers, including direct mail, telemarketing, customer service, point of sale, and Web interactions.

In CRM applications, the data mining prediction models are used to calculate a score, which is a numeric value assigned to each record in the database to indicate the probability that the customer represented by that record will behave in a specific manner. For example, when using DM to predict customer attrition or the likelihood that the customer will leave, a high score represents a high probability that the customer will indeed leave. The set of scores are then used to target customers for specific marketing campaigns.

Perhaps one of the best known innovative implementation of CRM is Harrah's Entertainment, one of the most recognized brand names in the casino entertainment industry. Harrah's comprehensive data warehouse and CRM implementation enabled them to keep track of millions of customers' activities allowing them to market more effectively, thus increasing the attraction and retention of targeted customers. Armed with deep knowledge about their customers' preferences, they customized their customer rewards program and were able to target promotions based on individual preferences. As an example, Harrah's provided hotel vouchers to their out-of-town guests and free show tickets to day-trip visiting customers. Harrah's CRM implementation won them national recognition in addition to an increase of their share of the gaming budget from 36 percent to 42 percent between 1999 and 2002 as well as 110 percent increase in their earnings per share between 1999 and 2002 (Lee et al. 2003). More recently, Hilton Hotels launched their "Customers Really Matter" (also abbreviated as CRM) strategy aimed at improving service delivery and consistency across the Hilton brand. The CRM strategy was viewed as "a way to use technology to give you the power to solidify relationships with our best customers" (Applegate et al. 2008) via the consolidation of far-flung customer data to produce comprehensive arrival reports of their top customers. This strategy aimed to achieve a "holistic view" of the customer and thus improve their experience at every one of their **customer touchpoints** and recognize them properly.

Consider the following scenario: The result of a DM study at a large national bank revealed that many of its customers only take advantage of the checking account services it provides. A typical customer at this institution would deposit their check, quickly moving the funds once they became available to mutual funds accounts and other service providers outside the bank. Using the integrated capabilities for campaign management, the software automatically triggers a direct marketing piece for those customers with a sizable deposit to encourage them to keep their money at the bank. DM and campaign management software can work together to sharpen the focus of prospects, therefore increasing marketing response and effectiveness. For more details about the relationship between DM and CRM, please refer to Berson et al. (2000).

The CRM market is expected to continue to expand in the foreseeable future. Even in times of economic slowdown, worldwide CRM software revenue grew to a total of US$8.1 billion in 2007, a 23.1 percent increase from 2006 revenue of $6.6 billion (Gartner 2008).

BARRIERS TO THE USE OF KNOWLEDGE DISCOVERY SYSTEMS

Possibly two of the barriers that prevented earlier deployment of knowledge discovery in the business arena, versus what we have witnessed in the scientific realm, relate to the prior lack of data in business to support the analysis and the limited computing power to perform the mathematical calculations required by the DM algorithms. Clearly, with the advent of more powerful computers at our desktops and the proliferation of relational databases, data warehouses, and data marts, these early barriers have been overcome. In fact according to the **Storage Law** (Fayyad and Uthurusamy 2002), the capacity of digital data storage worldwide has doubled every nine months for the last decade at twice the rate predicted by **Moore's Law** for the growth of computing power. But by and large, this growing capacity has resulted in phenomena called **data tombs** (Fayyad and Uthurusamy 2002) or **data stores** where data are deposited to "merely rest in peace." This means there's no possibility that these data will be used and the opportunity to discover new knowledge that could be used to improve services, profits, or products, will be lost.

In addition, although many of the DM techniques have been around for more than ten years for scientific applications, only in the past few years have we witnessed the emergence of solutions that consolidate multiple DM techniques in a single software offering. Probably one of the most significant barriers to the explosion of the use of knowledge discovery in organizations relates to the fact that still today implementing a data mining model is still considered an art. Although a number of software packages exist that bundle data mining tools into one software offering, adequately implementing the knowledge discovery models requires intimate knowledge of the algorithmic requirements in addition to familiarity of how to use the software itself and a deep understanding of the business area and the problem that needs to be solved. In addition, a successful DM study typically requires a number of actors to partake in the activity including the project leader, the DM client, the DM analyst, the DM engineer, and the IT analyst (Jackson 2002). The project leader has the overall responsibility for the management of the study. The DM client understands the business problem, but in general doesn't have the adequate technical skills to carry out the study. The DM analyst translates the business needs into technical requirements for the DM model. The DM engineer develops the DM model together with the DM client and analyst. The IT analyst provides access to hardware, software, and data needed to carry out the project. In some large projects, a number of DM analysts and engineers may be involved. Clearly managing the number of actors involved in the study is indeed a challenging task that must be carefully coordinated by the project leader.

Perhaps one of the most interesting dilemmas facing KDD today is its basic definition of being an "interactive" process versus the notion that for the technology to be successful it must become "invisible." KDD can't be both interactive and invisible at the same time. Advocates of making KDD invisible argue that DM is primarily concerned with making it easy, convenient, and practical to explore very large databases without years of training as data analysts (Fayyad and Uthurusamy 2002). In fact, according to this view this goal requires that the following challenges be addressed:

1. *Scaling analysis to large databases:* Current DM techniques require that data sets be loaded into the computer's memory to be manipulated. This requirement offers a significant barrier when very large databases and data warehouses must be scanned to identify patterns.

2. *Scaling to high-dimensional data and models:* Typical statistical analysis studies require humans to formulate a model and then use techniques to validate the model via understanding how well the data fit the model. But it may be increasingly difficult for humans to formulate models *a priori* based on a very large number of variables, which increasingly add dimension to the problem. Models that seek to understand customer behavior in retail or Web- based transactions may fall in this category. Current solutions require humans to formulate a lower dimensional abstraction of the model, which may be easier for humans to understand.

3. *Automating the search:* DM studies typically require the researcher to enumerate the hypothesis under study *a priori.* In the future, DM algorithms may be able to perform this work automatically.

4. *Finding patterns and models understandable and interesting to users:* In the past, DM projects focused on measures of accuracy (how well the model predicts the data) and utility (the benefit derived from the pattern, typically money saved). New benefit measures like understandability of the model and novelty of the results must also be developed. Also DM techniques are expected to incorporate the generation of meaningful reports resulting from the study.

Some of these current challenges are being resolved today through the increasing availability of "verticalized" solutions. For example in CRM software, KDD operations are streamlined through the use of standardized models which may include the most widely used data sources. For instance, a standardized model for financial services would most likely include customer demographics, channel, credit, and card usage as well as information related to the promotion and actual response. In order to streamline the KDD process, the metadata type for each table must be predefined (nominal, ordinal, interval, or continuous) while subsequent KDD operations are based on this information including the prespecification of algorithms that are appropriate to solve specific business problems (Parsa 2000). For example, based on the results presented earlier in Table 9.5, a verticalized application to predict which loan customers are considered a "good" risk will automatically implement the C5.0 algorithm if the input **variables** are continuous and the outcome is discrete.

An additional limitation in the deployment of DM today is the fact that the successful implementation of KDD at any organization may require the integration of disparate systems, since there are few plug-and-play solutions. All of these requirements translate into dollars, making many DM solutions sometimes quite expensive. Making the business case based on realistic estimations of ROI is essential for the success of the knowledge discovery initiative. Finally, effective application of the KDD to business applications requires the solution to be seamlessly integrated into existing environments. This requirement makes the case for vendors, researchers, and practitioners to adopt standards like the CRISP-DM standard discussed earlier.

CASE STUDIES

AN APPLICATION OF RULE INDUCTION TO REAL ESTATE APPRAISAL SYSTEMS

In this section we describe an example of how data mining, specifically rule induction, can be used to infer new knowledge, specifically the contribution of an individual piece of data on a data set or the incremental worth of the individual component on an aggregate set (Gonzalez et al. 1999). For example when performing real estate appraisals, it is necessary to know the incremental worth that a specific feature may have on a house—say for example a swimming pool or garage. Property appraisers face this dilemma, and typically it is the market and not the feature construction cost that determines the incremental worth of the feature on the house. For instance, the incremental worth of an additional bedroom when going from 3 to 4 bedrooms may be different from the incremental worth of going from 4 to 5 bedrooms.

Property appraisals estimate property values via market analysis, which means comparing a house with other similar houses sold recently in the same area. Property appraisers typically use databases of recently sold properties to establish a basis of sales comparables. Market changes are reflected on these databases, although there may be a lag before the market effects are reflected. Sometimes, depending on market conditions, it may be difficult to make such comparisons. For example, during the economic downturn of the housing market it may be hard to find comparable sales because homes are just not selling. On the flipside during the height of the housing market bubble, past sales comparables didn't match what the market, based on supply and demand, estimated were adequate property values.

The technique that we focus on here is described as calculating the *incremental* or *relative* worth of components of **aggregate sets**, where an aggregate set represents a collection, assembly or grouping of member components that have a common nature or purpose (Gonzalez et al. 1999). Based on this definition, a house constitutes an aggregate set of features such as number of bedrooms, number of bathrooms, living area, and so forth. In this example, the term *worth* is used to represent the price of the house, and discovering the incremental worth that a particular feature (e.g., an extra bedroom) will contribute to the price of a house.

In the research cited in this case study, the authors use the technique called difference-based induction (DBI)[2] to calculate the incremental worth of a feature, given the database has similar attributes (e.g., bedrooms) that may have dissimilar impact on the price of the house. The induction algorithm used in this example identifies aggregate sets in the database that contribute slight differences in their attributes' values, thereby identifying which are the most significant attribute/value combination of nearly similar aggregate sets of individual houses. In this example, *value* is associated with each attribute (or feature) in the database, while *worth* is associated with the value of the aggregate set (or house). For each house attribute, the *value* of the attribute is specified (for example area = 1,500 square feet, or number of bedrooms = 4) as well as how each one contributes to the house's *worth*. In this example, the individual worth of an attribute is the amount that it contributes to the overall worth of the house.

The procedure to create the decision tree based on the induction techniques presented earlier is as follows:

1. **Data preparation** and preprocessing—For example there may be missing values in the database, there could be data-entering errors, or lack of consistency with other sets. Therefore they will need to be identified and eliminated, otherwise they could have a distorting effect on the outcome worth of the house.
2. **Tree construction**—Houses are progressively assigned to each of the nodes at each of the tree levels. Branches represent each range of values of the attribute represented in that node, and the branch through which each house is routed depends on the value that each particular house has for the attribute represented in the parent node.
3. House pruning—**Heuristics** are applied to identify and discard those houses whose worth are not consistent with those of other houses in the same leaf-level group.
4. **Paired leaf analysis**—Any difference in worth between houses in two sibling leaves is directly caused by the difference in their values of the critical attribute. For example, two houses are identical in all features, but one has three bedrooms and the other four. If the four-bedroom house sells for $75K and the three-bedroom one for $73K, the extra bedroom is attributed the difference of $2K.

Figure 9.4 and Table 9.6 represent the partial decision tree resulting from the induction algorithm applied to a small sample database of 84 sold homes. The incremental worth computed with the induction algorithm was validated by opinions of real estate appraisal experts. For additional details on this case study please refer to Gonzalez et al. (1999).

AN APPLICATION OF WEB CONTENT MINING TO EXPERTISE LOCATOR SYSTEMS

One application of Web content mining methods is in the construction of **expertise locator knowledge management systems**. A KM system that locates experts based on published documents requires an automatic method for identifying employee names, as well as a method to associate employee names with skill keywords embedded in those documents. Although we discuss expertise locator systems in general in Chapter 8, we include in this section a discussion of the system's Web text mining component.

An example of an expertise locator KM system is the NASA Expert Seeker Web Miner,[3] which required the development of a name-finding algorithm to identify

Figure 9.4 **Partial Decision Tree Results for Real Estate Appraisal**

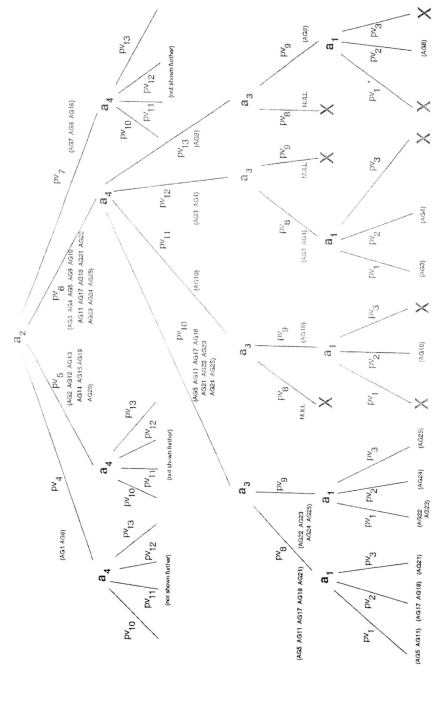

Source: Gonzalez et al. 1999.
Key: a = attribute, X = dead end

Table 9.6

Summary of Induction Results

Attribute	Induction Results	Expert Estimate	Difference
Living Area	$15–$31	$15–$25	0–2.4%
Bedrooms	$4,311–$5,212	$2,500–$3,500	49–72%
Bathrooms	$3,812–$5,718	$1,500–$2,000	154–186%
Garage	$3,010–$4,522	$3,000–$3,500	0.3–29%
Pool	$7,317–$11,697	$9,000–$12,000	2.5–19%
Fireplace	$1,500–$4,180	$1,200–$2,000	25–109%
Year Built	1.2–1.7%	1.0–1.2%	20–42%

Source: Gonzalez et al. 1999.

names of NASA employees. Traditional IR techniques[4] were then used to identify and match skill keywords with the identified employee names. An IR system typically uses as input a set of inverted files, which is a sequence of words that reference the group of documents in which the words appear. These words are chosen according to a selection algorithm that determines which words in the document are good index terms. In a traditional IR system, the user enters a **query** and the system retrieves all documents that match that keyword entry. Expert Seeker Web Miner is based on an IR technique that goes one step further. When a user enters a query, the system initially performs a document search based on user input. However, since the user is looking for experts in a specific subject area, the system returns the names of those employees whose names appear in the matching documents (excluding Webmasters and curators). The employee name results are ranked according to the number of matching documents in which each individual name appears. The employee information is then displayed to the user.

The indexing process was carried out in four stages. First, all the relevant data were transferred to a local directory for further processing. In this case, the data included all the Web pages on the NASA-Goddard Space Flight Center domain. The second stage identifies all instances of employee names by programmatically examining each HTML file. The name data are taken from the personnel directory databases (based on the X.500 standard). All names in the employee database are organized into a map-like data structure beforehand that is used in the Web content mining process. This map consists of all employee names referenced by their last name key. In addition, each full name is stored in every possible form it could appear. For example, the name John A. Smith is stored as

- John A. Smith,
- J. A. Smith,
- J. Smith,
- Smith, John A.,
- Smith, J.A., and
- Smith J.

An individual document is first searched for all last name keys. Subsequently, the document is again searched using all values of the matching keys. Name data organized in this way can increase the speed of the text search. Using one long sequence containing all names in every possible form as search criteria would slow down processing time.

The third stage involves identifying keywords within the HTML content. This is done using a combination of word stemming and frequency calculation. First the text is broken up into individual words through string pattern matching. Any sequence of alphabetical characters is recognized as a word while punctuation, numbers, and white-space characters are ignored. The resulting list of words is processed to determine if a word was included in a stoplist. The resulting list of words was then processed with a **stemming algorithm**. This is done to group together words that may be spelled differently but have the same semantic meaning. A person who types "astronomical" as a query term would most likely also be interested in documents that match the term "astronomy." Once the stemming process is completed, the algorithm calculates the frequency of each term. Word frequency was used during the keyword selection process in the determination of good index terms. However, other indexing algorithms could have been used instead with comparable results.

It is important to note that the degree of relation between an employee name and a keyword within an individual document is not considered. Rather, expertise is determined based on the assumption that if an employee recurrently appears in many documents along with a keyword, then that person must have some knowledge of that term. Theoretically, a large document count for a search query should produce more accurate results.

The chosen keywords have a twofold purpose. First, they are used to quickly associate employees with recurring skill terms. These keywords can also be used in future work for clustering similar documents into topic areas. Finally, **knowledge taxonomy** can be constructed from the mined keywords such that an appropriate query relevance feedback system can be developed that suggests **query terms** that are related to the query entered by the user. Details about the role of taxonomies on the development of expertise locator systems are presented in Chapter 8.

Next, we discuss the role that the Web and search engines play in knowledge discovery.

NOVEL-KNOWLEDGE DISCOVERY ON THE WEB

The Web is a rich source of information for knowledge discovery.[5] Organizations and individuals search the Web for different types of knowledge and to answer different types of questions. For example, individuals typically use the Web to find specific answers—also known as focused search—and to uncover patterns and trends about a topic—also known as scanning. Google (www.google.com) is the most popular Web-searching tool and is most suited to focused searching and discovering deep knowledge. Tools such as Kartoo (www.kartoo.com) and Clusty (www.clusty.com), which provide knowledge maps and clustered categories, are more suitable for scanning and discovering broad knowledge.

In addition to deep and broad knowledge, individuals and organizations sometimes seek to discover novel knowledge—knowledge that is surprising and unknown to them yet interesting and relevant. The challenge with discovering novel knowledge on the Web is that the question posed in the search is usually very vague, therefore creating appropriate search terms may be virtually impossible. Essentially, it's like searching for "what you don't know you don't know"! In addition, novel knowledge may be difficult to locate amongst the vast amount of content returned; one of the many challenges posed by the information overload that may result from the Web search. In most instances, the content returned may be highly related to the search terms provided. Thus, discovering novel knowledge may be more like looking for a needle in a haystack—except you may not know what the needle looks like. In other words, because of its novelty, individuals have a difficult time differentiating purely irrelevant results ("junk") from surprising and interesting results ("novel knowledge"). Furthermore, what's interesting, surprising, and relevant differs from individual to individual based on what they already know; novel knowledge to one person may be considered deep knowledge to another person. Thus, novel knowledge is basically "in the eye of the beholder."

Novel knowledge can be valuable to organizations for many reasons, for example, for the discovery of new strategic opportunities, for development of learning capabilities, and to support the creative thinking leading to innovation or solving "wicked" problems (for more on wicked problems see Chapter 13). Researchers at Queen's University in Kingston, Ontario, have been investigating the importance of novel knowledge to organizations and how they currently go about discovering novel knowledge. Their findings show that organizations do consider novel knowledge important, especially in industries where innovation is critical. However, in many of the organizations investigated, the discovery of novel knowledge was purely serendipitous. Unlike deep and broad knowledge, they found that there are currently no specialized tools to support the discovery of novel knowledge on the Web, motivating the development of Athens (Jenkin 2008a; Jenkin et al. 2007; Vats and Skillicorn 2004a; Vats and Skillicorn 2004b). The Athens prototype uses text and data mining techniques such as clustering, singular-value decomposition, and spectral graph partitioning to find content on the Web that is indirectly connected yet contextually related to what the individual knows. In essence, the individual specifies to Athens the specific topic of interest and Athens finds content on the Web that is literally two steps away from it, that is, related to the area of knowledge familiar to the individual. Thus, Athens tries to find what you don't know you don't know but would find interesting and relevant.

An example using a popular knowledge discovery case will help to illustrate how Athens works. Don Swanson, an information scientist, made an important discovery about Raynaud's Syndrome (a condition that results in intermittent restriction of blood flow to fingers and toes) by exploring the medical literature (Gordon and Lindsay 1996; Swanson 1986; Swanson 1990). Swanson did not know what to look for specifically, so he began by reviewing the Raynaud's literature and found a connection between Raynaud's Syndrome and blood viscosity. He then reviewed the blood-viscosity literature and found that dietary fish oil lowers blood viscosity. He then hypothesized that fish oil may be a useful dietary supplement to help decrease the blood viscosity in humans and therefore alleviate symptoms of Raynaud's Syndrome (Swanson 1986). At the time, this was novel knowledge and not explicitly mentioned in any of the source documents Swanson had previously reviewed. Using this manual approach, Swanson spent a significant amount of time reviewing different bodies of literature in order to make this important novel-knowledge discovery.

If Don Swanson had used Athens for this task rather than a manual approach, he would have provided Athens with terms to describe what he knows or, rather, his focal topic—*Raynaud's Syndrome*. Athens, using an iterative clustering approach, would discover content that is directly connected to Raynaud's Syndrome—in this case, *blood viscosity*. Next, Athens would repeat this iterative clustering step, using blood viscosity as the starting point, in order to find content that is indirectly connected to the original topic of Raynaud's Syndrome—in this case, *fish oil*. Thus, the final result is content that is two steps away from original topic area. It would be up to the user to hypothesize how Raynaud's Syndrome and fish oil might be related.

The Athens prototype is an example of a new tool to discover novel knowledge. However, current research findings show that the innovative aspects of the tool may present some problems. For most individuals and organizations, the concept and task of searching for novel knowledge is new. The popularity of Web-search tools like Google has trained us to view Web searching as a focused search activity. Thus, the initial reaction when using Athens is to view it as a focused search tool yielding a specific result, essentially comparing its features and output to those of Google. Despite these challenges, organizations that have been experimenting with the Athens prototype see the potential of the tool's capabilities. For example, they were impressed with how quickly they were able come up with new and innovative ideas for the topics investigated—something that would have taken a lot of time, effort, and serendipity to do before (Jenkin 2008b). Athens promises to be a useful tool for organizations interested in discovering novel knowledge on the Web or within their own internal information repositories. Figures 9.5 and 9.6 show the outcomes of using Athens for a search using the terms *digital music* and *portable audio player.*

SUMMARY

In this chapter you learned what knowledge discovery systems are, the design considerations for such systems, and specific types of data mining techniques that enable such systems. Also the chapter discusses the role of DM in customer relationship management. Three case studies that describe the implementation of knowledge discovery systems are presented, each based on different methodologies and intelligent technologies. The first system is based on the use of decision trees, or rule induction as a knowledge-modeling tool, and is described in the context of a real estate appraisal system. The second system is based on the use of Web-content mining to identify expertise in an expertise locator system. The third tool presents the use of an innovative tool used to improve the discovery of novel knowledge on the Web. Finally, the use of socialization in organizational settings is discussed as a mechanism to help discover new knowledge and catalyze innovation.

Figure 9.5   Examples of Search with Terms "Digital Music" and "Portable Audio Player"

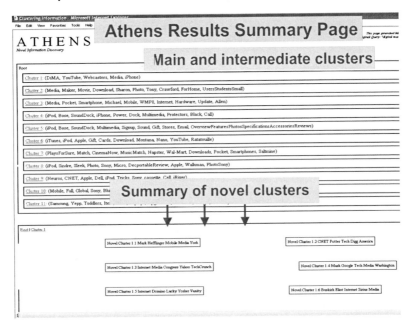

Figure 9.6   **Novel Clusters Resulting from the Search with Terms "Digital Music" and "Portable Audio Player"**

KEY TERMS

Aggregate sets
Analytical CRM
Back-of-the-napkin diagrams
Back-propagation algorithm
Business understanding
Clustering techniques
Combination
Creative brainstorming
CRISP-DM
Customer profile exchange (CPEX)
Customer relationship management (CRM)
Data collection
Data description
Data mining (DM)
Data preparation
Data quality and verification
Data stores
Data tombs
Data warehouse
Enterprise application integration (EAI)
Expertise locator knowledge
  management systems (ELS)
Human computer interface (HCI)
Inferential DM techniques
Information retrieval (IR)
Knowledge discovery in databases (KDD)

Knowledge discovery
  mechanisms (KDM)
Knowledge discovery technologies
Knowledge taxonomy
Lateral thinking
Linguistic analysis
Link analysis/NLP
Market basket analysis
Moore's Law
Operational CRM
Paired leaf analysis
Personal profile
Potential predictors
Predictive DM techniques
Rule induction algorithms
Sample set
Semantic analysis
Similarity functions
Socialization
Storage Law
Target-sell
Tenfold (n-fold) cross validation
Touchpoints
Term frequency inverse document
  frequency (TFIDF)
Tree construction

REVIEW

1. How do socialization techniques help to discover tacit knowledge?
2. Describe the six steps in the CRISP-DM process.
3. Why is understanding of the business problem essential to knowledge discovery?
4. Describe the three types of Web DM techniques. Which one is used in the Expert Seeker case study?
5. Describe some of the barriers to the use of knowledge discovery.

APPLICATION EXERCISES

Identify which DM techniques would be selected to solve the following problems. Explain your answer. Include a description of the input and output variables that would be relevant in each case. Note that more than one technique may apply for each of these problems.

1. Predict fraudulent credit card usage based on purchase patterns.
2. Predict instances of fraud related to Medicare claims.
3. Predict which customers are likely to leave their current long-distance provider.
4. Predict whether a person will renew their insurance policy.
5. Predict who will respond to a direct mail offer.
6. Predict that a generator is likely to fail.
7. Predict which specialized voice services a person is likely to purchase from their local telecommunications provider.
8. Identify factors resulting in product defects in a manufacturing environment.
9. Predict the expected revenue from a customer based on a set of customer characteristics.
10. Predict cost of hospitalization for different medical procedures.
11. Create customer segments in a marketing campaign.
12. Segment among university graduates those that are likely to renew their alumni membership.

NOTES

1. For an extensive review of articles on data mining techniques and applications, see: Bishop 1994; Smith and Gupta 2000; Widrow et al. 1994; Wong et al. 1997.

2. DBI builds a classification tree similar to that used in other induction algorithms like ID3 and C4.5. More details on the tree-building process may be found in Gonzalez et al. (1999).

3. This version of Expert Seeker was developed to support the needs of Goddard Space Flight Center. Expertise locator systems in general are discussed in detail in Chapter 8.

4. See for example Selection by Discriminant Value in Frakes and Baeza-Yates 1992, an algorithm for selecting index terms.

5. We acknowledge Tracy Jenkin, Yolande Chan, and David Skillicorn of Queen's University for this case study.

REFERENCES

Applegate, L., Piccoli, G., and Dev, C. 2008. *Hilton Hotels: Brand differentiation through customer relationship management.* Harvard Business School Case Study #809029, July 23.

Becerra-Fernandez, I., Zanakis, S., and Walczak, S. 2002. Knowledge discovery techniques for predicting country investment risk. *Computers and Industrial Engineering,* 43(4), 787–800.

Berry, M. and Linoff, G. 1997. *Data mining techniques for marketing, sales, and customer support.* New York: John Wiley & Sons.

Berson, A., Smith, S., and Thearling, K. 2000. *Building data mining applications for CRM.* New York: McGraw-Hill.

Bishop, C. 1994. Neural networks and their applications. *Review of Scientific Instruments,* 65(6), 1803–1832.

Brachman, R. and Anand, T. 1996. The process of knowledge discovering in databases. In *Advances in knowledge discovery and data mining,* ed. Usama M. Fayyad et al., 37–57. Menlo Park, CA: AAAI Press.

Chapman, P., Clinton, J., Kerber, R., Khabaza, T., Reinartz, T., Shearer, C., and Wirth, R. 2000. *CRISP-DM 1.0: Step-by-step data mining guide.* SPSS Technical Report.

Chen, H. 2001. *Knowledge management systems: A text mining perspective.* Tucson, AZ: The University of Arizona.

Edelstein, H.A. 1999. *Introduction to data mining and knowledge discovery,* 3d ed. Potomac, MD: Two Crows Corporation.

———. 2001. Pan for gold in the clickstream. *Information Week,* March 12.

Fayyad, U., Piatetsky-Shapiro, G., Smyth, P., and Uthurusamy, R. 1996. From data mining to knowledge discovery: An overview. In *Advances in knowledge discovery and data mining,* eds. Usama M. Fayyad et al., 1–33. Menlo Park, CA: AAAI Press.

Fayyad, U. and Uthurusamy, R. 2002. Evolving data mining into solutions for insights. *Communications of the ACM,* 45(8), 28–21.

Frakes, W. and Baeza-Yates, R. 1992. *Information retrieval: Data structures and algorithms.* Upper Saddle River, NJ: Prentice Hall.

Gartner. 2008. Gartner says worldwide customer relationship management market grew 23 percent in 2007. Press release, *Gartner.com,* July 7. http://www.gartner.com/it/page.jsp?id=715308 (accessed January 3, 2009).

Gilbert, A. 2002. Smart carts on a roll at Safeway. *CNET News,* October 28. http://news.cnet.com/2100–1017–963526.html (accessed August 24, 2008).

Gonzalez, A., Daroszweski, S., and Hamilton, H.J. 1999. Determining the incremental worth of members of an aggregate set through difference-based induction. *International Journal of Intelligent Systems,* 14(3), 275–294.

Gordon, M.D. and Lindsay, R.K. 1996. Toward discovery support systems: A replication, re-examination, and extension of Swanson's work on literature-based discovery of a connection between Raynaud's and fish oil. *Journal of the American Society for Information Science,* (47)2, 116–128.

Gray, P. and Watson, H.J. 1998. *Decision support in the data warehouse.* Upper Saddle River, NJ: Prentice Hall.

IBM. 2004. *IBM and Safeway create enjoyable grocery shopping experience.* IBM White Papers, March 2. http://www-1.ibm.com/industries/wireless/doc/content/bin/Safeway_1.pdf (accessed August 24, 2008).

Jackson, J. 2002. Data mining: A conceptual overview. *Communications of the Association for Information Systems,* 8, 267–296.

Jenkin, T.A. 2008a. How IT supports knowledge discovery and learning processes on the Web. In *Proceedings of the 41st Hawaii International Conference on System Sciences* (HICSS). Waikoloa, HI.

———. 2008b. *Using information technology to support the discovery of novel knowledge in organizations.* PhD Thesis (Management), Queen's University.

Jenkin, T.A., Chan, Y.E., and Skillicorn, D.B. 2007. Novel-knowledge discovery—challenges and design theory. In *Proceedings of the Annual Conference of the Administrative Sciences Association of Canada.* Ottawa, Canada.

Kovalerchuk, B., Triantaphyllou, E., Ruiz, J., Torvik, V., and Vityaev, E. 2000. The reliability issue of computer-aided breast cancer diagnosis. *Journal of Computers and Biomedical Research,* 33(4), 296–313.

Lamont, J. 2002. CRM around the world. *KM World,* 11(9; October).

Lawrence, R., Almasi, G., Kotlyar, V., Viveros, M., and Duri, S. 2001. Personalization of supermarket product recommendations. *Data mining and knowledge discovery,* 5, 11–32.

Lee, H., Whang, S., Ahsan, K., Gordon, E., Faragalla, A., Jain, A., Mohsin, A., and Shi, G. 2003. *Harrah's Entertainment Inc.: Real-time CRM in a service supply chain.* Harvard Business School Case Study #GS50, October 27.

Le Storti, A.J. 2003. *When you're asked to do the impossible: Principles of business teamwork and leadership from the U.S. Army's Elite Rangers.* Guilford, CT: The Lyons Press.

Nonaka, I. and Takeuchi, H. 1995. *The knowledge creating company.* New York: Oxford University Press.

Parsa, I. 2000. Data mining: Middleware or middleman, panel on KDD process standards (position statement). In *Proceedings from the Sixth ACM SIGKDD International Conference on Knowledge Discovery and Data Mining,* ed. R. Ramakrishnan and S. Stolfo. New York: ACM.

Salton, G. 1989. *Automatic text processing.* Reading, MA: Addison-Wesley.

Schwenk, H. 2002. Real-time CRM analytics: The future of BI? *KM World,* 11(2), (February).

Smith, K.A. and Gupta, J.N.D. 2000. Neural networks in business: Techniques and applications for the operations researcher. *Computers and Operations Research,* 27, 1023–1044.

SPSS. 2000. *Data mining: Modeling.* Chicago, Illinois.

Stevens, L. 2001. IT sharpens data mining's focus. *Internet Week,* August 6.

Swanson, D.R. 1986. Fish oil, Raynaud's Syndrome, and undiscovered public knowledge. *Perspectives in Biology and Medicine,* (30)1, 7–18.

———. 1990. Medical literature as a potential source of new knowledge. *Bulletin of the Medical Library Association,* 78(1), 29–37.

Vats, N. and Skillicorn, D.B. 2004a. The ATHENS system for novel information discovery. Department of Computing and Information Science, Queen's University, Technical Report 2004–489.

———. 2004b. Information discovery within organizations using the Athens system. In *Proceedings of the 2004 Conference of the Centre for Advanced Studies on Collaborative Research,* ed. H. Lutfiyya, J. Singer, and D.A. Stewart, 282–292. Markham, Ontario.

Widrow, B., Rumelhart, D.E., and Lehr, M.A. 1994. Neural networks: Applications in industry, business and science. *Communications of the ACM,* 37(3), 93–105.

Witten, I. 2000. Adaptive text mining: inferring structure from sequences. In *Proceedings of the 34th Conference on Information Sciences and Systems.* Princeton University, NJ, March 15–17.

Wong, B.K., Bodnovich, T.A., and Selvi, Y. 1997. Neural network applications in business: A review and analysis of the literature (1988–1995). *Decision Support Systems,* 19, 301–320.

Zanakis, S. and Becerra-Fernandez, I. 2005. Competitiveness of nations: A knowledge discovery examination. *European Journal of Operations Research,* 166(1), 185–211.

Zanasi, A. 2000. Web mining through the Online Analyst. In *Proceedings of the first Data Mining Conference.* Cambridge University, Cambridge, UK.

Zdanowicz, J. 2004. Detecting money laundering and terrorist financing via data mining. *Communications of the ACM,* 47(5).

PART III

MANAGEMENT AND THE FUTURE OF KNOWLEDGE MANAGEMENT

10 Emergent Knowledge Management Practices

In the last chapter, we discussed knowledge discovery systems. In this chapter we introduce emergent knowledge management practices. In particular we focus in the discussion of social networks, how they facilitate knowledge sharing, and how they benefit from communication technologies. We start with a discussion of emerging technologies such as social networks, wikis, and blogs, followed by a description about how they enable collaboration and knowledge sharing. Finally, we present the business implications of open source development and virtual worlds.

WEB 2.0

For those of us who were entering the field of computers in the 1980s, we witnessed a revolution that would forever change the world of computing as we saw it back then. This revolution consisted of the transformation of the computing platform from the traditional mainframe to the PC. This change took many by surprise, including Thomas Watson, then chairman of IBM, who in 1943 uttered one of the most famous technology quotes: "I think there is a world market for maybe five computers."

We're currently witnessing a new computing revolution that has been given the name Web 2.0. According to Wikipedia, a Web 2.0 service, the term **Web 2.0** "is a living term describing changing trends in the use of World Wide Web technology and web design that aims to enhance creativity, information sharing, collaboration, and functionality of the web. Web 2.0 concepts have led to the development and evolution of Web-based communities and hosted services such as social-networking sites, video sharing sites, wikis, blogs, and folksonomies." The term Web 2.0 is credited to Tim O'Reilly, who used it during the first Web 2.0 conference in 2004 to describe the Internet as a platform. O'Reilly (2005) first described Web 2.0 via an example that contrasted a set of popular applications in the new platform from their counterparts in the Web 1.0 platform. See a comparison of Web 2.0 and Web 1.0 technologies in Table 10.1 and Figure 10.1.

Web 2.0 was made possible through the development of Ajax (asynchronous JavaScript and XML), which enabled Web-based applications to be made to work much more like desktop ones. Ajax (Garret 2005) refers to several technologies, which combined together provide the possibility to create much more interactive applications for the user. Ajax incorporates:

Table 10.1

Web 2.0

	Web 1.0		Web 2.0
	DoubleClick	→	Google AdSense
	Ofoto	→	Flickr
	Akamai	→	BitTorrent
	mp3.com	→	Napster
	Britannica Online	→	Wikipedia
	personal Web sites	→	blogging
	evite	→	upcoming.org and EVDB
	domain name speculation	→	search engine optimization
	page views	→	cost per click
	screen scraping	→	web services
	publishing	→	participation
	content management systems	→	wikis
	directories (taxonomy)	→	tagging ("folksonomy")
	stickiness	→	syndication

Source: O'Reilly 2005.

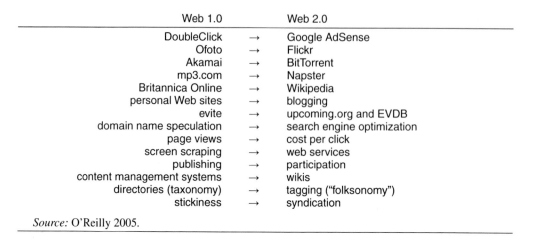

Figure 10.1   **Web 2.0 Technologies Compared to Web 1.0 Technologies**

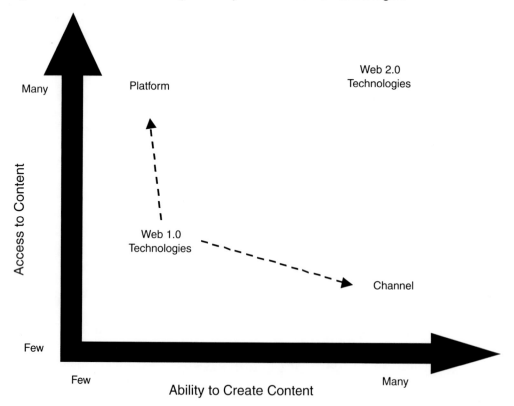

Table 10.2

Web 2.0 Applications

Blogs	(short for Web logs) are online journals or diaries hosted on a Web site and often distributed to other sites or readers using RSS (see below).
Collective intelligence	refers to any system that attempts to tap the expertise of a group rather than an individual to make decisions. Technologies that contribute to collective intelligence include collaborative publishing and common databases for sharing knowledge.
Mash-ups	are aggregations of content from different online sources to create a new service. An example would be a program that pulls apartment listings from one site and displays them on a Google map to show where the apartments are located.
Peer-to-peer networking	(sometimes called P2P) is a technique for efficiently sharing files (music, videos, or text) either over the Internet or within a closed set of users. Unlike the traditional method of storing a file on one machine—which can become a bottleneck if many people try to access it at once—P2P distributes files across many machines, often those of the users themselves. Some systems retrieve files by gathering and assembling pieces of them from many machines.
Online games	include both games played on dedicated game consoles that can be networked and "massively multiplayer" games, which involve thousands of people who interact simultaneously through personal avatars in online worlds that exist independently of any single player's activity.
Podcasts	are audio or video recordings—a multimedia form of a blog or other content. They are often distributed through an aggregator, such as iTunes.
RSS (Really Simple Syndication)	allows people to subscribe to online distributions of news, blogs, podcasts, or other information.
Social networking	refers to systems that allow members of a specific site to learn about other members' skills, talents, knowledge, or preferences. Commercial examples include Facebook, MySpace, and LinkedIn. Some companies use these systems internally to help identify experts.
Virtual worlds	Virtual worlds, such as Second Life, are highly social, three-dimensional online environments shaped by users who interact with and receive instant feedback from other users through the use of avatars.
Web services	are software systems that make it easier for different systems to communicate with one another automatically in order to pass information or conduct transactions. For example, a retailer and supplier might use Web services to communicate over the Internet and automatically update each other's inventory systems.
Widgets	are programs that allow access from users' desktops to Web-based content.
Wikis	Wikis (such as Wikipedia) are systems for collaborative publishing. They allow many authors to contribute to an online document or discussion.

Source: Mc Kinsey 2007a, 2007b.

- standards-based presentation using XHTML and CSS;
- dynamic display and interaction using the Document Object Model;
- data interchange and manipulation using XML and XSLT;
- asynchronous data retrieval using XMLHttpRequest; and
- **JavaScript** binding everything together.

Another essential ingredient of Web 2.0 applications is that this type of computer application will essentially get better the more people use it. In fact, the most significant aspect of Web 2.0 is its ability to harness **collective intelligence**—building databases that get better the more people use them. For example, Amazon's ability to garner user reviews of their products improves the user experience who is seeking to buy their products. Table 10.2 provides a short definition for a type of Web 2.0 application.

This exciting collaboration infrastructure is not just an entertainment medium for young adults. Many organizations are beginning to ponder how this new collaboration medium can add value to businesses. In a recent McKinsey & Company survey (2008), businesses confirm a wide support for the use of Web 2.0 applications which many organizations consider being "strategic." More than three-fourths of the executives who responded confirmed they would maintain or increase their investments in technology that encourages user collaboration such as **peer-to-peer social networking**, social networks, and **Web services**. The report confirmed that "companies aren't necessarily relying on the best-known Web 2.0 trends such as blogs; instead, they place the greatest importance on technologies that enable automation and networking," revealing that of the firms surveyed only 32 percent were using blogging technologies as compared to more popular collective intelligence (48 percent) and peer-to-peer networking (47 percent; McKinsey 2008). Furthermore, of the firms surveyed 43 percent were not considering the use of blogs, which is a large percentage as compared to the number of firms that will not be using the more popular collective intelligence (26 percent) and peer-to-peer networking technologies (28 percent). These trends remained the same as compared to those same trends in 2007.

The rise of Web 2.0-like applications within the organization has received the label of **Enterprise 2.0** (McAfee 2006). Traditionally knowledge workers use information technology for two main uses: as *channels,* to create and distribute digital information that is visible by few people via technologies like e-mail and instant messaging; or as *platforms,* which enable content to be widely visible via technologies like intranets and information portals. Enterprise 2.0 technologies focus on: search, links, authoring (via wikis and blogs, discussed in the next section), tags (to categorize content), extensions (such as recommendations matched to user preferences), and signals (like **RSS** feeds and aggregators). The biggest difference between Enterprise 2.0 technologies and traditional KM systems is that the latter are typically highly structured and users typically can't influence this structure. Enterprise 2.0 technologies on the other hand provide users the potential to create intranets built by distributed autonomous peers and are subject to network effects, which means the more that people participate in authoring the better the content will get.

In the next section, we describe one of the most popular Web 2.0 applications: social networking.

SOCIAL NETWORKING

User-driven online spaces have redefined the meaning of the word "socializing" for most teenagers in the United States, primarily due to the emergence of Web 2.0 applications such as Friendster, MySpace, Facebook, LinkedIn, and YouTube. In a sense Web 2.0 enables widely available knowledge management systems that deliver value to communities that have sufficient incentives to provide content to these popular social sites.

Friendster was founded in 2002 and became a well-known social network dating Web site in addition to allowing users to sharing online content and media such as videos, photos, messages, and comments among friends. One of Friendster's moves to gain notoriety among all other **social networking** sites was its feature "Who's Viewed Me," which allowed users to see who else had viewed their profile (Mintz 2005). What made social network sites so unique was their ability to grow in terms of user base through the use of human relationships without the need of traditional marketing methods (Barnett et al. 2006).

MySpace, which according to its Web site it touts itself as "a place for friends," was founded in 2003 and quickly became a well-known social networking service that combined the features of user profiles, blogs, groups, photos, and videos with music discovery. In particular, MySpace established itself as a niche player in the popular music distribution space by allowing both unsigned artists and major label musicians to feature music streams and downloads. The power of social networking sites became evident on July 11, 2006, when MySpace, a popular social networking site, became the number one visited domain by users in the United States according to Hitwise (Tancer 2006), a phenomenal growth from 2004 when MySpace.com had represented only 0.1 percent of all Internet visits, achieving a 4,300 percent increase in visits over two years and 132 percent increase in visits since the same time the prior year.

LinkedIn was launched in 2003 as a business-oriented social networking site for professional networking, allowing users to maintain a detailed list of business contacts. In 2004 another prominent social network site, which would later capture most of the Brazilian and Indian market space, made its debut—the Google-owned Orkut. YouTube was launched in 2005 as a videosharing Web site where users could upload, share, and view video clips. Essentially, YouTube established the infrastructure that made it possible for anyone to post a video that millions of users across the world could view in a matter of minutes.

In 2004, Facebook.com was launched by Harvard student Mark Zuckerberg as a social network that offered school members access to the profiles of other classmates who were members of their same school network. In the past, paper-based student directories (called facebooks) were circulated among freshman college students as a means to help newcomers establish new friends, and who knows, perhaps even find a date. Facebook enables users to keep a personal profile and interact with other people within their same social networks that are organized by school, workplace, city, and region. Facebook users keep up with their friends and send them messages, upload photos and links to videos, and simply learn about people whom they meet. Probably one of the most captivating features of social network sites is the integration of a News Feed functionality, which essentially allow users to keep up with every little change in their friends' profile pages, what Zuckerberg describes as "a stream of everything that's going on in their lives" (Thompson 2008). One of the most remarkable characteristics of Facebook is its "stickiness" in the sense that about two-thirds of its total user base comes back to the site within a day, a measure of daily retention, which serves as a contrast with most sites which measure monthly retention (Barnett et al. 2006).

Social networks research focuses on the knowledge held by entities (called *nodes,* meaning people or information systems) and the relationships between them (*ties*). Ties are characterized by type (friendship, advice, professional), strength (intensity

Box 10.1

The Power of Social Networks: Operation Burnt Frost

In December 2007, the U.S. Strategic Command was charged by President Bush to mitigate the danger posed by a bus-sized satellite falling out of orbit, commissioning Operation Burnt Frost. The satellite hurled through space at 17,000 MPH and posed a danger to people around the globe, due to the fact that its fuel tank contained nearly 1,000 lbs. of hydrazine fuel, which is highly toxic. The complex problem required expertise to calculate the satellite's trajectory and to understand the likelihood of success. The mission's success required the ability to successfully reach out and connect with the appropriate subject-matter experts. A major factor in the success of the operation was leveraging expertise through individual social networks. The mission required the successful collaboration of hundreds of subject-matter experts representing more than two dozen federal agencies that were spread around the United States. Last February 20, 2008, a single Standard Missile 3 (SM3), which was launched from the Pacific Ocean aboard the USS Lake Erie, shot down a National Reconnaissance Office satellite that was falling out of orbit. Extensive social networking played a key role in the success of this mission (Steinhauser and Thon 2008).

or reciprocity between two nodes, which could be strong or weak), and density (the ratio of actual ties to the possible number of ties in a network and is defined as high or low). Nodes could represent individuals as well as organizations, and researchers may focus on dyadic analysis (two nodes), ego network (all the relationships maintained by one node), or whole network analysis (all the nodes and ties among them). Knowledge sharing researchers have concluded that strong and weak ties have different effects on knowledge sharing relationships, and strong ties are better for cultivating trust and reliability while weak ties are more appropriate for searching for different types of knowledge (Alavi and Kane 2008). In addition, the position of the individual within the network (central or peripheral) is also important in knowledge sharing effectiveness, whereas individuals in central positions act as knowledge brokers in the network and pose knowledge sharing benefits in terms of timing, access, and referral of knowledge.

The recognition that business is built on relationships as much as on information has spawned a new set of software offerings that range from contact management (both inside and outside the enterprise) to social network-based enterprise solutions for knowledge sharing. These new software offerings may, for example, calculate the strength of the business relationship by measuring the frequency of e-mail message flows outside of the enterprise. For instance, users may enter the name of an individual or organization and the software would return a list of people within the firm who have connections with the target prospect. Furthermore, social networking solutions have also made an inroad into the world of talent management, and organizations are increasingly using these products in order to build relationships with current employees, alumni, and retirees (Lamont 2008). In Box 10.1, we explore an example of how social networks can help solve business problems.

Perhaps social networking has delivered the dreams that KM has forged over the last ten years and the Internet is no longer a collection of static Web sites hijacked by powerful Web masters. Instead social networking is a mechanism to voice the collective wisdom of communities that use the Internet to voice their opinions on a myriad of topics from the best Web sites, articles, blogs, and music (http://www.del.icio.us.com/), the best restaurants (www.zagat.com), the best pictures (http://www.flickr.com/), and those guys you shouldn't date (http://www.dontdatehimgirl.com).

In the next section, we discuss two specific types of Web 2.0 technologies used to generate content: wikis and blogs.

WIKIS AND BLOGS

According to Wikipedia, one of the best-known wikis, a **wiki** "is a page or collection of Web pages designed to enable anyone who accesses it to contribute or modify content, using a simplified markup language. Wikis are often used to create collaborative Web sites and to power community Web sites." Wikipedia is a free online encyclopedia that was launched on January 10, 2001. Wikipedia grew to approximately 20,000 articles, by the end of 2001, and 18 language editions—numbers that would grow to 2 million and 161 respectively by 2004. Articles in Wikipedia do not go through a formal peer-review process and are created by its users, who volunteer endless hours to create or edit articles. One of the interesting characteristics of Wikipedia is that it fosters a cooperative and helpful culture among its users, since articles that annoy others can easily be erased by one click therefore offering an opportunity for reaching decisions based on consensus among community members (McAfee 2006). In terms of quality of its entries, an article published in *Nature* (Giles 2005) compared Wikipedia's accuracy with that of *Encyclopedia Britannica,* finding the former to have four serious errors and the latter three in 42 science entries, and 162 versus 123 minor errors respectively, proving that while the collective wisdom of the Wikipedia contributors may not be perfect it's perhaps good enough. Contributors to Wikipedia must abide by a set of policies and guidelines, which fall in one of the following areas (Wikipedia 2009b):

- *Global:* General principles about how Wikipedia operates.
- *Behavioral:* Standards for behavior while on Wikipedia to make it a pleasant experience for everyone.
- *Content and style:* Define which topics are welcome on Wikipedia, and provide quality and naming standards.
- *Deletion:* The body of policies dealing with page deletion.
- *Enforcement:* What actions editors can take to enforce other policies.
- *Legal and copyright:* Law-based rules about what material may be used here and remedies for misuse.

Blogs (a contraction between Web and log) refer to a form of online digital diary and in essence is a Web site where an individual makes regular written journal entries that comprise a statement of opinion, a story, an analysis, description of events, or other material. Blogs typically display an entry in reverse chronological order, with the most recent entries at the top.

Blogging techniques offer tremendous opportunities for businesses. For example, firms can take advantage of Web 2.0 technologies such as blogs for agile new product development. Consider for example the case of The GorB (a contraction of 'Good or Bad'), a social network startup that offered users the opportunity to rate others on both their personal and professional reputation. The team that designed the site spent countless hours developing the algorithm that would be used to accurately calculate this reputation, placing a higher value on those reputation opinions that accurately predicted the opinions of others. But such an important endeavor (at least that's what the development team thought) would meet considerable pushback, and some critics considered that the GorB had just gone too far![1] In order to respond to its public constituency, the GorB published a blog on the site and used it to communicate how the product was being redesigned in order to address its user concerns.

Blogs have played a significant role in chronicling the events of the Iraq war, from the abuse of prisoners at Abu Ghraib first reported by Chris Missick, a soldier with the Army's 319th Signal Battalion and author of the blog "A Line in the Sand" (Missick 2008). Missick's account of the events in Iraq perhaps summarizes best the impact of this particular technology:

> Never before has a war been so immediately documented, never before have sentiments from the front scurried their way to the home front with such ease and precision. Here I sit, in the desert, staring daily at the electric fence, the deep trenches and the concertina wire that separates the border of Iraq and Kuwait, and write home and upload my daily reflections and opinions on the war and my circumstances here, as well as some of the pictures I have taken along the way. It is amazing, and empowering, and yet the question remains, should I as a lower enlisted soldier have such power to express my opinion and broadcast to the world a singular soldier's point of view? To those outside the uniform who have never lived the military life, the question may seem absurd, and yet, as an example of what exists even in the small following of readers I have here, the implications of thought expressed by soldiers daily could be explosive (Hockenberry 2005).

Blaming a breach of security and the potential leak of sensitive wartime information, the U.S. Army ordered in April 2007 that soldiers stop posting to blogs or sending personal e-mail messages, unless the content was first cleared by a superior (Shachtman 2007). A lawsuit ensued under the Freedom of Information Act, which concluded that the real security breach came from official Army Web sites and not blogs. Another example that brought popularity to blogging was the blog by American soldier Alex Horton: "Army of Dude—Reporting on Truth, Justice and the American Way of War" (Horton 2008). His site won the second place for "best military blog" in the 2007 WebLog Awards, perhaps due to his crude pictures, unfiltered war accounts—including posts about a day in which he and other soldiers were being shot at by insurgents with machine guns, and his open cynicism about the war.

New online tools, for example, Twitter, are also enabling users to *microblog,* which refers to posting frequent tiny (140 characters) updates of what they're doing. This technology is enabling users to have what social scientists are calling *online awareness,* which refers to incessant online contact with their friends (and even strangers who may choose to follow you if you allow them). The continuing rise of online awareness begs the question: Are these technologies helping increase the number of

Figure 10.2 **Blogalaxia**

friends people have? In 1998, anthropologist Robin Dunbar theorized that humans had an upper limit on the maximum social connections they had: 150—hence called the Dunbar number. A closer look at the effect of these tools seems to suggest that perhaps their biggest contribution is in helping people keep up with their weak ties, for example, someone they may have met at a conference, high school, or at a party. Sociologists also have found that weak ties may be important to help people solve problems, for example finding a new job (Thompson 2008). Box 10.2 describes two sites that provide an interesting service to bloggers in Latin America. Figures 10.2 and 10.3 represent these two innovative Web sites.

Box 10.3 describes how a traditional investment bank launched corporate wikis as a means to allow employees to work together and share important insights that made investment traders more productive, alleviating some of the e-mail overload that many employees deal with these days.

In the next section, we describe the open source movement and its role in business today.

OPEN SOURCE DEVELOPMENT

The Open Source movement was introduced to the general public by Tim O'Reilly who organized the first Open Source Summit, as a means to bring together open source software developers and supporters together from across the world. **Open source**

Figure 10.3 **Telurica**

software development refers to "Internet-based communities of software developers who voluntarily collaborate in order to develop software that they or their organizations need" (von Krogh 2003).

Historically, open source development dates back to the early days of the Internet, when the U.S. Defense Advanced Research Projects Agency (DARPA) helped launch the first transcontinental high-speed computer network called ARPAnet. One of the most important reasons for establishing ARPAnet was to allow researchers at universities, government, and corporate labs to share software code. The Free Software Foundation was established in 1985 as a mechanism to allow developers to preserve the "free" status of their software in the face of increasing pressure from commercial software firms that sought to restrict the access to source code. Later on the free software movement would become known as the "open source" software movement, a term that encompassed the right to use it at no cost, the right to study and modify the source code, and the right to distribute modified or unmodified versions to others at no cost (von Krogh 2003). The definition of open source, according to the Open Source Initiative that is the steward of the Open Source Definition, doesn't denote just free software and encompasses the following criteria:

1. Free Redistribution—The license shall not require a royalty for any sale.
2. Source Code—The program must include source code, so the programmer may be able to modify the program.
3. Derived Works—License allows modifications and derived works.

Box 10.2

Blogalaxia and Telurica: Adding Value for Latin American Bloggers

So, how do you resolve the problem of indexing the phenomenal number of blogs across 28 Latin American countries? Enter Blogalaxia, a directory of blogs, which ranks blogs on the basis of popularity. Blogalaxia features the top 512 blogs through a popularity ranking that is based not only on the number of visitors but also integrates the concept of "authority," meaning it takes into consideration the number of links that other blogs make to a particular blog. The popularity concept reflects how a particular blog influences the content of other blogs, or the "referential" characteristic of a particular blog. Blogalaxia counts with more than 44,000 registered blogs, all contributing to over 1,000 daily posts and more than 7.2 million unique visitors each month. Blogalaxia accounts for 81 percent of all the total registered blogs in Mexico, Argentina, and Spain (the three top visit source countries) in addition to Peru, Chile, and Venezuela.

Telurica is an Internet TV program, which emits each day its program "video blog" about Internet and Web culture. The sources of information for this TV program are the blogs featured in Blogalaxia, and it serves to diffuse Latin American information in an entertaining fashion. Telurica is daily the most viewed video in YouTube (in Spanish) and features each day stories from the blogs registered in Blogalaxia. Telurica was the first video aggregator in Latin America, and it already counts with over 9.1 million total views as a channel in YouTube.[1]

[1] We acknowledge Leonard Boord, director of Blogalaxia and Telurica, for the information in this box.

Box 10.3

Wikis at Dresdner Kleinwort Wasserstein: Are Bankers and Wikis Ready for Each Other?

Dresdner Kleinwort Wasserstein (DrKW) investment bank was one of the first firms to launch a corporate wiki for employees to contribute and edit their corporate Web site without the need of special permissions or knowledge of HTML or Web-authoring skills. Wiki use at DrKW first started within the IT department as a means to keep their online training schedules up-to-date (McAfee and Sjoman 2006). A corporate blog would not provide the needed functionality since it would still require one person to consolidate all the schedule changes, which was a daunting task. RSS feeds are an important complement to the wiki, because they can alert all the people that want to learn about new training. Even though wikis come with the ability for users to edit, and potentially destroy, the content of the wiki, it would be easy to correct it as the technology provides the capability to restore the previous version of the wiki page. Following the initial success of the use of wikis at the IT department, the bank introduced a bankwide wiki that provided access to most bank employees. Wikis have been successful at DrKW because it had an initial structure, it provided for a more effective form of collaboration, and because it helped reduce the amount of e-mail.

4. Integrity of the Author's Source Code—License permits the distribution of software built from modified source code.
5. No Discrimination Against Persons or Groups.
6. No Discrimination Against Fields of Endeavor—License doesn't restrict anyone from making use of the program in a specific field.
7. Distribution of License—Rights apply to all to whom the program is redistributed.
8. License Must Not Be Specific to a Product—All parties to whom the program is distributed to have the same rights.

9. License Must Not Restrict Other Software—No restriction on other software distributed along the licensed software.
10. License Must Be Technology-Neutral—No restrictions based on type of technology or interface.

But the most interesting fact about open source is that all the projects including BIND (the Berkeley Internet Name Daemon which runs the Domain Name System), Sendmail (which routes Internet e-mail), Apache (the world's most used Web server), and Linux (the operating system that became the backbone of the Internet) were developed by thousands of loosely coordinated individuals (Collis and Montgomery 2004). The open source movement is what has allowed the development for protocols that make all of these programs interoperable. Open source developers embrace co-operation and collaboration as a source of competitive advantage. In the open source movement value is added through architecture of participation, which takes advantage of network effects services that become more valuable the more people use them.

One successful product in the open source space is MySQL. The company was founded in the early 1990s, and by 2004 it was estimated that MySQL held two million out of the 12 million total relational database management systems (DBMS; Wittig and Inkinen 2004). One of the strategies that MySQL employed to penetrate markets was to use its open source status as a viral marketing vehicle. MySQL made its products available under a dual-licensing policy that allowed both open source and commercial users to have access to the same product either without fees or for purchase for a lower licensing fee than other commercial DBMS. But commercial users enjoyed special privileges including a warranty and development support. One of the competitive advantages that companies like MySQL enjoy is that unlike first-generation, nonprofit open source products like Linux in which the code was written by many, second-generation open source companies write and own all the code. The advantage that MySQL has is that each time it releases a new version, its vast number of users massively test and debug the product allowing for rapid stabilization of the product and thus faster development cycles. This means development costs at MySQL could be significantly lower (even up to 80 percent) than traditional development environments.

One of the important questions raised by the success of the open source movement is "why should thousands of top-notch programmers contribute freely to the provision of a public good" (von Krogh 2003). Research into this phenomenon suggests that open source software development is underpinned by the personal benefit that developers reap from developing complex software including gaining expertise, improving their reputation, and the sheer enjoyment of participating in this communal activity. Collaborating individuals obtain peer evaluation of their work as well as gain group-related factors such as indispensability to the team and loyalty among peer developers (von Krogh 2003). Other research projects have also confirmed this finding, namely that a significant predictor of individual knowledge contribution to electronic networks of practice, such as communities of practice discussion forums used by individuals to exchange advice and ideas with other strangers with common interests, is the perception that participation in these networks enhances one's professional reputation. Furthermore, the development of social capital may also play an important role in the underlying knowledge exchange; in addition, the opportunity of mastering the application of expertise and the understanding of what is relevant may be essentially what motivates users to contribute (Wasko and Faraj 2005). In summary, the motives for participating and contributing to open source software include (Shah 2003):

1. Need for product—create, customize, or improve a product or feature.
2. Enjoyment, desire to create and improve—one enjoys it; that is, finds creating or improving software creative and interesting.
3. Reputation and status within the community—build or maintain reputation or status within the community.
4. Affiliation—socialize or spend time with like-minded individuals.
5. Identity—reinforce or build a desired self-image.
6. Values and ideology—promote specific ideals, such as the free-software philosophy.
7. Training, learning, reputation outside the community and career concerns— improve one's skills, with the belief that it will lead to a better job or promotion.

Open source licenses guarantee the rights of future users against appropriation by private firms, guaranteeing the product will remain a public good. Open source development comes with its own set of challenges, such as how to monitor the programmers, in particular when participation is voluntary and not bounded by a formal contract. Also, even though mechanisms exist to limit "free riding" (those that download code without contributing to it) typically these measures are not closely watched. On the other hand, open source communities are known to be "meritocracies," meaning that technical knowledge and expertise will determine the impact of a contributor on the software (von Krogh 2003).

Open source development models are redefining business models for software companies based on the idea that software should be free and resistant to the monopoly power of large software development companies. Nonprofits may have been the early ventures, but for-profit ventures have also started to embrace an open source business model.

In the next section, we describe a technology that is poised to transform the way we do business today: virtual worlds.

VIRTUAL WORLDS

Virtual worlds have been touted as a "breakthrough idea" in the sense that it's destined to transform the way that businesses function, providing the infrastructure for innovative operational models as well as alternate realities for working and interacting with customers. In fact, virtual worlds today are compared to radio and TV broadcasting from the perspective that when the technologies first emerged, they both started as trivial content providers but eventually became the dominant medium for advertising (HBR 2008). The **metaverse**—a compound (known technically as *portmanteau*) of the words "meta" (an abstraction of) and "universe"—describes a multiplayer virtual

Figure 10.4 **Sky Dancers in a Second Life**

Shared Spaces based on (imaginative) Reality

"Sky Dancers" Live Music and Dance Performance

world where humans (as **avatars**) interact with each other and software agents in a three-dimensional world that is a metaphor of the real world (Wikipedia 2009a).

Virtual worlds such as Second Life and Sun Microsystems's Project Wonderland provide the infrastructure for users to build three-dimensional immersive virtual worlds where individuals represented by avatars socialize, explore, and conduct business. Virtual worlds are proving to be effective environments where remote users can spontaneously interact with goals that span agendas that span collaborative learning environments for college students to helping autistic children acquire skills they can transfer to the real world.[2]

Second Life, a metaverse launched by Linden Lab in 2003, provides its users (called *Residents*) the ability to interact via their personalized avatars, and provides Residents the ability to explore and meet other residents, socialize and have fun, participate in individual and group activities, create and trade virtual property and services purchased via its own currency (the Linden dollar), and travel through the world (called *Grid*). Second Life started as sixty-four acres of "virtual land" space that had grown to over 65,000 acres by 2008. Everything in Second Life is Resident-created, and Residents retain the intellectual property rights in their digital creations which they can buy, sell, and trade with other fellow Residents. Residents can trade their Linden dollars for real-world currency in their LindeX dollar exchange, while Second Life leases real estate according to their own published land pricing and use fees. As of November 2008,

Figure 10.5   **Flickr in Wonderland**

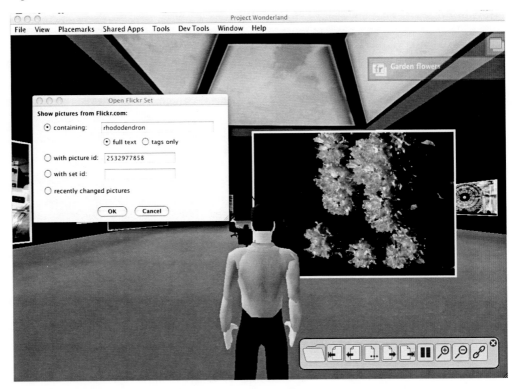

Second Life Residents represent an international multiuser community and spend about fifty-six hours per month in entertainment, education, work, advocacy, and entrepreneurial activities. Second Life Residents have a median age of 35 years old and are gender neutral by hours of use.[3] Figure 10.4 depicts a creative live music and dance performance by human-led avatars on Second Life known as Sky Dancers.[4]

Project Wonderland launched in 2007 by Sun Microsystems[5] is a 100 percent Java, free and open source toolkit for building three-dimensional immersive virtual worlds. Project Wonderland was developed to overcome some of the collaborative challenges that Sun employees face—of whom about 50 percent may be out of the office on any given day—including remoteness, management issues, difficulty brainstorming, and lack of social interactions. Project Wonderland was designed with a focus on business and education collaboration and provides a software platform for its users to develop virtual worlds in which avatars communicate with high-fidelity immersive audio and share applications like Open Office documents, Web browsers, and games. One of the advantages that Project Wonderland offers is to allow users to make changes to the virtual world using XML files instead of needing to modify the source code. The "world builder" functionality is integrated into the client to let users drag-and-drop import external work and arrange artwork and custom world components. One of the advantages that Project Wonderland offers is the ease of integration with web service applications such as Googlemaps, Flickr, etc.[6] Figure 10.5 presents the integration of the Flickr application to Wonderland.

Box 10.4

A Virtual Retail Store for UnME Jeans

Many established organizations ventured into Second Life to establish a virtual presence: Wells Fargo & Company developed *Stagecoach Island* which teaches young consumers about banking; American Apparel, Inc., established the first virtual retail store only to be quickly followed by Apple Inc., and Reebok International Ltd.; the Coca-Cola Company invited metaverse entrepreneurs to design virtual soda machines that dispensed *Coke experiences;* L'Oreal SA hosted the first *Miss Second Life* beauty contest for avatars; and future U.S. President Barack Obama held virtual town meetings (Steenburgh and Avery 2008). UnME Jeans, a successful player in the up-and-coming upscale junior denim market, had traditionally marketed to its target teenage consumer market via popular television programs, teenage magazines, and radio commercials on Top 40 stations. Like many other brands, UnME Jeans struggled with how to effectively spend its marketing dollars across the new spectrum of social media options including YouTube advertising videos, banner ads and branded content in Facebook and MySpace social network sites, and digital self expression via metaverses like Second Life and Zwinktopia (Steenburgh and Avery 2008). Given that Zwinktopia's main target market was girls between the ages of thirteen to twenty-four, UnMe Jeans considered the opportunity to develop a virtual jean store there where UnME jeans would be sold to avatars. Users (called Zwinky's) would be invited to design their own virtual jeans and enter a contest that would be judged by a panel of real-life celebrity judges and would be manufactured to be sold in the real world. Clearly this marketing option offered many benefits including (Steenburgh and Avery 2008):

- Zwinktopia offers a highly targeted environment that matches exactly the demographics of UnME Jeans.
- The initiative was innovative enough to generate buzz in the fashion press.
- Virtual products offer incremental sales prospects. Also virtual retail apparel stores are responsible for 34 percent of the products for sale on Second Life, offering users the opportunity to forge a relationship with the brand.
- Users feel a sense of ownership via the sharing of jean designs which can later be exported to Facebook and MySpace.
- Since only some retail stores are there, UnME Jeans can get a "first-mover advantage" that requires a minimal upfront investment.

On the other hand, this idea also offered certain barriers, mainly how to effectively measure the impact of marketing dollars invested in a new medium, since traditional marketing metrics are not appropriate measures for this new medium.

One of the challenges that virtual worlds face in becoming pervasive platforms for business is that computers are not typically designed for three-dimensional inputs, and the fact that startup costs in developing these environments is high. In fact, people typically spend a lot more time than they anticipated when designing their avatars because most people feel a personal sense of identification with their virtual personae. On the other hand, virtual worlds are beginning to show promise in resolving issues in distributed collaboration that other technologies like videoconferencing just can't address, such as supporting multiple simultaneous conversations of remote coworkers. In addition, virtual worlds can also be an important informal communication infrastructure to build human relationships. Finally, virtual worlds can also help its users develop new skills that can later be transferred to the real world. Is *The Matrix*[7] potentially a reality? Box 10.4 explores how one company UnME Jeans explores the use of virtual worlds for marketing their popular teenage jeans.

THE THREE WORLDS OF INFORMATION TECHNOLOGY: DOES IT REALLY MATTER?

In this chapter we have presented a group of breakthrough technologies that may be poised to be transformational, that is they may disrupt and redefine the way business is done today. As we look back at the history of another transformational technology, we learn that at first The Western Union Company rejected Alexander Graham Bell's offer to sell the patent for the telephone for a mere $100,000, commenting that the instrument was nothing but a toy—an offer that would translate to $25 million dollars only two years later. Similarly, many of these emerging Web 2.0 technologies are facing increasing resistance from their users as their management struggles with finding "appropriate" mechanisms to carry out business transactions on these platforms. One example was Facebook's release of the marketing initiative Beacon, which allowed external Web sites to publish a user's activities to their Facebook profiles in order to promote their products even if users tried to opt out of this feature. Beacon was met with such resistance from Facebook users and privacy advocate groups who pointed out that it violated Facebook's promise that "no personally identifiable information is shared with an advertiser." Zuckerberg publicly apologized and promised users a revamped Beacon where users would opt-in, rather than be expected to opt-out of this feature (Perez 2007). On the other hand, companies have already started to use virtual venues to collaborate and learn. For example, BP created an environment that allows engineers to roam freely around a future oil pipeline in a virtual representation of its existing surroundings in order to allow the engineers to effectively identify constructability and safety issues (Hemp 2008). Are social networks and virtual worlds, seen as the entertainment tools of our youngest generation, prepared to be the next disruptive business technologies in the near future?

It's easy to infer that IT has a positive influence on KM and organizational learning. For example, research supports the hypothesis that **groupware** systems contributed to improved organizational learning as compared to those individuals that didn't have access to those KM systems (Orlikowski 1996). In addition, studies have found that IT-enabled learning mechanisms facilitate capabilities that have an effect on exploration and exploitation dynamics in organizational learning (Kane and Alavi 2007). So IT can be used to improve organizational learning, in particular in times of turnover and turbulence.

Some skeptics of the potential transformational role that IT is positioned to play in the near future point out that the evolution of IT follows the same blueprint of earlier infrastructural technologies like railroads and electric power (Carr 2003). At first, these technologies provide opportunities for visionary companies that are quick to integrate them into their business processes and thus gain competitive advantages. But as their cost decreases and their availability become pervasive, the competitive advantages they offer are similarly eroded, commoditizing their value and becoming simply the cost of doing business. IT then no longer matters. Have we indeed reached the point where IT doesn't matter?

Recently IT spending is facing increasing criticism. A report by Computer Science Corporation, which surveyed 782 American executives in charge of IT, revealed that

51 percent of large-scale IT efforts finished later than expected and ran over budget, that only 10 percent of companies believed they were getting high returns from IT investments, and that 47 percent felt the returns were low or negative or unknown (McAfee 2006). Research has found that executives indeed have a critical role in the selection, adoption, and exploitation of IT in the organization. Furthermore, executives must adopt a comprehensive model of what IT does for their organization and what they must do to ensure those IT projects are successful (McAfee 2006).

Building a comprehensive model includes understanding not only the uses of IT innovations but how can they change the how the work is done. IT can in fact have different types of impacts in the organization because they fall in three different categories:

1. Function IT—refers to IT that helps with the getting a specific task done. This type of IT doesn't require modifications to business processes to maximize their utility, although their impact could increase when this happens. Function IT delivers productivity and optimization. It is not hard to implement; the manager's main role is to create business processes that will maximize their utility. Some examples are spreadsheets and simulation software.
2. Network IT—refers to IT that supports interaction. This type of IT doesn't require modifications to business processes, but these may evolve over time in order to gain additional advantages. Network IT delivers increased collaboration. Adoption is usually voluntary and their adoption isn't difficult. Some examples are wikis and blogs.
3. Enterprise IT—refers to IT that specifies business processes and thus must be accompanied by the specification of new tasks and sequences. Enterprise IT delivers standardization and monitors work. It is hard for companies to adopt, and employees usually dislike them thus requiring forceful intervention of the IT leader. Some examples include ERP and CRM.

Successful IT executives have three tasks: electing IT applications that deliver needed organizational capabilities, leading their adoption effort, and shaping their exploitations (McAfee 2006). Successful IT leaders are those that follow an "inside-out approach (that) puts the spotlight squarely on the business before evaluating the technology landscape; it focused on the capabilities that IT can provide rather than on the technologies themselves" (McAfee 2006).

So we conclude with the analysis of the question: Does IT no longer matter? Even if software is not rare and easy to imitate, successful system implementations are not necessarily easy to replicate. And as disruptive technologies continue to be developed, new business processes must be discovered in order for the organization to gain new competitive advantages.

SUMMARY

In this chapter, you learned what social networks are and how they are redefining the definition of collaboration both on the Internet and within organizations. We discussed emerging technologies such as wikis and blogs and how they enable knowledge management. Then we discussed the importance of open source development and its emergence as an important new business model for profitable firms across the world. We followed with a discussion of virtual worlds, including some of the challenges they face and the value they are already providing businesses. Finally, we closed this chapter with a discussion on how IT is still poised to act as a transformational technology for businesses that continue to find ways in which technology can continue to redefine the ways businesses operate proving that IT indeed still matters.

KEY TERMS

Avatars
Blogs
Collective intelligence
Enterprise 2.0
Groupware
JavaScript
Mash-ups
Metaverse
Online games
Open source

Peer-to-peer social networking
Podcasts
RSS
Social networking
Virtual worlds
Web services
Web 2.0
Widgets
Wikis

REVIEW

1. What is Ajax?
2. Describe the difference between wikis and blogs.
3. Describe the categories for the policies and guidelines for Wikipedia. Who developed these guidelines?
4. Define open source development.

APPLICATION EXERCISES

1. How could social networking redefine collaboration within organizations?
2. Give an example from the literature of how top organizations are deploying an enterprise 2.0 architecture.
3. Describe the process to make a new contribution or edit an entry in Wikipedia.
4. Make an entry, either a new contribution or edit an existing article, in Wikipedia. Since anyone can modify the contents of Wikipedia, then why is it that we can be confident that its contents are credible?

NOTES

1. See, for example, Michael Arrington, "Gorb: Taking Personal Reputation to a New Low," *Tech-Crunch*, March 12, 2007. http://www.techcrunch.com/2007/03/12/gorb-taking-personal-reputation-to-a-new-low/ (accessed September 15, 2008).

2. For details, see University of Missouri's iSocial at http://isocial.rnet.missouri.edu/.

3. We acknowledge John Lester of Linden Labs for this information. Additional information can be found at http://secondlifegrid.net/programs/education.

4. A video of this performance can be seen at http://www.youtube.com/watch?v=c_gT0YDAkec.

5. We acknowledge Jordan Slott and Nicole Yankelovich for this information. Additional information can be found at http://wiki.java.net/bin/view/Javadesktop/ProjectWonderlandResources.

6. A video explaining how to integrate services like Flickr can be seen at https://www.dev.java.net/files/documents/5924/109223/flickrapp.mov.

7. A science fiction film released in 1999 in which the reality perceived by humans is actually a virtual world created by intelligent computers in order to subdue the human population.

REFERENCES

Alavi, M. and Kane, G. 2008. Social networks and information technology: Evolution and new frontiers. In *Knowledge management: An evolutionary view,* Advances in Management Information Systems, vol. 12, ed. I. Becerra-Fernandez and D. Leidner, 63–85. Armonk, NY: M.E. Sharpe.

Barnett, W., Leslie, M., and Harkey, M. 2006. *Facebook.* Stanford Graduate School Case E-220, May 3.

Carr, N. 2003. IT doesn't matter. *Harvard Business Review,* May.

Collis, D. and Montgomery, C. 2004. Sharing to advantage: A new paradigm for business. *Strategy and Innovation,* July-August, 3–5.

Garrett, J.J. 2005. Ajax: A new approach to web applications. *Adaptive Path,* February 18. http://www.adaptivepath.com/ideas/essays/archives/000385.php (accessed September 12, 2008).

Giles, H. 2005. Internet encyclopaedias go head to head. *Nature,* December 15.

Harvard Business Review. 2008. The HBR list: Breakthrough ideas for 2008. *Harvard Business Review,* February.

Hemp, P. 2008. Getting real about virtual worlds. *Harvard Business Review,* October.

Hockenberry, J. 2005. The blogs of war. *Wired,* August 1.

Horton, A. 2008. Army of Dude website. http://armyofdude.blogspot.com/ (accessed September 15, 2008).

Kane, G. and Alavi, M. 2007. Information technology and organizational learning: An investigation of exploration and exploitation process. *Organization Science,* 18(5), 796–812.

Lamont, J. 2008. Contacts and connections: An array of options. *KM World,* July/August, 20–22.

McAfee, A. 2006. Enterprise 2.0: The dawn of emergent collaboration. *MIT Sloan Management Review,* 47(3), 21–28.

McAfee, A. and Sjoman, A. 2006. *Wikis at Dresdner Kleinwort Wasserstein.* Harvard Business School Case 9–606–074, January 29.

McKinsey. 2007a. How businesses are using Web 2.0: A McKinsey Global Survey. *The McKinsey Quarterly,* March. http://www.mckinseyquarterly.com/How_businesses_are_using_Web_20_A_McKinsey_Global_Survey_1913 (accessed September 12, 2008).

———. 2007b. How companies are marketing online: A McKinsey Global Survey. *The McKinsey Quarterly,* September. http://www.mckinseyquarterly.com/How_companies_are_marketing_online_A_McKinsey_Global_Survey_2048 (accessed September 12, 2008).

———. 2008. Building the web 2.0 enterprise: McKinsey Global Survey Results. *The McKinsey Quarterly,* July. http://www.mckinseyquarterly.com/Building_the_Web_20_Enterprise_McKinsey_Global_Survey_2174 (accessed September 12, 2008).

Mintz, J. 2005. Friendster's 'eww' moment. *Wall Street Journal,* December 8.

Missick, C. 2008. *Christopher Missick.* http://www.missick.com/Welcome.html (accessed September 15, 2008).

O'Reilly, T. 2005. What is Web 2.0: Design patterns and business models for the next generation of software. *Communications & Strategies,* January 1, 17.

Orlikowski, W. 1996. Improving organizational transformation over time: A situated change perspective. *Information Systems Research,* 7(1), 63–92.

Perez, J. 2007. Facebook's Beacon more intrusive than previously thought. *PC World,* November 30.

Shachtman, N. 2007. Army squeezes soldier blogs, maybe to death. *Wired,* May 2.

Shah, S. 2003. Understanding the nature of participation and coordination in open and gated source software. *COSPA Knowledge Base.* http://kb.cospa-project.org/retrieve/2743/shah3.pdf (accessed February 12, 2009).

Steenburg, T. and Avery, J. 2008. *UNME Jeans: Branding in Web 2.0.* Boston: Harvard Business School Publishing.

Steinhauser, L. and Thon, S. 2008. Operation Burnt Frost: The power of social networks. *NASA's Academy of Sharing Knowledge (ASK) Magazine,* Summer, 17–19.

Tancer, B. 2006. MySpace moves into #1 position for all Internet sites. *Hitwise Intelligence,* July 11. http://weblogs.hitwise.com/bill-tancer/2006/07/myspace_moves_into_1_position.html (accessed July 14, 2006).

Thompson, C. 2008. Brave new world of digital intimacy. *The New York Times,* September 7.

von Krogh, G. 2003. Open-source software development. *MIT Sloan Management Review,* 44(3).

Wasko, M. and Faraj, S. 2005. Why should I share? Examining social capital and knowledge contribution in electronic networks of practice. *MIS Quarterly,* 29(1), 35–57.

Wikipedia. 2009a. *Metaverse.* http://en.wikipedia.org/wiki/Metaverse (accessed January 19, 2009).

———. 2009b. Wikipedia: List of policies. http://en.wikipedia.org/wiki/Wikipolicy.

Wittig, C. and Inkinen, S. 2004. *MySQL open source database in 2004.* Stanford Graduate School of Business Case, SM-124, June.

11 Factors Influencing Knowledge Management

In the last chapter, we discussed some of the emerging trends in knowledge management. Earlier, in Chapter 5, we examined the impacts KM can have on companies and other private or public organizations. These impacts result either directly from KM solutions or indirectly through knowledge created by KM solutions. KM solutions include KM processes and systems, which were discussed in Chapter 4. In this chapter, we argue that various KM solutions may have different impacts on performance depending on the circumstances, and we examine the key factors affecting the suitability of KM solutions. This perspective, which is called *contingency perspective*, is discussed next and the overall approach in this chapter is outlined. The subsequent sections examine the effects of several important factors.

A Contingency View of Knowledge Management

A universalistic view of knowledge management would imply that there is a single best approach of managing knowledge, which should be adopted by all organizations in all circumstances. This seems to be implicit in the literature on knowledge management; for example, knowledge sharing is recommended as being useful to all organizations, although we believe that the use of direction may sometimes represent an equally effective but more efficient alternative. In contrast to this universalistic view, **contingency theory**, which has previously been used, for example, in the literature on organization design, suggests that no one approach is best under all circumstances. Whereas a universalistic view focuses on identifying a single path to successful performance, a contingency theory considers the path to success to include multiple alternative paths with success being achieved only when the appropriate path is selected. For instance an organization design with few rules or procedures is considered appropriate for small organizations, whereas one with extensive rules and procedures is recommended for large organizations.

We recommend the use of a similar approach based on contingency theory for identifying KM processes and solutions. When asked what kind of a KM solution should an organization use, we often find ourselves responding, "it depends," rather than unequivocally recommending a specific solution. We need to understand the specific circumstances within the organization and the ones surrounding it in order to identify the KM solution that would be most beneficial for those circumstances. This indicates that each KM solution is contingent upon the presence of certain circumstances—hence, the name. A contingency perspective for KM is supported by prior empirical research (Becerra-Fernandez and Sabherwal 2001; Sabherwal and Sabherwal 2005). For example based on a detailed study of Nortel Networks Corporation, Massey et al. (2002, p. 284) conclude: "Thus, a key finding of our study is that successful KM initiatives like Nortel's cannot be disentangled from broader organizational factors and changes."

Figure 11.1 summarizes the way in which the relationship between the contingency factors and KM solutions is examined in this chapter. As discussed in Chapters 3 and 4, KM solutions include KM systems and KM processes. Much of this chapter focuses on **knowledge management processes**, with the choice of appropriate KM process depending on contingency factors, as shown by arrow 1 in Figure 11.1. Once the appropriate KM processes are recognized, the KM systems needed to support them can be identified as well. Thus, the contingency factors indirectly affect KM systems and the mechanisms and technologies enabling KM systems, as shown using arrows 2 and 3. Moreover, the KM infrastructure supports KM mechanisms and technologies (arrow 4), which in turn affect KM systems (arrow 5) and KM systems support KM processes (arrow 6). Thus, the KM infrastructure indirectly affects KM processes (arrow 7).

Several contingency factors influence the choice of KM processes. They include characteristics of the tasks being performed, the knowledge being managed, the organization, and the organization's environment. Figure 11.2 summarizes these categories of contingency factors affecting KM processes. In the forthcoming sections, we will examine the effects of task characteristics and knowledge characteristics, respectively. And, we will also describe the effects of organizational and environmental characteristics.

In general, the contingency factors and KM infrastructure affect the suitability of KM processes in two ways: (a) by increasing or reducing the need to manage knowledge in a particular way; and (b) by increasing or reducing the organization's ability to manage knowledge in a particular way. For example, larger organizations have a greater need to invest in knowledge sharing processes, whereas an organization culture characterized by trust increases the organization's ability to use knowledge sharing processes. Consequently, the benefits from a KM process would depend on the contingency factors (Sabherwal and Sabherwal 2005).

THE EFFECTS OF TASK CHARACTERISTICS

The underlying argument here is that the KM processes that are appropriate for an organizational subunit (e.g., a department, a geographic location, etc.) depend on the nature of its tasks (Becerra-Fernandez and Sabherwal 2001; Haas and Hansen 2005). This involves viewing each subunit at the aggregate level based on the predominant nature of its tasks. This approach has considerable support in prior literature. For example, Van de Ven and Delbecq (1974) offered a contingency view of the relationship between subunit tasks and organization structure. They suggested that the structure appropriate for a subunit depends on task difficulty, or on the problems in

Figure 11.1 Contingency Factors and Knowledge Management

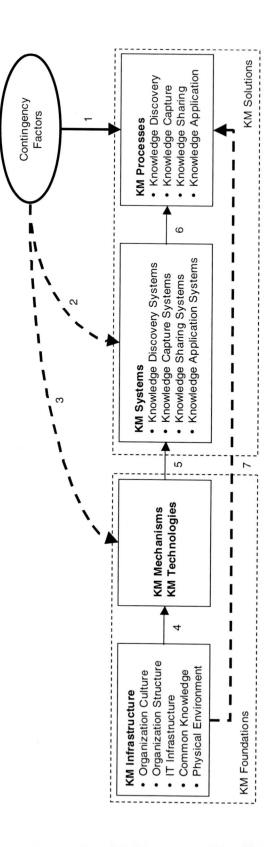

Figure 11.2 **Categories of Contingency Factors**

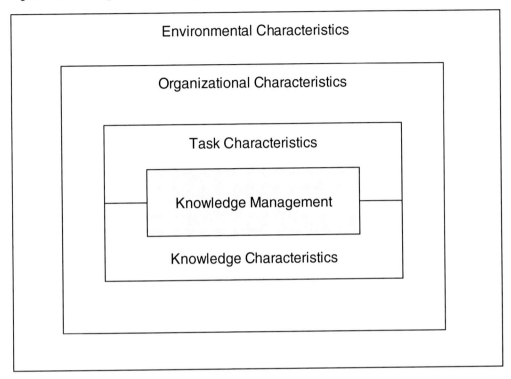

analyzing the work and stating performance procedures and task variability, or on the variety of problems encountered in the tasks. Lawrence and Lorsch (1967) also focused on a task characteristic—**task uncertainty**—at the subunit level, and found subunits that perform certain, predictable tasks to be more effective when they were formally structured. Thus, a number of task characteristics have been studied at the level of organizational subunits. Here, two task characteristics—task uncertainty and task interdependence—are considered as influencing the appropriate KM processes (Spender 1996).

Consistent with Lawrence and Lorsch (1967), greater task uncertainty is argued to reduce the organization's ability to develop routines, and hence knowledge application would depend on direction. Moreover when task uncertainty is high, **externalization** and **internalization** would be more costly due to changing problems and tasks. Under such circumstances knowledge is more likely to remain tacit, inhibiting the ability to use combination or exchange. Therefore under high task uncertainty, direction or socialization would be recommended. For example, individuals responsible for product design when customer tastes are expected to change frequently would benefit most from socializing with, and receiving directions from, each other.

On the other hand, when the tasks are low in uncertainty routines can be developed for the knowledge supporting them. Moreover, the benefits from externalizing or internalizing knowledge related to any specific task would accumulate through

Figure 11.3   **Effects of Task Characteristics on KM Processes**

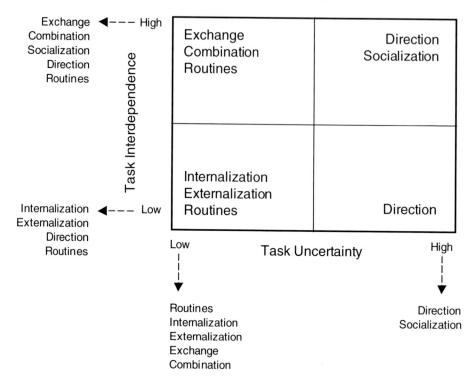

the greater occurrence of that task. Finally, exchange and combination would be useful due to the externalization of potentially tacit knowledge. Therefore under low task uncertainty, routines, exchange, combination, internalization, or externalization would be recommended. These conclusions are summarized in the bottom part of Figure 11.3.

For example, for individuals performing tasks related to credit and accounts receivables, considerable benefits would be obtained from the use of routines (e.g., those for credit-checking procedures), exchange (e.g., sharing of standards and policies), combination (e.g., integration of explicit knowledge that different credit analysts may have generated from their experiences), and from externalization and internalization (e.g., to facilitate training and learning of existing policies by new credit analysts).

The second important task characteristic is **task interdependence**, which indicates the extent to which the subunit's achievement of its goals depends on the efforts of other subunits (Jarvenpaa and Staples 2001). Performing tasks that are independent of others primarily requires the knowledge directly available to the individuals within the subunit. These tasks rely mainly on distinctive units of knowledge, such as "functional knowledge embodied in a specific group of engineers, elemental technologies, information processing devices, databases, and patents" (Kusonaki et al. 1998). They often require deep knowledge in a particular area. With internalization, such as when individuals acquire knowledge by observing or by talking to others, as well as with externalization, such as when they try to model their knowledge into analogies, metaphors, or problem-solving systems, the learning processes are personal and individualized. Through externalization, the individual makes the knowledge more agreeable and understandable to others in the group while through internalization the individual absorbs knowledge held by others in the group (Maturana and Varela 1987). Internalization and externalization are thus fundamental to KM in an independent task domain. Performance of interdependent tasks relies mainly on dynamic interaction in which individual units of knowledge are combined and transformed through communication and coordination across different functional groups. This creates greater causal ambiguity, since knowledge is being integrated across multiple groups that may not have a high level of shared understanding. Socialization and combination processes, both of which help synthesize prior knowledge to create new knowledge, are therefore appropriate for interdependent tasks (Grant 1996).

The left portion of Figure 11.3 shows that internalization and externalization should be preferred for independent tasks whereas **exchange**, **combination**, and **socialization** should be preferred for interdependent tasks. Moreover, **directions** and **routines** can be used for independent as well as interdependent tasks; their suitability depends more on task uncertainty, as already discussed.

Combining the arguments regarding the effects of task uncertainty and task interdependence, we obtain the four-cell matrix in Figure 11.3. As shown in the matrix, direction is recommended for uncertain, independent tasks; direction and socialization are recommended for uncertain, interdependent tasks; exchange, combination, and routines are recommended for certain, interdependent tasks; and internalization, externalization, and routines are recommended for certain, independent tasks.

THE EFFECTS OF KNOWLEDGE CHARACTERISTICS

Three knowledge characteristics—explicit versus tacit, procedural versus declarative, and general versus specific—were examined in Chapter 2. The first two of these knowledge characteristics directly affect the suitability of KM processes. The underlying contingency argument is that certain KM processes may have greater impact on the value that one type of knowledge contributes to the organization, while some other KM processes might affect the value of another type of knowledge (Spender 1996).

Figure 11.4 shows the KM processes that were presented earlier in Chapter 3 while also depicting the effects of the two knowledge classifications. The difference between KM processes appropriate for explicit and tacit knowledge is based directly on the main difference between these knowledge types.

For **knowledge discovery**, combination would be appropriate for integrating multiple streams of explicit knowledge, for example with knowledge discovery systems, where socialization would be suitable for integrating multiple streams of **tacit knowledge**. For **knowledge capture**, externalization would be appropriate for tacit knowledge as it helps convert tacit knowledge into **explicit knowledge**, for example in knowledge capture systems; whereas internalization would be appropriate for explicit knowledge, as it helps convert explicit knowledge into tacit knowledge, for example in learning. For **knowledge sharing**, exchange helps transfer explicit

264

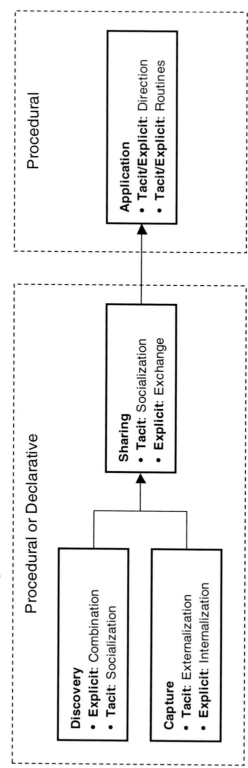

Figure 11.4 Effects of Knowledge Characteristics on KM Processes

knowledge whereas socialization is needed for tacit knowledge. These intuitively obvious recommendations are also based on the logic that a KM process would contribute much to the value of knowledge if it is both effective and efficient for managing that knowledge (Gupta and Govindarajan 2000). Some KM processes might not contribute to the value of a given type of knowledge either because they are not effective in managing it (e.g., combination and exchange would not be effective for managing tacit knowledge), or because they are too expensive or too slow—that is, an alternative process would be able to integrate it more quickly or at a lower cost (e.g., socialization would be too expensive and slow for sharing explicit knowledge, especially in comparison to exchange).

No difference between the suitability of direction and routines is expected between tacit and explicit knowledge. In other words, either direction or routines could be used to apply either tacit or explicit knowledge. This is the case because no knowledge is being transferred in either direction or routines; only recommendations based on the expert's knowledge (whether tacit or explicit) are being transferred. Both direction and routine processes are appropriate to be used mainly for **procedural knowledge**, or "know-how," which focuses on the processes or means that should be used to perform the required tasks—for instance how to perform the steps in performing a specific process, such as installing a piece of software. This is shown in the right portion of Figure 11.4. Procedural knowledge differs from **declarative knowledge**, substantive knowledge, or "know what," which focuses on beliefs about relationships among variables, as we discussed in Chapter 2. As shown in the left part of Figure 11.4, all the KM processes supporting knowledge discovery, capture, and sharing can be used for both declarative and procedural knowledge.

Thus, either direction or routines could be used to apply procedural knowledge, whether tacit or explicit. KM processes used to discover, capture, or share knowledge are the same for both procedural and declarative kinds of knowledge. However, these processes differ between tacit and explicit knowledge, as discussed and shown in Figure 11.4 within the boxes for knowledge discovery, capture, and sharing.

THE EFFECTS OF ORGANIZATIONAL AND ENVIRONMENTAL CHARACTERISTICS

Two organizational characteristics—size and strategy—and one environmental characteristic—uncertainty—affect the suitability of various knowledge management processes. Table 11.1 summarizes the effects of environmental and organizational characteristics.

Organization size affects KM processes by influencing the choice between the two processes supporting **knowledge application** (direction, routines) and the two processes supporting knowledge sharing (socialization, exchange). For knowledge application, large and more bureaucratic organizations would benefit more from routines because of their greater use of standards and their potential for reuse of these routines. Small organizations, on the other hand, are usually not very bureaucratic and have less potential for reusing processes and procedures coded as routines. They would therefore benefit more from direction, which does not rely on standardization and rules. The circumstances needed for direction—for example, the knowledge user's

Table 11.1

Effect of Environmental and Organizational Characteristics on KM Processes

Characteristic	Level/Type	Recommended KM Processes
Organization Size	Small	• Knowledge sharing (socialization) • Knowledge application (direction) • Knowledge discovery (combination, socialization) • Knowledge capture (externalization, internalization)
	Large	• Knowledge sharing (exchange) • Knowledge application (routines) • Knowledge discovery (combination) • Knowledge capture (externalization, internalization)
Business Strategy	Low cost	• Knowledge application (direction, routines) • Knowledge capture (externalization, internalization) • Knowledge sharing (socialization, exchange)
	Differentiation	• Knowledge discovery (combination, socialization) • Knowledge capture (externalization, internalization) • Knowledge sharing (socialization, exchange)
Environmental Uncertainty	Low	• Knowledge sharing (socialization, exchange) • Knowledge capture (externalization, internalization)
	High	• Knowledge discovery (combination, socialization) • Knowledge application (direction, routines)

trust in the individual providing direction (Conner and Prahalad 1996)—are also more likely to exist in smaller organizations. Large organizations are often globally distributed, therefore knowledge sharing across greater distances would be needed in large organizations; whereas knowledge is more likely to be shared across shorter distances in smaller co-located organizations. Therefore, knowledge sharing through exchange is recommended for large distributed organizations while socialization is recommended for small co-located organizations (Boh 2007). Socialization for knowledge discovery is also recommended for small organizations, although combination could be used in either small or large organizations. Finally, small and large organizations do not differ in terms of the suitability of the alternative knowledge capture processes (externalization, internalization).

For example, a small financial consulting firm with 25 employees would have only a few experts in any area—for instance, customer relations practices. Consequently, others in the organization are likely to trust these experts and depend on their direction. Moreover, the small number of employees would have frequent opportunities to interact with each other thereby enabling greater use of socialization for knowledge discovery as well as knowledge sharing. On the other hand, a large consulting firm with over 5,000 employees would find it infeasible or overly expensive to rely on socialization, especially across large distances. Instead, in such an organization, knowledge sharing would rely more on exchange of knowledge explicated in reports, lessons learned documents, and so on. In addition, large organizations may find it more likely to reuse knowledge that has been explicated previously, for example in lessons learned systems or best practices databases as described in Chapter 8. Furthermore, this firm would find it beneficial to develop and use routines for applying knowledge. Routines would be more economical due to their greater frequency of use in such larger firms and also needed by more individuals within the organization who may be seeking help.

The effect of **business strategy** may be examined using Porter's (1980, 1985) popular typology of low cost and differentiation strategies.[1] Organizations pursuing a low-cost strategy should focus on applying existing knowledge rather than creating new knowledge, whereas organizations following a differentiation strategy are more likely to innovate (Langerak et al. 1999), seek new opportunities (Miles and Snow 1978), and frequently develop new products (Hambrick 1983). They would therefore benefit more from knowledge discovery and capture processes (combination and socialization). Organizations pursuing either low-cost or differentiation strategy would benefit from knowledge capture and sharing processes, as these processes can be used to capture or share knowledge on ways of reducing costs as well as innovating with products or services.

For example, a supermarket chain competing through a low-cost strategy would seek to reuse prior knowledge about ordering, inventory management, supplier relations, pricing, and so on. This company would therefore use organizational routines (in case the company is large) or direction (if the company is small) to support the application of prior knowledge. In contrast, an exclusive fashion boutique, trying to differentiate itself from its competitors would seek new knowledge about attracting competitors' customers, and retaining its own customers, developing innovative products, and so on. This boutique would significantly benefit from socialization and combination processes for creating new knowledge about these aspects, using prior tacit and explicit knowledge, respectively.

The environmental uncertainty encountered by the organization also affects knowledge management (Hsu and Wang 2008), and the suitability of various KM processes (Sabherwal and Sabherwal 2005). Environmental uncertainty, which refers to the business context in which the firm operates, should not be confused with task uncertainty which refers to not having *a priori* knowledge of details involved in the steps required by a task. When the organization faces low levels of uncertainty, knowledge sharing and knowledge capture processes would be recommended because the captured and shared knowledge would be relevant for longer periods of time. On the other hand, under higher uncertainty, knowledge application and discovery would be recommended. Knowledge application contributes in an uncertain environment by enabling individuals to address problems based on existing solutions indicated by those possessing the knowledge, instead of more time-consuming processes like sharing knowledge (Alavi and Leidner 2001; Conner and Prahalad 1996). Knowledge discovery processes contribute by enhancing the organization's ability to develop new innovative solutions to emergent problems that may not have been faced before (Davenport and Prusak 1998).

For example, the environment would be rather certain and predictable for an automobile-manufacturing firm that has a relatively stable product line and competes with a small number of competitors especially when each firm has its own, clear market niche. For such an organization, knowledge about product design, manufacturing, marketing, sales, and so forth would be generally stable, benefiting from the sharing of prior knowledge through socialization or exchange and the capture of knowledge through internalization and externalization. Knowledge sharing, as well as internalization and externalization, would have long-term benefits, as the knowledge remains inherently stable. On the other hand, an international mobile phone manufacturer having a dynamic product line and evolving customer base would face a highly uncertain environment. This organization would seek to create new knowledge and quickly apply existing knowledge by investing in combination and socialization for knowledge discovery and routines and direction for knowledge application. For example, Canon Inc.'s success has been attributed to both creating new innovations, for example in the photography industry, and quickly applying these innovations to other relevant products like fax and copy machines.

The effects of contingency factors on the selection of knowledge management solutions at one leading consumer-goods company, Groupe Danone, is described in Box 11.1.

IDENTIFICATION OF APPROPRIATE KNOWLEDGE MANAGEMENT SOLUTIONS

Based on the above discussion, we recommend a **methodology** for identifying appropriate KM solutions. The methodology includes the following seven steps:

1. Assess the contingency factors.
2. Identify the KM processes based on each contingency factor.
3. Prioritize the needed KM processes.
4. Identify the existing KM processes.
5. Identify the additional needed KM processes.
6. Assess the KM infrastructure and identify the sequential ordering of KM processes.
7. Develop additional needed KM systems, mechanisms, and technologies.

These seven steps are now discussed.

STEP 1. ASSESS THE CONTINGENCY FACTORS

This step requires assessing the organization's environment in terms of the contingency factors—characterizing the tasks, the knowledge, the environment, and the organization—and how they contribute to uncertainty.

The variety of tasks for which KM is needed should be characterized in terms of task interdependence and task uncertainty. Furthermore, the kind of knowledge those tasks require should be classified as general or specific, declarative or procedural, and tacit or explicit. Environmental uncertainty may arise from changes in the firm's competition, government regulations and policies, economic conditions, and so on.

Additionally, the organization's business strategy—low-cost or differentiation—should be identified. Lastly, the organization should be classified as small or large relative to its competitors. In some instances, it may be labeled as midsized, in which

Box 11.1

Networking Attitude Fosters Knowledge Sharing and Creation at Danone

Groupe Danone is a leading consumer-goods company, with headquarters in Paris. Known as Dannon in the United States, it is among the world's leading producers of dairy products, bottled water, cereals, and baby foods. Danone is a fast-moving and entrepreneurial company, emphasizing differentiation rather than cost reduction. Although it is spread across 120 countries, it is smaller than its competitors and operates in a decentralized fashion with considerable emphasis on responsiveness to the needs of local markets. Most of the knowledge used at Danone is held in tacit form by its employees. Danone's business strategy (differentiation), environmental uncertainty (which is high because of its operating in numerous countries with changing products), and focus on tacit knowledge make it important for the company to share knowledge across countries and across divisions. However, the use of exchange through IT did not seem promising due to the tacit nature of their knowledge. Moreover, Danone's employees did not make much use of portals and information technologies in general.

Senior executives at Danone, including Frank Mougin Danone's executive vice president of human resources, recognized that using IT to share knowledge would not work as well for the company. Therefore, they have concentrated their KM efforts on using socialization for sharing existing knowledge as well as creating new knowledge using processes akin to their firm's characteristics. As a result, they launched the Networking Attitude Conference in the Fall of 2002. Networking Attitude was presented to the company's general managers as a mechanism for people in units distant from each other to share their knowledge. It focused on the following initiatives:

- "Marketplaces" were special events focusing on a theme, and involving "takers" who "pay" for best practices obtained from "givers," using a "check" and a facilitator tracking the number of checks acquired by each giver and using it as a way of evaluating the relevance of each best practice.
- A "message-in-a-bottle" session brought "takers" facing problems to a smaller audience of potential "givers," and with no observer to facilitate more spontaneous networking.
- A "T-shirt session" was incorporated into meetings or conferences, with the participants writing suggestions and problems on the front and back of their T-shirts, respectively.
- "Who's Who" was an internal directory on the company's Intranet.
- "Communities" were smaller networks (with a leader and about 10 to 15 members) who met regularly (every six months or so).

Although there was no formal tracking of its impact, the Networking Attitude Conference appears to have worked well for Danone, with people participating actively by sharing important knowledge and providing each other recommendations on directions. People seemed to like it, and marketplaces had especially become popular in Mexico and Hungary. From 2004 to 2007, Danone employees shared about 640 best practices with each other and made useful knowledge available to about 5,000 (out of a total of about 9,000) Danone managers around the world.

The success of Networking Attitude led to a demand for introducing additional networking opportunities. Danone was considering three ways of extending Networking Attitude: *deeper* (i.e., involving all the employees rather than only managers), *wider* (i.e., extending the use of networks to customers, consumers, suppliers, and partners), and *richer* (i.e., using it more explicitly for innovation by inviting employees to network with each other with the goal of identifying new products or processes).

Source: Compiled from Edmondson et al. 2008; Groupe Danone; Mougin and Benanti 2005.

case the KM processes would be based on considerations of both small and large organizations.

In using these contingencies, it is important to use the appropriate unit of analysis, which could be either the entire organization or a subunit depending on the specific context for which the KM solution would be developed. When deciding on KM processes that are intended to improve KM within a subunit, such as the accounting department of the organization, the contingency factors should be evaluated for that subunit. On the other hand, when deciding on KM processes that are intended to improve KM for the entire company, the contingency factors should be evaluated for the entire company.

STEP 2. IDENTIFY THE KM PROCESSES BASED ON EACH CONTINGENCY FACTOR

Next, the appropriate KM processes based on each contingency factor should be identified. In doing this, Table 11.2, which summarizes the effects of various contingency factors, should be useful. This table shows the seven contingency factors and the effects they have on the KM processes. It is important to note, however, that this table only provides some of the most important factors that need to be considered in making this choice. There are several other factors, such as the information intensity of the organization's industry, that would also affect the appropriateness of KM processes, but they have been excluded to simplify the presentation.

STEP 3. PRIORITIZE THE NEEDED KM PROCESSES

Once the KM processes appropriate for each contingency factor have been identified, they need to be considered together in order to identify the needed KM processes. In doing so, it is useful to assign a value of 1.0 to situations where a KM process is appropriate for a contingency variable and 0.0 where it is not appropriate. Moreover, where a KM process is appropriate for all possible states of a contingency variable, a value of 0.5 could be assigned. As a result, a prioritization of the importance of various KM processes can be developed, and a Cumulative Priority Score can be computed. For example, if KM process A has a composite score of 6.0 based on the seven contingency factors whereas another one (B) has a composite score of 3.0, greater attention is needed toward KM process A rather than B. This computation is shown in greater detail using an illustrative example in the next section.

STEP 4. IDENTIFY THE EXISTING KM PROCESSES

Next, the KM processes that are currently being used should be identified. In doing so, a short survey of some of the employees assessing the extent to which each KM process is being used may be helpful. Possible approaches for such assessments are discussed in detail in the next chapter.

STEP 5. IDENTIFY THE ADDITIONAL NEEDED KM PROCESSES

Based on the needed KM processes (identified in step 3) and the existing KM processes (identified in step 4), the additional needed KM processes can be identified. This comparison might also find some of the existing KM processes to not be very

Table 11.2

Appropriate Circumstances for Various KM Processes

Contingency Factors	KM Processes							
	Combination	Socialization for knowledge discovery	Socialization for knowledge sharing	Exchange	External-ization	Internalization	Direction	Routines
Task uncertainty	Low	High	High	Low	Low	Low	High	Low
Task interdependence	High	High	High	High	Low	Low	High/low	High/low
Explicit (E) or tacit (T) knowedge	E	T	T	E	T	E	T/E	T/E
Procedural (P) or declarative (D) knowledge	P/D	P/D	P/D	P/D	P/D	P/D	P	P
Organizational size	Small/large	Small	Small	Large	Small/large	Small/large	Small	Large
Business strategy (Low cost—LC; Differentiation—D)	D	D	LC/D	LC/D	LC/D	LC/D	LC	LC
Environmental uncertainty	High	High	Low	Low	Low	Low	High	High

useful. In other words, if a KM process is identified as needed (step 3) but it is not currently being used (step 4), it should be added; whereas if a KM process is not identified as needed (step 3) but it is currently being used (step 4), it could potentially be dropped—at least based on knowledge management considerations.

STEP 6. ASSESS THE KM INFRASTRUCTURE AND IDENTIFY THE SEQUENTIAL ORDERING OF KM PROCESSES

The KM infrastructure indirectly affects the KM processes as we discussed earlier. Specifically, organization culture, organization structure, and the physical environment can facilitate or inhibit knowledge sharing and creation. Additionally, information technologies can support all KM processes, and organizing knowledge can help enhance the efficiency of knowledge sharing (e.g., through common language and vocabulary) and application processes (e.g., by enhancing recognition of individual knowledge domains). These aspects of the KM infrastructure should be considered with respect to the additional KM processes needed (as identified in step 5) to identify the KM processes for which supporting infrastructure, mechanisms, and technologies currently exist. This step is especially important when deciding the sequence in which KM processes that are nearly equal in importance (step 3) should be developed.

STEP 7. DEVELOP ADDITIONAL NEEDED KM SYSTEMS, MECHANISMS, AND TECHNOLOGIES

Steps 1 through 6 have helped identify the KM processes and the order in which they should be developed. Now the organization needs to undertake steps to initiate the creation of KM systems, **mechanisms**, and technologies that would support those KM processes. This might require creation of teams, acquisition of technologies, development of systems, and so on. In the long run, these systems, mechanisms, and technologies would also contribute to the KM infrastructure.

ILLUSTRATIVE EXAMPLE

As an illustration, which is kept somewhat simple to prevent this discussion from becoming overly complex, let us consider the fictional Doubtfire Computer Corporation, a manufacturer of low-end personal computers for home users. A small player in this industry, Doubtfire has recently undergone some difficult times due to new competition for its product line. Competitors make frequent changes in technology in an attempt to gain the upper hand in the marketplace with more state-of-the-art products. Having belatedly recognized this, Doubtfire recently hired a new president and a new sales manager to turn the situation around. The new president called a meeting of the staff to discuss possible strategies for the financial turnaround of the company. The main thrust of this presentation was that the staff needed to better manage knowledge so as to creatively identify areas where new technology could improve the company's products and operations. Based on inputs from the senior management, the president hired a knowledge management consulting firm, KM-Consult Inc., to help improve its KM strategy.

A team of consultants from KM-Consult Inc. conducted an in-depth study of Doubtfire, using interviews with several employees and examination of company documents. Based on their investigation, they concluded that Doubtfire is a small organization that has pursued a low-cost business strategy to operate in an uncertain environment as is typical of high-tech firms. Knowledge management is needed for its tasks, which are highly interdependent and also highly uncertain due to changing components in the computer industry. Doubtfire relies mainly on the tacit, procedural knowledge possessed by its employees rather than seeking the explication of that knowledge or management of declarative knowledge. Then, based on Table 11.2, the consulting team arrived at the following conclusions.

First, based on Doubtfire's small organization size, socialization (for knowledge sharing or knowledge discovery) and direction processes would be appropriate. In addition, combination, internalization, and externalization could be used regardless of organization size. However, exchange and routines would be inappropriate due to Doubtfire being a small organization.

Moreover, considering Doubtfire's low-cost business strategy, direction and routines would be appropriate. In addition, socialization (for knowledge sharing), exchange, internalization, and externalization could be used regardless of strategy. However, combination and socialization (for knowledge discovery) would be inappropriate because they are not suitable for firms pursuing a low-cost strategy.

The consulting team also concluded that, based on the uncertain environment in which Doubtfire operates—which is characteristic of firms in the high-tech sector—direction, combination, and socialization (for knowledge discovery) would be appropriate. However, the remaining processes would be inappropriate as they are more suitable for certain, predictable environments.

The high task interdependence in Doubtfire suggests that socialization (for knowledge sharing or knowledge discovery), combination, and exchange would be appropriate. In addition, direction and routines could be used regardless of task interdependence. However, externalization and internalization would not be as useful. The high task uncertainty suggests that socialization (for knowledge sharing or knowledge discovery) and direction would be appropriate. However, the remaining processes would be less suitable.

The procedural nature of knowledge indicates that direction and routines would be useful for managing this knowledge. The tacit nature of knowledge suggests that socialization (for knowledge sharing or knowledge discovery) and externalization would be appropriate. In addition, direction and routines could be used regardless of tacit or explicit nature of knowledge.

Table 11.3 shows the results of this analysis by KM-Consult Inc. The cells in the columns for each contingency factor show the suitability of the KM process in that row for that contingency variable. More specifically, "Yes" indicates that KM process in that row is appropriate for the contingency variable in that column, which converts to a score of 1.0; "No" indicates that KM process in that row is inappropriate for the contingency variable in that column, which converts to a score of 0.0; and "OK"

Table 11.3

Prioritizing KM Processes for Doubtfire Computer Corporation

Contingency Factors	KM Processes							
	Combination	Socialization for knowledge discovery	Socialization for knowledge sharing	Exchange	Externalization	Internalization	Direction	Routines
Task uncertainty = High	No	Yes	Yes	No	No	No	Yes	No
Task interdependence = High	Yes	Yes	Yes	Yes	No	No	OK	OK
Tacit knowledge	No	Yes	Yes	No	Yes	No	OK	OK
Procedural knowledge	OK	OK	OK	OK	OK	OK	Yes	Yes
Organizational size = Small	OK	Yes	Yes	No	OK	OK	Yes	No
Business strategy = Low cost	No	No	OK	OK	OK	OK	Yes	Yes
Environmental uncertainty = High	Yes	Yes	No	No	No	No	Yes	Yes
Number of "Yes"	2	5	4	1	1	0	5	3
Number of "OK"	2	1	2	2	3	3	2	2
Number of "No"	3	1	1	4	3	4	0	2
Cumulative priority score ("Yes" = 1; "OK" = 0.5; "No" = 0)	3.0	5.5	5.0	2.0	2.5	1.5	6.0	4.0

indicates that KM process in that row can be used for all possible values of the contingency variable in that column, which converts to a score of 0.5.

The last four columns of the table show the computation of the Cumulative Priority Score for each KM process, based on the number of "Yes," "OK," and "No" responses for the suitability of that KM process for the seven contingency variables. Based on this analysis, direction has the highest Cumulative Priority Score (6.0), followed by socialization for knowledge discovery (5.5) and then socialization for knowledge sharing (5.0). Routines are at an intermediate level of priority with a Cumulative Priority Score of 4.0 whereas combination, externalization, exchange, and internalization have low Cumulative Priority Scores (3.0 or less).

Thus, the consideration of the contingency variables led KM-Consult Inc., to conclude that Doubtfire should focus its KM efforts primarily on direction and socialization (for both knowledge discovery and knowledge sharing), with attention being given to combination and routines if the resources so allow. However, recognizing the financial difficulties Doubtfire was facing, KM-Consult Inc., recommended that Doubtfire should focus its efforts on direction and socialization. Moreover, KM-Consult Inc., had found that the current KM initiative at Doubtfire was making little use of both socialization and direction. Therefore, KM-Consult Inc., recommended that Doubtfire should try to enhance the use of direction and socialization for knowledge management. Their report also identified the specific technologies and systems for Doubtfire to pursue. It recommended the establishment and use of communities of practice to support socialization and an expertise locator system to support direction. It also recommended that Doubtfire should enhance socialization through more frequent meetings, rituals, brainstorming retreats, and more. The consultants argued that this socialization would also enhance mutual trust among Doubtfire's employees, thereby increasing their willingness to provide and accept direction. Moreover, KM-Consult Inc., found Doubtfire to be currently making considerable use of internalization, and spending considerable resources on employee training programs. In the light of the low cumulative score for internalization, KM-Consult Inc., advised Doubtfire to consider reducing the budget allocated towards employee training.

SUMMARY

Following our discussion of knowledge management impacts in Chapter 5, we have described how an organization can seek to enhance these impacts by targeting its KM solutions according to the circumstances in which KM is being used. In doing so we have examined the variety of KM processes, systems, mechanisms, as well as technologies discussed in Chapters 3 and 4, while focusing mainly on the KM processes. Table 11.2 summarizes the conclusions regarding the suitability of the KM processes under various circumstances. A methodology for effectively targeting the KM solutions has also been described and illustrated using a detailed example. The next chapter examines how we can evaluate the contributions of KM solutions.

KEY TERMS

Business strategy
Combination
Contingency theory
Declarative knowledge
Directions
Exchange
Explicit knowledge
Externalization
Internalization
Knowledge application
Knowledge capture

Knowledge discovery
Knowledge management mechanisms
Knowledge management processes
Knowledge sharing
Procedural knowledge
Routines
Socialization
Tacit knowledge
Task interdependence
Task uncertainty

REVIEW

1. What is the contingency view of knowledge management? How does it differ from the universalistic view of knowledge management?
2. What do you understand by the terms task uncertainty and task interdependence?
3. What are the knowledge characteristics that affect the appropriateness of knowledge management processes? Explain why.
4. How does organizational size affect knowledge management processes?
5. In what way do organizational strategy and environmental uncertainty affect knowledge management processes?
6. What steps would one take in identifying appropriate knowledge management solutions? Briefly describe them.
7. Explain how a large organization operating in a highly uncertain environment should pursue a low-cost business strategy using knowledge management? State the assumptions made to arrive at your answer.
8. In the seven steps of identifying appropriate KM solutions, Cumulative Priority Score was computed. Describe the function of the score and its application.

APPLICATION EXERCISES

1. Visit local area companies to study their knowledge management practices. Determine how they decided on the type of KM solution they use.
2. Consider reasons why an organization would choose the universalistic view of KM over the contingency view.
3. Visit an organization with a high level of task uncertainty in their business. Explore the extent to which KM is helping or could help them.

4. Similarly visit an organization with high levels of task interdependence among the subunits. Explore the ways in which they have implemented KM to the benefit of the organization.

5. Visit any three organizations and identify their major areas of organizational knowledge and the prominently used KM processes. Next, classify the characteristics of their organizational knowledge into: explicit or tacit; procedural or declarative; and general or specific. Based on the data you collect, determine how appropriate their KM processes are.

6. Collect information from the Internet, *Business Week, Fortune,* and others on either Toyota Motor Corporation or Apple Inc. about the nature of these organizations. Based on this information and the contingency approach presented in this chapter, identify how knowledge should be managed at this company.

7. You are a KM consultant for BP (http://www.bp.com). BP is one of the world's largest petroleum and petrochemicals groups. Its main activities are exploration and production of crude oil and natural gas; refining, marketing, supply, and transportation of oil and gas; and selling fuels and related products. Due to current worldwide financial problems, environmental uncertainty is said to be relatively high these days.

   a. Gather information on BP and decide its task uncertainty and task interdependence whether high or low. Provide the reasons for your decision.

   b. What types of knowledge does BP use most? Suggest the appropriate KM process for each of these types of knowledge?

   c. Assess (i) the organization size of BP (Small or Large); (ii) Business strategy (Low cost or Differentiation); and (iii) Environmental uncertainty (High or Low).

   d. Next, compute the Cumulate Priority Score of each KM processes discussed in this chapter. Based on this analysis, what is your recommendation to BP of appropriate KM solutions?

NOTE

1. Another popular classification of business strategy focuses on classifying firms into Defenders, Analyzers, and Prospectors (Miles and Snow 1978). Defenders, Analyzers, and Prospectors have been found to differ according to the kind of KM efforts that would be most suitable in terms of their effects on the firm's stock market performance (Sabherwal and Sabherwal 2007).

REFERENCES

Alavi, M. and Leidner, D. 2001. Knowledge management and knowledge management systems: Conceptual foundations and research issues. *MIS Quarterly,* 25(1), 107–136.

Becerra-Fernandez, I. and Sabherwal, R. 2001. Organizational knowledge management processes: A contingency perspective. *Journal of Management Information Systems,* 18(1) (Summer), 23–55.

Boh, W.F. 2007. Mechanisms for sharing knowledge in project-based organizations. *Information and Organization,* 17, 27–58.

Conner, K.R. and Prahalad, C.K. 1996. A resource-based theory of the firm: Knowledge versus opportunism. *Organization Science,* 7(5), 477–501.

Davenport, T.H. and Prusak, L. 1998. *Working knowledge: How organizations manage what they know.* Boston: Harvard Business School Press.

Edmondson, A., Moingeon, B., Dessain, V., and Jensen, D. 2008. Global knowledge management at Danone. *Harvard Business Publishing,* 9-608-107, April 16.

Grant, R.M. 1996. Toward a knowledge-based theory of the firm. *Strategic Management Journal,* 17 (Winter), 109–22.

Gupta, A.K. and Govindarajan, V. 2000. Knowledge management's social dimension: Lessons from Nucor steel. *Sloan Management Review,* (Fall), 71–80.

Haas, M.R. and Hansen, M.T. 2005. When using knowledge can hurt performance: The value of organizational capabilities in a management consulting company. *Strategic Management Journal,* 26, 1–24.

Hambrick, D.C. 1983. Some tests of the effectiveness and functional attributes of Miles and Snow's strategic types. *Academy of Management Journal,* 26(1), 5–26.

Hsu, I-C. and Wang, Y-S. 2008. A model of intraorganizational knowledge sharing: Development and initial test. *Journal of Global Information Management,* 16(3), 45–73.

Jarvenpaa, S.L. and Staples, D.S. 2001. Exploring perceptions of organizational ownership of information and expertise. *Journal of Management Information Systems,* 18(1) (Summer), 151–184.

Kusonaki, K., Nonaka, I., and Nagata, A. 1998. Organizational capabilities in product development of Japanese firms: A conceptual framework and empirical findings. *Organization Science,* 9(6), 699–718.

Langerak, F., Nijssen, E., Frambach, R., and Gupta, A. 1999. Exploratory results on the importance of R&D knowledge domains in businesses with different strategies. *R&D Management,* 29(3), 209–217.

Lawrence, P.R. and Lorsch, J.W. 1967. *Organization and environment: Managing differentiation and integration.* Cambridge: Harvard University Press.

Massey, A.P., Montoya-Weiss, M.M., and O'Driscoll, T.M. 2002. Knowledge management in pursuit of performance: Insights from Nortel Networks. *MIS Quarterly,* 26(3) (September), 269–289.

Maturana, H. and Varela, F. 1987. *The tree of knowledge.* Boston: New Science Library.

Miles, R.E. and Snow, C.C. 1978. *Organizational strategy, structure, and process.* New York: McGraw-Hill.

Mougin, F. and Benenati, B. 2005. *Story-telling at Danone: A Latin approach to knowledge management.* Report by Sylvie Cherier, trans. Rachel Marlin. Report, École de Paris du management. http://innovation.zumablog.com/images/186_uploads/Networking_at_Danone.pdf (accessed February 16, 2009).

Nahapiet, J. and Ghoshal, S. 1998. Social capital, intellectual capital, and organizational advantage. *Academy of Management Review,* 23(2), 242–266.

Nonaka, I. 1994. A dynamic theory of organizational knowledge creation. *Organization Science,* 5 (1), 14–37.

Pisano, G.P. 1994. Knowledge, integration, and the locus of learning: An empirical analysis of process development. *Strategic Management Journal,* Winter, 85–100.

Porter, M.E. 1980. *Competitive strategy.* New York: Free Press.

———. 1985. *Competitive advantage.* New York: Free Press.

Sabherwal, R. and Sabherwal, S. 2005. Knowledge management using information technology: Determinants of short-term impact on firm value. *Decision Sciences,* 36(4), 531–567.

———. 2007. How do knowledge management announcements affect firm value? A study of firms pursuing different business strategies. *IEEE Transactions on Engineering Management,* 54(3), 409–422.

Spender, J.C. 1996. Making knowledge the basis of a dynamic theory of the firm. *Strategic Management Journal,* 17 (Winter), 45–63.

Van de Ven, A. and Delbecq, A. 1974. The effectiveness of nominal, delphi, and interacting group decision-making processes. *Academy of Management Journal,* 17, 314–318.

12 Leadership and Assessment of Knowledge Management

In Chapter 3 we discussed knowledge management foundations including infrastructure, mechanisms, and technologies, and how organizations manage it. In Chapter 4, we examined how organizations manage KM solutions, including KM systems and processes. In Chapter 11, we examined how organizations should consider the contingency factors in selecting KM solutions. We also examined the management of specific KM systems in Chapters 6, 7, 8, and 9. To complement these chapters and better understand the overall management of KM in an organization, this chapter examines the leadership of KM and the ways in which the value of KM can be assessed in an organization.

This chapter begins with a discussion of the overall leadership of KM in an organization. Next, it examines the reasons why a KM assessment is needed. It subsequently describes the alternative approaches to assessing KM in the organization, first for evaluating various aspects related to KM and then for the overall evaluation of KM effectiveness.

LEADERSHIP OF KNOWLEDGE MANAGEMENT

The **Chief Executive Officer (CEO)** and the executive board have a direct impact on how the organization views KM. In order for KM to be practiced across the organization, leaders at the top must endorse and stress the importance of KM programs (DeTienne et al. 2004). The CEO must be involved in the knowledge sharing efforts so that others in the organization can follow (Kluge et al. 2001). Also, "if KM doesn't permeate all levels of an organization, beginning at the top, it is unlikely that KM programs will ever catch on or be effective" (DeTienne et al. 2004, p. 34). In summary, the role of the CEO is critical to the success of KM in the organization: first to articulate a "grand theory" of the organization's vision for KM; second to incorporate this vision into the organization's objectives; and third to identify which KM initiatives support that strategy (Takeuchi 2001).

The CEO designates the leadership of the knowledge management function to another senior executive who could be the **Chief Knowledge Officer (CKO)**, Chief Learning Officer, and in some cases the Chief Information Officer. Whereas the Chief Knowledge Officer is usually expected to balance social and technical aspects of KM, the Chief Learning Officer and the Chief Information Officer are generally charged with KM in organizations where the emphasis is on the social aspects and technical aspects respectively.

Some CEOs might consider adding that responsibility of leading KM to the role of the **Chief Information Officer (CIO).** However, this may not be an appropriate decision: "While some CIOs might have the capabilities for the model CKO—entrepreneur, consultant, environmentalist, and technologist—most will score high on the technologist and consultant dimensions but be less accomplished on the entrepreneur and environmentalist dimensions. And CIOs are oriented toward directing a substantial function, rather than toward nurturing and leading a transitory team. Most CIOs have demanding enough agendas without adding the ambiguities of the CKO role" (Earl and Scott 1999, p. 38).

The **Chief Learning Officer (CLO)** is the "business leader of corporate learning" (Bersin 2007). At organizations like CIGNA Corporation (Conz 2008), HP (Kiger 2007), PriceWaterhouseCoopers LLP (Cencigh-Albulario 2008), Accenture Ltd (Meister and Davenport 2005), and many others the CLO is the business executive who leads the organization's learning and development strategy, processes, and systems. Thus, the CLO usually focuses on human resource development and employees' learning and training. For example, PriceWaterhouseCoopers hired a Chief Learning Officer in 2007 to work with its human resource development team and to lead the further study and training of its personnel (Cencigh-Albulario 2008). CLOs usually focus on people and on social aspects of KM, although the CLO's role increasingly involves utilizing ITs to improve KM, often in collaboration with the CIO.

Organizations that recognize the importance of knowledge management as a critical function that goes beyond either information management or human resource development appoint a CKO and charge that individual with the management of the organization's intellectual assets and knowledge management processes, systems, and technologies (Kaplan 2007). Appointing a CKO is "one way of galvanizing, directing, and coordinating a knowledge management program" (Earl and Scott 1999, p. 37).

A study of twenty CKOs in North America and Europe (Earl and Scott 1999) found that many of the CKOs were appointed by CEOs more through intuition and instinct than through analysis or logic, based on the understanding about the increasing importance of knowledge in value creation and the recognition that companies are not good about managing it. Therefore, CKOs were named with the purpose of correcting a perceived corporate deficiency: lack of formal management of knowledge in operations, failure to leverage knowledge in business development, inability to learn from past failures and successes, and not creating value from existing knowledge assets. This study also found that many CKOs did not have a formal job description and that their position was perceived as somewhat transient (three to five years), culminating in the expectation that KM would be embedded in all organizational work processes. Many of these individuals were tasked first with articulating a customized KM program. This study characterized a model CKO as being both a technologist and an environmentalist. CKOs are technologists because they invest in IT, and they are environmentalists because they also create social environments that stimulate conversations and knowledge sharing. In addition the model CKOs are also an entrepreneur, because they are visionary and starting a new activity; and at the same time that they are consultants, because they match new ideas with managers' business needs.

Two other studies, one based on a survey of 41 organizations in the United States and Canada (McKeen and Staples 2003) and the other based on announcements of

23 newly created CKO positions during the period 1995–2003 (Awazu and Desouza 2004), found additional insights regarding the backgrounds, roles, and challenges for CKOs. They found that CKOs usually possess postgraduate education in business or an allied discipline and include many former academics, mainly professors in the areas of information and knowledge management (Awazu and Desouza 2004). An analysis of the background of CKOs revealed that most had a nice blend of technical and management skills. Many CKOs spent their formative years in areas such as KM, management consulting, corporate planning, change management, customer research, marketing, human resource planning, and IT. Organizations were equally likely to promote from within for the CKO position or make an external hire for the job. In either case, the average CKO had about ten years of experience in the industry in which the organization operates (Awazu and Desouza 2004).

CKOs' budgets and staff are modest, because KM initiatives are typically corporately funded and they may have divisional knowledge managers appointed on a dotted-line basis (Earl and Scott 1999; McKeen and Staples 2003). But the most important resource for CKOs is CEO support and sponsorship. The critical success factors for CKOs to achieve their goal of managing knowledge in organizations are (Awazu and Desouza 2004; Earl and Scott 1999):

- Having high-level sponsorship that extends beyond the CEO support.
- Institutionalizing knowledge sharing incentives.
- Breaking knowledge bottlenecks in the organization that impede smooth knowledge flows.
- Embedding knowledge into the work practices and processes.
- Organizational slack time to think, dream, talk, and sell.
- Creating reference projects that demonstrate the value of KM.
- Documenting visible successes for their own performance.

The CKO continues to be an important position in contemporary organizations. It is sometimes combined with other important positions. For example, at Colliers International, the president of U.S. Brokerage Services also serves as the Chief Knowledge Officer and was instrumental in setting up Colliers University, which is the company's business development and training division (Business Wire 2009). Similarly, global management consulting firm Booz & Company announced the position of Chief Marketing and Knowledge Officer and the Symbio Group in China, which provides outsourced software development for companies such as IBM, Mercedes-Benz (a division of Daimler AG), and MasterCard, announced the appointment of their Chief Knowledge Officer (*Knowledge Management Review* 2008).

Box 12.1 describes the experience of the Chief Knowledge Officer (CKO) and Chief Operating Officer (COO) at Atlantis Systems International.

IMPORTANCE OF KNOWLEDGE MANAGEMENT ASSESSMENT

In any aspect of organizational or individual task performance, it is imperative to track whether the efforts are enabling the organization or the individual to achieve the

Box 12.1

Management of KM at Atlantis Systems International

In an interview in September 2006, Blake Melnick, the chief knowledge officer (CKO) and chief operating officer (COO) of Atlantis Systems, discussed his role in the company's knowledge management efforts and the way in which Atlantis deployed its strategic knowledge advantage to recover following the September 11 terrorist attacks. Melnick stated that he has "always been an active knowledge builder," but his formal KM work started in 1995 during graduate studies at the University of Toronto, where he helped to found the Institute for Knowledge Innovation and Technology. He served as the head of external relations and workplace research for this institute for five years before joining Atlantis.

After September 11, 2001, the company faced difficult financial times and changed ownership in 2004. The new CEO, Andrew Day a strong supporter of KM, hired Melnick as CKO and COO to develop and deploy KM initiatives intended to achieve internal change management. Melnick considered measuring and demonstrating the ROI associated with KM to be a major challenge. Another challenge related to externalizing KM and using it as a discriminator in Atlantis' current and targeted markets.

Melnick described an integrated systems approach to KM, Knowledge Exchange (KX), which has been developed at Atlantis. The KX system integrates facilities for content management, collaborative discourse, performance management, mentoring, and employee and customer satisfaction and is the key to KM at Atlantis. The KX system is supported by several analytic tools that track usage, idea development, knowledge clusters, and so forth.

Melnick champions several established KM methods at Atlantis:

- Democratization of knowledge by providing every employee with the ability to influence the company's direction.
- Iterative improvement by encouraging each employee to strive to progress beyond best practices and capture ideas for improvement as they perform their tasks and activities.
- Rewards and recognition for employees, which contributes to the company's collective knowledge.
- Incorporation of the customer into the improvement process by encouraging them to contribute to the company's knowledge base.
- Flattening of organizational hierarchy, thereby enabling people to talk to each other.

Melnick has learned three lessons about KM that might be valuable to others:

1. KM is not all about technology. Instead, it involves both information management (technology) and knowledge-building (people).
2. We cannot really "manage knowledge," but we can manage the process that helps convert information into knowledge.
3. For KM in any organization, it is essential to address the employees' primary concern, such as, "What's in it for me."

Melnick believes that since he joined Atlantis, KM at the company has progressed in terms of a greater appreciation for the "human dynamic" as an essential ingredient to successful KM implementation. Atlantis became more successful after making the various improvements in KM. The revenues grew by over 200 percent during the three years prior to 2007. During the same period the number of employees increased from 102 to 210, the retention rates remained stable at 3 percent, and the company successfully leveraged its knowledge of the aerospace sector to enter the nuclear energy sector.

Source: Compiled from *Knowledge Management Review* 2006; Melnick 2006; Melnick 2007.

underlying objectives. Without such assessment, it would be impossible to determine either the contribution of those efforts or whether and where improvements are needed. More specifically, a **knowledge management assessment** is aimed at evaluating the need for KM solutions—the knowledge these solutions can help discover, capture, share, or apply—and the impact they will have on individual or organizational performance. A KM assessment can help establish the baseline for implementing those KM solutions, including the existing infrastructure and technologies that can help support those efforts.

Overall, the assessment of knowledge management is a critical aspect of a KM implementation; what is not measured can't be managed well. A survey by Ernst & Young (1997) indicated that measuring the value and contribution of knowledge assets ranks as the second most important challenge faced by companies, with changing people's behavior being the most important. However, only four percent of the firms surveyed by Ernst & Young claimed to be good or excellent at "measuring the value of knowledge assets and/or impact of knowledge management." Several reasons attest to the need for conducting a KM assessment, as described below.

1. A KM assessment helps identify the contributions being currently made by KM. It helps answer the question: Is KM improving the individual's or the organization's ability to perform various tasks and thereby enhancing efficiency, effectiveness, and/or innovativeness?

2. A KM assessment enhances the understanding of the quality of the efforts being put into KM as well as the intellectual capital produced through these efforts. It helps answer the questions: Are the KM solutions being employed adequate for the needs of the individual or the organization? Do these efforts produce the intellectual capital required to perform individual or organizational tasks?

3. A KM assessment helps understand whether the costs of the KM efforts are justified by the benefits they produce. It helps answer the question: Do the direct and indirect benefits from KM together exceed or equal the various costs incurred? This is an important benefit for the overall KM solutions as well as the solutions pursued in a specific KM project. Thus, the overall KM solutions as well as specific KM projects can be cost-justified through careful KM assessment.

4. A KM assessment helps recognize the gaps that need to be addressed in the KM efforts by individuals or the organization. It helps answer the question: What kind of potentially valuable KM solutions do the individual and the organization currently lack? What potentially important knowledge is not adequately supported by the KM efforts?

5. Finally, a KM assessment can also help in making a business case to senior executives in an organization for additional investments in KM efforts. Based on the benefits currently provided by the organization's KM solutions (Point 1 above) and the gaps in the organization's KM efforts (Point 4 above), a business case can be built for the development of solutions that address these gaps.

Box 12.2

An Illustrative Tool for Assessing KM

Please indicate your level of agreement with each of the following statements by selecting a number from 1 (Strongly Disagree) to 5 (Strongly Agree).

1. I am satisfied with the availability of knowledge for my tasks.
2. It is easy for me to locate information I need to perform my job
3. I always know where to look for information.
4. The available knowledge improves my effectiveness in performing my tasks.
5. My supervisor encourages knowledge sharing within my subunit.
6. The members of my group consistently share their knowledge.
7. I am satisfied with the management of knowledge in my subunit.
8. The available knowledge improves my subunit's effectiveness.
9. The organization directly rewards employees for sharing their knowledge.
10. The organization publicly recognizes employees who share their knowledge.

Responses to the above statements may be averaged across a number of employees from various subunits of the organization. Averages for each subunit and the entire organization would then show where the individual subunits, as well as the overall organization, perform in terms of the overall quality of KM. Each assessment would be in terms of a number ranging from 1 (poor KM) to 5 (excellent KM).

Thus, knowledge management assessments are important because of several reasons, as described above. We next examine the different types of KM assessments and then examine the alternative KM assessment approaches in some detail.

TYPES OF KNOWLEDGE MANAGEMENT ASSESSMENT

KM assessments can be classified in a number of different ways. Three possible ways of considering alternative KM assessments are described here. They are related to the following aspects: (1) When is KM assessed? (2) How is KM assessed? (3) What aspects of KM are assessed?

THE TIMING OF KM ASSESSMENT

A KM assessment can be performed on different occasions. Three possibilities are especially noteworthy. First, a KM assessment may be performed *periodically for an entire organization or a subunit*. The objective of such an assessment is to evaluate the overall quality of KM solutions, intellectual capital, and their impacts. This could help identify any areas that need improvement in KM. Such an assessment can be performed, for example by surveying employees and inquiring about their degree of agreement with statements such as in Box 12.2.

KM assessments may also be conducted at *the start of a KM project* to build a business case for it. The purpose of such an assessment is to identify the gap in current KM at the organization and delineate the potential benefits of the proposed KM project. For example, for a firm focusing on new products and increasing market share, so that R&D represents a major cost center, the business plan might include the following statement describing the value of the proposed KM project:

> The target for the KM project will be to cut cycle time on specific new projects by 20 percent. In addition, . . . The project will identify cost savings and time savings for scientists in the unit of 25 percent (Wilson 2002, p. 17).

The above example illustrates the outcome of a KM assessment conducted at the start of the project. It indicates there are currently problems in KM within the R&D function, which is a critical component of the organization, and that addressing these problems through the proposed project would be highly beneficial.

A KM assessment may also be done *following the conclusion of a KM project*. Such assessment aims to determine the impacts of the KM project and may focus on the entire organization or a specific subunit. It may be necessary to establish historical KM performance in order to evaluate the effects produced by the KM project. Following are some of the aspects that can be evaluated during such a post-project assessment:

- Perceptions of improved knowledge management in the area focused on by the project.
- Perceptions of greater availability of knowledge in the area focused on by the project.
- Some evidence of financial return (e.g., cost savings, increased returns, ROI, etc.), either for KM function itself or for the entire organization.
- Increased awareness of the importance of knowledge management.
- Increased recognition of the different areas of knowledge and their importance to the organization.
- Greater knowledge sharing throughout the organization.
- Greater comfort level throughout the organization with the concepts of knowledge and knowledge management.

For example, a KM project at one large consulting firm caused a major transformation of the organization. This transformation was significant in both breadth and depth of impact across the organization. The KM project required line managers to re-engineer their business processes to draw heavily from the organization's centralized knowledge by accessing earlier client presentations, work plans, system specifications, and other important documents. Consequently, the consulting firm's "win rate" in client proposals increased as well (Davenport and Prusak 1998, p. 152). Box 12.3 describes a KM assessment that relies on measuring the effectiveness of one specific KM mechanism—communities of practice.

THE NATURE OF KM ASSESSMENT

KM assessments are also differentiated on the basis of the way in which KM assessment is done. There are two distinct and important methods to perform KM assessments: qualitative and quantitative.

Box 12.3

Assessment of KM Through Communities of Practice

1. What was the overall value of this community to you and your team?
2. When your community discussed "topic A," what specific knowledge, information or data did you use?
3. What was the value of this knowledge, information, or data for you as an individual? Can you express the value in numeric terms such as time saved?
4. Can you estimate the value of this knowledge, information, or data to your business unit in cost savings, reduced cycle time, improved quality of decision-making, or lower risk?
5. What percentage of this value was obtained directly from the community? What is the likelihood you would have learned it without the community?
6. How confident are you of the above estimate?
7. Who else in your team used this knowledge, information or data?

Source: Compiled from Wilson 2002.

Qualitative KM assessments aim to develop a basic understanding of whether the KM efforts are producing positive results. Qualitative assessments focus on signs, text, language, and so on instead of focusing on numbers, as is the case with quantitative assessments. Qualitative assessments focus involve such simple tasks as walking around the halls and buildings of the organization and informally chatting with the employees about how things are going for them. They also include more formal **interviews** based on semistructured or structured interview guides, individually conducted with a carefully selected set of employees. Regardless of the formality of these conversations, they are inherently qualitative, surfacing anecdotes about how well the KM efforts seem to be working as well as examples of situations where the KM efforts did not produce the desired results. Such anecdotes of successes (or problems) may concern the quality of decisions, innovations, and technology transfer at the organizational level. In addition they may point out issues related to career development, visibility, confidence, and staying up-to-date technologically at the individual level. Furthermore, such qualitative assessments can be performed at certain periodic intervals, such as at the start of a project or at the conclusion of a project as discussed before. Consequently, they may focus on the organization's overall strategy for KM or on more specific aspects, such as the development of a KM system like a community of practice or an expertise locator system.

Quantitative KM assessments, on the other hand, produce specific numerical scores indicating how well an organization, an organizational subunit, or an individual is performing with respect to KM. Such quantitative assessments may be based on a survey, such as the one described in Box 12.2. Alternatively, such quantitative KM assessments may be in financial terms, such as the ROI or the cost savings from a KM project. Finally, quantitative measures also include such ratios or percentages as employee retention rate (i.e., the percentage of employees most essential to the organization retained during the preceding year) or training expenditures as a proportion of payroll (i.e., total expenditures on training as a percent of the organization's annual payroll).

Quantitative measures are more difficult to develop during an organization's early experiences with knowledge management. During initial stages, qualitative assessments should be preferred, with greater use of quantitative measures as the organization gains experience with knowledge management. This is depicted in Figure 12.1. However, it is important to note that even when an organization is very experienced with KM, it can obtain considerable benefits from using qualitative assessment especially in uncertain environments that reduce the benefits from quantitative measurement.

DIFFERENCES IN THE ASPECTS OF KM ASSESSED

The third way of viewing knowledge management assessments, which is used to structure the rest of this chapter, focuses on the aspect being assessed. As discussed in Chapter 5, KM can directly or indirectly impact organizational performance at several levels: people, processes, products, and the overall organizational performance. These impacts either come about directly from the KM solutions or from the knowledge produced and shared through the KM solutions. Therefore, the KM assessment can focus on: (a) the KM solutions, as discussed in the next section—"Assessment of KM Solutions"; (b) the knowledge produced or shared through KM solutions, as discussed in the section entitled, "Assessment of Knowledge"; and (c) the impacts of KM solutions or knowledge on performance (including individuals or employees, processes, products, and the overall organizational performance), as discussed in the section entitled, "Assessment of Impacts."

ASSESSMENT OF KNOWLEDGE MANAGEMENT SOLUTIONS

Assessment of knowledge management solutions involves evaluating the extent to which knowledge discovery, capture, sharing, and application processes—discussed in Chapter 3—are utilized and how well they are supported by KM technologies and systems. Table 12.1 provides some illustrative measures of the four aspects of KM solutions—discovery, capture, sharing, and application. Although most of the measures given in this table are easy to quantify, some (e.g., extent of use of learning by doing) involve perceptions to some extent. Moreover, further research is needed to establish these measures, but some of them are based on prior empirical research.

Collison and Parcell (2001) describe another way of viewing KM solutions, especially for knowledge sharing in organizations that focus on organizational subunits and the key activities they perform. Such organizational activities include increased morale and motivation; plan, schedule, and work execution; management of spare parts and stores; and more. Once these activities are identified for the organization, interviews with managers from each subunit are used to evaluate each subunit's target performance as well as actual performance for each activity. This process helps identify, for each combination of subunit and activity, the gap between actual and target performance. For each activity, actual as well as target performance for various subunits can then be placed along a matrix as shown in Figure 12.2. Subunits that show a high level of actual performance and a high level of target performance, such as SU-1 in Figure 12.2, are the ones that both consider that activity as important and

Figure 12.1   **Qualitative and Quantitative Assessments of KM**

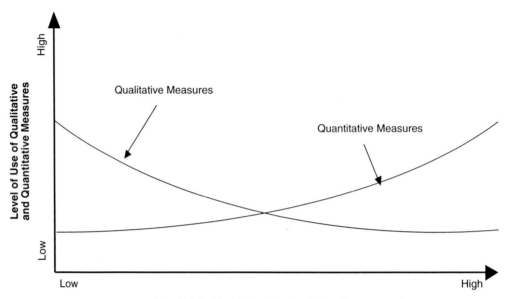

Table 12.1

Illustrative Measures of Key Aspects of KM Solutions

Dimension	Illustrative Measures
Knowledge Discovery	• Number of cooperative projects across subunits divided by the number of organizational subunits • Extent of use of apprentices and mentors to transfer knowledge • Employee rotation, i.e., number of employees who move to a different area each year • Annual number of brainstorming retreats or camps as a proportion of the total number of employees • Number of patents published per employee
Capture	• Average number of annual hits on each document in the document repository • Number of subscriptions to journals per employee • Attendance at group presentations as a proportion of invited attendees • Number of annual presentations per employee • Extent of use of learning by doing
Sharing	• Proportion of information used that is available on Web pages (Intranet and Internet) • Proportion of organizational information that resides in databases • Level of use of groupware and repositories of information, best practices, and lessons learned • Size of discussion databases • Annual number of shared documents published per employee
Application	• Frequency of advice seeking per employee • Corporate directory coverage, i.e., proportion of employees whose expertise areas are listed in the corporate directory • Annual number of improvement suggestions made per employee • Level of use of decision-support systems and expert systems • Frequency of hits on KM Web sites

Figure 12.2   **Identifying Knowledge Sharing Opportunities**

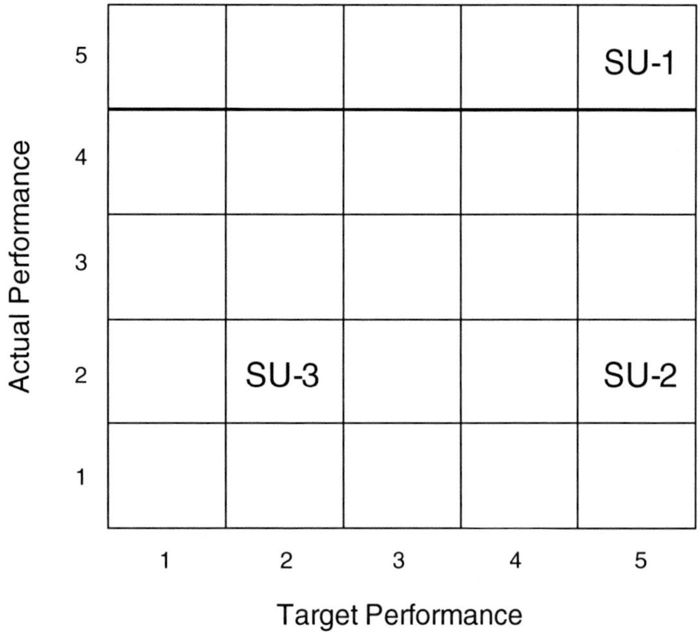

perform it well. These subunits should be emulated by subunits, such as SU-2, that consider that activity as important but perform it poorly as shown by a high level of target performance combined with a low level of actual performance. Therefore, the organization would benefit from knowledge sharing between these two kinds of subunits (SU-1 and SU-2), which both consider that activity as important (high level of target performance) but differ in actual performance. Subunits (such as SU-3) that consider the activity as less important (low level of target performance) may also benefit from knowledge sharing with subunits that consider that activity as important in case the focus of their operations changes.

Some specific tools for assessing KM solutions have also been proposed. One example is "Metrics that Matter"[1] from Knowledge Advisors, a Chicago-based company (PR Newswire 2001b), which provides a comprehensive solution to help training organizations measure their learning investments. This approach using **metrics** has three components—learner-based, manager-based, and analyst-based. Each component helps measure learning across five levels of evaluation: (1) did they like it? (2) did they learn? (3) did they use it? (4) what were the results? and (5) what is the return on investment?

ASSESSMENT OF KNOWLEDGE

Assessment of knowledge requires: (a) the identification of the various areas of knowledge that are relevant to the organization or a specific subunit, followed by (b) an evaluation of the extent to which knowledge in each of these areas is available. The first of these steps—*identification of the relevant areas of knowledge*—may be

---

Box 12.4

Assessment of Available Knowledge

On a 5-point scale, (ranging from 1 = Strongly disagree to 5 = Strongly agree), I can easily access knowledge in this area. Statements 1–4 are coded such that a *high* score indicates excellent availability of this knowledge, whereas statements 5 and 6 are reverse-coded so that a *low* score on these items indicates excellent availability of this knowledge. Therefore, ratings on items 5 and 6 should be subtracted from 6 and the results can then be averaged with the ratings on items 1 to 4. The resulting average would range from 1 to 5, with 5 indicating excellent availability of this knowledge.

1. I can easily access knowledge in this area.
2. Everyone in the organization (or the subunit) recognizes the experts in this area of knowledge.
3. Available knowledge in this area is of a high quality.
4. Available knowledge in this area helps improve the organization's (or subunit's) performance.
5. I often have to perform my tasks without being able to access knowledge in this area.
6. The performance of this organization (or subunit) is often adversely affected due to the lack of knowledge in this area.

---

performed using interviews with managers and other employees of that organization or subunit. In this step, it may be useful to first identify the *critical success factors* for the organization or the subunit. Critical success factors have been defined as "the limited number of areas in which results, if they are satisfactory, will insure successful performance for the organization" (Rockart 1979, p. 85). Organizations should therefore give special attention to them, trying to perform exceedingly well in the few areas they represent rather than seeking to perform a larger number of tasks only reasonably well. Asking the senior executives to identify six to eight critical success factors, and then asking them to identify the knowledge needed to succeed with respect to each critical success factor can thus obtain the most important knowledge areas.

Once the relevant knowledge areas have been identified, *the extent and quality of available knowledge* in each area needs to be assessed. This is often a very tricky issue, for such knowledge can reside in individuals' minds, corporate databases and documents, organizational processes, and so on. To some extent, such measurement of available knowledge may be conducted through surveys or interviews of organizational employees, asking them to evaluate items such as the ones in Box 12.4.

Another important aspect of KM assessment is the value each area of knowledge contributes to the organization. *Assessment of value of knowledge* is one way of attributing a **tangible measure** of benefits resulting from knowledge, which is often intangible (Sullivan 2000). In general, value has two monetary measures—cost and price. Price represents the amount a purchaser is willing to pay in exchange for the utility derived from that knowledge, whereas cost is the amount of money required to produce that knowledge. Both cost and price are direct, quantitative measures of value, but there are also other nonmonetary or indirect measures of value, such as the improvement in the quality of decisions enabled by this knowledge. Some of these benefits of knowledge are discussed in the next section. The Intangible Assets Monitor approach focuses on **intangible measures** of knowledge, This approach, and its use to evaluate the value of intellectual capital, is discussed later in the section entitled, "Overall Approaches for KM Assessment."

ASSESSMENT OF IMPACTS

As we discussed in Chapter 11, KM solutions and the knowledge they help to create, capture, share, and apply can impact individuals, products, processes, and the overall performance of organizations. A KM assessment, therefore, involves not only the evaluation of KM solutions and knowledge but also an evaluation of their impacts. This section describes how these impacts may be assessed.

ASSESSMENT OF IMPACTS ON EMPLOYEES

KM can impact an organization's employees by facilitating their learning from each other, from prior experiences of former employees, and from external sources. KM can also enable employees to become more flexible by enhancing their awareness of new ideas, which prepares them to respond to changes and also by making them more likely to accept change. These impacts, in turn, can cause the employees to feel more satisfied with their jobs due to the knowledge acquisition and skill enhancement and their enhanced market value. Thus, KM can enhance learning, adaptability, and job satisfaction of employees. Some illustrative measures of impacts on each of these three dimensions are given in Table 12.2.

ASSESSMENT OF IMPACTS ON PROCESSES

KM can improve organizational processes—for example marketing, manufacturing, accounting, engineering, public relations, and so forth. These improvements can occur along three major dimensions: **effectiveness**, **efficiency**, and degree of **innovation** of the processes as discussed in Chapter 4. For example, at HP, a KM system for computer resellers enhanced efficiency by considerably reducing the number of calls for human support and enabling the number of people needed to provide this support (Davenport and Prusak 1998). Table 12.3 lists some illustrative measures of the impacts that KM and organizational knowledge can have along each of these dimensions.

ASSESSMENT OF IMPACTS ON PRODUCTS

KM can also impact the organization's products by helping to produce either value-added products or inherently knowledge-based products. Value-added products are new or improved products that provide a significant additional value as compared to earlier products. Inherently **knowledge-based products** refer for example to products from the consulting and software development industries. These impacts were discussed in Chapter 4. Table 12.4 provides some examples of possible measures of the impacts that knowledge management can have on these two dimensions.

Table 12.2

Illustrative Measures of Impacts on People

Dimension	Illustrative Measures
Employee learning	• Average amount of time annually spent by an employee in being trained • Average number of conferences or seminars annually attended by each employee • Average amount of time annually spent by an employee in training others within the organization • Average of employees' annual assessment of their learning during the year
Employee adaptability	• Proportion of employees who have worked in another area (other than the area in which they currently work) for more than one year • Average number of areas in which each employee has previously worked • Number of countries in which each senior manager has worked as a proportion of the total number of countries in which the organization conducts business
Employee job satisfaction	• Proportion of employees who express high level of satisfaction with the organization and their jobs • Percentage of critical employees retained during the previous year • Percentage of openings requiring advanced degrees or substantial experience filled in the previous year

Table 12.3

Illustrative Measures of Impacts on Organizational Processes

Dimension	Illustrative Measures
Efficiency	• Reduced ratio of manufacturing costs to annual sales • Shortening proposal times • Quicker decisions • Faster delivery to market
Effectiveness	• Enhanced customer service • Improved project management • Fewer surprises due to external events • Percentage of customers reporting complaints about products/services
Innovativeness	• Percentage of all current products/services introduced in the previous year • Greater number of patents per employee • Organizational changes precede, rather than follow, competitors' moves • Number of new ideas in KM databases

ASSESSMENT OF IMPACTS ON ORGANIZATIONAL PERFORMANCE

KM can impact overall organizational performance either directly or indirectly. Direct impacts concern revenues and/or costs, and can be explicitly linked to the organization's vision or strategy. Consequently direct impact can be observed in terms of increased sales, decreased costs, and higher profitability or **return on investment**. For example, Texas Instruments Inc. generated revenues by licensing patents and intellectual property (Davenport and Prusak 1998). However, it is harder to attribute revenue increases to KM than cost savings (Davenport et al. 2001). Indirect impacts

Table 12.4

Illustrative Measures of Impacts on Organizational Products

Dimension	Illustrative Measures
Value-added Products	• Increased rate of new product launch • More frequent improvements in products • Average of the ratio of profit margin to price across the range of products offered by the organizations
Knowledge-based Products	• Increased information content in products • Greater product-related information provided to customers • Proportion of customers accessing product-related knowledge that the organization places on the Internet

on organizational performance come about through activities that are not linked to the organization's vision, strategy, or revenues and cannot be associated with transactions. As discussed in Chapter 5, indirect impacts include **economies of scale and scope**, and sustainable **competitive advantage**. Table 12.5 provides some examples of possible measures of these direct and indirect impacts that knowledge management can have on overall organizational performance.

The value of a KM investment should be evaluated based on how it affects discounted cash flow. Improved problem-solving, enhanced creativity, better relationships with customers, and employee's more meaningful work can all eventually be linked to real cash flows. Therefore, organizations can enhance their cash flow in the following ways:

- Reduce expenses by decreasing costs.
- Enhance margins by increasing efficiency to improve profit.
- Increase revenue through the sale of more products or services.
- Reduce taxes using smart strategies to minimize tax liabilities of the organization.
- Reduce capital requirements by lowering amount of capital needed by regulation.
- Reduce cost of capital by lowering the cost of loans, equity, and other financing. (Clare 2002; Wilson 2002)

It is important to keep the above drivers in mind during the implementation of knowledge management projects. In other words, if KM initiatives are observed to help increase the company's cash flow, executives will listen and therefore find a viable way to fund them.

CONCLUSIONS ABOUT KNOWLEDGE MANAGEMENT ASSESSMENT

We have examined and provided illustrative measures for KM assessments. We also discussed the direct and indirect impacts that KM assessments can have on the overall organizational performance. In this section, we examine and provide a broader discussion of KM assessment including a discussion of who performs KM assessment, some overall approaches for KM assessment, the approach for the implementation of a KM assessment, and some caveats regarding KM assessments.

Table 12.5

Illustrative Measures of Impacts on Organizational Performance

	Illustrative Measures
Direct Impacts	• Revenues: Increase in total revenues per employee compared to the previous year • Costs: Increase in total annual costs per employee compared to the previous year • ROI: Increase in ROI compared to the previous year
Indirect Impacts	• Economy of scale: Average (across all products offered by the organization) change in total cost per unit sold as compared to the previous year • Economy of scope: Average (across all products offered by the organization) change in the number of different products a salesperson can sell as compared to the previous year • Economy of scale: Average (across all products offered by the organization) of the difference between the price of the organization's product and the mean price of competing products • Economy of scope: Difference between the average number of different products produced in the organization's manufacturing plants and the average number of different products produced in the manufacturing plants of its main competitors • Competitive advantage: Difference between return on investment for the organization and its key competitors • Competitive advantage: Average number of years existing customers have been buying the organization's products/services • Competitive advantage: Percentage of top customers ending sales contracts in the previous year

WHO PERFORMS KM ASSESSMENT?

In order to perform a KM assessment, it is helpful to form a team that includes internal and external members. The internal members provide the necessary context and help retain within the organization the knowledge acquired from the assessment, whereas the external members can help identify KM-related assumptions and opportunities that may be missed by internal members. Overall, a KM assessment should incorporate: (a) peer review of internal performance; (b) external appraisal (by customers, suppliers, etc.) of the organization and its outputs; (c) business evaluation of effectiveness, efficiency, and innovativeness; and (d) evaluation of the knowledge assets created (Quinn et al. 1996).

The following example illustrates how these perspectives could be included and effectively integrated. Following each project a major investment banking firm asks all team members, the team leader, and its customer group to rank all project participants in terms of their exhibited knowledge, specific contributions to the project, and support for the team. Customers also rate their overall satisfaction with the firm as well as with the specific project. Annual surveys, ranking the firm against competitors on 28 key dimensions, complement these evaluations. The firm also measures costs and profits for each project and allocates them among participating groups based on a simple, pre-established formula. Annually, for each division the firm computes the net differential between its market value (if sold) and its fixed asset base. This net intellectual value of the division is tracked over time as an aggregate measure of how well the division's management is building its intellectual assets.

OVERALL APPROACHES FOR KM ASSESSMENT

In the preceding sections we have discussed a number of measures that can be used for KM assessment. Overall KM assessment approaches usually combine several of these measures, as illustrated above with the investment banking firm's example. One such approach involves the use of **benchmarking,** or comparing KM at an organization or subunit with other organizations or subunits. Adopted as a systematic technique for evaluating a company's performance in reaching its strategic goals, benchmarking is based on the recognition that best practices are often the same within a company or even within an industry. Benchmark targets could therefore include other units within the same company, competing firms, the entire industry, or in some cases, successful companies in other industries. For example, a leading manufacturer identifies outstanding operating units, formally studies them, and then replicates their practices throughout the rest of the company. This approach produced sales that exceed goals by five percent (PR Newswire 2001a). Box 12.5 provides information on a cross-industry survey that may be used as a benchmark in the arena of KM.

Another overall approach for KM assessment utilizes the **Balanced Scorecard**, which was originally developed by Kaplan and Norton (1996) to provide a more "balanced view" of internal performance rather than for KM assessment. The Balanced Scorecard provides a way of maintaining a balance between short-term and long-term objectives, financial and nonfinancial measures, lagging and leading indicators, and external and internal perspectives. It examines the goals, metrics, targets, and initiatives for the following four different perspectives (Tiwana 2002):

1. *The Customer Perspective:* How should our customers perceive us?
2. *The Financial Perspective:* What is the face that we want to present to our shareholders?
3. *The Internal Business Perspective:* Are our internal operations efficient and effective and performing at their best?
4. *The Learning and Growth Perspective:* How can we sustain our competitive advantage over time?

In employing the Balanced Scorecard for KM assessment, the above four perspectives are used in a series of four steps performed over time. The first step involves translating the KM vision (i.e., Why are we managing knowledge, and what is our vision for KM?). In the second step, this vision is communicated within the organization with rewards linked to knowledge use and contribution. The third step involves business planning, including the establishment of goals and the alignment of metrics and rewards to them. The fourth step—learning and feedback on whether KM is working and whether it can be improved— then feeds back to the first step to begin the cycle again. The above four complementary criteria from the Balanced Scorecard are used during each of these steps.

Like the Balanced Scorecard, the Intangible Assets Monitor Framework (Sveiby

---

Box 12.5

The Most Admired Knowledge Enterprises Survey

The Annual Most Admired Knowledge Enterprises (MAKE) survey by Teleos, an independent KM research company and leaders of the KNOW network, is based on a ranking of firms by a panel of CKOs and leading KM practitioners along eight criteria (Teleos 2009):

1. Ability to create and sustain an enterprise knowledge-driven culture.
2. Ability to develop knowledge workers through senior management leadership.
3. Ability to develop and deliver knowledge-based products/services/solutions.
4. Ability to manage and maximize the value of enterprise intellectual capital.
5. Ability to create and sustain an enterprise-wide, collaborative knowledge sharing environment.
6. Ability to create and sustain a learning organization.
7. Ability to manage customer knowledge to create value and enterprise intellectual capital.
8. Ability to transform enterprise knowledge into shareholder value (or societal value for non-profits and the public sector).

2000) also recognizes the importance of examining **intangible knowledge** assets rather than focusing only on financial or monetary assets. The Intangible Assets Monitor considers a firm's market value to depend on tangible net book value and **intangible assets** which include external structure (including relationships with customers and suppliers, brand names, trademarks, and image or reputation); internal structure (including the patents, concepts, models, and systems); and the competence of the organization's individual employees (including skills, education, experience, values, and social skills). Based on these factors, WM-Data, a Swedish computer software and consulting company,[2] designed a set of nonmonetary indicators that top management uses to supervise their operations on a weekly, monthly, and annual basis. The **Intangible Assets Monitor Framework**[3] evaluates growth, renewal, efficiency, and stability for tangible assets (financial value), external structure (customer value), internal structure (organizational value), and individuals' competence (individual value). Following are some of the questions that may be used to evaluate growth:

1. Is the existing customer base growing in value?
2. Are the support staff and administrative management improving their competence?
3. Are our tools and processes growing in value?

The **Skandia Navigator method** is another approach to KM assessment that gives considerable attention to intangible assets (Edvinsson and Malone 1997). The Swedish company, Skandia Insurance Company Ltd., developed this method in 1993 under the leadership of Leif Edvinsson, although it preferred using the term intellectual capital rather than knowledge. The Skandia Navigator included a number of ratios in which it looks at the past, present, and future. In the Skandia Navigator approach, the past is examined with an emphasis on financial aspects, the present is examined by focusing on customers, people, and processes, and the future is examined in terms of renewal and development.[4]

Figure 12.3   **KM Projects Mapped on the Option Space**

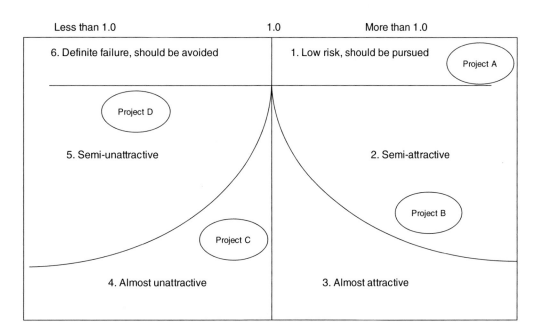

Value-to-cost Ratio

Another overall approach for KM assessment is the **real options approach**, which views KM initiatives as a **portfolio of investments** (Tiwana 2002). This approach focuses on the value-to-cost ratio—that is, the ratio of the net value to the total cost for each investment and the volatility faced by each investment. Using this approach, KM projects can be placed on an option space as shown in Figure 12.3. A clockwise move from region 1 to region 3 in the option space implies a shift from projects that are low-risk and attractive to projects that are fairly attractive. Continuing further to region 6, the projects reduce further in attractiveness. Thus, projects A and B in the figure are attractive, and projects C and D are not, with project A being the most attractive and project D being the least attractive. Such real options analysis combines strategic and financial approaches to evaluating investments. In positioning projects on the option space, it can benefit from the techniques discussed earlier in the chapter, especially for identifying the value-to-cost ratio. To conclude this section on overall KM assessment, Box 12.6 provides a summary of KM assessment at Siemens AG.

FURTHER RECOMMENDATIONS FOR KM ASSESSMENT

So far in this chapter we have described a number of KM metrics and assessment approaches. In developing these measures and approaches, the following eight suggestions should be carefully considered (Tiwana 2002; Wilson 2002).

Box 12.6

KM Assessment at Siemens

Siemens, a large firm in the electronics industry, has benefited considerably over the years from one of its knowledge sharing systems. Called "ShareNet," this system serves as the foundation for several communities of practice. To estimate ROI, Siemens computes the costs of a community of practice including labor, meetings, facilities, and the effort spent by KM experts. It also considers costs of the incentive program. Siemens then decides how much effort has been saved through the sharing of solutions in the community.

Siemens also considers subcommunities and their generation of solutions in terms of community projects. If a group needs a solution and embarks on a knowledge-creation effort, it can determine the savings in time-to-market, competitive positioning, and so forth. To further determine the value of KM, Siemens has developed a master plan of KM metrics that contains measures for each of four dimensions of its holistic KM system:

- *Knowledge community:* the organization, community, and people dimensions
- *Knowledge marketplace:* the IT involved in knowledge management
- *Key KM processes:* sharing and creation
- *Knowledge environment:* all of the above

Siemens has realized that it can assess the success of its communities and marketplaces with measures such as how much knowledge comes in or out of the community and the quality of feedback. Contracts that had been gained with the support of other divisions, or savings obtained through knowledge shared using the knowledge communities, were also included in the benefits. A contribution key, determined through a survey form that the ShareNet Managers fill out, indicated the proportion that ShareNet had contributed to the success of each initiative.

Siemens believes communities are the heart of their KM systems, and it has spent a great deal of time on communities-of-practice assessments—questionnaires for community members that provide ideas on how to improve each of the communities. Siemens has tried to check the health of KM processes to determine the performance of the sharing process. Ideally, the measures evaluate whether a person has managed the process correctly and set the right limits on it. This provides Siemens a good way to look at the marketplace and also to examine how much sharing and creation is taking place.

To monitor the entire KM systems, Siemens performs a KM maturity assessment that defines whether KM is still *ad hoc* and chaotic or has progressed to an optimized state. To do this, Siemens measures its four dimensions and 16 enablers, each of which has a set of questions.

Source: Compiled from Davenport and Probst 2002; MacCormack et al. 2002; Voelpel et al. 2005.

---

1. *Remember why you are doing KM:* When proposing a KM project, it is critical to define its measures of success based on things the organization cares about, such as: reducing waste, lowering costs, enhancing the customer experience, and so forth.
2. *Establish a baseline:* It is important to identify and develop a baseline measure when you begin efforts, rather than scrambling after the effort is completed to try to determine measures of success. Establishing a baseline is essential to prove successful results down the line.
3. *Consider qualitative methods:* KM is a qualitative concept and qualitative methods of measurement, such as analyzing the value of social networks, telling success stories, and others, should not be ignored.
4. *Keep it simple:* An organization does not need hundreds of measures. A handful

of the relevant, robust, and easily assessable ones are better in demonstrating to yourself and your organization that KM is indeed adding value.

5. *Avoid KM metrics that are hard to control:* KM assessment should use metrics that are specific and within the control of the organization's employees. Broad and grand statements, such as "enable the firm to become a one of the top learning organizations in the World by 2010" are visionary but impossible to control or measure.

6. *Measure at the appropriate level:* Measure at the project or application level in the beginning. Organizations that have implemented KM initiatives for a long time can then try to measure the total organizational value of KM or their program.

7. *Link rewards to KM assessment results:* KM assessment should not be an end in itself. Instead, it's the results of KM assessments that should be used to provide rewards and incentives thereby motivating improved KM results in the future.

8. *Be conservative in your claims:* When calculating a figure like ROI for KM projects, it is better to err on the higher side when estimating costs and to err on the lower side when estimating value in order to make the results more believable to management.

SUMMARY

This chapter complements our earlier discussion of management of KM foundations and KM solutions in Chapters 3 and 4, respectively; the effects of how contingency factors on KM solutions; and the management of specific KM systems in Chapters 6, 7, 8, and 9. To better understand the overall management of knowledge management in an organization, we have examined in this chapter the leadership of KM and the ways in which the value of KM can be assessed in an organization. We have discussed the assessment of KM systems and the impacts that assessments can have. We have also summarized some overall KM assessment approaches and how a KM assessment can be implemented.

KEY TERMS

Benchmarking
Balanced Scorecard
Chief Information Officer (CIO)
Chief Knowledge Officer (CKO)
Chief Learning Officer (CLO)
Competitive advantage
Intangible assets
Intangible Assets Monitor Framework
Intangible knowledge
Intangible measure

Knowledge management assessment
Knowledge-based products
Portfolio of investments
Qualitative KM assessments
Quantitative KM assessments
Real options approach
Return on investment
Skandia Navigator Method
Tangible measure

REVIEW

1. Distinguish between the roles of Chief Knowledge Officer and Chief Learning Officer.
2. Why is it important to perform KM assessment? Identify and discuss any three reasons.
3. Describe the different types of KM assessment in terms of (a) the timing of KM assessment; and (b) the aspects assessed.
4. What are the differences between quantitative and qualitative assessments of KM assessment? How does their use depend upon the organization's experience with KM?
5. Briefly describe some financial measures that can be used for KM assessment.
6. Briefly describe some nonfinancial measures that can be used for KM assessment.
7. Briefly discuss how the different impacts of KM on employees can be assessed?
8. How can the impacts of KM on efficiency, effectiveness, and innovation be evaluated?
9. How do the measures of the direct impacts of KM differ from the measures of its indirect impacts?

APPLICATION EXERCISES

1. Visit a local area firm to study its KM assessment process. Determine how they decided on the type of KM solution they use.
2. How would you conduct KM assessment at the firm you visited? Describe the suggested approach in some detail, making sure to connect this approach to the approaches described in this chapter.
3. Study how knowledge is managed at either your family physician's office or your dentist's office through 15-minute conversations with a few individuals who work at that office. Then recommend an approach for assessing KM at this office. Discuss the suggested approach with some senior employees (e.g., the family physician or the dentist) at this office, and seek their feedback concerning your suggestions.
4. Visit any three organizations of varying sizes and different industries. Identify who leads the KM function at each organization, and examine how these organizations perform their KM assessments. Compare the three organizations in terms of whether they use a Chief Knowledge Officer, a Chief Learning Officer, a Chief Information Officer, or an individual in some other position to lead the KM function. Discuss why the organizations might differ or be similar with respect to the leaders of their KM function.
5. For each of the organizations you visited in Question 4 above, examine how consistent the organization's KM assessment approach is with the recommendations in this chapter. Which organization seems most consistent with

the recommended approach? Of the three organizations, is this organization the one that has the most experience with KM?

NOTES

1. More details about this approach may be found at http://www.knowledgeadvisors.com/metrics-that-matter/.

2. Since October 10, 2006, WM-Data has become a subsidiary to LogicaCMG (www.logica.com/).

3. See http://www.sveiby.com/articles/EmergingStandard.html#TheIntang.

4. Edvinsson left Skandia in 1999. Although intellectual capital remained an important focus of Skandia's corporate philosophy until early 2000, Skandia has undergone considerable changes as a company, with a merger with Storebrand in 1999, followed by its acquisition by Old Mutual in 2006. See http://www.valuebasedmanagement.net/methods_skandianavigator.html and http://www.skandia.com/about/history.asp.

REFERENCES

Awazu, Y. and Desouza, K. 2004. The knowledge chiefs: CKOs, CLOs and CPOs. *European Management Journal,* 22(3), 339–344.

Bersin, J., 2007. *The new Chief Learning Officer: 2008 and beyond.* Bersin and Associates, July 21. http://joshbersin.com/2007/07/21/the-new-chief-learning-officer-2008-and-beyond/ (accessed February 17, 2009).

Business Wire. 2009. Colliers International appoints top executives to its USA management team. *Business Wire,* February 2.

Cencigh-Albulario, L. 2008. Now everyone is joining the rush to learn. *Weekend Australian,* November 22, 11.

Clare, M. 2002. Solving the knowledge-value equation: Part one. *Knowledge Management Review,* May/June.

Collison, C. and Parcell, G. 2001. *Learning to fly.* Milford, CT: Capstone Publishing.

Conz, N. 2008. CIGNA has launched a series of public-facing e-learning modules that leverage Web technologies to teach consumers about the basics of the health insurance system. *Insurance and Technology,* December 1, 13.

Davenport, T.H., Harris, J.G., De Long, D.W., and Jacobson, A.L. 2001. Data to knowledge to results: Building an analytic capability. *California Management Review,* 43(2), 117–138.

Davenport, T.H. and Probst, G. (Eds.). 2002. *Knowledge management case book: Siemens best practises,* 2d ed. New York: John Wiley & Sons.

Davenport, T.H. and Prusak, L. 1998. *Working knowledge: How organizations manage what they know.* Boston: Harvard Business School Press.

DeTienne, K., Dyer, G., Hoopes, C., and Harris, S. 2004. Toward a model of effective knowledge management and directions for future research: Culture, leadership and CKOs. *Journal of Leadership and Organizational Studies,* 10(4), 26–43.

Earl, M. and Scott, I. 1999. What is a chief knowledge officer? *Sloan Management Review,* Winter, 29–38.

Edvinsson, L. and Malone, M.S. 1997. *Intellectual capital: The proven way to establish your company's real value by measuring its hidden values.* London: Piatkus.

Ernst & Young. 1997. *Executive perspectives on knowledge in the organization.* Cambridge, MA: The Ernst & Young Center.

Kaplan, B. 2007. Creating long-term value as chief knowledge officer. *Knowledge Management Review,* (September/October), 30–33.

Kaplan, R.S. and Norton, D.P. 1996. *The Balanced Scorecard.* Boston: Harvard Business School Press.

Kiger, P.J. 2007. Precision-targeted development at HP. *Workforce Management,* June 25, 38.

Kluge, J., Shein, W., and Licht, T. 2001. *Knowledge unplugged: The McKinsey and Company Global Survey on knowledge management.* New York: Palgrave Macmillan.

Knowledge Management Review. 2006. Using knowledge as a competitive differentiator at Atlantis Systems. *Knowledge Management Review,* 9(4), 4.

———. 2008. Recent appointments demonstrate KM's continued influence. *Knowledge Management Review,* 11(5) (November/December), 4.

MacCormack, A., Volpel, S., and Herman, K. 2002. *Siemens ShareNet: Building a knowledge network.* Boston: Harvard Business School Publishing, Case 9-603-036, November 5.

McKeen, J.D. and Staples, D.S. 2003. Knowledge managers: Who they are and what they do. In *Handbook on knowledge management,* Vol. 1, ed. C.W. Holsapple, 21–41. Berlin: Springer.

Meister, D. and Davenport, T. 2005. *Knowledge management at Accenture.* Ivey Management Services, University of Western Ontario.

Melnick, B., 2006. Using knowledge as a competitive differentiator at Atlantis Systems. *Knowledge Management Review,* 9(5), 8–13.

———. 2007. Case study: Atlantis System International—Using KM principles to drive productivity and performance, prevent critical knowledge loss and encourage innovation. *International Atomic Energy Agency.* http://www.iaea.org/inisnkm/nkm/documents/nkmCon2007/fulltext/ES/IAEA-CN-153-2-P-17es.pdf (accessed February 20, 2009).

PR Newswire. 2001a. Knowledge management: Best practice sharing overcomes barriers. *PR Newswire,* November 1.

———. 2001b. Microsoft teams with knowledge advisors to measure training investments. *PR Newswire,* November 27.

Quinn, J.B., Anderson, P., and Finkelstein, S. 1996. Leveraging intellect. *Academy of Management Executive.* 10(3) 7–27.

Rockart, J.H. 1979. Chief executives define their own data needs. *Harvard Business Review,* 57(2), 81–92.

Sullivan, P.H. 2000. *Value-driven intellectual capital.* New York: John Wiley & Sons.

Sveiby, K-E. 2000. Measuring intangibles and intellectual capital. In *Knowledge management: classic and contemporary works,* ed. D. Morey, M. Maybury, and B. Thuraisingham, 337–353. Cambridge, MA: The MIT Press.

Takeuchi, H. 2001. Toward a universal management concept of knowledge. In *Managing industrial knowledge,* ed. I. Nonaka and D. Teece, 314–329. London: Sage Publications.

Teleos. 2009. Most admired knowledge enterprises. *The KNOW Network.* http://www.knowledgebusiness.com/knowledgebusiness/Screens/MakeSurvey.aspx?siteId=1&menuItemId=43 (accessed February 18, 2009).

Tiwana, A., 2002. *The knowledge management toolkit: Orchestrating IT, strategy, and knowledge platforms.* Upper Saddle River, NJ: Prentice Hall.

Voelpel, S.C., Dous, M., and Davenport, T.H. 2005. Five steps to creating a global knowledge-sharing system: Siemens' ShareNet. *Academy of Management Executive,* 19(2) (May), 9–23.

Wilson, J. (Ed.). 2002. *Knowledge management review: The practitioner's guide to knowledge management.* Chicago: Melcrum Publishing.

13 The Future of Knowledge Management

As we have seen throughout this book, knowledge management goals are for the members of an organization to discover, capture, share, and apply knowledge. However, the nature of KM is undergoing a dramatic change partly as a result of the emergence of Web 2.0 technologies, as discussed in Chapter 10. In this concluding chapter, we identify and discuss five critical issues for the future of KM. These five issues are discussed in the next five sections followed by some concluding remarks.

USING KNOWLEDGE MANAGEMENT AS A DECISION-MAKING PARADIGM TO ADDRESS WICKED PROBLEMS

The development of management information systems, decision support systems, and KM systems has been influenced by the works of five influential philosophers, namely Leibniz, Locke, Kant, Hegel, and Singer (Churchman 1971). Based on Churchman's definition of *inquiring organizations,*[1] a new paradigm for decision-making in today's complex organizational contexts has been developed (Courtney 2001).

In the conventional decision-making process, the emphasis is first on recognizing the problem, then on defining it in terms of a model. Alternative solutions are then analyzed, and the best solution is selected and implemented. Thus, KM systems have successfully supported solving semistructured problems, those characterized by a limited number of factors and a certain future. Recent developments in KM have helped extend the reach of those involved in the solution. But the jury is still out on how well KM systems support problems that are characterized as wicked (Rittel and Webber 1973). **Wicked problems** are unique and difficult to formulate. Their solutions are good or bad (rather than true or false) and generate waves of consequence over time. Solutions to wicked problems are accomplished in one-shot occurrences, and so there is no opportunity to learn from prior mistakes and solutions cannot be undone. Moreover, solutions to wicked problems are not a numerable set of solutions, and many may have no solutions.

For example, a project plan for an enterprise resource planning (ERP) system implementation is a wicked problem. ERP systems' implementations are one-shot occurrences, in the sense that organizations will typically only implement them once. Therefore, there's no opportunity to learn over time how to successfully implement these systems. Usually organizations only find out if their implementation was "good" or "bad" on the deployment or "go-live" date, and at this point "bad" implementations result in disastrous economic consequences for the organization.

The fact is that as globalization expands, the number of stakeholders affected by the organization increases; each one affected by different customs, laws, behaviors, and environmental concerns. Globalization also leads to wicked planning problems for organizations, and methods to help make decisions in such situations are greatly needed. The new paradigm for KM support, suggested by Courtney (2001), defines the decision-making process as starting with the recognition that the problem exists, but then rather than proceeding immediately into analysis the process consists of developing multiple perspectives. These multiple perspectives consider the following:

1. *Technical perspective:* Consists of analyzing the alternatives and implementing the chosen alternative. This perspective is the only one relevant to existing decision support and KM systems.
2. *Personal and individual perspective:* Complex problems involve a multiplicity of actors. Each sees the problem differently and generates a different perspective based on individual experiences, intuition, personality, and attitudes about risk.
3. *Organizational and social perspective:* Complex problems involve various organizations. Organizations also each view the problem in a different fashion, and thus generate a different perspective. Organizations may also consist of diverse members with different interests.
4. *Ethics and aesthetics perspective:* Complex problems involve business ethics and aesthetic issues that are so high that they require the involvement of key stakeholders since there are no simple solutions. Perhaps the utilitarian emphasis of the Industrial Age neglected the spirituality of the "rational man" and contributed to the demise of ethics and aesthetics in decision-making today (Courtney 2001).

This new paradigm bases decisions on the use of these multiple perspectives. The prior view of decision-making environments minimizes the importance of relationships, collaboration, and trust in the organization. Personal relationships define organizational boundaries to a large extent. The future calls for the development of KM systems that support the human aspects of decisions: the personal, organizational, ethical, and aesthetic perspective. Thus, KM systems should help decision-makers make more humane decisions and enable them to deal with wicked problems.

Further work is needed on how KM can be used to address problems that are not only wicked but also critical to humanity. Two of the biggest threats currently being encountered are the staggering global financial crisis and the escalating rise in terrorism. Could the kind of Web 2.0 technologies that have been successfully used in such diverse tasks as enabling common people to design T-shirts (online), creating an entire encyclopedia of knowledge and building grassroots support in the U.S. presidential elections, play a role in generating ideas and taking actions needed to address such wicked and crucial problems?

PROMOTING KNOWLEDGE SHARING WHILE PROTECTING INTELLECTUAL PROPERTY

Knowledge sharing could also bring forth certain risks, namely that the knowledge falls into the wrong hands either maliciously or accidentally. The same communication technologies that support the sharing of knowledge within an organization also enable the knowledge to leak outside the organization to its competing firms. Given the value of the knowledge, and the reliance that an organization places on this knowledge, losing this knowledge could have severe negative consequences for the organization. It is therefore critical for organizations to manage knowledge such that knowledge sharing is enhanced but **knowledge leakage** is controlled. This is not an easy balance to achieve. Below we discuss some of the ways in which knowledge leakage can be controlled.

Intellectual property (IP) can be defined as any results of a human intellectual process that has inherent value to the individual or organization that sponsored the process. It includes inventions, designs, processes, organizational structures, strategic plans, marketing plans, computer programs, algorithms, literary works, music scores, and works of art, among many other things. KM enables the effective use of IP, but it could also lead to loss of IP, which can damage the organization just as much as losing real capital property. In fact, in many cases IP is an organization's most valuable asset. One of the KM initiatives actively pursued by The Dow Chemical Company was harvesting little-used patents and intellectual assets (Davenport and Prusak 1998). Box 13.1 describes Dow Chemical's approach to KM.

As discussed in prior chapters, organizations often capture knowledge from documents stored in Web-based repositories. The more codifiable this knowledge is and the more it is documented and distributed, the greater the risk of losing this knowledge. IP losses can happen in many ways including the following:

1. Employee turnover. The employee may leave the organization to be hired by a competitor. The employee may deliberately or accidentally share her knowledge with her new employer.
2. Physical theft of sensitive proprietary documents, either by outsiders or by insiders.
3. Inadvertent disclosure to third parties without a nondisclosure agreement.
4. Reverse engineering or close examination of company's products.
5. The Web repository security is breached, and unauthorized access to the proprietary documents takes place.
6. Unauthorized parties intercept electronic mail, fax, telephone conversation, or other communications for the purpose of illicitly acquiring knowledge.
7. Attempts by insiders or outsiders to corrupt documents or databases with false data, information, or knowledge. This could be done directly via hacking into a database and effecting unauthorized modifications or indirectly via a virus. This is a variation of the electronic breach of data problem in item 5, but it is somewhat different in that the actions can destroy the system in question. There are significant criminal implications with this act.

Box 13.1

Dow Chemical's KM Initiative Captures Big Returns

In October 3, 1994, Dow Chemical's KM initiative under the direction of then director of intellectual asset management Gordon Petrash, achieved worldwide notoriety on the cover of *Fortune* Magazine (Stewart 1994). Petrash recognized that the intellectual capital represented in the company's 29,000 unused patents presented an underutilized opportunity that could bring back huge returns to the organization.

Unused patents can represent a sizable investment to an organization, since the expense associated with keeping the patents current could be quite high. Petrash's group first decided to develop a concerted effort to evaluate these patents. Patents were assessed to determine if they could be used, sold, or abandoned. During this process, Petrash was able to save the organization close to $US1 million in licensing fees that were being expended on patents that would return no value to the organization.

Note that the first four types of IP loss are not related to technology, while the last three are. Also, some of the intellectual capital losses are related to legal practices used to acquire sensitive competitive intelligence (items 1, 3, and 4), while the law prosecutes others (items 2, 5, 6, and 7). Clearly the losses related to technology are easier to prove and therefore easier to prosecute. Companies can take a number of steps to protect their organization against IP losses as follows.

1. Nondisclosure Agreements

A **nondisclosure agreement** is a contract between an organization that owns the IP and outside individuals to whom the organization's sensitive and proprietary information is disclosed on the condition that they maintain it as confidential. Divulging this knowledge to a third party constitutes a breach of confidentiality, and the offending party can be sued for damages. Employees of the organization owning the IP are by definition expected to maintain confidentiality not only while they are actively employed by that organization, but also after they terminate their association for whatever reason. Nondisclosure agreements can serve to protect against loss of knowledge via employee turnover as well as via covered disclosure to outsiders.

2. Patents

Patents are the oldest and most traditional means of protecting inventions. They grew out of the need to encourage exceptionally bright people to invent products and processes that benefit humankind. Patents do this by giving exclusive rights (a monopoly) to any product containing the patented works to the inventor, with all rights therewith. This means that an inventor, for a fixed period of either 16 or 20 years from patent issuance, can control the duplication of the patented works or process. Patent law can be quite complex in what can and cannot be patented, at what time, and for how long. However, as long as a patent is not overturned, it provides the most secure of protections. Unfortunately, this protection is only exercised through court action taken by the patent holder against the individual or organization allegedly infringing the patent. In some cases, small inventors holding valid patents cannot successfully sue large corporate entities with large legal staffs. Patents are excellent vehicles for protecting knowledge about technical innovations and products. They can protect against reverse engineering of a product as well as unauthorized acquisition of any design or other documents that detail the nature of the invention. In fact, loss of such documents is considered immaterial since the design of the patented invention is already part of the public record by virtue of its patented nature.

3. COPYRIGHTS

While patents protect the ideas behind the invention (the so-called claims), **copyrights** protect the expression of the work. They have been traditionally used to protect literary works, works of art, architecture, and music. However, they can also be used to protect computer programs albeit weakly. The advantage is that while patents require a rather rigorous process to be granted, a copyright can be done by merely stating on a copy of the body of the work that it is copyrighted. Registration of the copyrighted work with the government in the United States is not required, although it's highly advisable. Other countries require registration. This is done with the symbol ©. Copyrights typically last for the life of the creator plus up to 50 more years, depending on the country of filing. A copyright holder maintains the rights to publish, broadcast, reproduce, or copy the work. She has the exclusive right to translate it into another language, either wholly or in part. Copyrights can protect stolen or illicitly obtained IP only if it is valuable in its expression. For example, computer programs may fall into that category.

4. TRADE SECRETS

An organization may choose not to patent an invention but instead keep it as a **trade secret**. This invention may not fulfill all the criteria for patentability. Alternatively, the organization may want to avoid the legal process required to protect IP. Stealing trade secrets is illegal and punishable by law if the damaged organization takes legal action. However, said organization must make a strong effort to maintain confidentiality in order to maintain its legal rights. Organizations may accomplish this by instituting reasonable safeguards of its IP. Lacking that, a court may decide that it was not a very important trade secret to begin with.

We have discussed some legal avenues of IP protection. However, once the organization resorts to legal remedies, the damage has already been done and it most likely can only aspire to **damage recovery**. An effective KM initiative must include institutionalizing policies and safeguards that will prevent the loss of IP in the first place. Installing **firewalls** in computer systems, access controls, and protecting all the sensitive information through **encryption** can go a long ways towards this. Furthermore, organizations should clearly educate their employees of their responsibility for confidentiality and the consequences they could suffer if they violate this confidentiality whether accidentally or purposely.

As mentioned earlier, these avenues for IP protection should be used with some caution. Although they do help in preventing knowledge leakage, they may also inhibit the ability of the organization's own employees to seek knowledge from individuals outside the organization who may be able to provide them with helpful advice.

INVOLVING INTERNAL AND EXTERNAL KNOWLEDGE CREATORS

Two interrelated and emerging aspects of knowledge management focus on involving collaborations of a large numbers of individuals: (a) from across various levels within the organization; and (b) from outside the organization to share and create knowledge.

THE VALUE OF GRASSROOTS CONTRIBUTIONS

As discussed in Chapter 12, the democratization of knowledge refers to providing every employee within an organization with the ability to make grassroots contributions that stand the chance to influence the company's direction, much like Blake Melnick has championed at Atlantis Systems International. This ability is becoming increasingly valuable because people at the lowest levels of the organization are the ones who most commonly interact with customers, and are often the ones involved to the least extent in important decisions. Web 2.0 technologies enable widespread participation in decision-making, or at least the consideration of ideas from across the organization, by drastically reducing the time that it takes for such ideas to be communicated and aggregated. This could be done through blogs or wikis, for example, as they allow individuals across the organization to contribute to content and for individuals across the organization to access that content. Box 13.2 illustrates how such widespread contribution is being obtained at Northwestern Mutual Financial Network

Moreover, the success of Wikipedia, open-source software development, and innovative companies, such as Threadless,* led to the recognition of the potential for value creation through contributions from beyond traditional organizational boundaries (Cook 2008). Indeed, this has led to the emergence of the phenomenon called **crowdsourcing** or **community-based design**, which refers to the outsourcing of tasks to an undefined, large group of people or community in the form of an open call (Howe, 2006; Kaufman 2008; Wikipedia 2009a). Box 13.3 illustrates the use of such crowdsourcing, which has also been labeled as **collective intelligence** (Bonbeau 2009).

ADDRESSING BARRIERS TO KNOWLEDGE SHARING AND CREATION

Although it is important to involve internal and external knowledge creators and Web 2.0 technologies provide some interesting ways of doing so, it may not be easy to accomplish this. Three main problems constrain individuals' contributions to KM: (a) privacy concerns; (b) concerns related to "knowledge as power"; and (c) senior executives' reluctance to adapt. Each of these barriers is discussed next.

---

*Threadless is a community-centered online organized store that gets its T-shirt designs from members of their community who create and submit T-shirt designs online in exchange for a cash price and store credit.

Box 13.2

Spurring Grassroots Collaboration at Northwestern Mutual

Until 2005, one of the problems facing Northwestern Mutual was that the company's formal hierarchical structure and communication channels adversely affected information flow across departments. The employees were using e-mail and structured reporting systems to transfer information up the chain of command, while hoping that the senior executives would take appropriate actions and disseminate the results back down and across to other departments as well. This frequently led to one department not knowing about related ongoing projects in other departments, thereby inhibiting coordinated efforts or learning across departments.

Charged with the task of addressing such communication problems and promoting open communication, the Assistant Director of Corporate Communication found a solution in the form of corporate blogging, which would put information out in the open so that anyone could find it. In October 2005, she appeared in front of Northwestern Mutual's public affairs committee (a cross-functional steering committee created to track consumer and government trends that might affect the business) to discuss blogging opportunities and threats. As she described it, the problem with e-mail is one of reach: "You may be aware of only some subset of people that may have an interest in what you're working on." Sharing information through a blog helps in keeping everyone informed. "You're not determining and limiting who your potential audience may be," she remarked.

The committee found these ideas intriguing, and the Assistant Director of Corporate Communication returned in December to suggest alternative courses of action including various internal blogs and an external public-facing corporate blog. Although the communications department had been concentrating on external blogging, the CEO enthusiastically supported the notion of internal blogs. For Northwestern Mutual, blogging fit well into an overall corporate communications strategy that, according to the CEO, was intended to "open the windows" and foster a more honest and open dialogue within the company including between management and employees as well as among employees.

However, since it belonged to a highly regulated industry, Northwestern Mutual needed to be ready to produce a comprehensive record of all communications whenever needed. In January 2006, Northwestern Mutual selected the Customer Conversation System (from Awareness), which combines Web-based blogging and content management with enterprise security, workflow and regulatory compliance tools, and extensive versioning capabilities. A blogging solution (Mutualblog) was up and running four months later and was rolled out to 5,000 users across the organization in June 2006. About 100 people were actively blogging by September 2006. Although Northwestern was still in the early phase of its experience with blogging, it seemed to be working well in jump-starting collaboration and sparking a larger change in the corporate culture. "This is the first time we've had a grassroots application that allowed employees to share what they're working on directly," the Assistant Director of Corporate Communication remarked.

Source: Compiled from Spanbauer 2006; Young et al. 2007.

PRIVACY CONCERNS

Perceived threats to privacy may inhibit individuals from contributing knowledge both within the organization as well as across organizational boundaries. An individual may be less forthcoming with honest opinions if she believes that the recommendations she is providing for a decision would be compiled and potentially viewed in the future in the light of all other comments she makes over time, either within the organization or over the Internet, all the decisions she makes, and her demographic and other personal information. This is especially true when the individual perceives that the comments might not be liked by a powerful individual

---

Box 13.3

Open Innovation at InnoCentive

InnoCentive was founded in 2001, when pharmaceutical company Eli Lilly and Company funded its launch as a way to connect with people outside the company who could help in developing drugs and speeding them to market. InnoCentive is open to other firms eager to access the network's community of *ad hoc* experts. It connects public sector and nonprofit organizations, companies, and academic institutions all looking for breakthrough innovations, with a global network of over 160,000 creative thinkers (including engineers, scientists, inventors, and business people with expertise in life sciences, engineering, chemistry, math, computer science, and entrepreneurship) across the world. These creative thinkers, called "Solvers," join a community called "InnoCentive Solver" to address some of the world's toughest challenges posted by "Seeker" organizations, who offer registered Solvers considerable financial awards (anywhere from $5,000 to $100,000 per solution) for the best solutions. InnoCentive manages the entire process, while keeping the identities of Seekers and Solvers completely confidential and secure.

Companies like Boeing, DuPont, and Procter & Gamble also pay InnoCentive a fee to participate, post their most tricky scientific problems on InnoCentive's Web site, and anyone in InnoCentive's Solver community can try solving them. The Solvers are quite diverse. Many of them are hobbyists, such as a University of Dallas undergraduate student who identified which chemical to use in an art restoration project, or a patent lawyer from the Cary, North Carolina, who developed a creative way of mixing large batches of chemical compounds.

Dr. Karim R. Lakhani examined 166 problems posted by 26 research labs over four years on the InnoCentive site and found that an average of 240 people examined each problem, an average of 10 people offered answers, and about 30 percent of the problems were solved (Wessell 2007). During its seven-year history, InnoCentive has paid out more than $3.5 million in awards to over 300 winning Solvers (InnoCentive 2009).

Source: Compiled from the InnoCentive website at www.innocentive.com; Howe 2006; Wessell 2007.

---

within the organization. This applies to comments sent via e-mail as well as posted on blogs (DePree and Jude 2006).

People expect a certain level of privacy even beyond traditional organizational boundaries, such as in social networking sites, and are likely to react strongly to threats to privacy (McCreary 2008, Pottie 2004). Box 13.4 provides one illustrative example.

CONCERNS RELATED TO "KNOWLEDGE AS POWER"

KM mechanisms and technologies that help capture and store employee's knowledge reduce knowledge loss when expert employees leave the organization. However, this may lead to employees, who are not nearing retirement and are concerned about job security at the organization, being concerned about sharing their knowledge with others in the organization. The perception that "knowledge is power" could lead to the belief that by sharing one's privately held knowledge, one might become dispensable or lose some influence within the organization. Uniqueness is widely considered to be an important determinant of power within the organization (Hickson et al. 1971), and by sharing private knowledge individuals risk losing their unique contribution to the organization (Gray 2001).

Box 13.4

Privacy Concerns at Facebook

Facebook is a social networking Web site that provides free access to people who can join networks organized by interest, region, city, place of work, academic institution, and connect and interact with others. Users can also add friends and communicate with them and update personal profiles to inform friends about themselves. Operated and privately owned by Facebook, Inc., it currently has over 175 million active users worldwide (Facebook 2009).

In 2007, Facebook encountered problems with the default settings which provide to advertisers the product preferences that its users share with their friends. Users reacted negatively to this "privacy intrusion," and Facebook management had to change the default settings from "yes" to "no" (i.e., which meant that Facebook would not be able share these product preferences; McCreary 2008).

More recently, Facebook decided to change its policy on user-generated content, such that it would have a "perpetual" license to use any material uploaded by users for advertising or other venues, even if the user had subsequently deleted the content or even cancelled the account. However, Facebook backtracked the decision upon learning that the Electronic Privacy Information Center (EPIC), an advocacy group based in Washington, DC., was planning to file a formal complaint with the Federal Trade Commission over the changed license agreement.

The Executive Director of EPIC remarked: "What we sensed was taking place was that Facebook was asserting a greater legal authority over the user-generated content. It represented a fundamental shift in terms of how the company saw its ability to exercise control over what its users were posting, and that really concerned us." Credited for this protest against Facebook was a grassroots effort by Julius Harper, Jr., a 25-year-old who formed the "People Against the New Terms of Service" Facebook group, with over 80,000 members. This group started as a simple protest, and then submitted its major concerns to the service's legal team. The most significant concerns included why the revised terms of service appeared to give Facebook the right to use user photos if the company had no intention to utilize them, and what would occur if Facebook were to be acquired by another corporation in the future and the new owner wanted to utilize the user-generated content in ways the current Facebook leaders were not considering.

Source: Compiled from Facebook, 2009; McCreary 2008; Raphael 2009; Wikipedia 2009b.

When job security is low due to adverse economic conditions and frequent layoffs, workers have an even stronger motivation to attach greater utility to, and consequently withhold, their private knowledge (Davenport & Prusak 1998). By contrast, when the level of trust or care among employees in an organization is high, they may perceive a lower psychological cost of knowledge sharing due to greater concern about how they contribute to solving organizational problems and are useful to others (Constant et al. 1996).

A similar perception may inhibit knowledge sharing across departments. Therefore, managers need to be sensitive to issues related to power and control (Gray 2001). Incentives might help to some extent and only in some situations. Despite the progress in IT and in the field of KM, motivating employees to share private knowledge remains a critical issue.

SENIOR EXECUTIVES' RELUCTANCE TO ADAPT

As discussed above, individuals possessing the knowledge might be reluctant to do so due to concerns about privacy and perceived loss of power. In order to convince employees to share their knowledge and contribute to the creation of new organizational knowledge, senior executives need to play an important role. Senior executives should make considerable changes in organizational forums as well as in their own attitudes. Some of the important changes are:

1. The creation of a flatter organizational structure, because "most companies have hierarchical structures, and differences in status among people impede the exchange of ideas." (Amabile and Khaire 2008, p. 102)
2. The incorporation of diverse and multiple, and often starkly conflicting, perspectives to facilitate knowledge creation (Yoo 2008).
3. The willingness to allow redundancy and slack resources needed for the incorporation of these diverse and multiple perspectives.
4. The willingness to let go of their power, much more so than the traditional notion of "empowerment" might imply, as is needed for a true knowledge democracy.

Unfortunately, a number of senior executives are unwilling to recognize the importance of the above changes. A knowledge democracy in an organization cannot be achieved unless senior executives truly believe that people across the organization, including at the very lowest levels where interactions with customers most often occur, might have truly valuable ideas that would influence the organizational strategy, or product roadmap. For example, Scott Cook, the cofounder of Intuit Inc., wonders whether management is "a net positive or a net negative for creativity": "If there is a bottleneck in organizational creativity, might it be at the top of the bottle?" (Amabile and Khaire 2008, p. 102)

CONCLUDING REMARKS

The benefits from knowledge management are considerable, and progress in information technology as well as the experience gained within the field of knowledge management implies that there are also some valuable ways of managing knowledge so as to increase efficiency, effectiveness, and innovation for both organizations and individuals. However, KM is not easy, and encounters numerous challenges related to the adoption of technologies, motivation of individuals within and outside the organization, and the integration of people and technologies within the KM processes. In this book, we have tried to provide the reader with a comprehensive overview of the foundations of KM, the opportunities and challenges, as well as some of the important emerging and future directions.

In conclusion, the future of KM is one where people and advanced technology will continue to work together, enabling knowledge integration across diverse domains and with potentially high payoffs. However, the new opportunities and greater benefits will require careful management of people and technologies, synthesis of multiple perspectives, and effectively dealing with a variety of tradeoffs. Even though interesting challenges lie ahead for knowledge managers, the future of KM is clearly exciting because of the opportunities it promises for generations to come.

KEY TERMS

Collective intelligence
Community-based design
Copyrights
Crowdsourcing
Damage recovery
Encryption
Firewalls

Intellectual property (IP)
Knowledge leakage
Nondisclosure agreement
Patents
Trade secret
Wicked problems

REVIEW

1. Identify the one issue you consider most important for the future of knowledge management. Why?
2. How do you see organizations changing in the future, especially in terms of knowledge management but also in terms of their structure, as a result of Web 2.0 technologies?
3. Based on both Chapters 3 and 13, what role do you see top management playing in knowledge management in organizations in the future?
4. How might privacy concerns affect knowledge management in the future, both within organizations as well as in social networks?
5. Briefly identify any three ways in which you see employees changing their behaviors related to knowledge management in the future.

APPLICATION EXERCISES

1. Select any three topics on Wikipedia (http://en.wikipedia.org/) and track the identified pages for a week (visiting each page twice a day) to see how the knowledge changes on these pages. What lessons do you learn from this experience?
2. Select any one organization that utilizes crowdsourcing (such as Cambrian House [http://www.cambrianhouse.com/] or CrowdSpirit [http://www.crowd-spirit.com/]), and find our more information about whose knowledge is being managed at this organization through crowdsourcing. Then summarize the lessons you learn from this organization about the relationship between crowdsourcing and knowledge management.
3. Visit a local area firm to study how knowledge is being managed there at present, examine whether Web 2.0 technologies are being used, and talk to some of its people regarding how knowledge management might change in the future.
4. Visit a small local area firm and a large local organization, and talk to two individuals at each organization to examine whether concerns related to privacy and "knowledge is power" affect knowledge management at this organization.

5. Identify one wicked problem that seems really important to you. Investigate ways in which knowledge management, including knowledge management through crowdsourcing or collective intelligence, might help address this wicked problem.

Note

1. They have also been called *learning organizations.*

References

Amabile, T.M. and Khaire, M. 2008. Creativity and the role of the leader. *Harvard Business Review,* October, 100–109.

Bonbeau, E. 2009. Decisions 2.0: The power of collective intelligence. *Sloan Management Review,* 50(2) (Winter), 45–52.

Churchman, C. 1971. *The design of inquiring systems: Basic concepts of systems and organization.* New York: Basic Books.

Constant, D., Sproull, L., and Kiesler, S. 1996. The kindness of strangers: The usefulness of electronic weak ties for technical advice. *Organization Science,* 7(2), 119–135.

Cook, S. 2008. The contribution revolution: Letting volunteers build your business. *Harvard Business Review,* October, 123–131.

Courtney, J. 2001. Decision making and knowledge management in inquiring organizations: Toward a new decision-making paradigm for DSS. *Decision Support Systems,* 31, 17–38.

Davenport, T. and Prusak, L. 1998. *Working knowledge: How organizations manage what they know.* Boston: Harvard Business School Press.

DePree Jr., C.M. and Jude, R.K. 2006. Who's reading your office e-mail? Is that legal? *Strategic Finance,* 87(10).

Facebook. 2009. Statistics. Facebook Press Room. http://www.facebook.com/press/info.php?statistics (accessed February 21, 2009).

Gray, P. 2001. The impact of knowledge repositories on power and control in the workplace. *Information Technology and People,* 14(4), 368–384.

Hickson, D.J., Hinings, C.R., Lee, C.A., Schneck, R.E., and Pennings, J.M. 1971. A strategic contingencies theory of intra-organizational power. *Administrative Science Quarterly,* 16, 216–229.

Howe, J. 2006. The rise of crowdsourcing, *Wired,* June. http://www.wired.com/wired/archive/14.06/crowds.html (accessed February 20, 2009).

InnoCentive. 2009. FAQs. *Innocentive—Where the world innovates.* http://www.innocentive.com/crowd-sourcing-news/faq/.

Kaufman, W. 2008. Crowd sourcing turns business on its head. *NPR.* http://www.npr.org/templates/story/story.php?storyId=93495217 (accessed February 20, 2009).

McCreary, L. 2008. What was privacy? *Harvard Business Review,* October, 123–131.

Pottie, G.J. 2004. Privacy in the global e-village. *Communication of the ACM,* 47(2) (February), 21–23.

Raphael, J.R. 2009. Facebook's privacy flap: What really went down, and what's next. *PC World,* February 18. http://www.pcworld.com/article/159743/facebooks_privacy_flap_what_really_went_down_and_whats_next.html (accessed February 21, 2009).

Rittel, H. and Webber, M. 1973. Dilemmas in a general theory of planning. *Policy Sciences,* 4, 155–169.

Spanbauer, S. 2006. Modern knowledge management applications. *CIO.com,* December 1. http://www.cio.com/article/27087/Modern_Knowledge_Management_Applications.

Stewart, T. 1994. Intellectual capital: Your company's most valuable asset. *Fortune,* 10, 68–73.

Wessel, D. 2007. Prizes for solutions to problems play valuable role in innovation. *Wall Street Journal,* January 25.

Wikipedia. 2009a. *Crowdsourcing.* http://en.wikipedia.org/wiki/Crowdsourcing.

———. 2009b. Facebook. http://en.wikipedia.org/wiki/Facebook.

Yoo, Y. 2008. Mobilizing knowledge in a Yu-Gi-Oh! world. In *Knowledge management: An evolutionary view.* Advances in Management Information Systems, Vol. 12, ed. I. Becerra-Fernandez and D. Leidner, 127–144. Armonk, NY: M.E. Sharpe.

Young, G.O., Brown, M., Holmes, B.J., and Lawson, A. 2007. Forrester Research: How Northwestern Mutual deployed enterprise web 2.0. *CIO Zone.com.* http://www.ciozone.com/index.php/Editorial-Research/Forrester-Research-How-Northwestern-Mutual-Deployed-Enterprise-Web-2.0.html (accessed February 20, 2009).

Glossary

Access Control. Refers to mechanisms and policies that restrict access to computer resources.

Active Web Documents. Web documents received by a client from the WWW server, which contain programs that execute on the client's computer, continually changing the display.

Adaptation. The process of modifying a historical solution to solve the current problem when the current problem is not identical to the historical problem associated with that solution.

Algorithmic. A step-by-step problem-solving procedure for solving a problem in a finite number of steps.

Application Linking. Refers to when the enterprise shares business processes and data between two or more IT applications.

Artificial Intelligence (AI). The branch of computer science concerned with making computers behave like humans. John McCarthy coined the term in 1956 while at the Massachusetts Institute of Technology. It refers to the science that provides computers with the ability to solve problems not easily solved through algorithmic models.

Artificial Neural Networks (ANN). A type of artificial intelligence that attempts to simulate human intelligence by recreating the connective physiology of the human brain. It is a mechanism (either implemented in computer hardware or simulated using computer software) that can learn to map information between two vector spaces: *input* and *output*. Neural nets can be used to solve a large variety of problems, provided that it is possible to formulate the problem in terms of vector space-mapping.

Associational Expertise. Knowledge or heuristic ability acquired mostly through human experience and elicited through the knowledge engineering process.

Authorizer's Assistant. Assists the credit authorization staff to determine the credit level for credit card customers. The system takes information from a number of databases and approves or disapproves a telephone request from a merchant to authorize a large purchase from a cardholder.

Auxiliary Memory. The transfer of pages of data between a computer's main memory and a secondary medium of memory.

Avatar. Image of person in virtual reality; a movable three-dimensional image that can be used to represent somebody in cyberspace, for example, an Internet user.

Back-propagation Algorithm. An algorithm for efficiently calculating the error gradient of a neural network, which can then be used as the basis of learning.

Backward Reasoning. Reasoning from conclusions, or goals, to the inputs.

Benchmarking. A test used to measure performance.

Best Practices. An assessment recommending the most appropriate way of handling a certain type of task based on an observation of the way that several organizations handle that task.

Bi-directional Reasoning. Uses forward reasoning to propagate belief from the inputs and generate conclusions and backward reasoning to confirm the conclusions generated dynamically.

Blocks World. Early AI system. It used a robot arm to set blocks on a table. Demonstrated the feasibility of automated task planning.

Blogs. A contraction between Web and log, it refers to a form of online digital diary. In essence it is a Web site where an individual makes regular written journal entries that comprise a statement of opinion, a story, an analysis, description of events, or other material.

Brainstorming Camps. Company-organized social retreats designed to foster innovative ideas.

Business Intelligence (BI). Using information technologies to provide decisionmakers with valuable information and knowledge by utilizing a variety of sources of data and structured and unstructured information, via the discovery of the relationships that may exist between these sources of data and information.

Business Process. A network of activities performed by resources that transform inputs into outputs.

Campaign Management Software. Software used to manage and monitor a company's communications with its customers.

Case. A documented historical occurrence used for comparison to current problems, which is the basis of case-based reasoning (CBR).

Case-Based Reasoning (CBR). An intelligent reasoning process that seeks to solve new problems based on solutions of similar past problems, much like a lawyer seeks a new outcome on a trial based on precedents established by past legal cases.

Case Library. A database of historical cases containing the universe of knowledge in a CBR system.

Choosing Parameters from a Menu. In this method, the database system presents a list of parameters from which you can choose. This is perhaps the easiest way to pose a query because the menus guide you, but it is also the least flexible.

Churn. The turnover of users, for example on an online service, especially after the expiration of a free-trial period.

Classification. The grouping together of data sets according to some predefined similarity shared by all members of that set.

Clickstream Analysis. A virtual trail that a user leaves behind while surfing the Internet. A clickstream is a record of a user's activity on the Internet, including every Web site and every page of every Web site that the user visits, how long the user was on a page or site, in what order the pages were visited, any newsgroups that the user participates in, and even the e-mail addresses of mail that the user sends and receives. Both ISPs and individual Web sites are capable of tracking a user's clickstream.

Client. The client part of the client-server architecture. Typically, a client is an application that runs on a personal computer or workstation and relies on a server to perform some operations. For example, an e-mail client is an application that enables you to send and receive e-mail.

Close-ended Questions. Questions asked of an expert that require a short answer or a number for answers. Used for gathering specific problem-solving knowledge.

Cluster Analysis. The grouping together of data sets according to a natural but undefined parameter shared by all members of the set.

Codifiability. Reflects the extent to which knowledge can be articulated or codified, even if the resulting codified knowledge might be difficult to impart to another individual.

Collaborative-based Filtering. Recommends items (similar to the one being studied) that people have liked in the past.

Collaborative Computing. Software systems designed to help people involved in a project or common task collaborate, typically through the Web, to achieve their goals. Includes e-mails, calendars, text and chat, wikis, etc.

Collective Intelligence (or *crowdsourcing* or *community-based design*). Refers to the outsourcing of tasks to an undefined, large group of people or community in the form of an open call.

Combination. Explicit-to-Explicit knowledge conversion: Combination involves the synthesis of multiple bodies of explicit knowledge (and/or data and/or information) to create new, more complex sets of explicit knowledge. It is a process of systemizing concepts into a knowledge system. This may take place during activities such as sorting, adding, combining, and categorizing knowledge.

Common Knowledge. Refers to the organization's cumulative experiences in comprehending a category of knowledge and activities and the organizing principles that support communication and coordination. It provides unity to the organization and includes a common language and vocabulary, recognition of individual knowledge domains, common cognitive schema, shared norms, and elements of specialized knowledge common across individuals sharing knowledge.

Common Virtual System. The pinnacle of EAI; all aspects of enterprise computing are tied together so that they appear as a unified application.

Community-based design (or *crowdsourcing* or *collective intelligence*). Refers to the outsourcing of tasks to an undefined, large group of people or community in the form of an open call.

Community of Practice (CoP). An organic and self-organized group of individuals who are dispersed geographically or organizationally but communicate regularly to discuss issues of mutual interest.

Competitive Intelligence. A term that indicates knowledge leading to competitive advantages for a business organization.

Complex Knowledge. Draws upon multiple distinct areas of expertise. It involves mastering several different pieces of knowledge organized in the form of a system.

Computer-aided Design (CAD) System. A combination of hardware and software that enables engineers and architects to design everything from furniture to airplanes. In addition to the software CAD systems require a high-quality graphics monitor, a mouse, light pen, or digitizing tablet for drawing, and a special printer or plotter for printing design specifications. CAD systems allow an engineer to view a design from any angle with the push of a button and to zoom in or out for closeups and long-distance views. In addition, the computer keeps track of design dependencies so that when the engineer changes one value, all other values that depend on it are automatically changed accordingly.

Concept Learning System. An algorithm that classifies a set of example data by building an inductive tree and distributing the examples throughout the tree.

Concept Maps. These aim to represent knowledge through concepts and are enclosed in circles or boxes of some types, which are related via connecting lines or propositions.

Constrained Processing Tasks. Artificial tasks given to an expert for the purpose of observing him and learning from his performance. The expert is typically constrained in terms of time available for the solution.

Context. The background or environmental circumstances that surround a particular event or situation.

Content Based Filtering. Recommendations based on what a person has liked in the past.

Context-based Reasoning (CxBR). A human behavior representation paradigm specifically designed to effectively represent human tactical behavior.

Contextually Specific Knowledge. Refers to the knowledge of particular circumstances of time and place in which work is to be performed. It pertains to the organization and the organizational subunit within which tasks are performed.

Contingency View of KM. Suggests that no "one approach" to managing knowledge is best under all circumstances.

Cooker. Assists in the maintenance of soup-making equipment. It uses a personal computer as the delivery platform.

Critic. Rules used for adapting the solution of a similar historical case to the current problem.

Cross-Industry Standard Process for Data Mining (CRISP-DM). An industry-neutral and tool-neutral standard process for data mining. Starting from the embryonic knowledge discovery processes used in industry today and responding directly to user requirements, this project defined and validated a data mining process that is applicable in diverse industry sectors.

Crowdsourcing (or *community-based design* or *collective intelligence*). Refers to the outsourcing of tasks to an undefined, large group of people or community in the form of an open call.

Customer Profile Exchange (CPEX). An initial group of about 25 vendors who formed a working group with the goal of creating a unified view of business relationships and global privacy safeguards.

Customer Relationship Management (CRM). CRM entails all aspects of interaction a company has with its customer, whether it be sales or services related. Computerization has changed the way companies are approaching their CRM strategies because it has also changed consumer-buying behavior. With each new advance in technology, especially the proliferation of self-service channels like the Web, more of the relationship is being managed electronically. Organizations are therefore looking for ways to personalize online experiences (a process also referred to as mass customization) through tools such as help desk software, e-mail organizers, and Web development applications.

Customer Touchpoints. Refers to the steps in a business process, like a purchase transaction, or a software where it interfaces directly with the customer.

Daemons. Functions attached to a frame that assist in obtaining values for slots or to maintain consistency in the frame system.

Data. Comprise facts, observations, or perceptions (which may or may not be correct). By itself, data represent raw numbers or assertions and may therefore be devoid of context, meaning, or intent.

Data Mining (DM). A class of database applications that look for hidden patterns in a group of data that can be used to predict future behavior. For example, data mining software can help retail companies find customers with common interests. The term is commonly misused to describe software that presents data in new ways. True data mining software doesn't just change the presentation but actually discovers previously unknown relationships among the data.

Data Warehouse. A collection of data designed to support management decision-making. Data warehouses contain a wide variety of data that present a coherent picture of business conditions at a single point in time. The development of a data warehouse includes development of systems to extract data from operating systems plus installation of a warehouse database system that provides managers flexible access to the data. The term data warehousing generally refers to combining many different databases across an entire enterprise. A data mart is defined as a database, or collection of databases, designed to help managers make strategic decisions about their business. Whereas a data warehouse combines databases across an entire enterprise, data marts are usually smaller and focus on a particular subject or department. Some data marts, called *dependent data marts,* are subsets of larger data warehouses.

Database (DB). A large collection of data organized for rapid search and retrieval. Programs that manage data and can be used to store, retrieve, and sort information. You can think of a database as an electronic filing system. A relational database is a database that stores data in the form of related tables. Relational databases are powerful because they require few assumptions about how data are related or how they will be extracted from the database. As a result, the same database can be viewed in many different ways.

Database Linking. Databases that share information and duplicate information as needed.

Declarative Knowledge. Focuses on beliefs about relationships among variables. Characterized as "know what," it can be stated in the form of propositions, expected correlations, or formulas relating concepts represented as variables.

Deep Expertise. More theoretical knowledge acquired through formal training and hands-on problem-solving.

Deployment. Implementing the live model within an organization to aid the decision-making process.

Development Environment. A program used to develop the knowledge for the knowledge-based system and provides the inference mechanism used to exercise the knowledge to solve a problem or answer a question posed by the enduser.

Direction. Is the process through which the individual possessing the knowledge directs the action of another individual without transferring to him the knowledge underlying the direction.

Disjunctions. Otherwise identical cases with different solutions.

Document Management Systems. Computer systems that provide a Web-based repository accessible from multiple points. The systems also provide a collaborative environment for several clients to work on a document simultaneously.

Domain Expert. An individual who is both experienced and knowledgeable about a particular application domain.

Domain Knowledge. Relevant knowledge about a problem domain; knowledge embedded in the operators of the solution space.

Downsizing. To reduce in number or size.

Dynamic. Refers to actions that take place at the moment they are needed rather than in advance.

Dynamic Web Documents. Web pages created by the Web server in response to the specific request by the client.

Economy of Scale. A firm's output is said to exhibit economy of scale when as the amount of its output is increased, average costs (i.e., total costs divided by the output) decline.

Economy of Scope. A firm's output exhibits economy of scope when the total cost of that same firm producing two (or more) different products is less than sum of the costs that would be incurred if each product was produced separately by a different company.

Effectiveness. Performing the most suitable processes and making the best possible decisions.

Efficiency. Performing the processes quickly and in a low-cost fashion.

Eliza. Early AI implementation. It used a natural language interface to act as an artificial psychoanalyst, carrying on a dialogue with a patient.

EMYCIN. Knowledge-based system shell. Developed by removing the domain specific knowledge from MYCIN.

Encryption. The translation of data into a secret code. Encryption is the most effective way to achieve data security. To read an encrypted file, you must have access to a secret key or password that enables you to *decrypt* it. Unencrypted data is called *plain text;* encrypted data is referred to as *cipher text.*

Enduser. The person for whom the product was designed by the person who programs, services, or installs the product.

Enterprise Application Integration (EAI) Technology. EAI is the unrestricted sharing of data and business processes throughout the networked applications or data sources in an organization. Early software programs in areas such as inventory control, human resources, sales automation, and database management were designed to run independently with no interaction between the systems. They were custom built in the technology of the day for a specific need being addressed and were often proprietary systems. As enterprises grow and recognize the need for their information and applications to have the ability to be transferred across and shared among systems, companies are investing in EAI in order to streamline processes and keep all the elements of the enterprise interconnected.

Enterprise Resource Planning (ERP) System. A business management system that integrates all facets of the business including planning, manufacturing, sales, and marketing. As the ERP methodology has become more popular, software applications have emerged to help business managers implement ERP in business activities such as inventory control, order tracking, customer service, finance, and human resources.

Enterprise System. Literally, a business organization. In the computer industry, the term is often used to describe any large organization that utilizes computers. An Intranet, for example, is a good example of an enterprise computing system.

Evaluation. Evaluation of a case in the case library for similarity with the current problem.

Exchange. Is used for communicating or transferring explicit knowledge among individuals, groups, and organizations.

Expected Value. The sum of all possible values for a variable, each value multiplied by its probability of occurrence.

Experience Management. Encompasses the processes governing creation, storage, reuse, maintenance, dissemination, and evaluation of experience relevant to a particular situation or problem-solving context.

Expertise. Refers to knowledge of higher quality—that is, specific knowledge at its best. One who possesses expertise is able to perform a task much better than those who do not.

Expertise Locator Systems (ELS). A system to catalog knowledge competencies, including information not typically captured by human resources systems, in a way that could later be queried across the organization.

Explicit Knowledge. Refers to knowledge that has been expressed into words and numbers. Such knowledge can be shared formally and systematically in the form of data, specifications, manuals, drawings, audio-/videotapes, programs, patents, and so forth.

Exploratory Analysis of Data (with OLAP). Refers to the use of online analytical processing (OLAP) for creating complex queries across a multidimensional data model for the purpose of business reporting.

Externalization. Involves converting tacit knowledge into explicit forms such as words, concepts, visuals, or figurative language (e.g., metaphors, analogies, and narratives).

Facets. Subdivisions of a frame slot that contain various types of information related to the slot.

Facilitator. Leader or chairperson of a brainstorming session.

Fact Base. A data structure that holds all assertions made either by the system or provided as inputs. These assertions serve as facts for matching premises in an inference chain.

Fault Diagnosis. Software used to try to determine the causes of a malfunction, also known as a *fault*, in particular in a piece of equipment.

Firewall. A system designed to prevent unauthorized access to or from a private network. Firewalls can be implemented in both hardware and software or a combination of both. Firewalls are frequently used to prevent unauthorized Internet users from accessing private networks connected to the Internet, especially Intranets. All messages entering or leaving the Intranet pass through the firewall, which examines each message and blocks those that do not meet the specified security criteria.

Flat Case Libraries. Case library organization where all cases lie at the same hierarchical level in the case library.

Forward Reasoning. Reasoning from inputs to conclusions.

Frames. Structured framework for storing and retrieving knowledge best organized as attribute value pairs. Composed of slots.

Game-playing. Programming computers to play games such as chess and checkers.

GenAID. Remotely monitors and diagnoses the status of large electrical generators in real time. It issues a diagnosis with a confidence factor whenever the machine is operating outside its normal operating conditions. It is presently in commercial operation at various sites throughout the United States.

Generalization. The opposite of specialization. When a frame is more general than its child frame. This is the normal situation.

General Knowledge. Is possessed by a large number of individuals and can be transferred easily across individuals.

General Knowledge-gathering Interview Sessions. Interview sessions designed to elicit general domain knowledge from the expert.

General Problem Solver (GPS). Early AI implementation, which demonstrated ability to solve problems by searching for an answer in a solution space.

Goal State. Final desired state of a problem in the solution space.

Graphical User Interface (GUI). A program interface that takes advantage of the computer's graphics capabilities to make the program easier to use. Well-designed graphical user interfaces can free the user from learning complex command languages. On the other hand, many users find that they work more effectively with a command-driven interface, especially if they already know the command language.

Groupware. A class of software that helps groups of colleagues (workgroups) attached to a local-area network organize their activities.

GUIDON. An instructional program for teaching students therapy for patients with bacterial infections. GUIDON is a descendant of MYCIN and was developed as a research tool at Stanford University.

Hacking. The pejorative sense of the term *hacker* is becoming more prominent largely because the popular press has co-opted the term to refer to individuals who gain unauthorized access to computer systems for the purpose of stealing and corrupting data.

Help Desk Technologies. Software used to aid the operations of a *help desk,* which is used to troubleshoot problems with computers or other similar products. The help desk technologies help to track requests for service as well as to diagnose potential reasons for the problem.

Heterogeneous Networks. Networks consisting of computers with different processors and/or different operating systems.

Heuristic Functions. Used in solution space searches to compute the desirability of moving on to each of the possible next states based on some general knowledge. These states are ranked in order of decreasing desirability.

Heuristics. Common-sense knowledge drawn from experience to solve problems. Represents rules-of-thumb and other such shortcuts to the solution that are only learned through experience. This is in contrast to *algorithmic programming,* which is based on a deterministic sequence of steps procedures. Heuristic programs do not always reach the very best result but usually produce a good result.

Heuristic Search. A search that uses heuristic functions as a guide to determine where in the problem space to search next.

Hierarchical. Refers to systems that are organized in the shape of a pyramid with each row of objects linked to objects directly beneath it. Hierarchical systems pervade everyday life. The army, for example, which has generals at the top of the pyramid and privates at the bottom, is a hierarchical system. Similarly, the system for classifying plants and animals according to species, family, genus, and so on, is also hierarchical.

Human Computer Interface (HCI). The interface between a human and a computer; for example, a command line interface, a graphical user interface, virtual reality interfaces.

Hypertext Markup Language (HTML). A standard representation for text and graphics that allows the browser to interpret the intentions of the Web page designer.

Hypertext Transfer Protocol (HTTP). A transfer protocol used for exchanging hypertext.

Indexing. The act of classifying and providing an index in order to make items easier to retrieve.

Inference Chain. A sequence of rules in a rule-based system where the assertions of an upstream rule serve as the facts to match the premises of downstream rules.

Inferential DM. Models that explain the relationships that exist in data. They may indicate the driving factors for stock market movement or show failure factors in printed circuit-board production.

Information. Is a subset of data, only including those data that possess context, relevance, and purpose. Information typically involves the manipulation of raw data to obtain a more meaningful indication of trends or patterns in the data.

Information Retrieval. The science of searching for documents, information, or meta data within documents in the Web, as well as, for data within databases.

Information Technology (IT). The broad subject concerned with all aspects of managing and processing information, especially within a large organization or company. Because computers are central to information management, computer departments within companies and universities are often called *IT departments.* Some companies refer to this department as *IS* (Information Systems) or *MIS* (Management Information Systems).

Inheritance. The ability in frames and objects to conserve representational effort by having "children frame" contain all attributes and values possessed by its "parent frame."

Initial State. Starting problem definition in a solution space.

Innovation. Performing the processes in a creative and novel fashion that improves effectiveness and efficiency—or at least marketability.

Innovators. Those who brainstorm the solutions to the customer's problem.

Intellectual Capital. Knowledge that can be exploited for some moneymaking or other useful purpose. The term combines the idea of the intellect or brainpower with the economic concept of capital—that is, that intellect like capital can be used in service of the saving of entitled benefits so that they can be invested in producing more goods and services.

Intelligent Program. A concept where the enduser sees the knowledge-based system as a black box that provides intelligent problem-solving capability without the ability to see its components. It is composed of a knowledge base, an inference engine, and a development environment.

Internalization. Is the conversion of explicit knowledge into tacit knowledge. It represents the traditional notion of "learning."

Internet. A computer network protocol able to interconnect heterogeneous networks.

Inter-page Structures. Evaluates the arrangement of the various HTML or XML tags that connect one page to another.

Interviews. The time of interaction with an expert for the purposes of eliciting his/her knowledge.

Intra-page Structures. Evaluates the arrangement of the various HTML or XML tags within a page.

Inverse Document Frequency (IDF). Highlights terms that are frequently used in one document but infrequently used across the collection of documents.

Iterative. This is a programming term. It refers to a process that can be described by a fixed number of variables and a set of rules, which describe what happens to those variables to achieve the next step of the process. If the process is interrupted, it can be continued if the state of all the variables is known. Contrast this to a recursive process. Iteration is a single step.

Java. A programming language specifically designed to allow it to execute in any type of computer. This makes programs written in Java easily exchanged through the WWW.

Just-in-time (JIT) Manufacturing. An ideal method of manufacturing with minimal waste, short cycle times, and fast communication that can respond rapidly to changing circumstances.

Kickoff Interview. The first interview in the process of knowledge elicitation.

Knowledge. Is intrinsically different from information. Knowledge in an area is defined as justified beliefs about relationships among concepts relevant to that particular area.

Knowledge-based Systems. A computerized system that uses domain knowledge to arrive at a solution to a problem within that domain. This solution is essentially the same as one decided upon by a person knowledgeable about the domain when confronted with the same problem.

Knowledge Capture. The process of eliciting knowledge (either explicit or tacit) that resides within people, artifacts, or organizational entities and representing it in an electronic form such as a knowledge-based system, for later reuse or retrieval.

Knowledge Creation. An activity that catalyzes the innovation of knowledge.

Knowledge Discovery. Is the development of new tacit or explicit knowledge from data and information or from the synthesis of prior knowledge.

Knowledge Discovery in Databases (KDD). The process of data selection, data cleaning, transfer to a DM technique, applying the DM technique, validating the results of the DM technique, and finally interpreting them for the user.

Knowledge Elicitation. The process of obtaining tacit knowledge from an expert for the purposes of making that knowledge explicit.

Knowledge Engineering. The process of developing a knowledge-based system.

Knowledge Management (KM). Can be defined as performing the activities involved in discovering, capturing, sharing, and applying knowledge in terms of resources, documents, and people skills, so as to enhance, in a cost-effective fashion, the impact of knowledge on the unit's goal achievement.

Knowledge Management Foundations. Are the broad organizational aspects that support knowledge management in the long-term. They include knowledge management infrastructure, knowledge management mechanisms, and knowledge management technologies.

Knowledge Management Infrastructure. Is the long-term foundation on which knowledge management resides. It includes five main components: organization culture, organization structure, information technology infrastructure, common knowledge, and physical environment.

Knowledge Management Mechanisms. Are organizational or structural means used to promote knowledge management. They may (or may not) utilize technology, but they do involve some kind of organizational arrangement or social or structural means of facilitating KM.

Knowledge Management Processes. Are the broad processes that help in discovering, capturing, sharing, and applying knowledge.

Knowledge Management Solutions. Are the ways in which specific aspects of knowledge management (discovery, capture, sharing, and application of knowledge) can be accomplished. Knowledge management solutions include knowledge management processes and knowledge management systems.

Knowledge Management Systems (KMS). Integrate technologies and mechanisms to support KM processes.

Knowledge Repository. A system to share knowledge. Also known as a document management system and content management systems and serve primarily to share unstructured information.

Knowledge Sharing. Is the process through which explicit or tacit knowledge is communicated to other individuals.

Lateral Thinking. Using an entirely different approach to solve a problem. In any self-organizing system there is a need to escape from a local optimum in order to move towards a more global optimum. The techniques of lateral thinking, such as provocation, are designed to help that change.

Learning. The process of improving one's performance by experiencing an activity or observing someone else experience that activity. Learning has been one goal of artificially intelligent systems.

Lessons Learned Systems (LLS). The goal of LLS is to capture and provide lessons that can benefit employees who encounter situations that closely resemble a previous experience in a similar situation.

Limited Information Tasks. Artificial tasks given to an expert to perform with limited information. Used to place the expert in a situation where he will be challenged. Serve to observe the expert in problem-solving without danger of failure.

Linear Regression. A statistical procedure for predicting the value of a dependent variable from an independent variable when the relationship between the variables can be described with a linear model.

Machine Learning. Machine learning refers to the ability of computers to automatically acquire new knowledge—learning from, for example, past cases or experience, from the computer's own experiences or from exploration.

Many-on-Many Interviews. Interview sessions in which several knowledge engineers interact with several experts.

Market Basket Analysis. An algorithm that examines a long list of transactions in order to determine which items are most frequently purchased together.

Metadata. Data about data. Metadata describes how and when and by whom a particular set of data was collected and how the data are formatted. Metadata is essential for understanding information stored in data warehouses.

Metaphor. One thing conceived as representing another—a symbol.

Method of Least Squares. A statistical method of finding the best-fitting straight line or other theoretically derived curve for a group of experimental data points.

Methodology. A body of practices, procedures, and rules used by those who work in a discipline or engage in an inquiry; a set of working methods.

Metrics. A standard measurement.

Mission-Critical Objectives. A set of organizational goals that include both the purpose of the organization and its scope of operations critical to operationalize and accomplish the set of organizational goals. They must be measurable, specific, appropriate, realistic, and timely.

Model-based Reasoning (MBR). An intelligent reasoning technique that uses a model of an engineered system to simulate its normal behavior. The simulated operation is compared to the behavior of a real system and noted discrepancies can lead to a diagnosis.

Motor Skills Expertise. Physical rather than cognitive knowledge. This type of knowledge is difficult for knowledge-based systems to emulate. Examples include riding a bicycle or hitting a baseball.

MYCIN. Early knowledge-based system developed in the early 1970s. Developed to diagnose and specify treatments for blood disorders through a Q&A session with a physician. It is the most significant and renowned research system, for it pioneered the separation of the knowledge from the way it is used.

Narrative. A narrated account; a story.

Narrowcast. To send data to a specific list of recipients. Cable television is an example of narrowcasting since the cable TV signals are sent only to homes that have subscribed to the cable service. In contrast, network TV uses a broadcast model in which the signals are transmitted everywhere, and anyone with an antenna can receive them.

Natural Language. Programming computers to understand natural human languages.

Natural Language Processing (NLP). A branch of artificial intelligence that deals with analyzing, understanding, and generating the languages that humans use naturally in order to interface with computers in both written and spoken contexts using natural human languages instead of computer languages.

Normalization. In data processing, a process applied to all data in a set that produce a specific statistical property. For example, monthly expenditures can be divided by total expenditures to produce a normalized value that represents a percentage.

Object Oriented Programming (OOP). Refers to a special type of programming that combines data structures with functions to create reusable objects.

Observables. A physical property, such as weight or temperature, that can be observed or measured directly as distinguished from a quantity, such as work or entropy, that must be derived from observed quantities.

Observational Elicitation. The process of observing an expert perform a task in order to learn his/her process for performing the task. Can be quiet observation or interactive.

One-line Diagram. Drawing depicting the connectivity of an engineered system.

One-on-Many Interviews. Interview sessions in which one knowledge engineer interacts with several experts.

One-on-One Interview. An interview in which one knowledge engineer and one expert participate.

Online Analytical Processing (OLAP). A category of software tools that provides analysis of data stored in a database. OLAP tools enable users to analyze different dimensions of multidimensional data. For example, it provides time series and trend analysis views. The chief component of OLAP is the OLAP server, which sits between a client and a database management system (DBMS). The OLAP server understands how data are organized in the database and has special functions for analyzing the data. There are OLAP servers available for nearly all the major database systems. In essence OLAP enables to summarize, aggregate, or selectively extract data from different points of view.

Ontology. Description of the concepts and relationships that can exist for an agent or a community of agents.

Open-ended Questions. Questions asked of the expert, which require a narrative and/or long explanation. Used for gathering general domain knowledge.

Open Source. A broad general type of software license that makes source code available to the general public with relaxed or nonexistent copyright restrictions.

Output-Input-Middle Method. Method used to organize knowledge elicited during expert interviews.

Predictive DM. Models may or may not explain relationships. Primarily, they make predictions of output conditions given a set of input conditions.

Probability. A number expressing the likelihood that a specific event will occur, expressed as the ratio of the number of actual occurrences to the number of possible occurrences.

Procedural Knowledge. Focuses on beliefs relating sequences of steps or actions to desired (or undesired) outcomes. It may be viewed as "know-how."

Proposition. A statement that affirms or denies something.

Prospector. A system that assists geologists in identifying geological formations that may contain mineral deposits. The program elicited, preserved, and reused geologic formation knowledge to assist in mineral exploration.

Prototype. An original type, form, or instance serving as a basis or standard for later stages.

Proxy Server. A server that sits between a client application, such as a Web browser, and a real server. It intercepts all requests to the real server to see if it can fulfill the requests itself. If not, it forwards the request to the real server.

Quantitative KM Assessments. Produce specific numerical scores indicating how well an organization, an organizational subunit, or an individual is performing with respect to KM. They may be based on a survey, in financial terms, such as the ROI or cost savings, or may include such ratios or percentages as employee-retention rate.

Query. A request for information from a database.

Query by Example (QBE). In this method, the system presents a blank record and lets you specify the fields and values that define the query.

Query Language. Many database systems require you to make requests for information in the form of a stylized query that must be written in a special query language. This is the most complex method because it forces you to learn a specialized language, but it is also the most powerful.

Radio Frequency Identification (RFID). The combination of radio broadcast with radar technology and consists of two parts. First is an RFID tag, which is an integrated circuit that modulates and demodulates a radio frequency signal and processes and stores information. The second part is an antenna that receives and transmits the signal.

Random Search. A search that has no specific pattern, purpose, or objective.

Re-contextualized Knowledge. Existing knowledge is re-created using alternative and innovative knowledge technologies and mechanisms.

Repertory Grids. Table associating attributes of several subjects with respect to two diametrically opposed extremes. Used to organize elicited knowledge. Its use can be easily automated.

Retrieval. Obtaining a case from the library that matches the description of the current problem.

Reverse Engineering. The process of recreating a design by analyzing a final product. Reverse engineering is common in both hardware and software.

Rocketry. The science and technology of rocket design, construction, and flight.

Role Reversal. Elicitation technique where the expert and the knowledge engineer exchange roles, and the expert interviews the knowledge engineer. Can serve to verify already elicited knowledge.

Routines. Involves the utilization of knowledge embedded in procedures, rules, and norms that guide future behavior.

Search-Retrieve-Propose. The process upon which CBR is founded. A case is sought, compared to the current problem, retrieved if it is similar, and its solution proposed as the solution to the current problem.

Security. Refers to techniques for ensuring that data stored in a computer cannot be read by unauthorized users or compromised. Most security measures involve data encryption and passwords. Data encryption is the translation of data into a form that is unintelligible without a deciphering mechanism. A password is a secret word or phrase that gives a user access to a particular program or system.

Semantic Networks. A directed graph in which concepts are represented as nodes and relations between concepts are represented as links.

Server. A computer or device on a network that manages network resources. For example, a file server is a computer and storage device dedicated to storing files. Any user on the network can store files on the server. A print server is a computer that manages one or more printers, and a network server is a computer that manages network traffic. A database server is a computer system that processes database queries.

Shell. Development environment designed to exercise domain knowledge expressed as rules and to arrive at solutions or answers to questions.

Shifting character or context. Fictional anecdotes where the characters may be shifted to study the new perspective of the story.

Simple Knowledge. Focuses on one basic area.

Slot. The attribute of a frame to which a value or set of values is assigned. Consists of facets.

Socialization. Involves the integration of multiple streams of tacit knowledge for the creation of new knowledge; tacit-to-tacit knowledge conversion. Socialization is the process of sharing experiences and thereby creating tacit knowledge, such as shared mental models and technical skills.

Social Networks. User-driven online spaces.

Solution Space. Contains the actions, states, or beliefs that represent the status of the problem. The solution is a sequence of steps through these actions, beliefs, or states starting from the initial state to the goal state.

Specialization. When a child frame is more specific than its parent frame; the basis for inheritance.

Specific Knowledge. Possessed by a very limited number of individuals and is expensive to transfer.

Specific Problem-solving Interview Sessions. Interview sessions where the objective is to gather specific problem-solving knowledge.

Stakeholder. One who has a share or an interest as in an enterprise.

Static Web Documents. Web documents designed *a priori,* consisting of nonactive HTML.

Stemming Algorithm. Used to remove the suffix of a word.

Stoplists. Used to eliminate words that are not good concept descriptions. A group of words that are not considered to have any indexing value. These include common words such as "and," "the," and "there."

Storage Law. Data storage capacity doubles every 9 months. This law has been in operation for over 10 years now. Storage Law is related to Moore's Law, which states that the number of transistors on CPUs doubles about every 18 months.

Storytelling. The act or practice of telling a story.

Strategic Knowledge. Pertains to the long-term positioning of the organization in terms of its corporate vision and strategies for achieving that vision.

Structured Knowledge. Knowledge best represented through attribute value pairs; knowledge not conditional in nature.

Support Knowledge. Relates to organizational infrastructure and facilitates day-to-day operations.

Surrogates. Replacing someone else or used instead of something else.

Symbol Manipulation. Refers to using symbols for solving problems; basis of symbolic AI.

Synergy. The interaction of two or more agents or forces so that their combined effect is greater than the sum of their individual effects.

Systematic Blind Search. Follows a systematic, exhaustive method to find target. Does not use any knowledge. Can be very time-consuming.

Tacit Knowledge. Includes insights, intuitions, and hunches. It is difficult to express and formalize and therefore difficult to share.

Tactical Knowledge. Knowledge used to decide course of action to achieve a specific goal in a dynamically changing environment; pertains to the short-term positioning of the organization relative to its markets, competitors, and suppliers.

Talking Head. A *talking head* or *avatar* is an image selected to represent oneself. Talking heads could be a photograph, cartoon character, or an animated image driven by the user's voice including lip-synchronization.

Task Interdependence. Indicates the extent to which the subunit's achievement of its goals depends on the efforts of other subunits.

Task Uncertainty. Represents the extent to which the organizational subunit encounters difficulty in predicting the nature of its tasks. High uncertainty implies changing problems and tasks, which reduces the unit's ability to develop routines.

Teachability. Reflects the extent to which the knowledge can be taught to other individuals through training, apprenticeship, and so on.

Technically Specific Knowledge. Deep knowledge about a specific area. It includes knowledge about the tools and techniques that may be used to address problems in that area.

Tenfold (n-fold) Cross Validation. Cross-validation and bootstrapping are both methods for estimating generalization error based on re-sampling. For *ten-(n)-fold* cross validation the database is divided, with random selection of examples into ten (n) partitions (folds) of equal sizes.

Term Frequency (TF). How frequently a term occurs in the text.

Text Mining. Automatically reading large documents of text and deriving knowledge from the process.

Touchpoints. Refers to the steps in a business process, like a purchase transaction, or software when it interfaces with the customer directly.

Uniform Resource Locator (URL). A format for specifying Internet addresses; the global address of documents and other resources on the World Wide Web.

Universalistic View of KM. Implies that there is a single best approach of managing knowledge that should be adopted by all organizations in all circumstances.

User Interface. The screen and dialogue format seen by the user when working with a particular computer program.

Value-added Products. New or improved products that provide a significant additional value as compared to earlier products. Value-added products benefit from knowledge management due to increased knowledge or enhanced organizational process innovation.

Variable. A symbol or name that stands for a value.

Virus. A program or piece of code that is loaded onto your computer without your knowledge and runs against your wishes. Viruses can also replicate themselves. All computer viruses are manmade. A simple virus that can copy itself over and over again is relatively easy to produce. Even such a simple virus is dangerous because it will quickly use all available memory and bring the system to a halt. An even more dangerous type of virus is one capable of transmitting itself across networks and bypassing security systems.

Weak-theory Domains. Domains where robust theoretical explanations do not exist, or if they exist, they contain uncertainty.

Web 2.0. A term describing changing trends in the use of World Wide Web technology and Web design that aims to enhance creativity, information sharing, collaboration, and functionality of the Web.

Web Content Mining. Discovers what a Web page is about and how to uncover new knowledge from it.

Web Crawlers. Computer programs that visit Web sites continuously and regularly, acquiring information for use in search engines.

Web Mining. Web crawling with online text mining.

Web Structure Mining. Examines how Web documents are structured, attempts to discover the model underlying the link structures of the Web.

Web Usage Mining. Identification of patterns in user navigation through Web surfing.

Wicked Problem. Describes a problem that is one-of-a-kind and is difficult or impossible to solve, or one that may have contradicting requirements. For example, ERP implementations offer have both financial and accuracy requirements that contradict each other: accuracy requires more time to implement, but low cost requires expedited completion.

Wiki. A page or collection of Web pages designed to enable anyone who accesses it to contribute or modify content using a simplified markup language.

Workflow Management System (WfMS). A system that provides procedural automation of a business process by managing the sequence of work activities and by managing the required resources (people, data, and applications) associated with the various activity steps. Computer programs that provide a method of capturing the steps, which lead to the completion of a project within a fixed time frame.

World Wide Web (WWW). A format that enables large-scale storage of documents to be easily accessed by a user via a browser.

XCON. One of the earliest commercially successful systems, XCON assists in the configuration of newly ordered VAX computer systems. Developed by Digital Equipment Corporation (DEC) in conjunction with Carnegie-Mellon University XCON elicited, preserved, and reused the knowledge of human configurators of computer systems in order to automate and duplicate their functions.

SOURCES

The American Heritage Dictionary of the English Language, 4th ed. 2000. Boston: Houghton Mifflin.

Cambridge Dictionaries Online. Cambridge University Press. http://dictionary.cambridge.org/.

CRoss Industry Standard Process for Data Mining (CRISP-DM). http://www.crisp-dm.org/.

Dictionary.com—An Ask.com Service. http://dictionary.reference.com/.

Flake, Gary William. 2002. Glossary. In *The computational beauty of nature: Computer explorations of fractals, chaos, complex systems, and adaptation.* . Cambridge, MA: The MIT Press. http://mitpress.mit.edu/books/FLAOH/cbnhtml/glossary.html.

Geek.com. www.geek.com.

Knowledgepoint Australia. www.knowledgepoint.com.au.

Nonaka, Ikujiro, and Takeuchi, Hirotaka. 1995. *The knowledge creating company: How Japanese companies create the dynamics of innovation.* New York: Oxford University Press.

OneLook® Dictionary Search. www.onelook.com.

The Oxford American desk dictionary and thesaurus, 2d ed. 2001. New York: Berkley Books.

Stottler Heck Associates, Inc. 2002. *Glossary.* http://www.stottlerhenke.com/ai_general/glossary.htm.

WebMediaBrands. Wĕbopēdia™—The only online dictionary and search engine you need for computer and Internet technology definitions. www.webopedia.com.

Whatis?com—The leading IT encyclopedia and learning center. http://whatis.techtarget.com/.

Wikipedia—The Free Encyclopedia. http://en.wikipedia.org/wiki/Main_Page.

YourDictionary.com—The last word in words. www.yourdictionary.com.

About the Authors

Dr. Irma Becerra-Fernandez is Professor and Director of the Pino Global Entrepreneurship Center and the Knight Ridder Research Professor of Management Information Systems at Florida International University College of Business Administration, Decision Sciences and Information Systems department. She was the Spring 2009 MIT Sloan Visiting Scholar with the Center for Information Systems Research. Also she's the 2007 Kauffman Entrepreneurship Professor. Her research focuses on knowledge management (KM), KM systems, enterprise systems, disaster management, and information technology entrepreneurship. She has studied and advised organizations, in particular NASA, about KM practices. She founded the FIU Knowledge Management Lab eight years ago and has obtained funding as principal investigator for over $1.8 M from the National Science Foundation, NASA (Kennedy, Ames, and Goddard Space Flight Center), and the Air Force Research Lab to develop innovative KM systems. She has published extensively in leading journals including the *Journal of MIS, Decision Sciences, Communications of the ACM, European Journal of Operational Research, IEEE Transactions on Engineering Management, ACM Transactions on Internet Technology, Knowledge Based Systems, International Journal of Expert Systems Research & Applications,* and others. Dr. Becerra-Fernandez is an author of the book *Knowledge Management: Challenges, Solutions, and Technologies* (Prentice Hall 2004) and co-editor of the monograph *Knowledge Management: An Evolutionary View* (M.E. Sharpe 2008*)*. She has delivered invited presentations at many NASA Centers, the Naval Research Lab, universities around the world, and many international conferences with both an academic and a practitioner focus. Dr. Becerra-Fernandez was the recipient of the 2004 Outstanding Faculty Torch Award presented by the FIU Alumni Association, the 2006 FIU Faculty Teaching Award, and the 2001 FIU Faculty Research Award. She was the prior faculty director for the Masters in MIS and the MIS Ph.D Program, and serves on the editorial board of the *International Journal of Knowledge Management, International Journal of Knowledge and Learning, and* the *International Journal of Mobile Learning and Organisation* among others. Dr. Becerra-Fernandez earned her Ph.D from Florida International University in 1994 in electrical engineering and her Masters and Bachelors, also in electrical engineering, from the University of Miami.

Dr. Rajiv Sabherwal is University of Missouri System Curators' Professor, Emery C. Turner Professor of Information Systems, and the Director of the Ph.D Program in

Business Administration at the University of Missouri, St. Louis. He has previously taught at Florida State University and Florida International University and served as a visiting professor at National University of Singapore. He will be the Fulbright-Queen's School of Business Research Chair at Queen's University in Canada during the 2009–2010 academic year. Dr. Sabherwal was inducted as a Fellow of the Association for Information Systems in December 2008. He is currently Senior Editor for a special issue of *Information Systems Research* and serves on the editorial board for *Journal of MIS*. He has previously served as Departmental Editor of *IEEE Transactions on Engineering Management,* Senior Editor of *MIS Quarterly,* and editorial board member of *Management Science, Information Systems Research,* and *Journal of AIS.* He will be Conference Co-chair for the International Conference on Information Systems 2010 (ICIS 2010) in St. Louis. Dr. Sabherwal conducts research on knowledge management and business intelligence; strategic management of information systems; and development, adoption, and success of information systems. His papers have appeared in numerous journals including *Management Science, Information Systems Research, MIS Quarterly, California Management Review, Organization Science, Journal of MIS,* and *IEEE Transactions on Engineering Management.* In addition to this textbook on knowledge management, he is also writing a textbook on business intelligence. He received his Ph.D in Business Administration from the University of Pittsburgh, a Post Graduate Diploma in Management from the Indian Institute of Management, Calcutta, and a bachelor of engineering from Bhopal University, India. He is a member of AIS, Academy of Management, IEEE, and INFORMS.

Index

Italic page references indicate charts and graphs.

Declarative knowledge, 25
Deep and broad knowledge, 228
Deep expertise, 30, *30*
DeepGreen Financial, 64, *65*
Defense Advanced Research Projects Agency
    (DARPA), 245–246
Delbecq, A., 259
Denning, Steve, 128–129
Department of Energy (DOE), 160
Department of Homeland Security, 152
Deployment of data, 208
Depth aspect of information technology
    infrastructure, 47
Derr, Kenneth T., 81
Description of data, 205–206
Descriptive statistics, 211, *215*
Developer's risk, 212
Development Forum (DevForum), 187–188
Diagrammatic reasoning, 96
Difference–based induction (DBI), 223
Direction, 61, 64, 91, 263
Disjunctions, 117–118
Distribution tree, 116, *117*
Dit-spinning, 130
DM. *See* Data mining
DMG process methodology, 208
DOE, 160
Dolan, Tom, *73*
Domain experts, 94, 164
Domain knowledge, 6–7, 94
Domain Name System, 249
Doubtfire Computer Corporation, 272–273, *274,*
    275
Dow Chemical Company, 305, *306*
Downsizing, 7
Dresdner Kleinwort Wasserstein (DrKW), *247*
Drucker, Peter, 4
Dunbar number, 244
Dunbar, Robin, 244
Dyer, J.H., 77
Dynamic capabilities, 79

E

EAI, 219
eBags (Web-based retailer), 202
Economy of scale, 82, 293
Economy of scope, 82, 293
Effective transfer, 60
Effectiveness of processes, 76, *77,* 291
Efficiency of processes, 77–78, 291

Electric utility industry, 201
Electrical Power Research Institute to Results, 201
Electronic brainstorming, *199*
ELS. *See* Expertise locator systems
Emergent knowledge management practices
    blogs, 243–245, *245, 246, 247*
    information technology, 253–254
    open source development, 245–249
    overview, 237, 254–255
    social networking, 240–242
    virtual worlds, 249–252, *250, 252*
    Web 2.0 technologies, 237–240, *239*
    wikis, 243–245, *247*
Employees. *See also* People
    adaptability, 73–74
    job satisfaction, 74–75
    knowledge management assessment impact on,
        291, *292*
    learning, 72–73
    turnover, 7–8
Encryption, 307
Enduser, 116
Enterprise 2.0 technology, 240
Enterprise application integration (EAI), 219
Enterprise resource planning systems (ERPs), 47,
    303
Environment, physical, 48–49
Environmental characteristics, 259, *261,* 265–268,
    266
Environmental Protection Agency, 152
Ernst & Young, 152, *153*
ERPs, 47, 303
Ethics perspective, 304
Evaluation of data, 208
Exchange, 60, 61, 263
Executive Decision Centre (Queens University),
    199
Exemplar-based reasoning, 96
Expert Seeker, 173–176, *174, 177,* 178–179, *178,*
    180, 181, 224–225
Expertise, 26, 28–30, *30,* 141
Expertise locator systems (ELSs)
    aggregating knowledge and, 47
    characteristics of various systems, 166–168, *169*
    functions of, 165
    as knowledge sharing system, 159, 165–168, *167,*
        169, 170, 171, 172
    knowledge taxonomy and, 168, 170, *171,* 172
    names for, 47
    ontology and, 168, 170, 172
    Web content mining and, 202, 224, 226–227, *226*